What Works in Stepfamilies

This book uses a strengths-based approach and resilience perspective to offer guidance on what works in creating effective stepfamily relationships, sharing findings and empirically supported best practices for stepfamily members and the family professionals that work with them.

Drawing from over 2,500 studies, Ganong, Coleman, and Sanner present a comprehensive overview of research on what works to create positive and satisfying stepfamily relationships. Chapters address how to work with stepcouples, stepparents, biological parents, co-parents, stepsiblings and half-siblings, and biological and stepgrandparents, with illustrative case studies throughout. It emphasizes the diversity and complexity of stepfamilies, including work with LGBTQ+ stepfamilies, stepfamilies from various racial and ethnic groups, and stepfamily relationships across the life course, from childrearing stepfamilies to those formed later in life.

This book is essential reading for students, researchers, and practitioners interested in strengthening stepfamily relationships, such as those studying or working in family science, marriage and family therapy, psychology, and social work.

Lawrence Ganong, Ph.D., is internationally recognized as a leading stepfamily scholar. He has coauthored ten books and over 350 articles about family relationships, winning numerous awards for his work.

Marilyn Coleman, Ed.D., is a celebrated researcher with an international reputation for her work on stepfamilies. She has published 11 books and hundreds of articles and book chapters.

Caroline Sanner, Ph.D., is an award-winning family scientist and one of the leading stepfamily scholars of her generation.

"What Works in Stepfamilies is an excellent contribution to our understanding of stepfamily strengths—with a practical and evidence-based focus on what works. This important and insightful volume is useful for scholars studying stepfamilies, for clinicians working with stepfamilies, and for stepfamily members."

Dawn O. Braithwaite, *Ph.D., Willa Cather Professor of Communication Emerita, University of Nebraska, NE*

"Recognized as the most accomplished researchers on stepfamily life in the world, these authors have shifted focus to findings that support "what works" in these families. The result is a remarkably rich collection of useful research findings with clear clinical implications. Anyone interested in conducting evidence-based treatment for stepfamilies and their members will find *What Works in Stepfamilies* provides a step-by-step guide to relationships within this complex family type."

Scott Browning, *Ph.D., ABPP Professor Emeritus, Chestnut Hill College, PA*

"What Works in Stepfamilies is an indispensable resource. With a passionate strengths-based orientation and resilience perspective, the authors distill from the best available evidence clear insights about "what works" in stepfamily life and relationships to promote well-being. I could not recommend this book more highly!"

Todd Jensen, *Ph.D., MSW, University of North Carolina, NC*

"What Works in Stepfamilies is a gift. These stepfamily scholars have gathered a treasure trove of research about evidence-based "best practices" that support resilience and well-being in stepfamilies. This lucidly written, clearly organized volume will be indispensable for researchers, therapists, and others involved with stepfamilies."

Patricia Papernow, *Ed.D., psychologist and author of Surviving and Thriving in Stepfamily Relationships*

What Works in Stepfamilies

Creating and Maintaining Satisfying and Effective Relationships

Lawrence Ganong, Marilyn Coleman and Caroline Sanner

Routledge
Taylor & Francis Group
NEW YORK AND LONDON

Designed cover image: Kali9@ Getty Images

First published 2025
by Routledge
605 Third Avenue, New York, NY 10158

and by Routledge
4 Park Square, Milton Park, Abingdon, Oxon, OX14 4RN

Routledge is an imprint of the Taylor & Francis Group, an informa business

Library of Congress Cataloging-in-Publication Data
Names: Ganong, Lawrence H., author. | Coleman, Marilyn, author. |
Sanner, Caroline, author.
Title: What works in stepfamilies : creating and maintaining satisfying
and effective relationships / Lawrence Ganong, Marilyn Coleman and
Caroline Sanner.
Description: New York, NY : Routledge, 2025. | Includes bibliographical
references and index.
Identifiers: LCCN 2024028708 (print) | LCCN 2024028709 (ebook) |
ISBN 9781032438382 (hardback) | ISBN 9781032438375 (paperback) |
ISBN 9781003369073 (ebook)
Subjects: LCSH: Stepfamilies. | Interpersonal relations.
Classification: LCC HQ759.92 .G363 2025 (print) |
LCC HQ759.92 (ebook) | DDC 306.874/7--dc23/eng/20240718
LC record available at https://lccn.loc.gov/2024028708
LC ebook record available at https://lccn.loc.gov/2024028709

ISBN: 978-1-032-43838-2 (hbk)
ISBN: 978-1-032-43837-5 (pbk)
ISBN: 978-1-003-36907-3 (ebk)

DOI: 10.4324/9781003369073

Typeset in Caslon
by KnowledgeWorks Global Ltd.

CONTENTS

ABOUT THE AUTHORS

Lawrence Ganong, Ph.D., is Emeritus Professor of Human Development and Family Science and Nursing at the University of Missouri, USA. He has co-authored over 325 journal articles and chapters and ten books and has received multiple grants from public and private institutions. Ganong's research program has focused on how post-divorce families, particularly stepfamilies, develop and maintain satisfying and effective relationships. Ganong is a Fellow in the National Council on Family Relations and in the Gerontological Society of America. He has served on the Board of Directors of the National Council on Family Relations, the Council on Contemporary Families, and The Stepfamily Association of America. Ganong serves or has served on the editorial boards of *Journal of Marriage and Family, Family Relations, Journal of Family Issues, Journal of Family Theory and Review, Journal of Family Nursing, Journal of Social and Personal Relationships,* and *Journal of Family Transitions.*

Dr. Marilyn Coleman is a Distinguished Curators' Professor Emerita of Human Development and Family Science at the University of Missouri. She is a Fellow in the National Council on Family Relations. Coleman has conducted research on stepfamilies for over 45 years. Her recent work with Lawrence Ganong has focused on: (1) intergenerational family responsibilities following divorce and remarriage and (2) the development and maintenance of positive stepfamily relationships. She and Ganong have published several books, including *Stepfamilies: Development, Dynamics, and Intervention* (2017), *Families in the 20th Century* (2007), *Changing Families, Changing Responsibilities* (1999), *Remarried Family Relationships* (1994), and *Bibliotherapy with Stepchildren* (1988). They are the editors of *Points and Counterpoints: Controversial Relationship and Family Issues in the 21st Century* (2003) and *The Handbook of Contemporary Families* (2004). Dr. Coleman is a past editor of the *Journal of Marriage and Family*.

Dr. Caroline Sanner has been an active stepfamily researcher since her undergraduate years. She is an Assistant Professor of Family Science at Virginia Tech. Her research program explores resilience and successful adaptation in post-divorce families and stepfamilies, with an emphasis on how parents create healthy environments for their children during and after family structure transitions. Dr. Sanner has published 30 articles across 12 journals, and her work has been recognized at the national level; in 2018, she received the National Council on Family Relations (NCFR) Student Award, given annually to a graduate student who has demonstrated excellence and shows high potential for contribution to the field of family science.

PREFACE

Our careers have focused on researching resilience processes in step-families. Our approach to studying stepfamilies has differed from the dominant approaches to studying stepfamilies, which tend to focus on problems, challenges, and negative aspects of stepfamily life. Although we agree that stepfamilies face unique challenges and often lack cultural support, instead of problematizing stepfamilies, we have taken a *normative-adaptive* approach to studying them. This approach, while not ignoring the possibility of stepfamily challenges, does not focus solely on problems. Instead, we examine both positive *and* negative experiences, with an interest in the processes that contribute to *resilience* in stepfamilies, such as how stepfamilies develop close relationships and how they positively adapt to change (Ganong & Coleman, 2017; Sanner et al., 2022).

For several decades, there has been a movement among social and behavioral scientists to emphasize resilience processes and the positive aspects of individual and relational development (Masten, 2018). These researchers argue that studying positive adjustment yields as much or more generalizable knowledge as investigating problems or pathology. Although this approach is seldom applied to stepfamily research, from the start of our careers, our position has been that learning "what works" in stepfamilies is an effective way of drawing useful conclusions.

We found that asking questions about resilience in stepfamilies was intellectually stimulating and rewarding to us. It also was of interest, engaging, and useful both to stepfamily members and those family professionals who work with them.

We also have personal interests in studying stepfamilies, as we have either grown up in a stepfamily (CS, LG) or created a stepfamily as adults (MC, LG). No doubt our own experiences have somewhat shaped our approach to investigating stepfamilies. Our personal backgrounds, combined with our training as family scientists who were taught to value conducting and utilizing research that can be helpful and applicable to "real-life" contexts, have led to this book.

As stepfamily researchers, we have gathered data from a variety of stepfamily perspectives – parents, stepparents, stepgrandparents, stepchildren, half-siblings, stepsiblings, and more. We have interviewed individual stepfamily members, stepcouples, and even entire stepfamily households. We decided early in our careers that we wanted our studies to be grounded in data collected directly from stepfamily members themselves. We have used a wide variety of research techniques, including face-to-face interviews, mailed surveys, online surveys, phone calls, focus groups, and observations of dyadic and family interactions. Always collecting data for our own studies (i.e., primary data) makes us somewhat unique in that we have not used data collected by others (i.e., secondary data). We also have been ecumenical in our research methods, employing quantitative, qualitative, and mixed-method designs, all informed by a normative-adaptive framework.

In addition, part of our scholarly work has been to systematically review research on stepfamilies and stepfamily relationships with an emphasis on drawing inferences from this scholarship that address the "so what?" question of social and behavioral science research (e.g., Coleman, Ganong, & Gingrich, 1985a; Coleman et al., 2012; Ganong & Coleman, 1986, 1987; Sanner et al., 2018). The "so what?" question refers to the practical implications of a study's findings, as in, "OK, so you found that X is significantly related to Y, but why does this matter?" To us, whether conducting primary research or reviewing the research literature, our goal has been to glean insights into how study findings can be used to make substantive differences in the lives and relationships of stepfamily members – to answer the "so what" question. In addition to the reviews already cited, we have conducted decade reviews of research (Coleman & Ganong, 1990; Coleman et al., 2000), systematic reviews of research (Ganong & Coleman, 1984; Hadfield et al., 2018; Sanner et al., 2018), meta-analyses (Ganong & Coleman, 1993; Ganong et al., 1990; Vemer et al., 1989), reviews of the development of stepfamily scholarship (Ganong & Coleman, 2018), textbook critiques (Nolan et al., 1984), methodological reviews (Jensen & Sanner, 2021; Sanner & Jensen, 2021; Sanner et al., 2021), reviews of self-help books (Coleman & Ganong, 1989), reviews of books for adolescents (Coleman et al., 1986), and traditional literature reviews (Coleman & Ganong, 2012; Coleman, Ganong, & Gingrich, 1985a, 1986; Ganong, Coleman, & Sanner, 2019; Ganong, Sanner, & Coleman, 2019; Russell et al., 2018). Clearly, making sense of the research on stepfamilies has been our priority.

Relatively early in our careers (LG and MC) we began looking for stepfamily strengths in empirical research. We presented this work at conferences (Coleman et al., 1985; Coleman, Ganong, & Gingrich, 1985b) and in publications (Coleman, Ganong, & Gingrich, 1985a; 1986). In a sense, this early focus on strengths, or positive dimensions of stepfamilies, was our way of choosing to examine resilience instead of problems and was the beginning of our use of a normative-adaptive approach to understanding stepfamily dynamics. Unfortunately, other research projects consumed much of our time, and 15 years passed before we formally returned to searching for studies that yielded findings about what was working for stepfamilies. Early in this searching, we presented a paper at a national conference entitled, *"What distinguishes stepfamilies that 'work' from those that don't?"* (Ganong & Coleman, 1999). This paper was so well received that we left the conference energized, intending to continue to systematically review research on *what works* in stepfamilies. Once again, however, other projects, some funded by grants, took precedence. The "what works" review project kept slipping to the bottom of the long list of studies we were conducting. We never lost the enthusiasm for this project, renewing it again a few years later for an international audience (Coleman & Ganong, 2011), and for the first time used the label of "what works." It took a few more years before the What Works Project was renewed, this time adding a younger colleague, Dr. Caroline Sanner, and two graduate students (Steve Berkley and Olivia Landon). We started with a review of what works in childrearing in stepfamilies, which resulted in a symposium presented at the National Council on Family Relations Annual Conference (Ganong et al., 2020). This time, the initial review of *what works* was just the start of a bigger endeavor that was not interrupted by other projects.

As two of us near the end of our scholarly lives (LG, MC), while the third is in the early stages of an extremely productive research career (CS), it made sense to us to embark on an extensive project in which we examined hundreds of studies to cull findings about what works in stepfamilies. The *What Works* book project was based on reviewing over 2,500 English-language publications on stepfamilies and stepfamily relationships. Our goal was to identify research findings about what stepfamily members did that promoted positive individual and relational wellbeing. We wanted to find empirical evidence of what worked for people – not self-help advice, not clinical experts' views about effective stepfamily living, and not scholars' or practitioners' opinions – but phenomena grounded in research from around the world, using all kinds of investigative methods.

We began by examining research on childrearing in stepfamilies which yielded conference presentations and a series of articles published in the academic journal, *Family Relations* (Ganong, Berkley, Coleman, & Sanner, 2022; Ganong, Coleman, Sanner, & Berkley, 2022a, 2022b; Ganong, Sanner, Berkley, & Coleman, 2022; Sanner et al., 2022). These papers and presentations were so well received that it was clear to us that we needed to finish the project by also reviewing research on couples in stepfamilies, stepgrandparents and grandparents, and half- and stepsiblings. This volume represents newly updated material on parenting, stepparenting, and coparenting, along with new material on other stepfamily relationships.

Early into the project, we noticed how easy it was for us to go from reporting evidence-based results to framing these results in sentences that seemed more prescriptive and consistent with self-help literature than scientific reports. For example, it is a small step from "researchers found that stepparents who engaged in fun leisure activities with their stepchildren had closer relationships with them than stepparents who did not engage in such activities" to "stepparents should play fun games with their stepchildren." It seems clear that one statement is a study *finding* and the other is an *inference* that could be drawn from the finding. As scholars with a "so, what?" bent, we want to share the results of research as clearly as possible, accounting for the contexts within which investigators obtained their findings. We believe that drawing inferences from results of studies and engaging in controlled speculations about the meanings of study results are part of the scientific approach. It is our responsibility as scholars to carefully make sense of empirical results, taking note of contexts, limits to generalizability, and applicable "if – then" conditions as we do so. As much as we possibly can, however, we want research evidence to speak for itself in this book.

Any scholarly work is the outcome of collective efforts. In addition to the collaborative work of the three authors of this book, we want to thank Dr. Steven Berkley, Olivia Landon, and Matt Ogan for their help in finding, coding, and making sense of the research. We have been helped by a small army of students and colleagues over the years, many of whom have become members of our chosen (and academic) families. They are too numerous to mention by name, but they know who they are.

Finally, we want to thank our extended stepfamilies. It is not a cliché to say we would not be writing this book without them – we love them and are grateful to them. Our lives with them were our first clues into what works!

References

Coleman, M., & Ganong, L. (1989). Stepfamily self-help books: Brief annotations and ratings. *Family Relations, 38*, 91–96. https://doi.org/10.2307/583616

Coleman, M., & Ganong, L. (1990). Remarriage and stepfamily research in the '80s: New interest in an old family form. *Journal of Marriage and the Family, 52*, 925–940. https://doi.org/10.2307/353311

Coleman, M., & Ganong, L. (2011, July). *What works in stepfamilies.* Presented at the US-Japan Stepfamily Conference: A Special Event for the Stepfamily Association of Japan's 10th Anniversary, Tokyo, Japan. https://doi.org/10.1007/978-1-4419-9112-6_1

Coleman, M., & Ganong, L. (2012). Relationships in older stepfamilies. In R. Blieszner & V. Bedford (Eds.). *Handbook of families and aging* (2nd ed., pp. 213–242). NY: Praeger.

Coleman, M., Ganong, L., & Fine, M. (2000). Reinvestigating remarriage: Another decade of progress. *Journal of Marriage and the Family, 62*, 1288–1307. https://doi.org/10.1111/j.1741-3737.2000.01288.x

Coleman, M., Ganong, L., & Gingrich, R. (1985a). Stepfamily strengths: A review of the popular literature. *Family Relations, 34*, 583–589. https://doi.org/10.2307/584023

Coleman, M., Ganong, L.H., & Gingrich, R. (1985b, November). *An evaluation of the stepfamily self-help books.* Paper presented at the National Council on Family Relations Annual Conference, Dallas, TX. https://doi.org/10.2307/583616

Coleman, M., Ganong, L., & Gingrich, R. (1986). Strengths of stepfamilies identified in professional literature. In S. van Zandt (Ed.), *Building family strengths, Vol. 7* (pp. 439–451). Lincoln, NE: University of Nebraska.

Coleman, M., Ganong, L., Jamison, T., & Feistman, R. (2012, October). *Post-divorce co-parenting: What is working?* Presented at the National Council on Family Relations Annual Conference, Phoenix, AZ. https://doi.org/10.1111/j.1741-3729.2012.00706.x

Coleman, M., Ganong, L.H., & Vemer, E. (1985, May). *Stepfamilies from different perspectives.* Paper presented at Building Family Strengths, The Eighth National Symposium, Lincoln, NE.

Coleman, M., Marshall, S., & Ganong, L. (1986). Beyond Cinderella: Relevant reading for young adolescents about stepfamilies. *Adolescence, 21,* 553–560.

Ganong, L. Berkley, S., Coleman, M., & Sanner, C. (2022). Effective stepparenting: Empirical evidence of what works. *Family Relations, 71*(3), 900–917. https://doi.org/10.1111/fare.12624

Ganong, L., & Coleman, M. (1984). Effects of remarriage on children: A review of the empirical literature. *Family Relations, 33,* 389–406. https://doi.org/10.2307/584710

Ganong, L., & Coleman, M. (1986). A comparison of clinical and empirical literature on children in stepfamilies. *Journal of Marriage and the Family, 48,* 309–318. https://doi.org/10.2307/352398

Ganong, L., & Coleman, M. (1987). Effects of stepfamilies on children: A comparison of two literatures. In K. Pasley & M. Ihinger-Tallman (Eds.), *Remarriage and stepparenting: Current research and theory* (pp. 94–140). Guilford. https://doi.org/10.2307/2072511

Ganong, L., & Coleman, M. (1993). A meta-analytic comparison of the self-esteem and behavior problems of stepchildren to children in other family structures. *Journal of Divorce and Remarriage, 19,* 143–163. https://doi.org/10.1300/j087v19n03_10

Ganong, L., & Coleman, M. (1999, November). *What distinguishes stepfamilies that "work" from those that don't?* Paper presented at the National Council on Family Relations Annual Conference, Irvine, CA.

Ganong, L., & Coleman, M. (2017). *Stepfamily relationships: Development, dynamics, and intervention* (2nd ed.). Springer. https://doi.org/10.10078/978-1-4899-7702-1

Ganong, L., & Coleman, M. (2018). Studying stepfamilies: Four eras of scholarship. *Family Process, 57,* 7–24. https://doi.org/10.1111/famp.12307

Ganong, L., Coleman, M., & Mapes, D. (1990). A meta-analytic review of family structure stereotypes. *Journal of Marriage and the Family, 52,* 287–297. https://doi.org/10.2307/353026

Ganong, L.H., Coleman, M., Sanner, C. (2019). Divorced and remarried parenting. In M.H. Bornstein (Ed.), *Handbook of Parenting. Vol. 3. Being and Becoming a Parent* (3rd ed., pp. 311–344). Routledge. www.taylorfrancis.com/books/e/9780429433214/chapters/10.4324/9780429433214-9

Ganong, L., Coleman, M., Sanner, C., & Berkley, S. (2022a). Childrearing in stepfamilies: Empirical answers about "what works." *Family Relations, 71*(3), 876–883. https://doi.org/10.1111/fare.12634

Ganong, L., Coleman, M., Sanner, C., & Berkley, S. (2022b). Summary of what works in stepfamily childrearing. *Family Relations, 71*(3), 935–952. https://doi.org/10.1111/fare.12674

Ganong, L., Coleman, M., Sanner, C., Landon, O., Berkeley, S., & Jensen, T. (2020, November). *Childrearing in stepfamilies: Answers about "What works" drawn from forty years of research.* Invited symposium at the National Council on Family Relations Annual Conference, St. Louis., MO. https://doi.org/10.1111/fare.12634

Ganong, L., Sanner, C., Berkley, S., & Coleman, M. (2022). Effective coparenting in stepfamilies: Empirical evidence of what works. *Family Relations, 71*(3), 918–934. https://doi.org/10.1111/fare.12607

Ganong, L., Sanner, C., & Coleman, M. (2019). Divorce and stepgrandparents. In C. Fruehauf & B. Hayslip (Eds.), *Handbook of grandparenting: The changing dynamics of family relationships* (pp. 111–130). Springer. https://doi.org/10.1891/9780826149855.0007

Hadfield, K., Ungar, M. Gosselin, J., Heffernan, M., & Ganong, L. (2018). Do changes to family structure affect child and family outcomes? A systematic review of the instability hypothesis. *Journal of Family Theory & Review, 10,* 87–110. https://doi.org/10.1111/jftr.12243

Jensen, T.M., & Sanner, C. (2021). A scoping review of research on well-being across diverse family structures: Rethinking approaches for understanding contemporary families. *Journal of Family Theory & Review, 13,* 463–495. https://doi.org/10.1111/jftr.12437

Masten, A.S. (2018). Resilience theory and research on children and families: Past, present, and promise. *Journal of Family Theory & Review, 10*(1), 12–31. https://doi.org/10.1111/jftr.12255

Nolan, J., Coleman, M., & Ganong, L. (1984). The presentation of stepfamilies in marriage and family textbooks. *Family Relations, 33,* 559–566. https://doi.org/10.2307/583835

Russell, L., Coleman, M., & Ganong, L. (2018). Family structure as a structural determinant of health. *Journal of Family Theory & Review, 10,* 735–748. https://doi.org/10.1111/jftr.12296

Sanner, C., Ganong, L., & Coleman, M. (2021). Families are socially constructed: Pragmatic implications for researchers. *Journal of Family Issues, 42*(2), 422–444. https://doi.org/10.1177/0192513X20905334

Sanner, C., Ganong, L., Coleman, M., & Berkley, S. (2022). Effective parenting by biological parents in stepfamilies. *Family Relations, 71*(3), 884–899. https://doi.org/10.1111/fare.12703

Sanner, C., & Jensen, T. (2021). Towards more accurate measures of family structure: Accounting for sibling complexity. *Journal of Family Theory & Review, 13*(1), 110–127. https://doi.org/10.1111/jftr.12406

Sanner, C., Russell, L., Coleman, M., & Ganong, L. (2018). Half-sibling and stepsibling relationships: A systematic integrative review. *Journal of Family Theory & Review, 10,* 765–784. https://doi.org/10.1111/jftr.12291

Vemer, E., Coleman, M., Ganong, L., & Cooper, H. (1989). Marital satisfaction in remarriage: A meta-analysis. *Journal of Marriage and the Family, 51,* 713–725. https://doi.org/10.2307/352170

1

EMPIRICAL ANSWERS ABOUT WHAT WORKS IN STEPFAMILIES

"What advice would you give someone who was about to become a stepparent?" As researchers who have studied stepfamilies for over four decades, we often are asked this question by journalists who are writing articles about "best practices" in post-divorce families and stepfamilies.

Although often tempted to share advice drawn from our personal experiences, having lived in stepfamilies for decades, we try to limit the use of personal anecdotes. Advising people to do what we have previously done (using self as a positive example) or conversely sharing what not to do from our past experiences (using self as a negative example) is common among acquaintances, friends, and many authors of self-help books, but as researchers, we shy away from this approach, which we think of as generalizing from an extremely small sample. After all, we know how complex stepfamilies are, and that the sociocultural contexts surrounding families are important in understanding them, so generalizing from personal lives, while common, does not often lead to the best, most accurate answers.

Of course, we could share with journalists some of the information we have learned over the years from outstanding stepfamily therapists and clinicians whose work we have followed throughout our careers. Our research has been enriched by the insights of clinicians, who often think about stepfamily issues differently than we do as researchers. However, we

DOI: 10.4324/9781003369073-1

are reluctant to give our secondhand views of clinical wisdom, although we often cite clinicians' views as evidence of the validity of research findings.

Instead of personal anecdotes or clinical understandings, when asked about stepfamily best practices, as researchers our preferred "go-to" response is to share what is known from research on stepfamily dynamics and stepfamily relationships. So, we turn to research evidence about *what works* when we are asked questions like these:

- How do I get my stepchild to listen to me?
- How can I help my children learn to accept my new partner?
- How am I supposed to coparent with my ex-spouse, my ex-spouse's new partner, *and* my new spouse?
- I already have a dad – how can I convince my stepfather I don't need another one?
- My daughter is my best friend. How much should I tell her about what goes on between me and my new husband?

Our answers always begin with something like, "Well, the research indicates …" and then we share the best scientific evidence known about what works well in building effective and satisfying stepfamily relationships, focusing as much as possible on the situation presented to us. We think of this as **evidence-based knowledge** about *what works* for real stepfamilies facing life's challenges. Our careers have centered on conducting research on stepfamilies framed from what we call a *normative-adaptive, resilience perspective* aimed at examining positive, effective, and adaptive dynamics rather than focusing mainly or solely on stepfamily problems and deficits.

Some Background: Why Evidence-Based Answers Work for Us

Stepfamilies are common family structures that have been prevalent throughout history in every corner of the world (Kurosu et al., 2014; Stykes & Guzzo, 2015; Warner & Erdelyi, 2022). Although remarriage rates have been falling for decades (Westrick-Payne, 2023), the number of children residing with a remarried or unmarried cohabiting stepparent has remained steady at about 11% in the United States (Juteau et al., 2023), and about 9–10% in Canada, England and Wales, New Zealand, and Australia (Australian Bureau of Statistics, 2016; Gath, 2016). In the United States, 78% of unmarried cohabiting family households include stepchildren (Eickmeyer, 2019), and 44% of all U.S. stepchildren live with an unmarried cohabiting parent and stepparent (Payne, 2019). Among coresidential unions (marital or cohabiting), 24% of first unions, 65% of second unions, and 74% of third unions form stepfamilies (Guzzo, 2016). Among American adults under age 50 who were living with a partner in 2017, 35% of women and 25% of men were in a stepfamily (Aldrich et al., 2022). We repeat – stepfamilies are common family forms.

In the early 1970s, for the first time ever in the United States, more remarriages took place after divorce than after the death of one of the spouses. Prior to this, stepfamilies had been part of every society in the world, but they had been formed primarily because parents died young, leaving young children in the home, and surviving spouses needed to remarry or repartner to survive (Kurosu et al., 2014; Wilson, 2014). In these post-bereavement stepfamilies, the new stepparent essentially was a substitute for the deceased parent, replacing them pragmatically, if not always replacing them emotionally. Sociologists in the mid-20th century referred to these families as *reconstituted* families, because structurally and often functionally, the remarriage represented a "return" to a nuclear family household.

The rising divorce rates of the last decades of the 20th century led to a profound demographic shift in how stepfamilies were created. Stepfamilies formed after divorce were substantively different from step-families formed after a parent's death. Post-divorce stepfamilies were more complex and confusing than post-bereavement stepfamilies. Instead of taking the place of a deceased mother or father, many stepparents were acting as *extra* parents to children from prior unions, in addition to the primary parents. Their existence as a third or fourth (if both divorced parents remarried) adult in a family system that often extended across two households, created confusion and uncertainty for stepfamilies and any-one who interacted with them (e.g., therapists, educators, clergy, policy makers). Therapists and other clinicians began writing about post-divorce stepfamilies and their problems almost at once. Interestingly, authors of fiction seemed to appreciate the emergence of this new family structure well before either clinicians or researchers (Coleman & Ganong, 1990). Although few studies had been conducted before 1980, many novelists had been writing about stepfamilies; 17 novels about stepfamilies written for adolescents were published in 1979 alone. Some of the more gifted novelists were proven to be unusually insightful about stepfamily dynamics by later scholars.

Researchers were slow to focus on stepfamily issues. In 1979, a review by the United States Department of Health and Human Services reported that only 11 studies, including unpublished dissertations, had examined stepfamilies, and those studies had sampled only 550 individuals (Espinoza & Newman, 1979). It is safe to conclude that little was known about these new post-divorce stepfamily forms. This was bad for stepfamilies but good for us, as two of us (LG and MC) began both our remarriage and our collaborative research careers shortly after this notable demographic change in American stepfamilies. We had personal interests in knowing more about stepfamilies, and as family scientists, we were surprised at how little was known. For social scientists, this was a perfect storm – high motivation to investigate and many, many questions to answer.

Perhaps because there was so much ambiguity surrounding stepfamily relationships and the roles and functions stepparents in post-divorce stepfamilies would have, early research seemed to focus almost exclusively on investigating stepfamily deficits, problems, and challenges (see decade reviews by Coleman & Ganong, 1990; Coleman et al., 2000; Raley & Sweeney, 2020; Sweeney, 2010). Invariably in these studies, stepfamilies were compared to first-marriage nuclear families, with the assumption that stepfamilies would fall short of the "gold standard" set by nuclear families. We called this the *deficit-comparison perspective* because researchers examined stepfamilies with methods that seemed aimed at illustrating how deviant and deficient they were compared to nuclear family households (Ganong & Coleman, 1994). For example, the most commonly investigated questions about stepfamilies involved (a) comparing the well-being of children in stepfamilies to children in first-married nuclear families and (b) comparing the quality of relationships in stepfamilies to the quality of relationships in first-married nuclear families (e.g., comparing remarried spouses to first-married spouses, or stepparent–stepchild relationships to biological parent–child relationships). Findings from these studies generally showed that stepchildren, on average, fared worse than children in nuclear families on whatever outcome variables were being examined, and step-relationships were less close than biological relationships (Raley & Sweeney, 2020; Sweeney, 2010). Several explanations for these individual and relational differences were offered. Researchers proposed that stepfamilies face challenges: (a) adapting to instability that can accompany family structure transitions; (b) merging two families with pre-established sets of traditions, routines, and patterns of interaction; (c) negotiating mutual understanding and communicating in the context of a system lacking shared family history; and (d) managing ambiguous social scripts for how to enact new family roles (e.g., stepparent, stepsibling) (Cherlin, 1978; Ganong & Coleman, 2017; Papernow, 1987). For instance, stepparents have described feeling unsure of how to effectively build relationships with stepchildren or how to navigate their roles without overstepping family boundaries (Ganong et al., 1999; Weaver & Coleman, 2005).

Given these challenges, it is perhaps not surprising that most stepfamily researchers have focused on deficits in stepfamilies and how they differ from the "nuclear family ideal," rather than how they are adaptive and resilient (Ganong & Coleman, 2018). For most of the past half-century, stepfamilies were seen as lacking social support and societal norms to guide behaviors (Cherlin, 1978), as dysfunctional family forms that harmed children and adults and were not beneficial to society, or they were judged on the basis of how successfully they "passed" as a nuclear family by recreating, as closely as possible, first-marriage family dynamics (Daly & Wilson, 1998; Ganong & Coleman, 2017; Sanner & Jensen, 2021). It has not been until the last few years that *normative-adaptive approaches* emerged as another perspective by which to examine stepfamily dynamics and relationships. The normative-adaptive perspective recognizes that although stepfamilies differ from first-marriage nuclear families, they "can function well and be effective living environments for children and adults" (Ganong & Coleman, 2017, p. 36).

Normative-Adaptive Perspective

Our approach has been to take a *normative-adaptive, resilience* perspective. Our work has emphasized identifying processes that contribute to effective, adaptive relationships and dynamics in stepfamilies and the positive well-being of stepfamily members. As part of a larger movement in the social and behavioral sciences to focus on resilience processes and positive aspects of individual and relational development and dynamics (Masten, 2018), we argue that studying positive examples of adaptation and adjustment yields as much or more generalizable knowledge as do studies investigating problems and dysfunctional behaviors. In short, our position has been that learning "what works" in studies is an effective way of drawing useful conclusions. The third author of this book (CS), a stepfamily member as well, also has used normative-adaptive perspectives to explore resilience processes in stepfamilies. The three of us are members of a growing group of stepfamily scholars employing this research perspective.

Answering the "So, What?" Question

Another aspect of our collective work has been to systematically review research on stepfamilies and stepfamily relationships with an emphasis on drawing inferences from this scholarship that address the "so, what?" question of social and behavioral science research (e.g., Coleman et al., 1985; Coleman et al., 2012; Ganong & Coleman, 1986; Sanner et al., 2020). The "so, what?" question refers to the practical implications of study findings, as in, "OK, you found that X is significantly related to Y – so what does this mean, and why does it matter?" To us, one of the main purposes of doing research was to discover the "so, what?" answers to questions about effective stepfamily relationships.

Many years ago, we conducted a literature review on scholarship about stepchildren's well-being in which we compared writings by clinicians and clinical scholars to researchers' findings (Ganong & Coleman, 1986). We found that these two bodies of literature were like ships passing in the night. Clinicians wrote about the issues and challenges stepfamilies were presenting to them in therapy, with a focus on preventing or resolving problems in relationships between family members. In contrast, researchers rarely focused on the issues thought relevant by clinicians. In fact, there was little evidence that researchers were reading clinicians' work, and rarely did researchers address the practical implications (i.e., the "so, what?" question) of their data. Fortunately, there is evidence that this situation has changed somewhat; greater numbers of researchers show commitment to conducting science that focuses on issues that are relevant and that matter for the stepfamilies being studied (Ganong & Coleman, 2018).

This Book

In this project, we present systematic reviews of research on effective relationships in stepfamilies. The aims of this book are: (a) to examine research evidence on building and maintaining effective stepfamily relationships; (b) to draw "best practice" guidelines for effective relationships in stepfamilies; and (c) to identify gaps in what is known empirically about effective stepfamilies. Our overarching goal was to present evidence-based statements about what stepfamily members *do* that "works" to enhance the positive development of individual and relational well-being in stepfamilies. This book is framed from a resilience perspective, even though studies included in the reviews may have been framed from other theories and approaches.

We start by examining research on *what works* for stepcouples, the remarried or repartnered adults who created their stepfamilies (Chapter 2). We then review research on parenting (Chapter 3), stepparenting (Chapter 4), and coparenting (Chapter 5). Our coparenting chapter includes research on coparenting between: (a) separated/divorced parents (i.e., former couples), (b) coresidential parent–stepparent dyads (i.e., stepcouples as coparents), and (c) two primary parents and one or more stepparents (i.e., cross-residential coparents). Next, we explore smaller bodies of research on half- and stepsibling relationships (Chapter 6), followed by an even smaller body of work on grandparents and step-grandparents (Chapter 7). We conclude by synthesizing and summarizing what is known from the research on what works in stepfamilies (Chapter 8). We also point out what is not yet known from research efforts. For researchers, we have an Appendix devoted to our search and coding methods. Readers interested in how we searched for studies, our criteria for including a study that yielded *what works* information, coding strategies, and other information about either this project or the body of research we used for this book, can find these details in the Appendix.

Summary of the What Works Project

Our project on stepfamily relationships is part of our personal and collective research agendas in which we have examined the empirical evidence of adaptive-normative, resilience processes in complex families. This project is one of the "negative spaces" of family scholarship. As in art, negative space not only helps to define links between objects but also helps in defining their limits (Daly, 2003). Focusing on what works in stepfamilies helps fill in the gaps and supplies alternative images to research focusing primarily on problems or challenges. Such alternative images or spaces are needed because they answer questions that are relevant and important to family members and clinicians, as well as to scholars and researchers. In the chapters that follow, we present findings on *what works* in building effective and satisfying stepfamily relationships and promoting the well-being of stepfamily members, followed by a general summary and a synthesis of what is known. We consider this project to be an example of an approach that other scholars and practitioners might use when examining other family forms as they explore what is working for individuals, relationships, and families in all areas of family science scholarship.

References

Aldrich, L., Guzzo, K.B., Brown, S.L., & Westrick-Payne, K.K. (2022). *Defining and measuring the complexity of stepfamilies in the United States.* https://mastresearch-center.org/wp-content/uploads/2022/09/stepfamilies-complexity-sep2022_final.pdf

Australian Bureau of Statistics. (2016). *Family blending.* Retrieved 11/6/2020 from https://profile.id.com.au/australia/family-blending

Cherlin, A. (1978). Remarriage as an incomplete institution. *American Journal of Sociology, 84,* 63–650. https://doi.org/10.1086/226830

Coleman, M., & Ganong, L. (1990). Remarriage and stepfamily research in the '80s: New interest in an old family form. *Journal of Marriage and the Family, 52,* 925–940. https://doi.org/10.2307/353311

Coleman, M., Ganong, L., & Fine, M. (2000). Reinvestigating remarriage: Another decade of progress. *Journal of Marriage and the Family, 62,* 1288–1307. https://doi.org/10.1111/j.1741-3737.2000.01288.x

Coleman, M., Ganong, L., & Gingrich, R. (1985). Stepfamily strengths: A review of the popular literature. *Family Relations, 34,* 583–589. https://doi.org/10.2307/584023

Coleman, M., Ganong, L., & Russell, L.T. (2012). Resilience in stepfamilies. In D. Becvar (Ed.), *Handbook on family resilience.* Springer. https://doi.org/10.1007/978-1-4614-3917-2_6

Daly, K. (2003). Family theory versus the theories families live by. *Journal of Marriage and Family, 65*(4), 771–784. https://doi.org/10.1111/j.1741-3737.2003.00771.x

Daly, M., & Wilson, M. (1998). *The truth about Cinderella: A Darwinian view.* Yale Press.

Eickmeyer, K.J. (2019). Composition of cohabiting families. *Family profiles*, FP-19-02. Bowling Green, OH: National Center for Family & Marriage Research. https://doi.org/10.25035/ncfmr/fp-19-02

Espinoza, R., & Newman, Y. (1979). *Stepparenting (DHEW Publication #48-579)*. U.S. Department of Health, Education, and Welfare.

Ganong, L., & Coleman, M. (1986). A comparison of clinical and empirical literature on children in stepfamilies. *Journal of Marriage and the Family, 48*, 309–318. https://doi.org/10.2307/352398

Ganong, L., & Coleman, M. (1994). *Remarried family relationships*. Newbury Park, CA: Sage.

Ganong, L., & Coleman, M. (2017). *Stepfamily relationships: Development, dynamics, and intervention* (2nd ed.). Springer. https://doi.org/10.10078/978-1-4899-7702-1

Ganong, L., & Coleman, M. (2018). Studying stepfamilies: Four eras of scholarship. *Family Process, 57*, 7–24. 10.1111/famp.12307. https://doi.org/10.1111/famp.12307

Ganong, L., Coleman, M., Fine, M., & Martin, P. (1999). Stepparents' affinity-seeking and affinity-maintaining strategies with stepchildren. *Journal of Family Issues, 20*, 299–327. https://doi.org/10.1177/019251399020003001

Gath, M. (2016). Identifying stepfamilies in longitudinal data. *Statistics New Zealand Working Paper No. 16-01*. Retrieved from www.stats.govt.nz

Guzzo, K.B. (2016). Stepfamilies in the U.S. *Family Profiles*. FP-16-09. Bowling Green, OH: National Center for Family Management & Marriage Research. www.bgsu.edu/ncfmr/resources/data/family-profiles/guzzo-stepfamilies-women-fp016-09.html https://doi.org/10.25035/ncfmr/fp-17-08

Juteau, G., Westrick-Payne, K.K., Brown, S.L., & Manning, W.D. (2023). Visualizing children's family structure. *Socius: Sociological Research for a Dynamic World, 9*, 1–3. https://doi.org/10.1177/23780231231205216

Kurosu, S., Lundh, C., & Breschi, M. (2014). Remarriage, gender, and rural households: A comparative analysis of widows and widowers in Europe and Asia. In C. Lundh & S. Kurosu (Eds.), *Similarity in difference: Marriage in Europe and Asia, 1700–1900* (pp. 169–208). MIT Press. https://doi.org/10.7551/mitpress/9780262027946.003.0006

Masten, A.S. (2018). Resilience theory and research on children and families: Past, present, and promise. *Journal of Family Theory & Review, 10*(1), 12–31. https://doi.org/10.1111/jftr.12255

Papernow, P.L. (1987). Thickening the "middle ground": Dilemmas and vulnerabilities of remarried couples. *Psychotherapy: Theory, Research, Practice, Training, 24*(3S), 630–639. https://doi.org/10.1037/h0085761

Payne, K.K. (2019). Children's family structure, 2019. *Family Profiles*, FP-19-25. Bowling Green, OH: National Center for Family & Marriage Research. https://doi.org/10.25035/ncfmr/fp-19-25

Raley, R.K., & Sweeney, M.M. (2020). Divorce, repartnering, and stepfamilies: A decade in review. *Journal of Marriage and Family, 82*(1), 81–99. https://doi.org/10.1111/jomf.12651

Sanner, C., Ganong, L.H., & Coleman, M. (2020). Shared children in stepfamilies: Experiences living in a hybrid family structure. *Journal of Marriage and Family, 82*, 605–621. https://doi.org/10.1111/jomf.12631

Sanner, C., & Jensen, T. (2021). Towards more accurate measures of family structure: Accounting for sibling complexity. *Journal of Family Theory & Review, 13*(1), 110–127. https://doi.org/10.1111/jftr.12406

Stykes, B., & Guzzo, K.B. (2015). Remarriage and stepfamilies. National Center for Family & Marriage Research. www.bgsu.edu/ncfmr/resources/data/family-profiles/stykes-guzzo-remarriagestepfamilies-fp-15-10. https://doi.org/10.25035/ncfmr/fp-17-08

Sweeney, M. M. (2010). Remarriage and stepfamilies: Strategic sites for family scholarship in the 21st Century. *Journal of Marriage & Family*, *72*, 667–684. https://doi.org/10.1111/j.1741-3737.2010.00724.x

Warner, L., & Erdelyi, G. (2022). Stepfamilies across Europe and overseas, 1550–1900. *The history of the family*. https://doi.org/10.1080/1081602X.2022.2101502

Weaver, S., & Coleman, M. (2005). A mothering but not a mother role: A grounded theory study of the nonresidential stepmother role. *Journal of Social and Personal Relationships*, *22*, 477–497. https://doi.org/10.1177/0265407505054519

Westrick-Payne, K.K. (2023). Remarriage rate, 2021. *Family Profiles, FP-23-19*. National Center for Family & Marriage Research. https://doi.org/10.25035/ncfmr/fp-23-19

Wilson, L. (2014). *A history of stepfamilies in early America*. University of North Carolina Press.

2

WHAT WORKS IN REMARRYING AND REPARTNERING IN STEPFAMILIES

Effective Stepcouples

The interactions between the adults who form stepfamilies are important, not only for the well-being of the two adults involved, but also for their children's well-being and that of the entire family system. We think of adults as the "captains" of their families – the ones who oversee operations, make decisions, and maintain the health, safety, and general well-being of all family members. Family therapist Virginia Satir (1972) referred to committed romantic couples as "the architects" of the families they make because they are responsible for designing and building the family environment and family culture into which children are socialized. If the couple is thriving, the thinking goes, then so too will the family.

In first-union families, married or cohabiting, couples usually form their relationships prior to childrearing, and children are eventually added to the family culture the couple created. In stepfamilies, however, repartnered couples seldom have the luxury of building the foundation of a family culture before adding children. Instead, one or more children belonging to either or both partners are present when stepfamilies are formed. In some stepfamilies, children from prior unions are merely interested observers in the couple's development and creation of a stepfamily culture, but sometimes the children are actively involved in influencing couple dynamics and the stepfamily culture. If remarried and

DOI: 10.4324/9781003369073-2

repartnered cohabiting couples are "architects" of their stepfamilies, they are architects with motivated consultants. Former spouses who are coparents to children from earlier unions also may be thought of as interested observers, if not motivated consultants to these stepfamily architects.

In this chapter, we examine research on *what works* when parents repartner or remarry. We begin by looking at effective practices in dating and the courtship dynamics of single parents and how they prepare for stepfamily repartnerships or remarriage. We then look at personal characteristics of partners that contribute to success in stepfamily couple relationships and couple dynamics that are effective. Finally, we examine research findings on how other people positively influence repartnering quality and stability. The outcomes explored in these *what works* studies are measures of individual well-being, such as mood, affect, perceived relationship quality (e.g., happiness, satisfaction, adjustment) and perceived relationship stability (i.e., thoughts and beliefs about whether the couple will survive in the future or not).

Dating and Courtship

Most people who separate or divorce go on to cohabit or remarry with a new partner (Guzzo, 2016, 2018). The failure of one or more romantic relationships does not seem to deter divorced and separated parents from wanting to engage in another couple bond, lending credence to Samuel Johnson's famous statement in the 18th century that "remarriage is the triumph of hope over experience." Parents whose spouses die are less likely to remarry (James & Shafer, 2012), but finding a new partner after bereavement is not rare, especially for younger widow(er)s (James & Shafer, 2012). In the United States, the most common sequence of courtship after relationship dissolution is dating, followed by cohabitation for a time, and then remarriage (Montgomery et al., 1992). Of course, for some parents, cohabitation is not a phase or step toward remarriage, but a relational end (Smock & Schwartz, 2020). It should be noted also that some parents find new partners before separating from their spouses or cohabiting partners. Given that researchers have not studied these individuals as a unique group of divorcing/separating parents, however, there is little we can say about *what works* in these situations. It is likely that some of these parents are included in samples of formerly married parents who are dating.

In the United States, parental dating after divorce is widespread, and individuals seldom wait long after separation to begin dating. Roughly 50% of mothers date within 60 days of filing for divorce (Anderson et al., 2004), and up to 85% report dating within two years of filing (Langlais et al., 2015). It is common for divorced individuals to date more than one person – in one study mothers reported an average of 2.5 new dating partners in the first year following their divorce (Anderson et al., 2004), and in another study, divorced mothers reported more than 10 dating relationships before they remarried (Montgomery et al., 1992). Mothers who had multiple dating partners either dated more than one person during the same period (i.e., simultaneous dating) or dated only one partner at a time but replaced them with a new partner when those relationships ended (i.e., sequential monogamous dating; Langlais et al., 2015).

Parents' dating relationships after separation and divorce are known to be a source of stress for parents (Langlais et al., 2016) and children (Langlais et al., 2017) as they adjust to the changes accompanying divorce. Children and adults are aware that there is a possibility that parental dating may lead to more serious romantic unions, such as cohabitation or remarriage (Anderson et al., 2004), and the possibility that a new dating partner might become a stepparent/partner is sometimes unnerving. For children, a parent's dating may be a symbol that the divorce is permanent (Langlais et al., 2015).

Each new dating relationship represents further transitions that require children and parents to adjust (Anderson & Greene, 2005, 2011; Miller-Ott, 2013). For example, when parents have multiple dating partners who are around for a while and then leave, children and adults often have to adjust emotionally and interpersonally to these transitions. If children bond with a parent's new dating partner, serial dating relationships may feel like added losses and greater instability. This may aggravate the possible negative effects of divorce on children's well-being and adjustment, such as more frequent internalizing and externalizing behavior problems (DeAnda et al., 2021; Langlais et al., 2017) and less social competence (Montgomery et al., 1992). However, dating also potentially provides benefits. If a divorced parent's new dating partner becomes a serious romantic companion and a stable part of children's lives, the parent may benefit by receiving additional support, companionship, and affection.

Nonetheless, children are faced with adjusting to the new individual, and everyone is met with adapting to new relational dynamics in the family or household (Ganong & Coleman, 2017). The bottom line is that dating is an important part of the process of finding a new partner/stepparent, but it is not without risks for children.

What Works in Dating and Courtship

Nine studies have explicitly examined *what works* in the dating dynamics of single parents. Five studies were based on a longitudinal investigation of 319 post-divorce mothers in Texas (Anderson & Greene, 2011; DeAnda et al., 2021; Langlais et al., 2015, 2016, 2017), two studies were grounded in qualitative, in-depth interviews with 35 divorced coparents (Miller, 2009a, 2009b), and two studies were of remarried older adults who retrospectively looked back on what worked and what did not work when they were seeking new partners after the death of a spouse (Carr & Boerner, 2013; Nice et al., 2021). All studies were conducted in the United States.

Dating Patterns

In the longitudinal Texas Family Project, the effects of dating patterns on the well-being of divorced mothers were explored (Langlais et al., 2015). Mothers' dating patterns included: (a) no dating, (b) dating one partner only, (c) dating multiple partners serially, and (d) dating multiple partners simultaneously. Mothers' reports were obtained from monthly diaries written over three years. Although differences in mothers' well-being and dating relationship quality between dating patterns were small, suggesting that variations in dating patterns do not matter much, mothers who dated monogamously (i.e., one partner only or one at a time serially) were less likely to engage in risky behaviors (e.g., getting drunk, having unprotected sex) than mothers who dated multiple partners simultaneously. For mothers who want to date, monogamy or serial monogamy appear to be less personally risky than seeing multiple dating partners concurrently (Langlais et al., 2015).

Dating Orientations

Another way of thinking about dating patterns is to examine what researchers have called dating orientations, defined as an attitude or approach to dating in which parents prioritize either self-interests or child interests (Anderson & Greene, 2011). Mothers who agreed with such sentiments as, "I would not marry someone my child disliked," "I need to focus my time and attention on my child because she has had a hard time since the divorce," and "my child's welfare is my top priority," are thought to have child-focused approaches to dating. In contrast, other mothers were more adult-focused when dating (i.e., thinking more about finding a partner that met their needs, rather than their children's needs). Regardless of dating orientation, the mothers in this study saw themselves and their children as a "package deal" when dating (Anderson & Greene, 2011). However, mothers' dating orientations influenced how they managed problems between their dating partners and their children. Child-focused mothers more actively tried to facilitate better relationships between their children and their significant other when their children did not like their new partners. In contrast, mothers with more adult-focused orientations became more involved in helping improve partner–child ties when they perceived that dating partners did not like their children. Both dating approaches potentially help develop partner–child relationships that may lead to positive stepfamily bonds, so either an adult focus or a child focus to dating can be effective.

Quality of Dating Relationships

Research evidence suggests that the quality of relationships with dating partners matters more than other aspects of dating for mothers' well-being (DeAnda et al., 2021; Langlais et al., 2016). Mothers' rapport with partners, frequency of spending time together, getting along well with the dating partner, and commitment to and satisfaction with the dating relationship were associated with fewer depression symptoms (DeAnda et al., 2021) and greater life satisfaction for mothers (Langlais et al., 2016). In addition, high-quality dating relationships can help offset the negative effects of children's internalizing behaviors (e.g., sadness, withdrawal) on mothers' depression symptoms (DeAnda et al., 2021). Mothers in high-quality dating relationships are more satisfied with their lives than mothers who are not dating (Langlais et al., 2016). The researchers speculated that high-quality dating partners provide mothers with financial, emotional, and parental support that help improve their quality of life

(DeAnda et al., 2021; Langlais et al., 2016). In contrast, low-quality dating relationships can make mothers' lives worse; in fact, non-daters are more satisfied with their lives than women in lower-quality dating relationships (Langlais et al., 2016). Being alone was better for mothers' well-being than being with a bad dating partner, which suggests that mothers should be discriminating in whom they choose to date.

Keep Searching

How does a divorced or separated person find high-quality partners? Although little direct research evidence addresses this question, findings suggest that parents may need to date until they find someone they like, enjoy spending time with, and who meets their needs (Langlais et al., 2017). Unless a parent is fortunate, and their first dating partner is a good match, parents, and indirectly their children, likely will experience one or more dating breakups as they search for a partner that meets their needs.

The good news from research is that dating breakups are not particularly stressful (Langlais et al., 2016, 2017). In fact, life satisfaction improves after ending a dating relationship, regardless of whether a mother stays single and does not date (Langlais et al., 2017) or finds a new dating partner (Langlais et al., 2016). Researchers speculate that mothers who date multiple partners and who have multiple breakups with low stress may be the ones who initiate the breakups and who are more confident in their abilities to find other people to date (Langlais et al., 2017). These mothers keep searching for a good match for them and their children. See Box 2.1 for a brief list of *what works* findings about parental dating.

Box 2.1 *What works* in dating

What works in dating and courtship

- Think carefully about when to introduce your children to dating partners.
- Make a list of desired attributes you want in a new partner and seek dating partners who have those attributes.
- Date one person at a time to reduce risks related to dating (e.g., drunkenness, unprotected sex).

- Be selective when choosing dating partners. Being alone is better than being with a bad dating partner.
- Focus on either children or yourself when dating – both orientations work.
- Be persistent when searching for quality dating partners. Do not settle and do not hesitate to end a bad dating relationship.

What works in dating and coparenting

- Be sensitive to coparent's feelings when dating (help them save face).
- Be sensitive to children's feelings and keep them out of coparenting and dating issues.
- Limit dating information revealed to coparents but continue to share information related to the children.
- Use email and text to help control what is communicated about dating.
- Set rules for yourself regarding how much you will communicate to the coparent about dating.
- If possible, negotiate and agree on what information about dating will be shared with coparent.
- Confront and discuss with coparents any violations of privacy rules. Negotiate new privacy rules and make the new rules explicit.
- Try not to stress about coparents' reports of their dating activities.

What works in post-bereavement dating

- Wait to date and allow time to grieve.
- Grieve with children; talk to them about the deceased loved one and your feelings.
- Talk with children about the possibility of dating.
- Apologize and share feelings and grieve with the children to repair relationships if they are upset because they think dating was too soon after their parent's death.

A Big Caution

Advising divorced parents to search for a partner who is a good match is common sense that is supported by research. However, dating research leaves many important unanswered questions.

First, none of the post-divorce dating research examines the effects on children of being exposed to multiple potential stepparents. Clinicians warn that bonding with a parents' dating partner who is then removed because the parent and partner breakup may result in long-term issues for children. For instance, they may learn not to attach to people they like, not to invest emotionally in relationships because of concerns those relationships will not last, and to become cynical about marriage and other committed relationships (Ganong & Coleman, 2017).

Divorced mothers vary widely in their approach to exposing children to dating partners (Anderson et al., 2004). In what researchers called the *encapsulated approach*, mothers do not communicate anything about their dating activities to their children, regardless of how casual or serious those relationships are. In the *graded approach*, mothers do not introduce children to dating partners until the relationships become more serious, whereas in the *transparent approach*, children are told about every date and generally meet all dating partners from the start (Anderson et al., 2004). Other researchers found that most divorced parents feel that dating partners should be introduced to their children early in the relationship and more information shared with children *only* if the dating partner is perceived to potentially be helpful to the parent in coparenting (Kang et al., 2023). Parents generally feel that children should not be told much about casual partners, such as those that parents view as romantic or sexual partners only (Kang et al., 2023). As noted, the effects of these parental approaches on children are not known, so we cannot say *what works* from an evidence-based position.

Second, there is evidence from research on divorce dynamics that the spouse who decides to end the marriage (i.e., *the leaver*) has a different, less stressful experience than the spouse who does not initiate the dissolution (i.e., *the left*; Black et al., 1991; Buehler, 1987; Hopper, 1993). It seems probable to us that dating breakups of divorced parents are similar. *What works* behaviors and strategies for dating parents may depend on who initiates the breakup.

Finally, there is a general lack of research about dating dynamics – how often dating occurs, when, length of dating relationships prior to break-ups, children's contact with former dating partners, parents' transparency about dating – and the well-being of children, parents, and family relationships. In short, much needs to be known about *what works* for dating parents and their children prior to stepfamily formation.

Coparenting and Dating

After separation and divorce, parents are often challenged to redefine and renegotiate their relationships as coparents of their children (Ganong & Coleman, 2017). No longer romantic partners, parents must learn how to continue childrearing as coparents to their children while ending the intimate, sexual, and "couple" parts of their relationships. New dating relationships present parents with more challenges, as they try to build new romantic unions while maintaining coparenting relationships with exes. For example, how much to tell exes about dating, when to share dating information, and how to soften or diminish their concerns about dating and new partners, are all issues that dating parents face. What we know about *what works* for dating coparents comes from two papers by Aimee Miller, a communications scholar who investigated how divorced parents "save face" (i.e., maintain a favorable social impression on others) for themselves and their coparents (Miller, 2009a), and how they set and maintain boundaries (Miller, 2009b). See Box 2.1 for *what works* findings regarding coparenting and dating.

When a Parent Dates

One way that coparents engaged in face saving for their partners was to limit what they shared about their dating. One father in Miller's (2009a) study said:

> I didn't want to rub anything in her face and make her think that I had already found someone to take her place. I was very conscious of her feelings. She would ask me maybe what I did last weekend, and I would say I went out.
>
> (p. 166)

Parents develop personal "rules" about what and how much information about dating they will share (Miller, 2009b). They do this out of concern for sparing the former partner's feelings, keeping as much harmony in coparenting relationships as possible, and keeping children out of the middle of parental issues. Dating parents feel that it is important for them to communicate basic information about dating that affects their children (e.g., when they might be busy and unavailable), but they avoid sharing the specifics of dating, intimacy, or feelings about their dating partners. For some parents, communicating to ex-partners about their dating via email or text was a way of ensuring that shared information was limited and communicated carefully (Miller, 2009a). In deciding what to communicate to coparents, dating parents assess the risks and benefits of sharing specific types of information about dating. Risks included risk of damaging the coparenting relationship, risk of hurting their personal reputations, and fears about their personal security and safety if former partners become angry (Miller, 2009b).

Individuals who have amiable coparenting relationships are more able than parents with strained relationships to engage in conversations about dating where they could be more open about their own and their coparents' thoughts and feelings (Miller, 2009a). These in-depth conversations allow them to disclose dating information before the coparents learn about it from other people. In general, dating coparents are satisfied with how their personal privacy rules work (Miller, 2009b). When the personal privacy rules did not work, however, it was because coparents violated the typically unstated rules, perhaps because they did not understand them, the rules were unclear, or because the rules had not been explicitly communicated. When rule violations occur, effective coparents realize they need either to negotiate new privacy rules that both parents will follow or to make sure their personal privacy rules are clearly conveyed and mutually understood (Miller, 2009b).

When a Coparent Dates

Effective parents expect that former partners can be trusted to make good dating choices and that they are willing to disclose appropriate amounts of information about their dating (Miller, 2009b). If these assumptions prove to be untrue, with former partners divulging too much information, for instance, parents either express indifference and mask their feelings (e.g., "I would change the subject and say I had to go") to avoid conflict or they would directly confront the coparent to establish more comfortable information boundaries (Miller, 2009a). It should be noted that masking feelings, sometimes called expressive suppression, is effective as short-term coping, but using this as a coping technique in the longer term prevents problem-solving and the resolution of bad feelings (Gross, 1999).

Dating After Bereavement

Unfortunately, no studies have explored dating by widows and widowers with younger children, though two studies shed light on *what works* for older bereaved parents and their adult children. One was a qualitative study of six father–adult child pairs (Nice et al., 2021), and the other was a longitudinal quantitative investigation of 276 widowed parents (Carr & Boerner, 2013). Despite different methods used and diverse samples, the findings of these studies converge to send simple messages about *what works*. Both studies show that the death of a loved family member is not only a life event faced by individuals; grieving and adjusting to loss also are relational dynamics embedded in longstanding family relationships. What this means for parents is that their own sadness and bereavement are not independent of adult children's grief and mourning, and being sensitive to children's feelings is a meaningful part of widowed parents' adjustments. Bereaved widows' dating and searching for a new partner, therefore, affects their children as well as themselves. See Box 2.1.

Take Time to Mourn

The biggest takeaway is that bereaved parents who take time to mourn their losses before dating and repartnering adjust better, as do their adult children, than those who start dating "too soon" (Carr & Boerner, 2013; Nice et al., 2021). Norms for what is a suitable time to spend grieving varies, and these studies do not stipulate a minimum threshold of time, although Carr and Boerner (2013) suggest parents wait a year or more to date because 18 months was too soon for some adult children. Instead, these researchers recommend that parents allow themselves and their children adequate time to process the death before dating or even thinking about dating (Carr & Boerner, 2013). Effective parents judge when it is the right time to date by mourning with their children, talking with them about their memories of the deceased loved one, their sadness and loneliness, and, at some point, seeking adult children's thoughts about the widowed individuals' dating.

Repair Relationships

So, what happens when widowed parents do not take sufficient time to mourn? In one study, fathers who had dated and remarried within 18 months after bereavement regretted this later because relationships with children were strained (Nice et al., 2021). They were able to retroactively understand how painful the spouse's death had been for the children. One father noted, "I did not take enough time to mourn her passing and that was not helpful" (Nice et al., 2021, p. 10). Another stated, "Dating again was just too soon. I was lonely, but I just should have accepted loneliness as what I needed" (p. 11). In *healing conversations*, fathers worked through this hurt with their adult children by talking to them about mistakes they made, sharing feelings, and grieving together as they repaired relationships.

Cohabitation Prior to Remarriage

Once dating relationships become serious, many partners decide to move in together, initiating stepfamily formation. For some couples, living together without being married is an alternative to remarriage (Guzzo, 2018). For other couples, cohabitation is a stepping stone to remarriage; more than half of couples who remarry live together prior to remarriage (Sobotka & Berghammer, 2021). Premarital cohabitation is common enough that for many couples it is a predictable stage of the courtship process for single adults who have children. This process typically involves meeting the potential partner, dating while living apart, keeping separate households but spending overnights together a few times a week, moving in together and merging possessions into one household, and then, for many, legally marrying (Montgomery et al., 1992).

There are many reasons why divorced and separated individuals with children live together before they decide to remarry. Some parents see living together as easing into sharing a household with a new partner without contending with the added pressure of legal obligations (Xu et al., 2006). Living together is seen as a testing ground for lifestyle compatibility, learning about how the other lives, and working out relationship kinks prior to remarriage (Ganong & Coleman, 1989). As couples gradually spend more time with each other and with their partner's children from prior unions, living together becomes more convenient and logical than living apart, and may be seen as financially cost-effective because they save money and time by not commuting between households and paying two rents or mortgages (Hetherington & Kelly, 2002).

Mixed Evidence for the Benefits of Cohabitation

The research evidence on the effects of cohabiting prior to remarriage is decidedly mixed. Some scholars have found that cohabitation benefits remarriages (Crapo et al., 2022; Ganong & Coleman, 1989; Hanna & Knaub, 1981; Higginbotham et al., 2009; Montgomery et al., 1992) while some describe negative effects of cohabitation (King, 2009; Langlais et al., 2016; Stanley et al., 2010; Tach & Halpern-Meekin, 2009; Thomson et al., 2001; Xu et al., 2006). Other researchers report that premarital cohabitors do not differ from non-cohabitors in either positive or negative ways after remarriage (Langlais et al., 2017; Skinner et al., 2002), and still others report cohabitation benefits some but not others (Turner et al., 2021).

It should be noted that studies drawn from the same datasets have yielded mixed findings on the effectiveness of cohabitation prior to remarriage. For example, using data from the U.S. National Study of Families and Households, Xu et al. (2006) reported that cohabitors experienced lower remarital quality and happiness and more doubts that the relationship will last, while Skinner et al. (2002) did not find differences between those that cohabited prior to remarriage and those that did not. Studies drawn from the longitudinal Texas Family Project also returned mixed findings (Langlais et al., 2016, 2017), as did two studies drawn from the same longitudinal data set of newly remarried couples in Utah (Crapo et al., 2022; Turner et al., 2021). Their inconsistent results led Crapo and colleagues (2022) to reason that the effects of cohabitation on remarriage may be an issue of when remarriage occurs, the characteristics of couples, what outcomes are examined (positive or negative), and what other variables are controlled for in the study. In short, the research findings on if and how premarital cohabitation effectively prepares couples for remarriage and stepfamily living are unclear.

There is evidence from older studies for why cohabitation may work for some remarried individuals, however (Ganong & Coleman, 1989; Hanna & Knaub, 1981; Montgomery et al., 1992). For example, remarried husbands who cohabited had fewer marital disagreements, fewer marital problems, and more affection for their spouses than husbands who had not cohabited prior to remarriage, and wives who cohabited had fewer marital disagreements than those who had not (Ganong & Coleman, 1989; Hanna & Knaub, 1981). Cohabitators may be individuals who are concerned about avoiding a future divorce, so they live together and do other forms of preparation for remarriage, such as reading advice books (Hanna & Knaub, 1981). In another early study, in families where mothers cohabited prior to remarriage, children showed higher levels of social competence and lower levels of externalizing behaviors (i.e., acting out, misbehaving) over the first two years of remarriage compared to families in which mothers did not cohabit with stepfathers (Montgomery et al., 1992). Overall, cohabiting stepfamilies interacted more positively than did non-cohabiting stepfamilies one year after remarriage. The authors of this study reasoned that cohabitation may be a slower transition to remarried stepfamily life, allowing the stepfather to be gradually incorporated into family routines (Montgomery et al., 1992). Although researchers have examined the effects of cohabitation prior to remarriage, the evidence supporting cohabitation as an effective action that helps subsequent remarriages and stepfamilies is mixed. As the rates of cohabiting increase, there is a need for well-designed studies that address this issue. We return to this subject later in the chapter.

Preparation for Remarriage

Once couples become serious about the relationship, what do they do to prepare for remarriage? The few researchers that have tried to address this question (Ganong & Coleman, 1989; Higginbotham et al., 2009), despite being conducted decades apart, reached the same conclusion: "little is known about how remarried adults with children actually prepare for remarriage" (Ganong & Coleman, 1989, p. 28).

We do know that there are several educational programs designed for remarried couples in stepfamilies, as well as countless books, magazine articles, podcasts, and websites. Some counselors and therapists specialize in stepfamily issues, and it is likely that these family professionals also help their clients get ready for family life after remarriage (for example, see Browning & Artelt, 2012 and Papernow, 2013). There are also attorneys who specialize in family legal issues who help stepcouples in preparing wills, trusts, and prenuptial agreements. Unfortunately, what little evidence we have about the proportion of remarrying couples that try to prepare themselves and their children for stepfamily living shows that most do little, if anything, to prepare for remarriage (Ganong & Coleman, 1989; Higginbotham et al., 2009). Cohabiting (Ganong & Coleman, 1989) and talking with other couples, their parents, and religious leaders (Higginbotham et al., 2009) were the only sources of preparation engaged in by more than half of the remarried individuals in two investigations. We do not know of any investigations into the effectiveness of premarital stepfamily therapy or legal preparation.

Remarriage Preparation that Works

In one study, more than half of remarried men and women rated the following sources of information as "helpful" or "very helpful": reading books; receiving professional counseling; talking with religious leaders, other couples, and parents; and attending a class or workshop (Higginbotham et al., 2009). In general, most individuals thought that all forms of preparation were helpful to some degree, although none of the ten types of remarital preparation examined were predictive of adjustment in remarriage one year later (Higginbotham et al., 2009). The authors speculated that any form of preparation is likely to benefit stepcouples by making them aware of issues they may face.

Most educational programs and materials (i.e., books, articles, podcasts, websites) are aimed at couples who are about to remarry or who are living in stepfamilies (Adler-Baeder & Higginbotham, 2020). These educational endeavors usually cover stepfamily issues broadly, but most programs are designed for stepcouples only to attend (see Higginbotham & Skogrand, 2010 for an exception). Stepfamily education programs are usually based on family systems theory and address topics relevant to couples, stepparents and stepchildren, parents and children, coparenting, and children's developmental needs and adjustments to family transitions (Adler-Baeder & Higginbotham, 2020; Whitton et al., 2008). Evaluation studies of stepfamily education programs suggest that individuals who take part in them change how they interact as couples and as coparents in small, but statistically significant, degrees (Lucier-Greer et al., 2012; Lucier-Greer et al., 2014). Unfortunately, with rare exceptions (e.g., Lucier-Greer et al., 2014), evaluations have not employed comparison groups, nor have they used randomly assigned control groups in their efforts to assess the efficacy of programs, meaning that they cannot conclude with certainty that the programs are effective (Adler-Baeder & Higginbotham, 2020; Whitton et al., 2008). Also, with few exceptions, such as Higginbotham and colleagues' work in Utah with Hispanic stepcouples (e.g., Skogrand et al., 2009, 2014) and Adler-Baeder and colleagues' programs that have oversampled for African American couples (e.g., Lucier-Greer et al., 2012, 2014), participants in these programs generally have been White, further limiting the conclusions that may be drawn about their efficacy. Our conclusion is to agree with scholars who reason that participants benefit from stepcouple educational programs because sensitivity to stepfamily issues is raised, and participants are taught communication and problem-solving skills that promote relationship well-being. See Box 2.2 for lists of *what works* in preparing for remarriage.

Box 2.2 *What works* in preparing for remarriage and remarriage ceremonies

- Attend a workshop or educational program designed for repartnering couples. Stepfamily education can help increase sensitivity to stepfamily issues. Communication and problem-solving skills may be learned. Also, read books, articles, and blogs about stepcouples and stepfamilies, see a therapist or counselor knowledgeable about stepfamilies, and prepare for repartnering in other ways to increase awareness of issues.
- Inform and consult with stepchildren about the remarriage ceremony in advance.
- Include stepchildren in planning remarriage ceremonies.
- Focus the ceremony on new family, not just on the new couple.
- Recognize in the ceremony that stepchildren are going to be part of the new stepfamily.

Remarriage Ceremonies

Couples who decide to remarry may see the wedding celebrating their nuptials as a ceremony for themselves alone, but remarriage rituals can be an effective way to garner support from stepchildren (Baxter et al., 2009). In a qualitative study of stepchildren's perceptions of their parent's and stepparent's wedding, communication scholars found that there was no one right way to have a remarriage ceremony, but stepchildren are more supportive and see the remarriage as more legitimate when they are included in the planning of the ceremony and made a part of the ceremony itself (Baxter et al., 2009). They want to be informed and even consulted about the ceremony in advance, and they want to hear about the wedding plans directly from their parent and stepparent (as opposed to from grandparents or stepsiblings). Stepchildren want the ceremony to focus on the family as a whole and not just the couple, so ceremonies that recognize that children are a major part of the newly formed family are seen as more legitimate (Baxter et al., 2009). Wedding rituals also are more meaningful to stepchildren when adults take sufficient time *before* marriage to let stepchildren and stepparents get to know each other. In terms of the actual ceremony, stepchildren endorsed what the authors called the "Goldilocks Principle" (Baxter et al., 2009, p. 476), with not too much and not too little of the traditional wedding rituals included. The ambiguity of this principle, however, makes it hard for stepcouples to know what to do, other than to include children in planning ceremonies (see Box 2.2).

Individual Characteristics that Contribute to *What Works* in Repartnering

Stepfamily researchers have examined intrapersonal characteristics of individuals that contribute to successful remarriages and cohabiting repartnerships. In our review, we examined only variables that individuals have control over. As such, we excluded variables such as race, ethnicity, social class, or sex, instead focusing on self-awareness, attitudes, beliefs, general moods, and attachment styles (which are amenable to change).

Self-Awareness and Learning from the Past

Three studies, two employing qualitative methods with U.S. samples of post-divorce (Brimhall et al., 2008) and post-bereavement

(Brimhall & Engblom-Deglmann, 2011) remarried parents, and the third using a quantitative longitudinal design with a Dutch sample of both first marriage and repartnered parents (Ivanova, 2016), reported that prior marital experiences sensitize individuals to marital dynamics in ways that benefited the respondents or their partners. Self-awareness gained from past marital experiences led divorced individuals to deliberately seek partners who are different in meaningful ways from their first spouses (Brimhall et al., 2008). For example, some individuals made lists of attributes they wanted in their new partner that were lacking in their former spouse, and then sought potential partners with those desired characteristics (Brimhall et al., 2008). They were aware of what had gone wrong in their prior unions and were unwilling to tolerate behaviors in their new spouses that they disliked about old spouses. Consequently, these self-aware remarried individuals did not hesitate to share thoughts and feelings about what they had learned about unwanted spousal behaviors with their new partners. Further, they communicated what they would do if their new partners engaged in similar unwanted behaviors in the remarriage. In fact, more open communication was a goal for remarriage that was learned from prior dissatisfying marriages (Brimhall et al., 2008). As one remarried man said, "I'd have point blank addressed it right then and there ... I don't want that relationship again. I have been there, done that ... [I am] not going to tolerate the kind of crap [I] did the first time around" (Brimhall et al., 2008, p. 378).

These post-divorce remarried parents also were aware of their own contributions to past relational problems. Therefore, they paid attention to their emotional triggers and reactions to partners' behaviors and purposely did not respond as they had done in the past. As one remarried husband revealed to Brimhall and colleagues (2008, p. 379):

"We need to talk" ... when my first wife told me that, [it meant] there was hell to pay ... So, when Kay would say that, I went off the edge ... I got psyched up, pumped up, ready for war ... It took me a while to get past, "we need to talk."

They also avoided doing things that threatened their partner's sense of well-being and trust in them (Brimhall et al., 2008). For example, one woman said, "I will never cuss at him because I know that she did that" (p. 380). Being aware of a new partner's emotional triggers helped reduce conflicts and increased harmony in the remarriage.

Remarriages formed after the death of a spouse have different issues than do post-divorce couples, but self-awareness and learning from the past is still helpful (Brimhall & Engblom-Deglmann, 2011). Even widowed individuals who have had a long and satisfying marriage made lists of attributes they wanted in a new spouse, just as divorced individuals did (Brimhall & Engblom-Deglmann, 2011). Individuals change as they get older, and what they seek in a partner also may change, even when their first marriage was good. Self-awareness for widow(er)s entailed being sensitive to new spouses' insecurities about being compared unfavorably to a deceased, beloved spouse. Being aware of this led bereaved remarried partners to be frank about the good and bad in response to new spouses' questions about their prior marriages and their deceased spouses. Such openness had positive effects on the spouse's feelings and on the couple's interactions (Brimhall & Engblom-Deglmann, 2011). For example, one man said, "That was really when I started loving [her] is when she was so open about her husband" (Brimhall & Engblom-Deglmann, 2011, p. 55). Refraining from comparing deceased and new spouses in ways that might make new spouses feel insecure benefited the spouse and the remarriage (Brimhall & Engblom-Deglmann, 2011).

Beliefs and Attitudes about Repartnering

Beliefs and attitudes are relevant constructs to investigate because they are related to what people do and how they interact with others (Blumer, 1969). In other words, people act on their beliefs, attitudes, and cognitive constructions they hold to be true. By knowing what an individual's views are about remarriage and repartnered cohabitation, we understand more about how they will behave or engage in remarriage or cohabitation. Only a few stepfamily researchers have examined specific beliefs and attitudes that predict adjustment and satisfaction in remarriage

(Higginbotham & Adler-Baeder, 2008; Higginbotham & Agee, 2013; Slattery et al., 2011) and cohabitation (Slattery et al., 2011).

Higginbotham and colleagues created the Remarriage Belief Inventory (RMBI) to assess beliefs about remarriage and stepfamilies (Higginbotham & Adler-Baeder, 2008). Of the seven subscales of the RMBI, two predicted remarriage satisfaction and adjustment: (a) the belief that a couple's finances should be pooled, and (b) the belief that success in remarriage is likely (Higginbotham & Adler-Baeder, 2008). The authors speculated that beliefs about pooling finances may show commitment to working together as a couple to invest collectively in the future of the relationship. Believing that remarriages and stepfamilies can succeed suggests optimism about the future, a commitment to investing in and working on the relationship, and confidence in the ability to solve problems and overcome challenges (Higginbotham & Adler-Baeder, 2008).

In an investigation with another remarried sample, three RMBI subscales predicted couple cohesion (i.e., the degree to which couples engage in outside interests together and discuss stimulating ideas) and couple consensus (i.e., the degree to which couples agree on significant issues; Higginbotham & Agee, 2013). First, believing that their chances for success in remarriage were good was positively related to cohesion and consensus for both men and women. Feeling positive about your stepfamily's prospects may serve as self-fulfilling prophecies and encourage couples to invest more in the remarriage. Second, beliefs that children should not be prioritized over the new spouse also predicted cohesion and consensus. This supports the idea that new remarriages need to be nurtured by both partners and focusing primarily on children (to the exclusion of the marital relationship) makes this difficult. Third, believing that couple's finances should be pooled was predictive of positive outcomes for men and women. This belief may show a desire to commit to the partnership by investing "all-in" financially.

In an innovative Australian study in which the researchers employed oral history interviews and observations of couple interactions in remarried and cohabiting stepfamilies, two constructs were created that predicted relationship satisfaction and partners' views on how likely they were to stay together: *couple bond* and *stepfamily bond* (Slattery et al., 2011). An important part of the couple bond was a sense of "we-ness," or having shared goals and values as a couple. An important part of the stepfamily bond was having a shared stepfamily identity that included all family members (i.e., stepfamily cohesion). Strong couple bonds and strong stepfamily bonds for remarried couples and cohabiting stepcouples were related to relationship satisfaction and stability early in the relationship (Slattery et al., 2011). These researchers clearly saw attitudes and behaviors as linked phenomena that combine for a holistic depiction of *what works* for stepfamily couples.

A Special Belief – Confidence in Their Relationship Resilience

Two interrelated beliefs are often linked by researchers who study resilience dynamics of stepfamily couples. These interconnected beliefs are *confidence in their abilities to resolve problems as a couple* and the *belief that their relationships will last*. These beliefs have been variously conceptualized as *marital confidence* (Jensen & Ganong, 2023; Ganong et al., 2019), *expecting remarital success* (Higginbotham & Adler-Baeder, 2008; Higginbotham & Agee, 2013), *perceived stability* (Kopystynska et al., 2022; Turner et al., 2021), and *relationship stability* (Jackson et al., 2023; Pace et al., 2015; Petren et al., 2019). We think these combined beliefs form a productive and meaningful meta-belief that partners are *confident in their relationship resilience*. In short, individuals in successful repartnerships believe they can resolve problems they may face in the future; they expect to be successful in their romantic relationships and they expect the bonds to last forever. Perhaps not surprisingly, people who are confident in their relationship resilience are more satisfied with their relationships (Higginbotham & Adler-Baeder, 2008; Slattery et al., 2011), do more activities together as a couple (Higginbotham & Agee, 2013), and feel more support and togetherness with their partners (Jensen & Ganong, 2023). Confident couples do not just think their unions will last – they indeed stay together more often than less confident couples (Slattery et al., 2011), and they report fewer parenting and stepparenting difficulties (Pace et al., 2015; Turner et al., 2021).

How do couples acquire relationship confidence? The simple answer seems to be that they are confident in their future resilience because they get along, frequently express affection physically (e.g., hugs, kisses), enjoy doing things as a couple (e.g., working on household projects, going on dates, socializing with friends), talk to each other often, and express themselves clearly when it comes to their thoughts and feelings about the relationship (Ganong et al., 2019; Kopystynska et al., 2022; Pace et al., 2015; Slattery et al., 2011). The belief that one can resolve relational issues is characteristic of individuals who are open to discussing personal problems with their partners, say what they want clearly, and do not avoid difficult conversations with their partners (Pace et al., 2015).

Chicken or Egg?

Our careful reading of the research suggests that, in some studies, relationship confidence is conceptualized as a *predictor* of positive relationships (Jensen & Ganong, 2023; Higginbotham & Adler-Baeder, 2008; Higginbotham & Agee, 2013; Pace et al., 2015; Slattery et al., 2011; Turner et al., 2021), whereas in other studies, relationship confidence is thought to be an *outcome* of positive relationships (e.g., Crapo et al., 2022; Ganong et al., 2019; Jackson et al., 2023; Petren et al., 2018). Studies suggest that both are likely true (Petren et al., 2019; Turner et al., 2021). We cannot know for certain if marital confidence is cause or effect; we only know that marital confidence and positive relationships co-occur. Correlation does not mean causation, but the fact that confidence in relationship resilience is significantly related to positive couple and step-family dynamics in several investigations suggests that holding positive beliefs about relational resilience is an important phenomenon in effective repartnerships.

Attachment Style

Attachment theory initially proposed that infants and young children develop internal working models of relationships (i.e., cognitive representations of the world and other people, including themselves) that are shaped by their caregiver's emotional availability and responsiveness to their needs (Bowlby, 1969). For example, if caregivers are present, responsive, and supportive in children's formative years, then children are more likely to develop *secure* attachments, where they develop confidence and trust in the people around them (Bowlby, 1969). In contrast, when caregivers are inconsistently responsive or unresponsive to children's needs, then children are more likely to develop *insecure* attachments, where they become anxious or distrustful of people's ability to be there for them and meet their needs.

Researchers have uncovered robust evidence that attachments formed in early childhood carry over into adulthood, with implications for people's adult romantic relationships (Collins et al., 2002; Mikulincer & Shaver, 2012). In adulthood, securely attached individuals are those who are "comfortable with intimacy, willing to depend on others for support, and confident that they are loved and valued by others," and they are more likely to attract securely attached partners and to have satisfying unions (Collins et al., 2002, p. 969; Mikulincer & Shaver, 2012; Selcuk et al., 2010). People with insecure attachments are those who experience elevated levels of *attachment anxiety* because they fear rejection (Bartholomew & Horowitz, 1991; Brennan et al., 1998), and/or they show elevated levels of attachment *avoidance* because they are uncomfortable with emotional closeness (Brennan et al., 1998). Adult attachment researchers have documented that attachment styles are stable, but may be changed, either positively or negatively, due to life experiences (Guerrero, 2018), including therapy. For this reason, we include attachment styles as phenomena that fit our *what works* criteria.

Securely attached remarried adults report greater commitment to their marriages than do those with less secure attachments (Ehrenberg et al., 2012). Individuals whose attachment styles are oriented to seeing relationships in positive ways construct more positive interpretations of their spouses' repair messages (Bello et al., 2008; Brandau-Brown et al., 2010). Repair messages are efforts to restore a partner's positive feelings about the relationship after an argument, misunderstanding, or miscommunication (Bello et al., 2008), which are important for maintaining positive connections in marriages. When remarried individuals perceive their partners as caring, responsive, and helpful, then they attribute greater honesty, politeness, and competence in efforts to repair transgressions (Bello et al., 2008; Brandau-Brown et al., 2010).

The ability to dissolve attachments also may help stepcouples. In a Dutch study, researchers examined the effects of lingering attachment to the former spouse on remarried individuals' later relationships (Buunk & Mutsaers, 1999a). The authors defined continued attachment as still missing the former partner, being in love with them, feeling dependent on them, and fearing that the relationship might end (Buunk & Mutsaers, 1999a). Remarried men and women who no longer felt attached to their former spouses were more satisfied in their remarriages, as were their current spouses.

Tolerance for Ambiguity

Tolerance for ambiguity refers to the extent to which individuals are comfortable with ambiguous or uncertain situations and can operate effectively in uncertain environments by considering a range of creative solutions or options (Albertini, 2022). The extent to which a person can tolerate ambiguity is related to their problem-solving skills in situations where there is uncertainty and change (Albertini, 2022). The absence of societal norms that apply to stepfamily relationships (e.g., What does it mean to be a "good stepmother?" What guidelines exist for how fathers and stepfathers should relate to one another?) may serve as a source of anxiety for stepfamily members who are uncomfortable with unclear guidelines. Like attachment styles, tolerance for ambiguity is not necessarily a permanent individual trait but is a dimension of character modifiable by effort or therapy.

Remarried individuals who had high tolerance for ambiguity interpreted partners' repair messages as more competent and polite than remarried individuals with low tolerance for ambiguity (Brandau-Brown et al., 2010). In other words, individuals who are comfortable with ambiguous information or social situations were more tolerant of their partner's attempts to rectify relationship problems that were vague or unclear, and they attributed more positive meanings to those messages (Brandau-Brown et al., 2010). This is potentially useful information to partners of spouses who may be less uncomfortable with ambiguity, in that they can take care to clearly state their repair communications in ways that will be better received. See Box 2.3 for individual attributes that work.

Box 2.3 *What works* **in repartnering: Individual attributes**

Individual attributes that contribute to *what works* include:

- Awareness of what went wrong in the first marriage, including what you and former partner did that was damaging.
- Awareness of what personal and spousal behaviors you do not want in remarriage.
- Awareness of your emotional triggers and reactions to a partner's behaviors.
- Awareness of and sensitivity to the new partner's insecurities and needs for support.
- Optimism about the future of your marriage.
- Identifying as a couple, an effective parenting team, and a stepfamily.
- Confidence in your resilience as a couple.
- Confidence that you and your partner can solve problems you face.
- Comfort with emotional intimacy, willingness to depend on others, and confidence that you are loved and valued (i.e., have a secure attachment style).
- Tolerance of ambiguity.

Effective Couple Dynamics

In addition to exploring *individual characteristics* that are linked to couple satisfaction (e.g., attachment style, tolerance for ambiguity, confidence in relationship resilience), researchers also have identified *couple dynamics* that are linked to satisfying and effective romantic unions in stepfamilies. Half of the investigations on *what works* for stepcouples focus on successful couple dynamics, including how they spend leisure time, divide household chores, manage money and childrearing, and communicate. Given the importance of communication in relationship health, researchers examined multiple aspects of constructive partner communications, such as communicating clearly, responding in ways that foster greater closeness, and promoting problem-solving.

Sharing Leisure Activities and Having Fun Together

Partners who share similar ideas about how much time they want to spend together report higher marital adjustment and satisfaction (Allen et al., 2001; Weston & Macklin, 1990). Couples who spend more time together in leisure and fun activities, including physical intimacy, going out, and working on hobbies, are happier in their remarriages (Bryant et al., 2016; Ivanova, 2016; Leigh et al., 1985; Turner et al., 2023). These couples also are more committed to their marriages and are more trusting of their spouses (Bryant et al., 2016). Doing fun things together is seen as one of the major rewards of being married, and the more activities shared, the greater the perceived rewards (Ivanova, 2016).

Sharing Household Tasks and Decision-Making

Couples increasingly desire and expect more egalitarian marriages today than in the past (Gerson, 2011). Studies show that all romantic relationships benefit from equitable divisions of labor (Carlson et al., 2018; Waddell et al., 2021). When couples share housework more equally, they report greater sexual intimacy, greater relationship satisfaction, and less marital discord (Carlson et al., 2018). Of all chores, dishwashing appears to be the most consequential to relationship quality, especially for women – in different-gender partnerships, the percentage of women who say that their relationship is in trouble more than doubles when she does more of the dishwashing compared to when dishwashing is shared equally (Carlson et al., 2018). These studies included couples in first unions and those in repartnering relationships, but research focused on stepfamily couples corroborate these findings. For instance, remarried spouses who perceive equitable division of household duties are more satisfied with their marriages (Guisinger et al., 1989; Leigh et al., 1985). Remarried women often want more power and autonomy than they experienced in their first marriages (Allen et al., 2001; Pyke, 1994), and they expect to share decision-making responsibilities with their spouses, so they are happier when these expectations are realized (Guisinger et al., 1989; Leigh et al., 1985). Remarried men also are happier when they perceive that marital decision-making is shared equitably (Guisinger et al., 1989).

Although situations arise when stepparents should take a step back from being a major decision-maker (Kelly & Ganong, 2010, 2011) – see

Chapter 5 on coparenting – there is evidence that shared marital decision-making contributes to a sense of equity and unity that nurtures the couple bond in stepfamilies. Couples who share decision-making compromise and cooperate with each other as they make decisions, and *agreeing* on decisions about marriage and raising stepchildren is a significant predictor of remarital satisfaction (Orleans et al., 1989). In general, perceiving that one's donations to the relationship are balanced by the benefits one receives contributes to greater satisfaction and stability (Buunk & Mutsaers, 1999b; Ivanova, 2016).

Of course, equitable couple dynamics do not appear magically, especially if couples practiced more traditional (i.e., imbalanced) power distributions in their prior relationships. One study that tracked the housework behavior of individuals who had been in relationships and then repartnered found that women did the majority of housework in both partnerships (Ophir, 2022). Repartnered individuals who wish to establish more equitable relationships may need to work deliberately to unlearn old models of housework in favor of more flexible, shared alternatives.

Managing Money

Financial issues are common sources of problems and stress in remarriages (Ganong & Coleman, 2017). Money management is an important aspect of any marriage but may be more challenging for couples in stepfamilies because finances are more complex. For instance, money to support children can potentially flow into and out of stepfamily households. In addition, prior divorces negatively affect wealth accumulation, which carries over into later unions (Kapelle & Baxter, 2021). Worries about finances are related to relationship dissatisfaction (Turner et al., 2023) and intimacy (Crapo et al., 2022) among remarried couples. It makes sense that successful stepcouples effectively manage their finances.

Inspired by an early study's conclusion that couples who pooled their money had closer, more unified family relationships than couples who kept their money in separate accounts (Fishman, 1983), several researchers compared "one-pot" and "two-pot" couples to see which management style was better (Coleman & Ganong, 1989; Lown & Dolan, 1994; van Eeden-Moorfield et al., 2007). Coleman and Ganong (1989) reported that money management was unrelated to marital satisfaction for men, but that wives who pooled resources with husbands were more satisfied with their remarriages than women who had separate accounts from their spouses. For both men and women, couples who combined resources (i.e., "one pot") had more positive feelings about stepchildren than did two-pot spouses (Coleman & Ganong, 1989). This study lent partial support for Fishman's (1983) conclusion that combining resources had benefits for relationships but was not a total confirmation.

Another study attempting to reassess Fishman's (1983) conclusion examined three strategies of financial management – one-pot, two-pot, and mixed (i.e., some assets were held by one partner and some owned jointly) – and found that two-pot families were more cohesive and more adaptable than couples who used other strategies (Lown & Dolan, 1994). The magnitude of differences in cohesion and adaptability between strategies was quite small, however, and did not indicate a lesser commitment to the stepfamily, leading the researchers to conclude that financial management strategies have more to do with the *degree of complexity* of couple's financial needs and how flexibly they can address those needs (Lown & Dolan, 1994). Another group of scholars, using a similar three-group categorization of fiscal management (i.e., separate, joint, and combination accounts) reported that couples using a joint (i.e., one-pot) strategy were more secure than couples who had both separate and joint accounts (i.e., combination accounts; van Eeden-Morefield et al., 2007). The length of time between marriages moderated the effects of financial management strategies, however, with separate accounts associated with greater financial security when individuals had been single between marriages for longer than five years, and individuals with joint accounts being more secure when they had been single less than five years after divorce (van Eeden-Morefield et al., 2007). The findings of this study, therefore, lent partial support for Fishman's assertion that one-pot financial strategies were better, while also echoing Lown and Dolan's (1994) conclusion that couples with varying stepfamily contexts chose different money management approaches that worked well for their family's needs, suggesting that one method of handling financial resources does not necessarily fit every stepfamily. Finally, as we noted earlier in this chapter, remarried couples who believed that pooling incomes is better money management reported greater marital satisfaction (Higginbotham & Adler-Baeder, 2008) and agreed more often on major decisions (Higginbotham & Agee, 2013). Men who believed that pooling is better also engaged in more activities with their wives than men who did not believe that pooling was the best approach (Higginbotham & Agee, 2013).

In general, most stepcouples seem to prefer to pool their financial resources, and there is evidence that pooling is conducive to remarital closeness and satisfaction. Pooling money may be a way that partners show commitment to the remarriage. However, there also is evidence that stepfamily complexity may make it hard for all stepcouples to pool their money. In addition, remarried individuals want more decision-making autonomy than in their first marriages (Allen et al., 2001), which may be another reason some couples prefer separate accounts or a combination of joint and separate accounts. The presence of nonresidential children of one or both partners (Eickmeyer et al., 2019), court-ordered child support flowing into and out of the stepfamily household (Petren et al., 2018), and the number of children for whom parents are fiscally responsible, all are factors that may prevent couples from pooling money without maintaining additional, separate funds. Jackson and colleagues (2023) found that it was not the amount of money remarried couples had or how many financial demands a couple faced that mattered for remarital satisfaction, it was how much spouses agreed on financial issues. Couples who can agree on a money-management strategy that works for their stepfamilies' needs likely are the happiest, regardless of whether that strategy involves one shared account or multiple accounts.

It should be noted that the studies of *what works* in economic management have been limited to remarried couples. Although one study reported that unmarried low-income cohabiting stepfathers who are employed have greater relationship stability over time than non-working cohabiting stepfathers do (Petren et al., 2018), little is known about *effective* money-management approaches of cohabiting stepcouples.

Agreeing on Childrearing Responsibilities

Remarried couples who agree on how childrearing responsibilities will be negotiated are happier in their marriages than those who disagree (Guisinger et al., 1989; Leigh et al., 1985). Discussing childrearing responsibilities prior to remarriage or in the early days of living together helps couples reach consensus on childrearing duties (Mangarun, 2020). Stepcouples who explicitly discuss and agree on how they will approach childrearing of children from prior unions enjoy better relationships (Guisinger et al., 1989; Mangarun, 2020; Orleans et al., 1989; Slattery et al., 2011). Stepparents appreciate being consulted as coparents (Guisinger et al., 1989), and they want more input into how they can be involved in childrearing (Guisinger et al., 1989; Orleans et al., 1989; Slattery et al., 2011). Although parents may function as the primary decision-makers and disciplinarians of their own children, asking their partners for advice ("What should I do with her?") or feedback about childrearing issues ("How could I have handled that situation better?") helps stepparents feel they have a role in childrearing. When stepparents feel they have greater input into decisions about stepchildren and are more involved as coparents, they are more satisfied with their romantic relationships. In short, there is robust evidence that consensus on childrearing and coparenting issues has positive effects on couple satisfaction, children's and adults' well-being, and step-relationship quality.

Having a Child Together

One aspect of childrearing among repartnered couples involves the decision of whether to have a child together. Couples have children together for many reasons. For stepcouples in which only one partner brought children into the relationship, the other partner may desire to experience parenthood by having a child with their new partner. For other couples, having a child may be an attempt to save the marriage by creating bonds between partners and between stepparents and stepchildren, who would share genetic ties to the mutual child. A child of the repartnership would have a genetic link to everyone, thus cementing relationship bonds in stepfamilies, at least according to some self-help authors (Coleman & Ganong, 1987). Clinicians have long asserted that the effects of a mutual child vary, depending on the motives to reproduce, the quality of stepfamily relationships before the birth, the ages of stepchildren, and other factors (e.g., Visher & Visher, 1979). So, what does the research say about the effects of stepcouples having a child together?

The findings are mixed. In one qualitative investigation of 55 remarried and cohabiting individuals that had a child together, all reported feeling happier and closer as a result of having the child (Bernstein, 1989). However, they also admitted that having a child together increased their marital stress, mentioning issues related to money, time, and sex. In a quantitative study, repartnered individuals who had a child together were happier and closer than those who had not had a shared child (Ivanova & Balbo, 2019). A third study reported that 91% of people who had a shared child in their second marriage thought their remarriage was better than their first marriage, compared to a slightly lower 86% of people who did not have a shared child in their second marriage (Albrecht, 1979). Another researcher found that stepfathers were happier in their marriages if they had reproduced, but stepmothers were not (Ambert, 1986). Finally, one study found no difference in remarital satisfaction between couples who had or had not reproduced (Ganong & Coleman, 1988). It should be noted that all but one of the studies about having a child together are more than 30 years old, and only one reported statistically significant differences in relationship satisfaction between couples who had children together and those who did not (Ivanova & Balbo, 2019). Given the long-term implications of having a shared child, and the divergent and complicated findings, we do not think there is enough evidence to support a conclusion that having a child together benefits all stepcouples. More research on this subject is needed (see Box 2.4).

Box 2.4 *What works* in repartnering: Effective couple dynamics
- Spend time having fun together (e.g., go on dates, hang out, work on projects).
- Express physical affection frequently (e.g., hugging, kissing, having sex).
- Share household tasks equitably.
- Share decision-making equitably.
- Pool financial resources, if possible.
- Agree on money management as a couple, whether finances are combined or not.
- Agree on childrearing responsibilities.

Communicating

Communication is at the heart of relationship development and maintenance. It may be a cliché to say that frequent communication promotes marital well-being, but this is, in fact, what researchers have found (Bryant et al., 2016; Mangarun, 2020). Not surprisingly, stepfamily researchers have focused attention on effective communication dynamics among stepcouples, exploring clarity of communication, self-disclosure, how individuals respond to a new partner, and how problems are resolved in the relationship.

Communicating Clearly

Communication skills contribute significantly to explaining long-term marital satisfaction for remarried men and women. For example, in one Canadian sample, individuals whose partners showed effective communication skills when interacting with their spouses reported greater marital satisfaction one year later (Beaudry et al., 2004). In another study, *expressiveness*, defined as being able to talk openly, telling each other personal problems, and beginning discussions easily, was predictive of marital quality for both husbands and wives (Ganong et al., 2019). Kurdek (1989) also found that expressiveness was related to marital happiness for remarried husbands and wives, but he defined expressiveness slightly differently, as showing tenderness and compassion.

A study by Pace and colleagues (2015) provided a definition of clear communication that is helpful from a *what works* perspective. They defined clear communication as the degree to which individuals are "able to discuss personal problems with their partners, say what they want in a clear manner when talking to the partner, easily find words to express themselves to partner, able to sit down with partner and just talk things over, and talk over pleasant things that happen during the day with partner" (Pace et al., 2015, p. 32). These researchers found that clear communication helped remarried couples maintain relationship quality even when they faced problems involving stepchildren. In other words, clear communication between spouses reduced the negative influence of stepparenting problems on marital quality and stability (Pace et al., 2015). Clear marital communication helps make couples feel closer and more satisfied in their roles as parents and stepparents, and this greater closeness contributes to remarital adjustment and satisfaction (Roberts & Price, 1989).

Topics that remarried couples need to discuss openly and clearly include (a) roles and expectations about childrearing, and (b) ambiguity surrounding family membership (i.e., who is a member of the family and who is not; Brimhall et al., 2008; Kim, 2010). Rarely do couples have explicit conversations about these topics, but doing so early in stepfamily formation is critical for getting couples on the same page. For example, do you want your new partner to be a parent figure to your children, or do you want your new partner to act more like a friend? Who will discipline your children? Who will discipline your partner's children? What are the rules and expectations for how children will behave? Remarried spouses who clearly communicate their thoughts and feelings about each of these topics are more satisfied with their remarriages, feel more supported, and have fewer disputes with each other (Kim, 2010).

One aspect of clear communication in remarriage is to be open about one's thoughts and feelings, and to disclose those thoughts and feelings to one's partner (Brimhall et al., 2008). Self-disclosures that are purposeful, honest, and positive contribute to remarital satisfaction (Bograd & Spilka, 1996) and aid couple bonding (Slattery et al., 2011).

Communicating Support and Affection

Remarried individuals who are affectionate and who engage in positive behaviors toward their spouses (e.g., talking about the day, sharing emotions, and problem-solving) are more confident about the future of the relationship and less likely to consider divorce (Kopystynska et al., 2022). Couples who express fondness for each other and who show it by joking, touching, and laughing together, foster couple bonding and relationship satisfaction (Slattery et al., 2011).

Positive Messages about Coparenting

In other studies, remarried couples who enjoy higher marital satisfaction express support for each other as coparents and minimize criticism about how they are coparenting stepchildren (Schrodt & Braithwaite, 2011). These positive, supportive communications about coparenting also enhance the mental health of parents and stepparents, although stepparents who are asked to shoulder more childrearing responsibilities report more mental health symptoms (Schrodt & Braithwaite, 2011). It is important to note that childrearing activities are stressful, but supportive and cooperative communications help enable personal and marital well-being.

Remarried or repartnered relationship satisfaction also is related to evaluations of how appropriate the current partners' attachments are with their ex-spouses and how cooperative their partners' coparenting involvements are with ex-partners (Buunk & Mutsaers, 1999a; Weston & Macklin, 1990). Couples who agree on how much interaction with former partners is appropriate are more satisfied (Weston & Macklin, 1990). Stepparents' relationships with their partner's ex also predicts remarital quality (Schrodt, 2010). When communications between these individuals are supportive and nonantagonistic (i.e., business-like and calm), then stepparents are more satisfied with their remarriages and report more positive mental health (Schrodt, 2010).

Communicating in Response to Partners

Stepfamily researchers have examined effective ways in which repartnered adults respond to each other's needs. For instance, researchers have explored what is useful or helpful to say or do when: (a) a partner is sad or anxious (empathic responding); (b) a partner wants to engage in problem-solving (demand–engage patterns); (c) the relationship has been damaged in some way (relational repair messages); and (d) tensions are running high and there is conflict or disagreement (emotion regulation). In addition, we noted earlier in this chapter that self-awareness and having learned from prior relationships what to do and not to do was important in creating effective stepcouple relationships, but here we emphasize that such awareness and learning from the past are only effective insofar as a remarried/repartnered person uses that knowledge to respond *positively* to new partners. For example, when a partner feels threatened or scared, responding with reassuring messages is a constructive approach, or when a partner has doubts about the fidelity of the relationship, responding by encouraging trust. Certainly, clarity of responsive communications is important, but what is said and done in response to partners' communications also contributes to couple and partner well-being.

Empathic Responding

During stressful times, one way of maintaining satisfying relationships may be the extent to which partners respond with empathy to each other (O'Brien et al., 2009). Empathic responding during stressful encounters or situations is therefore a critical part of what has been called *relationship-focused coping* (O'Brien et al., 2009). This type of coping refers to efforts to sustain ties while also trying to resolve problems, deal with stress-producing situations, and manage emotions (O'Brien et al., 2009). In an intensive study of how remarried and repartnered cohabiting couples coped with stress, researchers found that empathic responding was related to lowered marital tensions the day after a stressful marital encounter for both men and women (O'Brien et al., 2009). These researchers defined empathic responding as having both cognitive and behavioral dimensions. Cognitively, empathic responding involves imagining yourself in the partner's shoes, trying to see things from the partner's perspective, and trying to understand how the other person feels. Behaviorally, it involves trying to help the partner by doing something for them, listening to them, or comforting them and expressing support (O'Brien et al., 2009).

Empathic responding is an adaptive way of coping with everyday relationship stress. Men may need help seeing the benefits of empathic responding, however, because when couples' interactions were stressful, men who responded empathically also experienced greater tension while doing so, while women who responded empathically to their partners reduced their tension immediately (O'Brien et al., 2009). The positive effects of empathic responding may take longer for men to notice, but engaging in empathic responding pays off because it seems to help couples manage conflicts more effectively and leads to greater emotional intimacy and stronger couple bonds.

Listening is an important communication skill that helps when responding effectively to a partner's concerns, thoughts, and feelings (Mangarun, 2020). Effective listening involves focusing on what the partner is saying (rather than thinking about our own response), asking good questions, listening non-judgmentally, empathizing, and paraphrasing (e.g., "You seem frustrated about that. Is that because…?"; "Tell me about what happened next"; "How did that make you feel?"; "What do you think we should do?"). A good listener does not merely listen to reply, but rather, listens to *understand*.

Relational Repair Messages

When something has happened in a relationship to create emotional distance, hurt feelings, anger, or anxiety, efforts by either partner to mend the rift are known as relational repair messages (Bello et al., 2008). Relational repair may include apologies, asking to discuss an issue calmly, making amends by correcting a past transgression, honoring your partner's perspective, and taking responsibility for any wrongdoing (Brittle, 2023). Earlier in this chapter we wrote about how attachment styles (Bello et al., 2008) and tolerance of ambiguity (Brandau-Brown et al., 2010) are related to the interpretation of relational repair messages among remarried individuals. Unfortunately, no researchers have examined relational repair messages directly in remarried couples. Two studies, based on the same sample, asked remarried individuals to respond to hypothetical repair messages, and these responses provided indirect support for the notion that individuals who are satisfied with their remarriages perceive repair messages more favorably than individuals who are less satisfied (Bello et al., 2008; Brandau-Brown et al., 2010). In first marriages, relational repair messages are positively related to marital satisfaction (Weigel & Ballard-Reisch, 2001), so it is likely that relational repair messages also work for remarried couples.

Regulating Emotions

During stressful encounters with partners, such as when couples are arguing, emotion regulation strategies are efforts to influence what emotions are being experienced, when, and how those emotions are communicated (Gross, 1999). Two emotion regulation strategies are widely used. *Cognitive reappraisal* entails reframing, defined as thinking about a situation in a different, more positive light to create more constructive responses. *Expressive suppression* occurs after an emotion has been experienced and involves inhibiting, concealing, or shortening the emotional response (Frye et al., 2020). Suppressing emotions does not alter the emotions being felt and is not an effective strategy in the long run, but it may be useful in stressful situations when calmer responses are immediately needed (Gross, 1998), such as when a couple is in the middle of an argument.

In one study, both remarried and first-married couples in which spouses used cognitive reappraisal of either the problem or of their partner were less stressed by marital conflicts than spouses who did not reframe (Frye et al., 2020). For example, reframing a spouse's grouchiness by reframing it as, "my partner is having a lot of problems with coworkers and this stress is affecting how we get along," reduced marital tensions better than an initial attribution that, "my partner is a cranky and mean person." On the other hand, suppressing their emotional expressions lowered marital satisfaction after marital conflict (Frye et al., 2020). Remarried and first-marriage husbands who used cognitive reappraisal had wives who were more satisfied with the marriages (Frye et al., 2020), lending more support for the idea that reframing works better than hiding one's emotions. One implication from this study is that expressive suppression of emotions is to be avoided by all couples, regardless of their marital status.

Reassuring Messages

One type of communication that might be particularly important in remarriages are messages aimed at reassuring the partner about the stability of the relationship when partners are feeling insecure (Brimhall et al., 2008). For example, it is not unusual for remarried spouses to ask questions about prior marriages and partners. When this happens, effective responses are to reassure the remarried partner that they are loved and that the spouse is committed to the union (Brimhall & Engblom-Deglmann, 2011). Being honest in answering questions about the former spouse is good practice, particularly when answers do not contain comparisons between former and current partners that favor the former partner (Brimhall & Engblom-Deglmann, 2011).

Encouraging Trust

Also relevant to remarriages are exchanges that create and preserve trust (Brimhall et al., 2008). This may involve being aware of one's physical and emotional reactions based on interactions in prior marriages, and re-setting upsetting thoughts and feelings when a remarried spouse's behavior triggers bad feelings (Brimhall et al., 2008). It also involves being sensitive to a new partner's insecurities and responding with expressions of love and support. Finally, trying to avoid repeating behaviors that threatened their partner's sense of trust is also significant (Brimhall et al., 2008).

Promoting Problem-Solving

Conflict theorists propose that conflicts are inevitable in any relationship and facing problems is a universal experience (Sprey, 1979), so being able to cooperatively resolve problems is critical for resilience. One simple thing that seems to work for remarried couples is to encourage efforts to solve problems, rather than avoiding them (Allen et al., 2001; Bograd & Spilka, 1996). For example, if a partner makes a request or tells their partner what they need or want and suggests a course of action, it is beneficial for partners to engage by responding in ways that show an effort to help or to reply in an affirming manner (King & DeLongis, 2013). For instance, if a wife shares her thoughts and feelings about needing help keeping the kitchen clean, her husband could ask her what he could do to help or suggest that they hire housecleaners. In one study, remarried couples had less marital distress when partners responded with a willingness to engage in discussion when their spouse wanted to talk about serious topics with them (Allen et al., 2001). Willingness to engage in discussion that addresses the problem at hand is critical for productive problem-solving (Allen et al., 2001; Bograd & Spilka, 1996; Pasley & Ihinger-Tallman, 1990).

In a study of mid-life and late-life remarried couples, Bograd and Spilka (1996) found that remarried individuals tried to engage in communication strategies that promoted problem-solving more than they had done in their previous marriages. These individuals had learned from their former relationships new ways to manage stressors and deal with problems, and they valued honesty in their own and their partner's disclosures (Bograd & Spilka, 1996).

Coming Out for LGBTQ Stepcouples

LGBTQ-parent stepfamilies face the same challenges as cisgender- and heterosexual-parent stepfamilies, but with added stressors of navigating heterosexist stigma and discrimination (Lynch & Murray, 2000). One issue faced by same-sex stepcouples involves whether and how to navigate levels of "outness" as a queer stepfamily (Lynch & Murray, 2000). Coming out is a major decision, and one not taken lightly, particularly when there are children involved. Lynch and Murray (2000) examined the processes by which gay and lesbian stepcouples decided to come out to others, exploring the consequences of doing so for all stepfamily members. These researchers found that the process of coming out lacks a single, uniform, identifiable pattern that similar adults in stepfamilies can imitate successfully. Instead, parents usually adopt a stance of flexibility regarding their level of outness to others to ensure that their children feel secure both developmentally and situationally (Lynch & Murray, 2000). For example, partners in these stepfamilies selectively chose to be out in varying levels to significant people in their lives, such as parents, ex-spouses, coworkers, and children's teachers, and they were careful about the contexts in which they disclosed this information (Lynch & Murray, 2000). Coming out had benefits, however. Couples who came out were able to express affection in their households more freely, and coming out created a sense of openness for children as well as adults in the family. For example, children of parents who are out are more comfortable in discussing their problems with parents, perhaps because their parents are better able to empathize with children who feel different (Lynch & Murray, 2000). Gay and lesbian parents also believed their children would grow up accepting diversity and appreciating differences in people, and they believed that their children learned strategies for coping with opposition and disapproval (Lynch & Murray, 2000). Another study found that gay men in first romantic partnerships, repartnerships without children, and repartnerships with children from prior relationships (i.e., stepfamilies) who were more out to others reported higher relationship quality and cohesion than more closeted gay men (van Eeden-Moorefield et al., 2012). Gay men in stepfamilies were more satisfied than gay men in first partnerships and repartnerships without children.

Given the serious implications of coming out for LGBTQ parents and stepparents, more evidence is needed about specific ways in which gay and lesbian stepcouples reveal their situations to others, and the effects of coming out under diverse scenarios. It seems likely that no general conclusion may be drawn at this time about *what works* in coming out for LGBTQ stepcouples.

Box 2.5 *What works* in stepcouple communication

- Talk to your partner often about daily topics as well as about thoughts, feelings, concerns about the relationship.
- Share thoughts and feelings with the new partner clearly and honestly.
- Discuss personal problems with partner, say what you want clearly, do not avoid difficult conversations.
- Discuss openly and clearly marital and stepfamily roles, expectations about childrearing, and family boundaries (i.e., membership – who is in and who is out).
- Frame thoughts and feelings positively.
- Avoid doing things that threaten partner's sense of trust in you.
- Be frank in answering the new partner's questions about your prior marriages and former partners.
- Refrain from comparing deceased and new partners in ways that make the new partners feel insecure.
- Communicate to new spouse your expectations for what you want from them.
- Respond differently than in first unions when you are emotionally triggered in negative ways by new spouse.
- Respond with empathy during stressful situations with the partner.
  - Imagine yourself in the partner's shoes, try to see things from the partner's perspectives, and try to imagine how partner feels.
  - Help the partner, listen to them, and comfort them.
- Engage with the partner after he or she makes a demand, complains, or confronts you.
- Reassure the partner when he or she is feeling insecure.
- Avoid doing things that have upset your partner in the past.
- Think about situations, events, or persons in new ways that gives more positive meanings to those phenomena (cognitive reappraisal or reframing).

- Express emotions in positive ways or wait until stressful situations have calmed down to express them.
- Communicate supportive messages about coparenting stepchildren.
- Encourage efforts to solve problems.
- Avoid negative conflict-resolution strategies (e.g., sulking, hitting, slamming doors, and storming out of the house).
- Talk about childrearing of stepchildren.
- Find ways for the stepparent to be involved without being the disciplinarian.
- Consult with stepparents about decisions involving stepchildren.
- Treat stepchildren kindly, try to bond with them, and play with them.
  - Express love and affection to stepchildren.
  - Engage in affinity-seeking activities.
  - Help the parent in childrearing.
- Interact cooperatively with former spouses as coparents.
  - Be supportive when possible.
  - Agree on coparenting with nonresidential parents.
  - Set clear boundaries with former partners.
  - Encourage children to be in contact with nonresidential parents when safe for them to do so.
- Maintain social networks and keep communication open with network members.
- Spend time with members of your supportive social networks.
- Be open to offers of help from friends and extended family.
- Seek help and support from friends and extended family when needed.

Third Party Influences on Repartnering

In any social system, dyadic relationships are influenced by outside parties (Smith & Hamon, 2012). In stepfamily systems, couple relationships are affected mainly by interactions with children, former spouses, and extended family members. For instance, when remarried parents have close relationships with their children from prior unions and with their ex-partners, they are more satisfied in their remarriages (Jensen, 2017; Schrodt, 2010; Weston & Macklin, 1990). Close stepparent–stepchild relationships also are linked to closer couple relationships in stepfamilies; stepparents who play with stepchildren, read to them, and show affection (e.g., telling the stepchild he/she is loved, expressing appreciation for something the child did) have better and more stable remarriages and cohabiting unions (Petren et al., 2018). Stepparents spending quality time with stepchildren facilitates closer emotional connections between them, and closer stepparent–stepchild relationships are related to closer relationships between the stepcouple (Bray & Berger, 1993; Bryant et al., 2016; Jensen, 2017; Mangarun, 2020; Orleans et al., 1989; Petren et al., 2019; Slattery et al., 2011). Even positive bonds among other stepfamily members indirectly help stepcouples; in one study, nonresidential parents' close ties with children predicted positive stepparent–stepchild closeness, which in turn was related to remarital and cohabiting satisfaction for residential parents and stepparents (Petren et al., 2019). In short, stepcouple relationships are stronger when other stepfamily relationships also are strong. In later chapters, we review evidence on *what works* in strengthening stepparent–stepchild relationships (Chapter 3), parent–child relationships (Chapter 4), and coparenting relationships (Chapter 5), all of which can directly or indirectly help strengthen the stepcouple bond.

Support from Extended Family and Friends

"It takes a village" is a phrase about childrearing, but it could also apply to creating satisfying remarriages, as in, "It takes a village to create a happy remarriage." Individuals who are more satisfied in their remarriages report receiving greater social support from family members (Kim, 2010) and friends (Roberts & Price, 1989). Remarried partners with larger social support networks (Johnson et al., 2008) that are responsive to their requests for help are more satisfied with their remarriages (Kurdek, 1989). Social support involves family members and friends showing approval of the relationship, spending quality time with the couple, and comforting them in times of stress (Roberts & Price, 1989). Social support networks are significant because they lower stress for remarried individuals, which in turn raises marital happiness and adjustment (Johnson et al., 2008;

Kurdek, 1989). Although support from family and friends is not under the control of stepcouples, being open to receiving help and support from network members *is* under the control of stepcouples, as is actively seeking assistance from friends and extended kin networks, and therefore may be a part of *what works.* The *what works* implications for stepcouples include seeking help and being open to support offered to them from friends and loved ones.

Implications for Practice

Helping Single Parents with Dating

The studies reviewed in this chapter yielded valuable information about *what works* for single parents who date. Not all parents, however, are able to figure out what to do about dating amidst the many changes they face when marriages and intimate relationships end. Some need assistance. Below we highlight target areas where helping professionals can help parents navigate post-separation dating, repartnership, and remarriage.

Helping Parents Grieve

Family professionals can assist newly single individuals to slow down, think about transitions they are facing, and attend to themselves and their children before looking ahead toward acquiring new partners. Bereaved individuals may need grief counseling and assistance in helping their children and grandchildren in grieving. Therapists with knowledge about stepfamilies after bereavement can potentially help widows and widowers avoid family stress and parent–child conflicts related to dating. This is true no matter the age of the children.

Grief counseling is also appropriate for divorced and separated individuals. Both death and dissolution entail losses, although people dissolving a marriage or cohabiting union may not be aware of the need to mourn the prior union. This type of grief support is more important for the one who is "left" than the "leaver" because it is likely that the leaver has spent more time thinking about the ending of the relationship. Family professionals can acknowledge the loss that accompanies divorce, provide space for divorced or separated adults to mourn, and assist them in the grieving process.

Helping Raise Awareness

Stepcouples who are happy and satisfied are mindful, thoughtful, and introspective about their remarriages/repartnerships. They have thought about previous romantic relationships, asking themselves questions like: What worked? What did not work? What can I do to make this current relationship happier, more satisfying, and longer lasting than prior relationships? What can my partner and I do together to make this work? Clinicians can help individuals who are not prone to introspection be more effective at self-examination by asking them these questions and helping them explore takeaways from the past and present. It may take a trained family professional to encourage parents to consider each partners' role in the break-up and get past blaming the other partner entirely for the dissolution, or solely blaming themselves for their perceived relational transgressions. Helping parents become more aware of their own relational wants and needs allows them to learn from the past and prepares them for future intimate relationships. Happy partners in stepcouples are open to learning and willing to change their thoughts, emotions, and behaviors, if necessary.

Making Attribute Lists

Years ago, we asked Terri Orbach, a sociologist who studies divorce, to speak on our campus. Unbeknownst to us, she was also a public scholar, answering questions about relationships and presenting information to the public as "Dr. Love." In her visit to our campus, she shared with graduate students her Dr. Love advice to single adults to make lists of desired characteristics they wanted in a partner. The idea of concretely writing down a list of the 10 or 20 most sought attributes was eye-opening for the students, and some of them also created lists of attributes that were "deal breakers" for them. This simple task, making lists of wanted and unwanted characteristics in a partner, was exactly what divorced and bereaved parents did that worked for them. Although anyone can make a list without a "Dr. Love" advising them, some parents may need help in thinking about what they want and do not want. Feedback and coaching may help improve the list-making experience for adults who are not inclined toward introspection or who may need support thinking that they deserve to have such a list. Honing a well-crafted list of realistically obtainable attributes takes effort, and helping professionals can provide advice and feedback.

Helping with Dating Disclosures

Dating parents may need assistance in knowing how much information, and what information, to share with children and coparents. Unfortunately, the body of *what works* research does not shed light on the best practices for disclosing dating information to children; we only know that there is a wide range of behaviors among parents, from full disclosure of every dating encounter to keeping dating a secret from children (Anderson et al., 2004). There is some evidence, however, that parents who are sensitive to their children's feelings and emotional maturity try to keep them from knowing more than they can handle about dating (Miller, 2009b). It may take professional assistance for parents to think carefully about each child and to create plans for disclosing dating information to each child that fits their unique needs. Children of different ages and of diverse temperaments may be able to manage differing amounts of information about parental dating; therapists may help parents consider these and other pertinent factors in their lives. We have interviewed stepchildren who were never told about a parent's dating, finding out about a parent's new spouse only after the remarriage; these stepchildren resented not knowing and were generally unaccepting of the new partner and the remarriage. Clinicians can help parents to think about appropriate times and ways to introduce a serious dating partner to their children before remarriage or cohabitation.

Clinicians also can assist parents in deciding what and how much to share with coparents (i.e., exes) about dating. Cooperative coparents may choose to discuss and negotiate informal rules about sharing information; mediators or therapists may help them do this. Mediators and therapists also may be able to assist coparents in renegotiating privacy rules when there have been violations.

Helping Children Adjust

When parents begin dating after divorce – especially if dating happens relatively quickly – family professionals can help parents engage in perspective-taking on behalf of their children. Children adapt to their parents' marital dissolutions at different rates than do parents, so children often are not ready for parents to date when parents feel ready. Expecting children to be happy for a parents' dating journey or expecting them to be excited to meet new partners is likely to set parents up for disappointment and put strain on the parent–child relationship. Even if parents have taken substantial time before dating again, children might have big feelings about this transition, and there is healing power in acknowledging and validating children's feelings and perspectives. Helping professionals can aid parents in perspective-taking and help family members discuss their thoughts and feelings about the past, present, and future.

Helping Couples Prepare for Stepfamily Living

It is likely that there are more ways for stepcouples to prepare for remarriage than ever before, and many of these resources are based fully or partly on research evidence (Adler-Baeder & Higginbotham, 2020). At this point in time, until there are more and better studies that indicate which preparatory and educational resources are effective, we will only say that the research evidence suggests that individuals planning to remarry who participate in remarriage education programs benefit by gaining awareness of what they might encounter (Higginbotham et al., 2009), and they are taught valuable communication and problem-solving skills (Lucier-Greer et al., 2014). These findings suggest that stepcouples benefit from enrolling in evidence-based programs prior to remarriage.

Marriage contracts also offer a way of preparing for remarriage. Sager (1976) proposed that remarrying couples create a contract, putting on paper what they were willing to do for the partner as well as what they expected from the partner. He suggested that a therapist or mediator could assist couples in discussing and modifying their individual lists into a joint marital contract, which would not be a legal document but would clearly state what they wanted, needed, and could provide in the marriage (Sager, 1976). A clear and concrete template with an easy-to-follow process for creating marriage contracts is presented in Sager's (1976) book.

We are less positive about blanket endorsements for other sources of pre-stepfamily preparations, such as self-help books, websites, podcasts, and blogs, since many of these resources are based on the providers' personal experiences, biases, or inaccurate understandings of the research evidence. Because of these problems, we fear that some preparation materials may do more harm than good.

Consulting on Ceremonies

We know there are professionals who help stepcouples plan weddings, but we do not know how many of them incorporate *what works* evidence into their consulting. This seems like a niche that family professionals and clerics could fill. Helping stepcouples expand their ideas about weddings and commitment ceremonies by consulting with children and including children in some meaningful ways in the ceremony may make these ceremonies more meaningful. Some stepchildren may be reluctant to participate in a remarriage wedding ceremony, so adults may need professional help to negotiate their participation. Wedding preparation may seem minor and even frivolous, but these ceremonies matter to stepchildren (Baxter et al., 2009) and are worthy of attention by family professionals.

Helping Couples Communicate and Interact Effectively

Some of the skills needed to have a satisfying remarriage (e.g., spending time together, having fun, discussing personal problems clearly, framing thoughts and feelings in a positive way) are not unique to stepfamily couples and are sound practices for any relationship. Other issues – such as fiscal management, expectations for childrearing, and relations with former spouses and children from prior unions – are unique or are especially relevant to stepcouples, and marriage and family therapists should be familiar with these common stepcouple challenges. Seeing all marriages or romantic partnerships as the same, regardless of whether partners have been married previously or had children in prior relationships, leaves helping professionals with blind spots and limits their ability to assist stepcouples prevent and remediate problems. Remarried couples have different and more complex family histories than couples in first marriages. Even a generic task of couplehood, such as dividing household responsibilities, is performed within different contexts from that of first unions, and clinicians should be aware of these stepfamily contexts and how they affect individual and partner well-being. For this reason, we encourage family clinicians to seek training about stepfamilies and their unique challenges and potential strengths before working with stepcouples.

Partners in stepcouples are forming and building their relationships within a web of close, emotionally charged ties with people who love them, or who used to love them, and who may or may not want the best for them in their new love relationship. Clinicians can encourage stepcouples to think about their relationship as being linked to and embedded within other individuals and relationships. Clinicians can help couples plan and negotiate how to build their love relationship while sustaining other close relationships (i.e., with children), and while setting or confirming boundaries between those other important relationships and the remarriage or repartnership. Boundary setting is not easy for everyone, and clinicians can assist couples in these tasks. In other words, clinicians can help newly repartnered individuals who may want to focus their energies on each other be cognizant of the necessity of concurrently focusing on other family relationships. In other chapters we review *what works* for stepparents, primary parents, and coparents, so we will not repeat those findings and implications for practitioners here. We will only say that clinical attention should be paid to building positive ties between stepparents and stepchildren, nurturing ties between parents and children, and figuring out how to coparent because these relationships will increase marital happiness.

With ex-spouses, the main concern for stepcouples is boundary management – not being too emotionally involved with ex-spouses but staying connected for the well-being of the children. Clinicians can help members of stepcouples resolve lingering attachments and heal old wounds with ex-spouses. They can also assist with boundary setting and maintaining those boundaries.

Future Research

In general, more research is needed that aims to identify *what works* for stepcouples. Although existing evidence gives us a good start on knowing what successful and effective stepcouples do, this body of literature is small, and opportunities are ripe for identifying specific behaviors that contribute to flourishing stepcouple relationships. There is a particular need for more research on what works in cohabiting stepfamilies, as most research has focused on remarried stepcouples only. We offer some specific suggestions for areas of investigation needed and methods to use that will enrich what is known.

Research on Dating

Most of what is known about parents' post-divorce dating is based on mothers' reports; research is needed that explores fathers' and children's perspectives on what works for them. We encourage researchers to explore underexamined but consequential processes such as how parents introduce their dating partners to their children, what parents do to encourage relationship development between dating partners and children, and how children are included in the courtship processes with prospective new spouses/partners. More research on outcomes associated with these processes also is needed, so that we can help single parents be better informed about what works and what does not.

Research on Preparing for Repartnering

Studies are needed about stepcouple preparation and education that have well-designed evaluations which will allow researchers to draw causal conclusions about what is working. Ideally, evaluation studies would contain randomly assigned treatment and control groups or they would compare treatment groups to carefully matched comparison groups (Adler-Baeder & Higginbotham, 2020). In addition to evaluation studies, surveys that ask stepcouples what would help them prepare for stepfamily living would add to what is known.

More research is needed on how divorced, and even bereaved, individuals draw "lessons" from earlier relationships that help them in remarriages/repartnerships. We know some partners are introspective and thoughtful about what has worked for them and what has not, but how did this happen? Did they receive help from therapists, clerics, or self-help books, or were these lessons learned through trial and error? What kinds of introspection help and what kind does not? We present these "lessons learned" as an individual phenomenon, but some lessons may be learned as a couple. How purposeful are couples in looking back together as a way of improving their current bond? Many questions are left to be addressed.

Research on Ceremonies

Family rituals are symbolic events that honor something sacred (Braithwaite et al., 1998). In all families, rituals contribute to a sense of family identity and cohesion, but this is especially salient for stepfamilies. There is a small but helpful body of work on rituals in stepfamilies reviewed in this book (see Chapter 5, Effective Coparenting in Stepfamilies), but more research is needed on how remarriage or commitment ceremonies offer opportunities for co-creating rituals, and how rituals can meaningfully set the stage for stepfamily life. Investigations that examine *how* stepcouples plan and conduct this ritual successfully may yield insights that extend to other ritualized behaviors, such as those around holidays, birthdays, and rituals of daily living (shared meals, game nights, sporting events, and so on).

Research on Intrapersonal Qualities

Relatively few studies have identified how personal attributes – particularly those that are changeable over time and amenable to a degree of individual control – are associated with success in stepfamily relationships. For example, researchers could explore how attributes such as flexibility (e.g., openness, willingness to try new things), responsibility (e.g., conscientiousness), likability (e.g., agreeableness), and mental health (e.g., neuroticism) are predictive of relationship interactions that influence stepcouple effectiveness. In addition, research on how partners in stepcouples adapt to and respond to their partners' intrapersonal qualities may yield useful *what works* findings.

Research on Communication and Couple Interactions

We know a great deal about *what works* in stepcouple communication and couple interactions, but more research would deepen our knowledge in this area. Studies are needed that focus on everyday interactions and their outcomes. Researchers have relied heavily on self-reports, so using daily diary methods, observations of couples interacting, and longitudinal designs would be helpful. More dyadic research that treats the couple as the unit of analysis would enhance our understanding of couple dynamics. Examining couple dynamics is difficult, so mixed method designs that utilize both quantitative and qualitative methods may be beneficial to researchers studying *what works* for stepcouples.

References

Adler-Baeder, F., & Higginbotham, B. (2020). Efforts to design, implement, and evaluate community-based education for stepfamilies: Current knowledge and future directions. *Family Relations, 69*(3), 559–576. https://doi.org/10.1111/fare.12427

Albertini, E. (July 18, 2022). Tolerance of ambiguity: A critical future fit skill for the evolved world of work. www.linkedin.com/pulse/tolerance-ambiguity-critical-future-fit-skill-evolved-eric/

Albrecht, S. (1979). Correlates of marital happiness among the remarried. *Journal of Marriage and the Family, 41*, 857–867.

Allen, E.S., Baucom, D.H., Burnett, C.K., Epstein, N., & Rankin-Esquer, L.A. (2001). Decision-making power, autonomy, and communication in remarried spouses compared with first-married spouses. *Family Relations, 50*, 326–334. https://doi.org/10.1111/j.1741-3729.2001.00326.x

Ambert, A.-M. (1986). Being a stepparent: Live-in and visiting stepchildren. *Journal of Marriage and the Family, 48*, 795–804.

Anderson, E.R., Greene, S.M. (2005). Transitions in parental partnering after divorce. *Journal of Divorce & Remarriage, 43*, 47–62. https://doi.org/10.1300/J087v43n03_03

Anderson, E.R., Greene, S.M. (2011). "My child and I are a package deal.": Balancing adult and child concerns in repartnering after divorce. *Journal of Family Psychology, 25*, 741–750. https://doi.org/10.1037/a0024620

Anderson, E.R., Greene, S.M., Walker, L., Malerba, C., Forgatch, M.S., & DeGarmo, D.S. (2004). Ready to take a chance again: Transitions into dating among divorced parents. *Journal of Divorce & Remarriage, 40*, 61–75. https://doi.org/10.1300/J087v40n03_04

Bartholomew, K., & Horowitz, L.M. (1991). Attachment styles among young adults: A test of a four-category model. *Journal of Personality and Social Psychology, 61*, 226–244.

Baxter, L.A., Braithwaite, D.O., Kellas, J.K., LeClair-Underberg, C., Normand, E.L., Routsong, T., & Thatcher, M. (2009). Empty ritual: Young-adult stepchildren's perception of the remarriage ceremony. *Journal of Social and Personal Relationships, 26*(4), 467–487. https://doi.org/10.1177/0265407509350872

Beaudry, M., Boisvert, J.-M., Simard, M., Parent, C., & Blais, M.-C. (2004). Communication: A key component to meeting the challenges of stepfamilies. *Journal of Divorce & Remarriage, 42*(1/2), 85–104. https://doi.org/10.1300/J087v42n01_04

Bello, R.S., Brandau-Brown, F.E., & Ragsdale, J.D. (2008). Attachment style, marital satisfaction, and communal strength effects on relational repair message interpretation among remarrieds. *Communication Quarterly, 56*(1), 1–16. https://doi.org/10.1080/01463370701838968

Bernstein, A.C. (1989). *Yours, mine, and ours.* Scribner.

Black, L E., Eastwood, M.M., Sprenkle, D.H., & Smith, E. (1991). An exploratory analysis of the construct of leavers versus left as it relates to Levinger's social exchange theory of attractions, barriers, and alternative attractions. In C. Everett (Ed.), *Marital instability and divorce outcomes: Issues for therapists and educators* (pp. 127–139). Routledge. https://doi.org/10.4324/9781315801414-8

Blumer, H. (1969). *Symbolic interactionism: Perspective and method.* Prentice-Hall.

Bograd, R., & Spilka, B. (1996). Self-disclosure and marital satisfaction in mid-life and late-life remarriages. *International Journal of Aging and Human Development, 42*(3), 161–172.

Bowlby, J. (1969). *Attachment and loss: Vol. 1. Attachment.* Basic.

Braithwaite, D.O., Baxter, L.A., & Harper, A.M. (1998) The role of rituals in the management of the dialectical tension of "old" and "new" in blended families. *Communication Studies, 49*(2), 101–120. https://doi.org/10.1080/10510979809368523

Brandau-Brown, F.E., Bello, R.S., & Ragsdale, J.D. (2010). Attachment style and toler-ance for ambiguity effects on relational repair message interpretation among remar-rieds. *Marriage & Family Review, 46,* 389–399. https://doi.org/10.1080/01494929.2010.528311

Bray, J.H., & Berger, S.H. (1993). Developmental issues in stepfamilies research project: Family relationships and parent-child interactions. *Journal of Family Psychology, 7*(1), 76–90.

Brennan, K.A., Clark, C.L., & Shaver, P.R. (1998). Self-report measurement of adult attachment: An integrative overview. In J.A. Simpson & W.S. Rholes (Eds.), *Attachment theory and close relationships* (pp. 46–76). Guilford.

Brimhall, A.S., Engblom-Deglmann, M.L. (2011). Starting over: A tentative theory exploring the effects of past relationships on post-bereavement remarried couples. *Family Process, 50*(1), 47–62. https://doi.org/10.1111/j.1545-5300.2010.01345.x

Brimhall, A., Wampler, K., & Kimball, T. (2008). Learning from the past, altering the future: A tentative theory of the effect of past relationships on couples who remarry. *Family Process, 47*(3), 373–387. https://doi.org/10.1111/j.1545-5300.2008.00259.x

Brittle, Z. (2023). R is for repair. www.gottman.com/blog/r-is-for-repair/

Browning, S., & Artelt, E. (2012). *Stepfamily therapy: A 10-step clinical approach.* APA. https://doi.org/10.1037/13089-000

Bryant, C.M., Futris, T.G., Hicks, M.R., Lee, T.-Y., & Oshri, A. (2016). African American stepfather-stepchild relationships, marital quality, and mental health. *Journal of Divorce & Remarriage, 57*(6), 375–388. https://doi.org/10.1080/10502556.2016.119852

Buehler, C. (1987). Initiator status and the divorce transition. *Family Relations, 36*(1), 82–86.

Buunk, B.P., & Mutsaers, W. (1999a). The nature of the relationship between remar-ried individuals and former spouses and its impact on marital satisfaction. *Journal of Family Psychology, 13*(2), 165–174.

Buunk, B.P., & Mutsaers, W. (1999b). Equity perceptions and marital satisfaction in former and current marriage: A study among the remarried. *Journal of Social and Personal Relationships, 16*(1), 123–132.

Carlson, D.L., Miller, A.J., & Sassler, S. (2018). Stalled for whom? Change in the di-vision of particular housework tasks and their consequences for middle- to low-income couples. *Socius: Sociological Research for a Dynamic World, 4,* 1–17. https://doi.org/10.1177/2378023118765867

Carr, D., & Boerner, K. (2013). Dating after late-life spousal loss: Does it compromise relationships with adult children? *Journal of Aging Studies, 27,* 487–498. https://doi.org/10.1016/j.jaging.2012.12.009

Coleman, M., & Ganong, L. (1987). An evaluation of the stepfamily self-help literature for children and adolescents. *Family Relations, 36,* 61–65.

Coleman, M., & Ganong, L. (1989). Financial management in stepfamilies. *Lifestyles: Family and Economic Issues, 10*(3), 217–232.

Collins, N. L., Cooper, M. L., Albino, A., & Allard, L. (2002). Psychosocial vulnerabil-ity from adolescence to adulthood: A prospective study of attachment style differ-ences in relationship functioning and partner choice. *Journal of Personality, 70*(6), 965–1008. https://doi.org/10.1111/1467-6494.05029

Crapo, J.S., Turner, J.J., Bradford, K., & Higginbotham, B.J. (2022). The impacts of postdivorce cohabitation and relationship duration on the early marital climate of remarriages. *The Family Journal: Counseling and Therapy for Couples and Families, 30*(3), 307–315. https://doi.org/10.1177/10664807211054155

DeAnda, J.S., Langlais, M.R., Anderson, E.R., & Greene, S.M. (2021). Examining children's problem behaviors and mothers' depressive symptoms following divorce.

Journal of Child and Family Studies, 30, 2165–2179. https://doi.org/10.1007/s10826-021-02029-8

Ehrenberg, M.F., Robertson, M., & Pringle, J. (2012). Attachment style and marital commitment in the context of remarriage. *Journal of Divorce & Remarriage, 53,* 204–219. https://doi.org/10.1080/10502556.2012.663270

Eickmeyer, K.J., Guzzo, K.B., Manning, W.D., & Brown, S. L. (2019). A research note on income pooling in partnerships: Incorporating nonresident children. *Journal of Family Issues, 40*(18), 2922–2943. https://doi.org/10.1177/0192513X19868270

Fishman, B. (1983). The economic behavior of stepfamilies. *Family Relations, 32,* 359–366.

Frye, N., Ganong, L., Jensen, T., & Coleman, M. (2020). A dyadic analysis of emotion regulation as a moderator of associations between marital conflict and marital satisfaction among first-married and remarried couples. *Journal of Family Issues, 41*(12), 2328–2355. https://doi.org/10.1177/0192513X20935504

Ganong, L.H., & Coleman, M. (1988). Do mutual children cement bonds in stepfamilies? *Journal of Marriage and the Family, 50*(August), 687–698.

Ganong, L.H., & Coleman, M. (1989). Preparing for remarriage: Anticipating the issues, seeking solutions. *Family Relations, 38*(1), 28–33.

Ganong, L., & Coleman, M. (2017). *Stepfamily relationships: Development, dynamics, and intervention* (2nd ed.). Springer. https://doi.org/10.10078/978-1-4899-7702-1

Ganong, L., Jensen, T., Sanner, C., Russell, L., Coleman, M., & Chapman, A. (2019). Linking stepfamily functioning, marital quality, and steprelationship quality. *Family Relations, 68,* 469–483. https://doi.org/10.1111/fare.12380

Gerson, K. (2011). *The unfinished revolution: Coming of age in a new era of gender, work, and family.* Oxford University Press.

Gross, J.J. (1999). Emotion regulation: Past, present, future. *Cognition & Emotion, 13*(5), 551–573.

Guerrero, L. (2018). Attachment theory in families: The role of *communication.* In D.O. Braithwaite, E.A. Suter, & Floyd, K. (Eds.), *Engaging theories in family communication* (2nd ed., pp. 38–50). Routledge. https://doi.org/10.4324/9781315204321-4

Guisinger, S., Cowan, P., & Schuldberg, D. (1989). Changing parent and spouse relations in the first years of remarriage of divorced fathers. *Journal of Marriage and the Family, 51,* 445–456.

Guzzo, K.B. (2016). Stepfamilies in the U.S. *Family Profiles.* FP-16-09. Bowling Green, OH: National Center for Family Management & Marriage Research. www.bgsu.edu/ncfmr/resources/data/family-profiles/guzzo-stepfamilies-women-fp016-09.html

Guzzo, K.B. (2018). Marriage and dissolution among women's cohabitations: Variations by stepfamily status and shared childbearing. *Journal of Family Issues, 39*(4), 1108–1136. https://doi.org/10.1177/0192512X16686136

Hanna, S.L., Knaub, P.K. (1981). Cohabitation before remarriage: Its relationship to family strengths. *Alternative Lifestyles, 4*(4), 505–522.

Hetherington, E.M., & Kelly, J. (2002). *For better or for worse.* Norton.

Higginbotham, B.J., & Adler-Baeder, F. (2008). Assessing beliefs about remarriages and stepfamilies: The remarriage belief inventory. *Journal of Divorce & Remarriage, 48*(3/4), 33–54. https://doi.org/10.1300/J087v48n03_03

Higginbotham, B., & Agee, L. (2013). Endorsement of remarriage beliefs, spousal consistency, and remarital adjustment. *Marriage & Family Review, 49,* 177–190. https://doi.org/10.1080/01494929.2012.733325

Higginbotham, B.J., Miller, J.J., & Niehuis, S. (2009). Remarriage preparation: Usage, perceived helpfulness, and dyadic adjustment. *Family Relations, 58,* 316–329. https://doi.org/10.1111/j.1741-3729.2009.00555.x

Higginbotham, B.J., & Skogrand, L. (2010). Relationship education with both married and unmarried stepcouples: An exploratory study. *Journal of Couple & Relationship Therapy*, 9(2), 133–148. https://doi.org/10.1080/15332691003694893

Hopper, J. (1993). Oppositional identities and rhetoric in divorce. *Qualitative Sociology*, 16, 133–156.

Ivanova, K. (2016). Relationship satisfaction of the previously married: The significance of relationship specific costs and rewards in first and repartnering unions. *Journal of Social and Personal Relationships*, 33(5), 559–580. https://doi.org/10.1177/0265407515583942

Ivanova, K., & Balbo, N. (2019). Cementing the stepfamily? Biological and stepparents' relationship satisfaction after the birth of a common child in stepfamilies. *Journal of Family Issues*, 40(10), 1346–1363. https://doi.org/10.1177/0192513X19836456

Jackson, J.J., Carrese, D.H., & Willoughby, B.J. (2023). The indirect effects of financial conflict on economic strain and marital outcomes among remarried couples. *International Journal of Stress Management*, 30(1), 69–83. https://doi.org/10.1037/str0000277

James, S.L., & Shafer, K. (2012). Temporal differences in remarriage timing: Comparing divorce and widowhood. *Journal of Divorce & Remarriage*, 53, 543–558. https://doi.org/10.1080/10502556.2012.719388

Jensen, T. (2017). Constellation of dyadic relationship quality in stepfamilies: A factor mixture model. *Journal of Family Psychology*, 31(8), 1051–1062. https://doi.org/10.1037/fam0000355

Jensen, T., & Ganong, L. (2023). Associations between dyadic relationship quality and stepfamily functioning: A common fate modeling approach. *Family Process*. https://doi.org/10.1111/famp.12803

Johnson, A.J., Wright, K.B., Craig, E.A., Gilchrist, E.S., Lane, L.T., & Haigh, M.M. (2008). A model for predicting stress levels and marital satisfaction for stepmothers utilizing a stress and coping approach. *Journal of Social and Personal Relationships*, 25(1), 119–142. https://doi.org/10.1177/0265407507086809

Kang, Y., Ko, K., & Ganong, L. (2023). Divorced parents' perceived benefits and risks of dating and sharing dating information. *Family Relations*. https://doi.org/10.1111/fare.12735

Kapelle, N., & Baxter, J. (2021). Marital dissolution and personal wealth: Examining gendered trends across the dissolution process. *Journal of Marriage and Family*, 83(1), 243–259. https://doi.org/10.1111/jomf.12707

Kelly, K.P., & Ganong, L. (2010). Moving to place: Childhood cancer treatment decision making in single-parent and repartnered family structures. *Qualitative Health Research*, 21, 349–364. https://doi.org/10.1177/1049732310385823

Kelly, K., & Ganong, L. (2011). 'Shifting family boundaries' after the diagnosis of childhood cancer in stepfamilies. *Journal of Family Nursing*, 17, 105–132. https://doi.org/10.1177/1074840710397365

Kim, H. (2010). Exploratory study on the factors affecting marital satisfaction among remarried Korean couples. *Families in Society*, 91(2), 193–200. https://doi.org/10.1606/1044-3894.3977

King, D.B., & DeLongis, A. (2013). Dyadic coping with stepfamily conflict: Demand and withdraw responses between husbands and wives. *Journal of Social and Personal Relationships*, 30(2), 198–206. https://doi.org/10.1177/0265407512454524

King, V. (2009). Stepfamily formation: Implications for adolescent ties to mothers, nonresident fathers, and stepfathers. *Journal of Marriage and Family*, 71, 954–968. https://doi.org/10.1111/j.1741-3737.2009.00646.x

Kopystynska, O., Bradford, K., Higginbotham, B., & Whiteman, S. (2022). Impact of positive and negative socioemotional behaviors on remarried instability. *Journal of Family Issues*, 43(12), 3194–3217. https://doi.org/10.1177/0192513X211042851

Kurdek, L.A. (1989). Relationship quality for newly married husbands and wives: Marital history, stepchildren, and individual-difference predictors. *Journal of Marriage and the Family, 51*, 1053–1064.

Langlais, M., Anderson, E., & Greene, S. (2015). Characterizing mother's dating after divorce. *Journal of Divorce and Remarriage, 56*, 180–198. https://doi.org/10.1080/10502556.2015.1012701

Langlais, M., Anderson, E., & Greene, S. (2016). Consequences of dating for post-divorce maternal well-being. *Journal of Marriage and Family, 78*, 1032–1046. https://doi.org/10.1111/jomf.12319

Langlais, M.R., Anderson, E.R., & Greene, S.M. (2017). Divorced young adult mothers' experiences of breakup: Benefits and drawbacks. *Emerging Adulthood, 5*, 280–292. https://doi.org/10.1177/2167696817696429

Leigh, G.K., Ladehoff, G.S., Howie, A.T., & Christians, D.L. (1985). Correlates of marital satisfaction among men and women in intact first marriage and remarriage. *Family Perspective, 19*(3), 139–149.

Lown, J.M., & Dolan, E.M. (1994). Remarried families' economic behavior: Fishman's model revisited. *Journal of Divorce & Remarriage, 22*(1/2), 103–119.

Lucier-Greer, M., Adler-Baeder, F., Harcourt, K., & Gregson, K.D. (2014). Relationship education for stepcouples reporting relationship instability—Evaluation of the Smart Steps: Embrace the Journey curriculum. *Journal of Marriage and Family Therapy, 40*, 454 – 469. https://doi.org/10.1111/jmft.12069

Lucier-Greer, M., Adler-Baeder, F., Ketring, S.A., Harcourt, K.T., & Smith, T. (2012). Comparing the experiences of couples in first marriages and remarriages in couple and relationship education. *Journal of Divorce & Remarriage, 53*, 55–75. https://doi.org/10.1080/10502556.2012.635970

Lynch, J.M., & Murray, K. (2000). For the love of the children: The coming out process for lesbian and gay parents and stepparents. *Journal of Homosexuality, 39*(1), 1–24. https://doi.org/10.1300/j082v39n01_01

Mangarun, A.J.S. (2020). Lived experiences of elderly remarried widows: Adjustment and coping to new roles as bioparent. *Belitung Nursing Journal, 6*(6), 203–208. https://doi.org/10.33546/bnj.1173

Mikulincer, M., & Shaver, P.R. (2012). Adult attachment orientations and relationship processes. *Journal of Family Theory & Review, 4*(4), 259–274. https://doi.org/10.1111/j.1756-2589.2012.00142.x

Miller, A. (2009a). Face concerns and facework strategies in maintaining postdivorce co-parenting and dating relationships. *Southern Communication Journal, 74*, 157–173. https://doi.org/10.1080/10417940802516842

Miller, A. (2009b). Revealing and concealing postmarital dating information: Divorced coparents' privacy rule development and boundary coordination processes. *Journal of Family Communication, 9*, 135–149. https://doi.org/10.1080/15267430902773287

Miller-Ott, A.E. (2013). Factors that influence separated and divorced parents' sharing of personal information with dating partners. *Journal of Divorce & Remarriage, 54*, 282–294. https://doi.org/10.1080/10502556.2013.780464

Montgomery, M.J., Anderson, E.A., Hetherington, E.M., & Clingempeel, G.C. (1992). Patterns of courtship for remarriage: Implications for child adjustment and parent-child relationships. *Journal of Marriage and the Family, 54*(August), 686–698.

Nice, L.A., Jenks, D.B., Saunders, C.A., & Quintero, L.C. (2021). Regret and repair: Experiences of adult children and parents when a father remarries soon after the death of a spouse. *Omega*, July, 1–15. https://doi.org/10.1177/00302228211036315

O'Brien, T.B., DeLongis, A., Pomaki, G., Puterman, E., & Zwicker, A. (2009). Couples coping with stress: The role of empathic responding. *European Psychologist, 14*(1), 18–28. https://doi.org/10.1027/1016-9040.14.1.18

Ophir, A. (2022). "Thank u, next"? Repartnering and the household division of labor. *Journal of Marriage and Family, 84*(2), 636–654. https://doi.org/10.1111/jomf.12816

Orleans, M., Palisi, B.J., & Caddell, D. (1989). Marriage adjustment and satisfaction of stepfathers: Their feelings and perceptions of decision-making and stepchildren relations. *Family Relations, 38*, 371–377.

Pace, G.T., Shafer, K., Jensen, T.M., & Larson, J.H. (2015). Stepparenting issues and relationship quality: The role of clear communication. *Journal of Social Work, 15*(1), 24–44. https://doi.org/10.1177/1468017313504508

Papernow, P. (2013). *Surviving and thriving in stepfamily relationships: What works and what doesn't.* Routledge. https://doi.org/10.4324/9780203813645-32

Pasley, K., & Ihinger-Tallman, M. (1990). Remarriage in later adulthood: Correlates of perceptions of family adjustment. *Family Perspective, 24*(3), 263–274.

Petren, R.E., Garneau-Rosner, C.L., & Yildirim, E.D. (2018). Union stability among mothers and stepfathers: Contributions of stepfathers and biological fathers. *Journal of Family Psychology, 32*(8), 1142–1151. https://doi.org/10.1037/fam0000482

Petren, R.E., Lardier, D.T., Bible, J., Bermea, A., van Eeden-Moorfield, B. (2019). Parental relationship stability and parent-adult-child relationships in stepfamilies: A test of alternative models. *Journal of Family Psychology, 33*(2), 143–153. https://doi.org/10.1037/fam0000481

Pyke, K.D. (1994). Women's employment as a gift or burden? Marital power across marriage, divorce, and remarriage. *Gender and Society, 8*, 73–91.

Roberts, T.W., & Price, S.J. (1989). Adjustment in remarriage: Communication, cohesion, marital and parental roles. *Journal of Divorce, 12*(1), 17–43.

Sager, C.J. (1976). *Marriage contracts and couple therapy: Hidden forces in human relationships.* Brunner/Mazel.

Satir, V. (1972). *Peoplemaking.* Science and Behavior Books.

Schrodt, P. (2010). Coparental communication with nonresidential parents as a predictor of couples' relational satisfaction and mental health in stepfamilies. *Western Journal of Communication, 74*, 484–503. https://doi.org/10.1080/10570314.2010.512282

Schrodt, S., & Braithwaite, D.O. (2011). Coparental communication, relational satisfaction, and mental health in stepfamilies. *Personal Relationships, 18*, 352–369. https://doi.org/10.1111/j.1475-6811.2010.01295.x

Selcuk, E., Zayas, V., & Hazan, C. (2010). Beyond satisfaction: The role of attachment in marital functioning. *Journal of Family Theory & Review, 2*(4), 258–279. https://doi.org/10.1111/j.1756-2589.2010.00061.x

Skinner, K.B., Bahr, S.J., Crane, D. R., & Call, V.R.A. (2002). Cohabitation, marriage, and remarriage: A comparison of relationships quality over time. *Journal of Family Issues, 23*, 74–90. https://doi.org/10.1177/0192513x02023001004

Skogrand, L., Barrios-Bell, A., & Higginbotham, B. (2009). Stepfamily education for Latino families: Implications for practice. *Journal of Couple and Relationship Therapy, 8*, 113–128. https://doi.org/10.1080/15332690902813802

Skogrand, L., Mendez, E., & Higginbotham, B. (2014). Latina women's experiences in a stepfamily education course. *Family Journal, 22*, 49–55. https://doi.org/10.1177/1066480713505053

Slattery, M.E., Bruce, V., Halford, W.K., & Nicholson, J.M. (2011). Predicting married and cohabiting couples' futures from their descriptions of stepfamily life. *Journal of Family Psychology, 25*(4), 560–569. https://doi.org/10.1037/a0024538

Smith, S.R., & Hamon, R.R. (2012). *Exploring family theories* (3rd ed.). Oxford.

Smock, P.J., & Schwartz, C.R. (2020). The demography of families: A review of patterns and change. *Journal of Marriage and Family, 82*(1), 9–34. https://doi.org/10.1111/jomf.12612

Sobotka, T., & Berghammer, C. (2021). Demography of family change in Europe. In N.F. Schneider & M. Kreyenfeld (Eds.), *Research handbook on the sociology of the family* (pp. 162–186). Edward Elgar Publishing. https://doi.org/10.4337/9781788975544.00019

Sprey, J. (1979). Conflict theory and the study of marriage and the family. In W.R. Burr, R. Hill, F.I. Nye, & Reiss, I. (Eds.), *Handbook of marriage and the family.* (pp. 130–159). Free Press.

Stanley, S.M., Rhoades, G.K., Amato, P.R., Markman, H.J., & Johnson, C.A. (2010). The timing of cohabitation and engagement: Impact on first and second marriages. *Journal of Marriage and Family, 72,* 906–918. https://doi.org/10.1111/j.1741-3737.2010.00738.x

Tach, L., & Halpern-Meekin, S. (2009). How does premarital cohabitation affect trajectories of marital quality? *Journal of Marriage and Family, 71,* 298–317. https://doi.org/10.1111/j.1741-3737.2009.00600.x

Thomson, E., Mosley, J., Hanson, T.L., & McLanahan, S.S. (2001). Remarriage, cohabitation, and changes in mothering behavior. *Journal of Marriage and Family, 63,* 370–380. https://doi.org/10.1111/j.1741-3737.2001.00370.x

Turner, J.J., Kopystynska, O., Bradford, K., Schramm, D.G., & Higginbotham, B. (2021). Predicting parenting and stepparenting difficulties among newly remarried parents. *Journal of Divorce & Remarriage, 62*(7), 511–531. https://doi.org/10.1080/10502556.2021.1925857

Turner, J.J., Crapo, J.S., Kopystynska, O., Bradford, K., & Higginbotham, B.J. (2023). Economic distress and perceptions of sexual intimacy in remarriage. *Frontiers in Psychology, 13,* 1–15. https://doi.org/10.3389/fpsyg.2022.1056180

van Eeden-Moorfield, B., Pasley, K., Crosbie-Burnett, M., & King, E. (2012). Explaining couple cohesion in different types of gay families. *Journal of Family Issues, 33*(2), 182–201. https://doi.org/10.1177/0192513X11418180

van Eeden-Moorefield, B., Pasley, K., Dolan, E.M., & Engel, M. (2007). From divorce to remarriage: Financial management and security among remarried women. *Journal of Divorce & Remarriage, 47*(3/4), 21–42. https://doi.org/10.1300/J087v47n03_02

Visher, E.B., & Visher, J.S. (1979). *Stepfamilies: A guide to working with stepparents and stepchildren.* Brunner/Mazel.

Waddell, N., Overall, N.C., Chang, V.T., & Hammond, M.D. (2021). Gendered division of labor during a nationwide COVID-19 lockdown: Implications for relationship problems and satisfaction. *Journal of Social and Personal Relationships, 38*(6), 1759–1781. https://doi.org/10.1177/0265407521996476

Weigel, D.J., & Ballard-Reisch, D.S. (2001). The impact of relational maintenance behaviors on marital satisfaction: A longitudinal analysis. *The Journal of Family Communication, 1*(4), 265–279. https://doi.org/10.1207/s15327698jfc0104_03

Weston, C.A., & Macklin, E.D. (1990). The relationship between former-spousal contact and remarital satisfaction in stepfather families. *Journal of Divorce & Remarriage, 14*(2), 25–47.

Whitton, S.W., Nicholson, J.M., & Markman, H.J. (2008). Research on interventions for stepfamily couples: The state of the field. In J. Pryor (Ed.), *The international handbook of stepfamilies: Policy and practice in legal, research, and clinical environments* (pp. 455–484). John Wiley & Sons, Inc. http://dx.doi.org/10.1002/9781118269923.ch19

Xu, X., Hudspeth, C.D., & Bartowski, J.P. (2006). The role of cohabitation in marriage. *Journal of Marriage and Family, 68,* 261–274. https://doi.org/10.1111/j.1741-3737.2006.00251.x

3

WHAT WORKS FOR EFFECTIVE STEPPARENTING

Effective Stepparenting

Stepparent–stepchild relationships are common throughout history and across the world. Among minor-age children, about one in 10 lives with a parent and stepparent in the United States (Juteau et al., 2023), Canada (Gath, 2016), England and Wales (Gath, 2016), New Zealand (Gath, 2016), and Australia (Australian Bureau of Statistics, 2016).

Stepparents are adults whose spouses or cohabiting partners have a child or children from prior relationships. A stepchild is someone whose parent has repartnered to someone who is not their other primary parent. Stepparents and stepchildren are brought together because of their connections to the primary parent. In other words, the stepparent–stepchild relationship is involuntary, at least at the start, created because the stepparent develops a romantic relationship with the parent of the stepchildren (Ganong & Coleman, 2017).

The success of the stepfamily, in many respects, hinges on the quality of the stepparent–stepchild relationships formed. Negative, hostile, or distant bonds create stress for all stepfamily household members, whereas close and affectionate bonds can serve as sources of comfort and strength that enhance other stepfamily ties (Blyaert et al., 2016; Bryant et al., 2016; Ganong et al., 2019a, 2019b; Guisinger et al., 1989; Jensen, 2017,

DOI: 10.4324/9781003369073-3

2021; Jensen & Ganong, 2019; King et al., 2020; Orleans et al., 1989). In fact, the entire stepfamily system benefits when stepparent-stepchild bonds are close (Crosbie-Burnett, 1984; Ganong et al., 2019a, 2019b; Jensen, 2019; Jensen & Ganong, 2023; Jensen & Weller, 2019; Petren et al., 2019). The quality of stepparent–stepchild relationships is also predictive of stepchildren's psychological health (Jensen, 2017, 2021; Jensen & Harris, 2017a; Jensen et al., 2017), physical well-being (Jensen & Harris, 2017b), and academic attainment (King et al., 2020). The stepparent–stepchild relationship is therefore extremely consequential in stepfamilies. Given this importance, it is perhaps not surprising that the processes by which stepparents and stepchildren form relationships with each other has been of interest to many family scholars, particularly to those who take a resilience approach to examining relational dynamics. In this chapter, we review studies in which effective stepparenting behaviors were investigated.

Researchers have focused mainly on stepparents' interactions and relationships with stepchildren, studying them from either the perspective of stepparents or stepchildren, or sometimes obtaining the perspectives of both. Some researchers have examined effective childrearing by stepparents within stepfamily dynamics that include all household members or all members of the larger stepfamily system. These studies fall broadly into two areas: (a) developing positive stepparent–stepchild relationships, and (b) creating clear roles for stepparents. We organize our examination of *what works* around these two topics.

Developing Stepparent-Stepchild Relationships

Stepparent Affinity-Seeking Strategies

Almost half of the studies about effective stepparenting addressed the development and maintenance of positive stepparent–stepchild relationships. For many stepparents, a critical part of effective childrearing is building emotional connections or bonds with stepchildren (Ganong et al., 1999; Oliver-Blackburn et al., 2022). Following early work by Stern (1982), stepfamily scholars often have used the term *affinity-building* to describe stepparents' efforts at bonding with stepchildren. Affinity-building consists of actions intentionally performed by individuals to get others to like them and feel positive towards them (Ganong et al., 1999).

The term affinity has the dividend of also being defined as "related by marriage or by ties other than blood" (Dictionary.com, n.d.), which accurately describes step-kin ties.

Research on relationship development in stepfamilies has yielded clear messages about *what works*. Scholars consistently find that stepparents who engage in affinity-seeking behaviors more frequently are more successful at building emotionally close bonds with stepchildren than stepparents who engage in such behaviors less frequently or not at all (Agar et al., 2010; Allan et al., 2011; Baxter et al., 1999; Braithwaite et al., 2018; Bronstein et al., 1994; Bzostek, 2008; Campbell & Winn, 2018; Cartwright et al., 2009; Crohn, 2006, 2010; Ganong et al., 1999, 2018, 2019a, 2019b, 2020; Gold & Edin, 2023; Golish, 2003; Hetherington, 1987; Ivanova & Kalmijn, 2020a; Jensen, 2019; Jensen & Pace, 2016; Kellas et al., 2014; King et al., 2015; Kinniburgh-White et al., 2010; Limb et al., 2020; Maier et al., 2019; Marsiglio, 2004; Metts et al., 2013, 2017; Nuru & Wang, 2014; Oliver-Blackburn et al., 2022; Salem et al., 1998; Schenck et al., 2009; Schrodt, 2016; Schrodt et al., 2008; Schrodt, 2006; Schwartz & Finley, 2006; Speer & Trees, 2007; Stern, 1982; Waldron et al., 2018, 2022; Weaver & Coleman, 2005; White & Gilbreth, 2001; Whiting et al., 2007; Willetts & Maroules, 2004). Moreover, stepparents' affinity-seeking efforts are more effective when stepparents engage in these efforts over a longer period with stepchildren and when they try to establish friendships before attempting to discipline them (Braithwaite et al., 2018; Ganong et al., 1999, 2020; Hetherington, 1987, 1993; Hetherington et al., 1992; Kinniburgh-White et al., 2010; McDougal et al., 2018; Oliver-Blackburn et al., 2022; Schrodt et al., 2008; Waldron et al., 2018). This approach imitates parent–child relational development by engaging in relationship-building and bonding before disciplining. After all, effective parents focus on building a nurturing, foundational relationship with children long before they ever attempt to discipline them. By the time children are old enough for parents to correct their behaviors and to set guidelines for how they should behave, children usually have established close emotional bonds with their parents after months of being cared for and supported. Children pay attention to their parents' directives in part because of this emotional bond between them. Effective stepparents try to emulate this developmental approach of bonding before disciplining. So, what specific behaviors have been found to work in creating closer bonds with stepchildren?

Spending Time Together

Spending time together is essential for stepparent–stepchild bonding (Ahrons, 2007; Ambert, 1986; Hutchinson et al., 2007; Perry & Fraser, 2020; Schmeeckle et al., 2006). Being together provides opportunities for stepparents to interact with stepchildren and express interest in building a relationship (Agar et al., 2010; Bronstein et al., 1994; Green & Chuang, 2021; McDougal & George, 2016; Oliver-Blackburn et al., 2022). Stepparents spending time with stepchildren has been associated with stepchildren's well-being (Agar et al., 2010; Gold & Edin, 2023; Jensen & Lippold, 2018; Salem et al., 1998; Sweeney, 2007) and closer stepparent–stepchild relationships (Ahrons, 2007; Baxter et al., 1999; Braithwaite et al., 2018; Cross & Zhang, 2022; Jensen, 2019; Oliver-Blackburn et al., 2022; Petren et al., 2019). For affinity-building, what is most salient are the interactions that happen when stepparents and stepchildren share time and space.

One-On-One Activities

One way that stepparents build closer relationships with stepchildren is interacting with them in one-on-one activities (Campbell & Winn, 2018; Ganong et al., 1999; Green & Chuang, 2021; Ivanova & Kalmijn, 2020a; Jensen & Pace, 2016; Kelley, 1992; Oliver-Blackburn et al., 2022). Often, dyadic activities are more effective at relationship-building when stepchildren choose the activities than when stepparents do (Ganong et al., 1999). For example, if a stepfather likes to hunt and his stepson dislikes hunting but enjoys playing basketball in the driveway, an effective stepfather becomes a rebounder, a passer, and a teammate. Choosing activities is easier when stepparents and stepchildren share interests (e.g., sports, music, computer games; Crohn, 2006; Ganong et al., 2018), but when they do not, letting the stepchild choose leisure-time pursuits with stepparents enhances the likelihood they will enjoy themselves, making it easier for stepparents to get to know them because children are relaxed and interacting with the stepparent in a situation of low stress (Ganong et al., 1999).

It also helps relationship-building when stepchildren have some control over the pace at which affinity-overtures occur (Limb et al., 2020). Preferences for how rapidly and how often stepparents approach stepchildren to do things together may reflect individual differences in children's temperament and tolerance for interactions. For example, some stepchildren may be shy or have low tolerance for engagement with new people in their lives; others may welcome the added stimulation a new stepparent brings. Stepchildren have reported appreciating stepparents who are mindful of their responses to stepparents' affinity-seeking behaviors and who are persistent, but cautious, when trying to befriend them (Braithwaite et al., 2018). By taking things slowly at first (Braithwaite et al., 2018) and being mindful of stepchildren's responses to affinity-seeking (Marsiglio, 2004), stepparents can maximize the benefits of their efforts to bond. Cohabiting stepfathers who are mindful, who bring full awareness and undivided attention to what they do, have better romantic and coparental relationships with mothers (Parent et al., 2014), which in turn may facilitate more positive step-relationships. There also is evidence that being a stepparent enhances mindfulness and self-awareness. For example, in an investigation of Black social fathers (i.e., men who fulfill a father-like role in children's lives [e.g., stepfathers, uncles, grandfathers]), one stepfather stated, "I think I'm really more aware of my actions and what I do. I be thinking how can I do things differently in my life so that I can set an example for the boys" (McDougal & George, 2016, p. 536).

Stepchildren's preferences for stepparents' affinity-building efforts also may have cultural roots. For example, Limb and colleagues (2020) found that, for Native American stepchildren, stepparents showing warmth behaviors (e.g., hugging, complimenting) that *exceeded* stepchildren's expectations negatively impacted their perceptions of stepfamily quality (the inverse relationship was found for non-Native American participants). The authors hypothesized that feelings of distrust or negative reactions to stepfamily formation may make Native American youth less receptive to affinity-building efforts. They added, "If negative feelings exist surrounding the stepfamily formation, support from elders, relatives or friends could create a safe environment for the family to communicate their needs" (p. 157).

Having Fun Together

Stepparents and stepchildren benefit from engaging in fun activities, which could include hanging out, watching television, shopping, listening to music, playing sports or games together, watching a sporting event, taking a hike, going to a movie, and more. Using humor is another common stepparent strategy (Ganong et al., 1999; Golish, 2003; Green & Chuang, 2021; Kelley, 1992). Joking with stepchildren and laughing along with them are also bonding activities that are linked to close relationships (Ganong et al., 1999; Golish, 2003; Green & Chuang, 2021; Kelley, 1992). In general, spending time together on activities children enjoy is satisfying to both stepparents and stepchildren and provides opportunities for them to get to know each other in relaxed settings (Baxter et al., 1999; Crohn, 2006; Erera-Weatherley, 1996; Ganong et al., 1999; Golish, 2003; Ivanova & Kalmijn, 2020a; Jensen & Pace, 2016; King et al., 2015; McDougal et al., 2018; Nuru & Wang, 2014; Perry & Fraser, 2020; Salem et al., 1998; Yuan & Hamilton, 2006).

Working Together

Stepparents and stepchildren also bond and develop close ties by working together (Allan et al., 2011; Blyaert et al., 2016; Campbell & Winn, 2018; Ganong et al., 1999; Kinniburgh-White et al., 2010; Maier et al., 2019; McDougal & George, 2016; McDougal et al., 2018). Working together can include stepparents helping stepchildren with their homework, sharing household chores, running errands, and working on projects for school and social clubs (e.g., scouts or 4H). Similar to having fun together, working together provides opportunities for quality-time interactions where the sole focus is not the relationship, but on joining efforts to accomplish a goal or finish a task. Working together also offers chances for stepparents to model behaviors, to mentor, and to teach stepchildren (Bzostek, 2008; Ganong et al., 1999; McDougal & George, 2016; Salem et al., 1998). Stepparents who teach their stepchildren knowledge and skills that stepchildren want to learn are more likely to bond with them (Crohn, 2006; Green & Chuang, 2021; McDougal et al., 2018; Stern, 1982).

Caregiving

In addition to spending leisure time with stepchildren, caregiving also presents opportunities for bonding and relationship development. When stepparents are with stepchildren, particularly younger stepchildren, there are ample opportunities to engage in caregiving tasks – making meals, helping them get dressed, reading aloud to children, comforting them when they are hurt or sad, and assuring they are safe (Allan et al., 2011; Bray, 1999; Bronstein et al., 1994; Bzostek, 2008; Cartwright et al., 2009; Crohn, 2006; Jensen & Harris, 2017a; Kinniburgh-White et al., 2010; Schwartz & Finley, 2006; Weaver & Coleman, 2005). Many of these caregiving behaviors may go unnoticed by stepchildren and may even be unwelcome (Hetherington, 1987), particularly if the caregiving behaviors are seen by stepchildren as attempts to replace an absent parent (Weaver & Coleman, 2005). Consequently, stepparents who fulfill caregiving roles may want to communicate to children they are not trying to replace a parent or usurp their roles. Stepmothers seem to be attuned to taking stock of how their affinity-seeking efforts affect their stepchildren and other family members. Effective stepmothers are careful to avoid intruding into mothers' parenting domains (Crohn, 2006, 2010; Weaver & Coleman, 2005; Whiting et al., 2007). There is evidence that stepfathers also monitor themselves to make sure they do not infringe on fathers' and mothers' roles, rights, and responsibilities (Blyaert et al., 2016; Marsiglio, 2004). Black social fathers, which include stepfathers, reported that they communicated directly with stepchildren, their partners, and the children's biological fathers when finding a place for themselves in the stepchildren's lives (Reid & Golub, 2018).

Giving Tangible Support

Stepchildren generally appreciate receiving tangible goods from stepparents such as money, toys, clothes, trips, and other wants if it occurs alongside emotionally-oriented affinity-building strategies (Baxter et al., 1999; Braithwaite et al., 2018; Ganong et al., 1999, 2011; Green & Chuang, 2021; Kinniburgh-White et al., 2010; Nuru & Wang, 2014; Oliver-Blackburn et al., 2022; Schwartz & Finley, 2006; Stern, 1982; Waldron et al., 2022). Supplying financial support is a common way in which stepparents can visibly support their stepchildren (Cartwright et al., 2009;

Crohn, 2006; Ganong et al., 2011; Green & Chuang, 2021; McDougal & George, 2016; Oliver-Blackburn et al., 2022; Reid & Golub, 2018; Schwartz & Finley, 2006). This financial support may be substantive, such as purchasing a family residence, paying for tuitions, and generally raising the stepchildren's standard of living, or financial support may be relatively minor, such as paying for meals or treats the stepchildren had not been able to afford before the stepparent joined the family (Braithwaite et al., 2018; Ganong et al., 1999; Waldron et al., 2022). For example, we once interviewed a stepfather who noted that a turning point in his relationship with his stepchildren was when he spontaneously bought them ice cream while they were out shopping. In a separate interview, his stepson also recalled this moment as an important one – ice cream had been a rare treat for him, and when the stepfather surprised them with this small, but to the child, exceptional "gift," he saw this man in a different light.

Beyond enjoying the tangible goods, financial support may carry symbolic weight for stepparents that is important to stepchildren. Providing financial support potentially has multiple meanings to stepchildren – that they belong in the family (Ganong et al., 1999, 2011; King et al., 2015), that the stepparent claims them as kin (Ganong et al., 2018; Marsiglio, 2004; McDougal & George, 2016), that they matter to the stepparent (Schenck et al., 2009), and that the stepparent cares about them (Braithwaite et al., 2018). Moreover, since financial support of children is a societal expectation of parents (Schwartz & Finley, 2006), assuming some monetary responsibility for stepchildren may be perceived by children and adults as parental duties engaged in by stepparents (Ganong et al., 2018; Marsiglio, 2004; McDougal & George, 2016). Although most studies of financial support have sampled stepfathers, studies of stepmothers (Whiting et al., 2007) and of stepparents in general have found that tangible support works for stepmothers, too.

Advocating for Stepchildren

Being an advocate for stepchildren is also an effective strategy for gaining affinity with them (Ganong et al., 1999, 2011; Oliver-Blackburn et al., 2022; Waldron et al., 2022). Being an advocate means the stepparents position themselves on the side of the stepchild, stand for the stepchild's desires/interests, protect them, and help them solve problems they have with others (Baxter et al., 1999; Ivanova & Kalmijn, 2020a; Oliver-Blackburn et al., 2022). For example, we once interviewed a stepdaughter in college who was grateful to her stepfather for helping her deal with a difficult landlord by making sure repairs were done that had been promised. Joining stepchildren in problem-solving helps build a sense of togetherness (Waldron et al., 2022). Advocating on behalf of stepchildren in discussions with parents (e.g., extending curfew for a special occasion) also is an effective affinity strategy if it does not occur too often or create spousal conflict (Crohn, 2010; Ganong et al., 2011; Oliver-Blackburn et al., 2022; Waldron et al., 2022; Weaver & Coleman, 2005).

In some stepfamilies, incidents in which stepparents protect or advocate for stepchildren are seen as notable turning points in relationship bonding (Oliver-Blackburn et al., 2022). For example, in one study, a stepfather recalled how he protected his stepson from witnessing volatile conflict between his mother and new stepmother, sharing: "I just removed him from that situation, took [him] to the truck, and [we] just sat and talked ... he really found comfort that I was just there to make sure he was okay" (Oliver-Blackburn et al., 2022, p. 1272). Passive forms of advocacy, actions such as attending stepchildren's sporting events or school activities, are ways in which stepparents show support for their stepchildren that facilitate connecting with them (Banker & Gaertner, 1998). By "being there" for stepchildren at sporting events and school functions, stepparents convey to stepchildren that they are invested, interested, and engaged in their lives (Ganong et al., 2011, 2018; Oliver-Blackburn et al., 2022; Waldron et al., 2022).

Communicating Effectively

Relationships are constructed and maintained via communication, and one-on-one communication is particularly important in affinity-seeking. Affinity communications may be brief (e.g., expressing love and affection) or lengthy (e.g., chatting over a meal), nonverbal (e.g., a hug or pat on the back) or verbal (e.g., praising the stepchild for doing something well), random (e.g., taking a moment to show the stepchild how to do something) or purposeful (e.g., setting aside time to have a quiet conversation). Indeed, researchers have found that stepparents who frequently and regularly communicate one-on-one with stepchildren as part of their relationship-building strategies create closer ties with them than stepparents who communicate infrequently and irregularly (Baxter et al., 1999; Braithwaite et al., 2018; Ganong et al., 1999; Golish, 2003; Jensen, 2021; Jensen & Harris, 2017a, 2017b; Schrodt, 2006, 2016).

Conveying Positive Messages

Stepparents who communicate positive messages to stepchildren are more successful at facilitating bonding; for instance, expressions of love, encouragement, and support to stepchildren are found to promote closer ties (Bronstein et al., 1994; Ganong et al., 1999, 2019b; Green & Chuang, 2021; Jensen & Harris, 2017a; Jensen et al., 2017; Schrodt, 2006; White & Gilbreth, 2001; Whiting et al., 2007). Talking about the relationship in positive ways and not focusing on problems was related to positive step-relationships (Braithwaite et al., 2018; Schrodt, 2016), as was communicating acceptance of stepchildren and offering emotional support (Cartwright et al., 2009; Crohn, 2006; Ganong et al., 2019b; Green & Chuang, 2021; Henry & Lovelace, 1995; Whiting et al., 2007).

Conveying Vulnerability

One-on-one communication that enhances relationship closeness is not limited to uplifting messages from stepparents to stepchildren. Being vulnerable with stepchildren by expressing sadness, apologizing for errors made, asking stepchildren for forgiveness, and forgiving stepchildren for their mistakes are examples of communications that enable stepparents and stepchildren to become closer (Baxter et al., 1999; Braithwaite et al., 2018; Ganong et al., 2019b; Waldron et al., 2018; Whiting et al., 2007). When stepparents are willing to share their own concerns, fears, and vulnerabilities, stepchildren perceive stepparents to be more open and authentic. In turn, stepchildren are more open to communicating with the stepparent (Afifi, 2003; Ganong et al., 2019b; Maier et al., 2019), which is important because stepchildren who disclose more to stepparents report greater stepfamily satisfaction (Metts et al., 2017) and enjoy emotionally closer step-relationships (Braithwaite et al., 2018).

Conveying vulnerability when resolving conflict may be especially beneficial. These instances can serve as powerful, positive turning points in stepparent–stepchild relationships (Baxter et al., 1999; Braithwaite et al., 2018;

Oliver-Blackburn et al., 2022). Forgiveness by either the stepparent or stepchild has positive healing effects that can reverberate throughout the stepfamily system (Schrodt, 2006; Waldron et al., 2018). Unexpected compassion on behalf of stepparents can be especially powerful in fostering forgiveness: "for example, the stern stepfather who unexpectedly cried at his stepdaughter's wedding, or the emotionally distant stepmother who shed tears on behalf of a distressed stepdaughter. These moments loomed large in some relational narratives and appeared to help forgiveness" (Waldron et al., 2018, p. 572). On the other hand, a stepmother who refused a corsage at her stepdaughter's wedding for fear it would poke holes in her silk blouse created hard feelings that continued to linger. When stepfathers apologize to stepchildren after a conflict, stepchildren feel better about themselves and their stepfathers (Cookston et al., 2014).

Engaging in Everyday Talk

Communication with stepchildren does not have to be intentionally aimed at enriching or improving the relationship. Everyday talk is also associated with closer stepparent–stepchild ties (Campbell & Winn, 2018; Golish, 2003; Green & Chuang, 2021; Jensen & Pace, 2016; King et al., 2015; Schrodt, 2016; Schrodt et al., 2008). Everyday talk primarily consists of regular, mundane encounters – talking about the days' events, making small talk, joking around. These often-brief social interactions connect stepparents and stepchildren and make them part of the daily routine of the household. When stepparents and stepchildren engage in everyday talk, stepchildren report more positive and respectful relationships with stepparents, are more satisfied with their stepparents, and respond more positively when stepparents ask them to do things (Schrodt, 2016).

Engaging in everyday talk may incorporate more than the mundane, however. Talking about relationships, checking in with how the other person is feeling, expressing love and affection, and making sure others are doing well, also are examples of everyday talk (Schrodt et al., 2008; Schrodt, 2006; Yuan & Hamilton, 2006). Everyday talk that incorporates *relationship talk* sends messages to stepchildren that stepparents care about them, are interested in their well-being, and that the stepchildren matter to them (King et al., 2015; Schenck et al., 2009). When adolescents perceive that they matter to stepparents, adolescent stepchildren report fewer mental health problems (i.e., depression, acting out in school), and stepparents report fewer problem behaviors (Schenck et al., 2009).

Indirect Relationship-Building Strategies

In addition to direct strategies, stepparents also engage in indirect ways of building positive bonds with stepchildren – behaviors that do not involve direct interactions with stepchildren but nonetheless send messages to stepchildren that facilitate bonding. For example, stepchildren find it easier to bond with stepparents when the stepparents treat the biological coparents with respect (Braithwaite et al., 2018; Green & Chuang, 2021; Marsiglio, 2004). One way they do this is by not intruding on parent–child relationships (Crohn, 2006, 2010; Marsiglio, 2004; Weaver & Coleman, 2005). For example, by encouraging parent–child activities, stepparents show support for these relationships. Another way of indirectly seeking a closer relationship with stepchildren is by leaving discipline to parents, particularly early in the stepfamily formation, and especially with adolescents (Hetherington, 1987, 1993; Kinniburgh-White et al., 2010). Stepchildren also are more likely to have closer relationships with stepparents, and to even change the trajectory of those relationships from distant to close, when they perceive that the stepparent's actions help the family (Waldron et al., 2022), their parent (Ganong et al., 2011), or an older half-sibling (Sanner et al., 2020). We call these indirect relationship-building efforts because the stepparent is not necessarily interacting with the stepchild, but their actions in helping other family members nevertheless encourage closer stepparent–stepchild ties.

Stepchildren's Receptivity to Stepparents' Efforts to Bond

Building a friendship is an interactive, interpersonal process; it takes someone to initiate relationship-building efforts and another person to respond favorably to those efforts. The relationship-building process of stepparents, in other words, is not complete until the stepchild responds in some fashion, and the process is only effective if the stepchild observes the stepparent's efforts, accepts those efforts, and reacts by feeling closer to the stepparent and repaying those efforts with their own relationship-building actions (Ganong et al., 2011). It is not enough, therefore, for stepparents to engage in bonding behaviors directed toward stepchildren – stepchildren must be receptive to and reciprocate those efforts. Unlike voluntary relationships in which both parties may be similarly motivated to become friends and build a closer bond, the involuntary nature of many early stepparent–stepchild ties may mean that stepparents are more motivated to befriend stepchildren than stepchildren are to befriend stepparents. The receptivity of stepchildren to stepparents' efforts is therefore a critically important element in the building of step-kin bonds that work (Allan et al., 2011; Baxter et al., 1999; Braithwaite et al., 2018; Bronstein et al., 1994; Brown et al., 1990; Campbell & Winn, 2018; Cartwright et al., 2009; Fang & Zartler, 2023; Ganong et al., 1999, 2011, 2018; King et al., 2015; Kinniburgh-White et al., 2010; Limb et al., 2020; Michaels, 2006; Schrodt, 2016; Waldron et al., 2022).

Stepchildren's receptivity to stepparents' efforts to build close relationships vary – some are responsive to stepparents from the start of the relationship, some take longer to warm up to the stepparents' efforts, and some never do respond affirmatively (Ganong et al., 2011; Fang & Zartler, 2023; Waldron et al., 2022). In one of six patterns of step-relationship development identified by Ganong, Coleman, and colleagues (2011), some stepchildren actively resisted and disliked their stepparents, sometimes for months or even years, until changing their minds and deciding that the stepparent meant well, was doing good for the family, and was making the child's parent happy. After this shift in awareness and appreciation for the stepparent, these stepchildren began repaying stepparents' efforts to bond with them. Those *changing trajectory* relationships became emotionally closer with time. In another study, four trajectories of stepparent–stepchild relationship development were identified; in two of them, relationships started as positive and stayed that way or became even closer over time, and in the other two, relationships shifted between negative and positive (Waldron et al., 2022). The common thread across these trajectories was how stepparents responded to stepchildren's vulnerability, stepchildren's perceptions that the stepparent added value to the family, and positive reframing of the stepparent's actions that occurred over time, likely because of stepchildren maturing (Waldron et al., 2022).

Stepchildren also may make attempts to get to know the stepparent in an effort to reduce or eliminate ambiguity surrounding the relationship (Fang & Zartler, 2023). For example, some adolescent stepchildren in Fang and Zartler's study described the uncomfortable, awkward, or unclear nature of relationships with stepparents; as one stepchild said, "The relationship with [my stepmother] is just so confusing, I don't really understand what is going on and how I could even begin to describe our relationship. It's just all very unclear to me" (p. 119). To reduce feelings of ambiguity, some participants decided to take a more active role in getting to know the stepparent and finding mutually interesting things to do together, such as sharing hobbies, which the researchers called *co-constructing a shared reality* (Fang & Zartler, 2023). These strategies reduced uncertainty in step-relationships and brought them closer together.

There is evidence from these and other studies that *what works* for stepparents is to be persistent in striving to build friendships or close bonds with stepchildren. For example, the closest step-relationships in another study were among *continuous affinity-seeking* stepparents and their stepchildren (Ganong et al., 1999). Continuous affinity seekers were stepparents who worked at building a friendship with stepchildren while they were dating the children's parent, and they continued working to build a close bond after remarriage. In contrast, stepparents who befriended stepchildren before remarriage but stopped doing so after, as well as stepparents who never engaged in affinity seeking, had more distant bonds with stepchildren (Ganong et al., 1999). This persistence can be difficult and challenging for stepparents, particularly when stepchildren do not respond to stepparents' efforts to become friends or to be close. In a longitudinal study of newly formed mother–stepfather households, researchers found that most stepfathers made attempts to befriend their stepchildren early in the remarriage, but two years later, many had stopped trying to bond with stepchildren because their stepchildren were not responding to them (Hetherington, 1987, 1993; Hetherington et al., 1992). As a result, these stepfathers became discouraged and discontinued efforts to bond. The *what works* takeaway from these studies is that stepparents' persistence in trying to bond with stepchildren, employing evidence-based ways of effective bonding, often pays (Ganong et al., 1999, 2011; Hetherington, 1987, 1993; Hetherington et al., 1992; Waldron et al., 2022). Stepparents should not give up attempting to bond, even after several years have passed.

Box 3.1 *What works* in effective stepparenting

Develop positive stepparent–stepchild relationships.

- Engage in affinity-seeking activities to build closer bonds with stepchildren.
  - Spend time together without the parent or other children being present.
  - Do one-on-one activities enjoying shared interests (e.g., hobbies).
  - Do one-on-one activities that the stepchild has chosen.
  - Be mindful of a child's responses to affinity-seeking – slow down, if necessary, but do not stop trying to make friends.
  - Be aware of any cultural norms that may affect efforts to befriend the stepchild.
  - Have fun together – do activities that you both like.
  - Work together on home or school projects, run errands together.
  - If the stepchild shows interest, teach them new knowledge or skills, but with low pressure.
  - Engage in caregiving tasks – make meals, do laundry, comfort children, etc.
  - Remind children that you are not trying to replace either parent when caretaking.
  - Give children tangible resources such as money, toys, clothes, snacks, and trips.
  - Defend the stepchild against others who want to harm them.
  - Let the stepchild know you are on their side in problems they have with others.
    - Be there for the stepchild by attending musical and sporting events, school functions, and other activities in which they participate.

- Communicate effectively.
  - ○ Convey positive messages to stepchildren.
    - ■ Express love and affection, praise and encourage them, say nice things.
    - ■ Convey vulnerability by expressing sadness, apologizing for errors made, asking for and granting forgiveness.
  - ○ Talk with the stepchild every day.
    - ■ Talk about mundane, everyday topics (e.g., school, hobbies, friends).
    - ■ Talk about family relationships, check on how they feel, tell them they matter.
- Engage in indirect ways of building relationships with stepchildren:
  - ○ Treat the stepchild's biological parents with respect.
  - ○ Respect the parent–child relationship by giving them space and time to be together without you.
  - ○ Leave discipline to parents.
    - ■ Make it clear by your actions that the interests of the family are a priority (e.g., be kind, be helpful, share resources).
- Bonding is a two-way street:
  - ○ Remember that resistant stepchildren may change their minds.
  - ○ Continue trying to build positive relationships with stepchildren. Persistence often pays.
  - ○ Avoid disciplining stepchildren until there is a close emotional connection with them.

Creating Clear Roles for Stepparents

Stepparents' roles have long been a focus of researchers and practitioners, in part because stepparent roles have changed over time. Since the early 1970s, most stepfamilies have been formed after parental divorce or separation rather than after a parent's death (Ganong & Coleman, 2018).

This demographic shift meant that stepparents were not replacing or substituting for a deceased parent, but instead were an additional parent figure, a role for which there were no clear social norms (Cherlin, 1978). Post-divorce stepfamilies (we include post-separation of cohabiting couples in this category) are more structurally and interpersonally complex than post-bereavement stepfamilies, mainly because of the *stepparent as extra adult* phenomenon. What roles should these stepparents enact with their stepchildren? Are they substitutes for absent parents? Bonus parents? Adult friends? Acquaintances? Clinicians addressed this phenomenon before researchers (e.g., Visher & Visher, 1979), but it did not take long for researchers to begin exploring answers to the questions facing stepfamilies about how to define and enact stepparents' roles (Ganong & Coleman, 2017, 2018).

Multiple Roles Work for Stepparents

One finding is that stepfamilies employ several diverse roles for stepparents that work for them (Blyaert et al., 2016; Crohn, 2006, 2010; Erera-Weatherley, 1996; Ganong et al., 2011; Kinniburgh-White et al., 2010; Schrodt, 2006; Weaver & Coleman, 2005). In short, one "size" does not fit all stepparents or all stepfamilies (Jensen, 2021). These roles include enacting: (a) a parental role, with the associated childrearing responsibilities (Berger, 1995; Erera-Weatherley, 1996; Forehand et al., 2014, 2015; Ganong et al., 2011; Green & Chuang, 2021; Hequembourg, 2004; Kinniburgh-White et al., 2010; Marsiglio, 1992; McDougal et al., 2018; Oliver-Blackburn et al., 2022; Parent et al., 2014; Schmeeckle et al., 2006), (b) a friend role, who is affable and supportive but not a parental authority or disciplinarian (Blyaert et al., 2016; Crohn, 2006; Erera-Weatherley, 1996; Ganong et al., 2011; Kinniburgh-White et al., 2010; Oliver-Blackburn et al., 2022; Waldron et al., 2022), (c) a nurturing stepparent role, or someone who engages warmly in childrearing while respecting parental boundaries (Crohn, 2006; Erera-Weatherley, 1996; Weaver & Coleman, 2005), (d) an "othermother" (Burton & Hardaway, 2012) or "otherfather" role – roles identified in communities of color that resemble parental roles without efforts to replace parents (Reid & Golub, 2018), (e) a mentor, who is something between a close friend and a family member (Blyaert et al., 2016; Crohn, 2006; Green & Chuang, 2021;

McDougal & George, 2016; Schmeeckle et al., 2006), (f) a casual acquaintance (Erera-Weatherley, 1996; Ganong et al., 2011; Kinniburgh-White et al., 2010), and (g) a distant stranger or ambivalent figure (Ganong et al., 2011). These various roles are identified as the main roles assumed by stepparents in these studies. It is likely, however, that each stepparent enacts multiple roles in their interactions with stepchildren (Oliver-Blackburn et al., 2022).

All roles except distant stranger and ambivalent figure were characterized by various degrees of positive feelings between the stepparent and stepchild. Further, in all role constellations, stepparents are not the primary disciplinarians, even when stepparents claimed parental status (Golish, 2003; McDougal & George, 2016; Reid & Golub, 2018). Across studies, effective stepparents, regardless of their roles, do not try to usurp the parents' authority or try to replace either biological parent in their stepchildren's lives (Burton & Hardaway, 2012; Blyaert et al., 2016; Crohn, 2006; Kinniburgh-White et al., 2010; Reid & Golub, 2018; Weaver & Coleman, 2005).

Another thing that effective stepparents have in common is that they are flexible in the roles they ultimately occupy (MacDonald & DeMaris, 2002; Oliver-Blackburn et al., 2022; Schrodt, 2021; Shapiro, 2014). This flexibility may be in response to the lack of clearly defined roles for stepparents (Cherlin, 1978). As a result, stepfamilies often have multiple, sometimes competing, perspectives within the family about what roles stepparents should fulfill. For example, stepmothers may find themselves at the intersection of opposing guidelines for expected behavior, as gendered norms suggest that they should be both highly involved as women in families while simultaneously less involved as stepmothers (Weaver & Coleman, 2005). Therefore, being flexible as these roles are negotiated is useful for stepparents. For example, stepparents who held flexible beliefs about gender and family roles had lower stress related to stepparenting than did those with less flexible beliefs (Shapiro, 2014). Stepparents also may occupy different roles for different stepchildren in the same family, particularly because stepchildren vary in how they respond to stepparents' overtures. For instance, the oldest stepchild sometimes is the most difficult for stepparents to develop a positive relationship with, while younger stepchildren may be more accepting of stepparents as friends or secondary parental figures.

Researchers often attribute challenges in stepfamily role definitions to their incompletely institutionalized status (Cherlin, 1978), but some stepfamilies use the lack of normative expectations in a positive way, creating roles that work for them without concerns about meeting societal expectations about parental roles and responsibilities (Goldberg & Allen, 2013). Creating roles that work may be easier for individuals and families who are marginalized by virtue of sexual orientation, race, or other factors, because they previously have learned to be flexible in defining themselves and their relationships as ones who stand outside of the mainstream. Galvin & Braithwaite (2014) called families located outside traditional structures, and who consequently lack social norms, *discourse dependent* families because they must engage in additional communicative labor to create and validate the family and its relationships (p. 29). Black families with stepfathers, social fathers, or othermothers (Burton & Hardaway, 2012; Cross & Zhang, 2022; Forehand et al., 2014, 2015, 2016; Green & Chuang, 2021; McDougal & George, 2016; McDougal et al., 2018; Reid & Golub, 2018) and families headed by same-sex couples (Goldberg & Allen, 2013) are discourse dependent, but they also are more likely to be flexible in creating roles and relationships that help meet their needs. Stepfamilies in general, of course, are discourse dependent families, which suggests that stepfamilies who engage in communication to define and modify roles for stepparents do better than those who do not (Oliver-Blackburn et al., 2022; Waldron et al., 2022).

Agreeing on Roles

Stepparents' roles, in whatever ways they are defined, work better when there is agreement among family members (Crosbie-Burnett, 1984; Jensen & Shafer, 2013; Quick et al., 1995; Saint-Jacques, 1995; Skopin et al., 1993; Whiting et al., 2007). When parents, stepparents, and stepchildren discuss, negotiate, and reach consensus on stepparents' roles, there are benefits for individuals, relationships, and overall stepfamily functioning (Brown et al., 1990; Erera-Weatherley, 1996). For example, stepfathers and adolescent stepchildren who agree on the kind of relationships they have together report greater overall satisfaction with the stepfamily and the step-relationship (Crosbie-Burnett, 1984). The parental role behaviors initiated by stepparents are less important than stepchildren's receptivity to those role behaviors (Brown et al., 1990). When figuring out what stepparenting style to adopt, communicating role expectations with partners and stepchildren reduces ambiguity (Erera-Weatherley, 1996; Reid & Golub, 2018; Whiting et al., 2007). When ambiguity of stepparents' roles and relationships persists, adolescent stepchildren cope by learning to live with it for the sake of their parents, and by doing what they can to avoid conflicts (Fang & Zartler, 2023).

In short, role clarity is key. It is not enough for stepparents to choose their roles; everyone in the stepfamily needs to understand and accept those roles for the whole family to benefit. For stepchildren, role clarity (i.e., having clear perceptions about how to relate to stepparents) is linked to more affinity-seeking behaviors toward stepparents, and fewer autonomy-seeking behaviors away from stepparents (Schwartz & Finley, 2006). Further, when the parent and stepparent agree on stepparent's roles in childrearing, stepchildren feel closer to the stepparent (Jensen & Shafer, 2013; Quick et al., 1995; Skopin, et al., 1993). Role clarity also predicts which stepfamilies have greater abilities to solve problems and are more satisfied with stepfamily functioning (Brown et al., 1990). The closer stepparents' actual role behaviors are to their ideal role performance goals (i.e., the type of stepparent they'd *like* to be), the more satisfied they are with their stepparenting, and the closer they are to stepchildren (Fine et al., 1997, 1998).

Context Matters

When discussing *what works* regarding stepparent roles, context matters. Several factors are relevant when stepfamilies decide on stepparent roles. For example, stepchildren's ages may be an important consideration – stepparents assuming a parental role appears to work better when stepchildren are younger than when they are older (Erera-Weatherley, 1996; Ganong et al., 2011; Kinniburgh-White et al., 2010; Schmeeckle et al., 2006). Involvement of nonresidential parents in childrearing also may be a factor in the negotiation and enactment of stepparents' roles – stepparents may be more inclined to fulfill a "friend" or "mentor" role if stepchildren already have two actively involved parents (Erera-Weatherley, 1996; Ganong et al., 2011; Kinniburgh-White et al., 2010; MacDonald & DeMaris, 2002; Reid & Golub, 2018). Multiple studies suggest that, although many stepparent roles work well for stepfamilies, a friend role may be the most effective choice for most stepfamilies, especially early in the stepfamily's development (Crohn, 2006, 2010; Erera-Weatherley, 1996; Ganong et al., 2011, 2018; Hetherington, 1987; Kinniburgh-White et al., 2010; Oliver-Blackburn et al., 2022).

Culture as Context

Earlier, we mentioned possible cultural differences in stepparent–stepchild bonding; for example, Native American youth have been found to respond differently to stepparents' efforts to bond than their peers, wanting stepparents to move more slowly in building close relationships (Limb et al., 2020). There are other examples of the importance of cultural context that should be noted. For example, studies of Black stepfathers and Black social fathers, many of whom are remarried or cohabiting stepfathers, reveal many findings about *what works* for them that also work for stepfathers of other racial backgrounds, but there are subtle differences as well. Many Black families in North America experienced forced migration from western African cultures in which the extended family was the norm, and collectivistic values prevailed. These cultural beliefs about extended kinship were adaptive for enslaved African Americans, who for centuries had to contend with attacks on their families (Green & Chuang, 2021; McDougal & George, 2016). Families of Black Americans and Afro-Caribbeans are rooted in cultural traditions in which extended kin networks were defined and sustained through flexibility, creativity, and persistence. These traditions, and the value of collectively looking out for others' well-being under conditions of White terrorism, may make it more likely that Black stepfamilies find it somewhat easier than other racialized groups to find supportive, adaptive roles for stepparents.

Parental roles for Black stepparents may be the preference for many families, with stepparents prepared to replace nonresidential parents (Green & Chuang, 2021; McDougal & George, 2016), but they are also willing to function in other roles, often negotiating with both biological parents to create *othermother* or *otherfather* roles (Burton & Hardaway, 2012; Reid & Golub, 2018). Discipline often is defined broadly to include teaching personal responsibility, serving as role models of how to navigate a hostile society, and supporting biological parents in keeping children safe and teaching children the values of hard work, education, and self-control (Green & Chuang, 2021; McDougal et al., 2018; Reid & Golub, 2018). Even for stepparents who see themselves as parental figures, punishment is directed by biological parents, with stepparents taking supporting roles, and disciplining only under the guidance and approval of the parent: "Her mother gives me that responsibility [to discipline] …. She gives me the green light to go ahead and discipline. She tells me to do it" (Reid & Golub, 2018, p. 970). Much of *what works* for Black stepparents, such as being innovative and flexible in creating a place for themselves in the stepfamily, works for all stepparents, but Black stepparents may be able to draw on cultural backgrounds that are less grounded in nuclear family models than are Eurocentric, individualistic approaches to family life (Hannon et al., 2023).

Box 3.2 *What works* **for creating clear roles for stepparents**

- Create clear stepparent roles.
  - ○ Remember that multiple roles may work for stepparents. Positive roles include:
    - Parental role
    - Friend role
    - Nurturing stepparent role
    - Othermother/Otherfather
    - Mentor role
    - Casual acquaintance
  - ○ Be flexible in the roles you take on.
    - Negotiate with other stepfamily members to agree on stepparent roles.
    - Make sure everyone knows and understands stepparent's roles.
    - Context matters: a stepparent's roles may depend on children's ages, the nonresidential parent's involvement, and other contextual factors.

Older Stepparents and Adult Stepchildren

Only a few studies of older stepparents and their adult stepchildren met our *what works* criteria. In general, studies of older stepfamilies are relatively few in comparison to studies of stepfamilies with children and adolescents, but there are signs that more researchers are examining later-life stepfamilies (see Chapter 7 on grandparents and stepgrandparents for more evidence of this interest). Most of what we know that works for older stepparents and adult stepchildren are based on studies of long-term step-relationships that began when stepchildren were minors and continued as stepchildren aged into adulthood.

Long-Term Stepparents

When relationships between aging stepparents and adult stepchildren are close, stepparents and stepchildren report better physical and mental health (Egginton et al., 2021; Ivanova, 2020; Ivanova & Kalmijn, 2020b; Jensen & Harris, 2017b). Relationship quality between older stepparents and adult stepchildren is primarily a consequence of the stepparent bonding with the stepchild when they were younger (Egginton et al., 2021; Ivanova & Kalmijn, 2020a). As such, *what works* for long-term stepparent–stepchild relationships often involves maintaining positive relationships that have been in existence for years if not decades. Other factors also shape long-term stepparent–stepchild relationships, however, such as exchanges of support between aging stepparents and adult step-children, as well as adult stepchildren becoming parents.

Adult stepchildren exchange resources like money and tangible help with older stepparents who have helped them in the past, both as children (Clawson & Ganong, 2002; Ivanova & Kalmijn, 2020a; Schmeeckle, 2007) and as adults (Clawson & Ganong, 2002; Coleman et al., 2015; Kalbarczyk, 2021; Schmeeckle, 2007; Vinick & Lanspery, 2000). In older step-relationships, the principle of reciprocity operates, as in, "You helped me as a child; I owe you help now that you are becoming older." In the absence of genetic or legal obligations, norms related to reciprocity function in positive step-kin relationships (Ganong & Coleman, 1999; Ivanova & Kalmijn, 2020a; Kalbarczyk, 2021). Some reciprocity is direct, as the example above, and some is indirect – for instance, a stepchild who repays an older stepparent for having enriched the biological parent's life (e.g., "I owe her for taking care of dad. She watches his health"; Clawson & Ganong, 2002, p. 64). Regardless of norms related to reciprocity, when adult stepchildren view their aging stepparents as family, familial obligations are in play, as in, "We are family to each other, so I will be there for you when you need me."

Regarding role enactment of long-term stepparents, older stepparents have been found to engage in gendered behaviors just as older parents do; stepmothers "kinkeep" by making sure stepchildren and fathers stay in friendly contact, even encouraging them to make amends and rebuild damaged relationships (Hornstra & Ivanova, 2023; Schmeeckle, 2007; Vinick & Lanspery, 2000), and stepfathers provide financial support, advice, and other tangible support to stepchildren (Coleman et al., 2015; Schmeeckle, 2007). Providing childcare for stepgrandchildren is common, and when stepgrandparents do this, they often receive financial and other aid from adult stepchildren (Kalbarczyk, 2021). In one study, the warm, loving interactions between stepgrandparents and stepgrandchildren served as a catalyst for middle-generation adult stepchildren to rethink their step-relationship and to make efforts to repair a distant connection that had existed since they were children (Clawson & Ganong, 2002).

Later-Life Stepparents

In contrast to long-term stepparents, who have known their stepchildren since they were young, later-life stepparents enter the family when their stepchildren (i.e., their partner's children) are adults. The only known study of later-life stepparents supported the idea that positive relationships are more likely to develop when stepchildren see that the new stepparent provides benefits to the parent (e.g., caregiving, companionship) or when their relationships with the parent improve due to the new stepparent's kinkeeping efforts (e.g., an adult child who sees their father more because the father's new wife encourages more frequent contact; Mikucki-Enyart & Heisdorf, 2020). Some adult stepchildren enjoy acquiring new extended family members (stepsiblings, stepgrandparents), and they appreciate being included in extended family rituals or having their own celebrations merged with those of the new stepparent (Mikucki-Enyart & Heisdorf, 2020). Apart from this investigation, little is known about *what works* for stepparents acquired in later life.

Names

Stepchildren who meet their stepparents when both are adults use first names when talking to or referring to each other (Mikucki-Enyart & Heisdorf, 2020). It is rare for stepfamilies that start in later life to think of themselves as forming step-relationships, so it is not surprising that they would not use familial labels for each other. For younger stepchildren, however, the use of family labels to address stepparents is more complicated (Kellas et al., 2008). How other people are addressed can be a symbolic way of indicating closeness and distance, so some stepchildren use address terms strategically, sometimes using familial terms to address stepparents and sometimes not, depending on the context, while other stepchildren purposefully use familial terms (e.g., mom, dad) to indicate solidarity with stepparents or intentionally use first names to suggest other types of relationships (Kellas et al., 2008). So, *what works* in naming? Stepchildren in one study advised others to "do what's comfortable," "don't force it," and "let kids decide" (Kellas et al., 2008, p. 257). Others suggested that stepfamilies discuss address terms before adopting specific language to use (Kellas et al., 2008).

Box 3.3 *What works* for older stepparents and adult stepchildren

Long-term stepparents:

- Maintain positive relationships developed when stepchildren were younger.
    - Take care of stepchildren when they are young.
        - Be kind.
        - Show affection.
        - Help them.
        - Support them emotionally, physically, and financially.
        - Teach them knowledge and skills.
    - Assist stepchildren in their adult years.
        - Babysit grandchildren.
        - Offer advice and emotional support.
        - Provide financial support (if possible and if needed).

○ Engage in kinkeeping.
  ▪ Keep in touch with family members.
  ▪ Arrange family gatherings.
  ▪ Remember birthdays and other celebrations.
○ Work through past conflicts by making amends and by apologizing.

Stepparents acquired in later life:
• Develop positive relationships with stepchildren.
  ○ Treat biological parents with respect and love.
  ○ Provide caregiving and companionship to the biological parent.
  ○ Encourage new partner to stay connected with their children or encourage them to re-connect.
• Call new step-kin by names that feel comfortable for everyone.
  ○ Let younger family members decide on names for new stepparents and stepgrandparents.
  ○ Do not force younger family members to use familial names and labels for new step-kin.

Implications for Practice

With an understanding of research findings of *what works* for stepparents, we turn now to a discussion of how these findings can be leveraged by helping professionals, such as therapists working with stepfamilies. One of the most robust findings about effective childrearing in stepfamilies is that stepparents who work at developing close bonds with stepchildren are more effective than stepparents who do not. These closer bonds are related to greater well-being for stepchildren, stepparents, and parents, and better overall functioning for stepfamilies. These empirical findings are good news, because it is likely that most stepparents have the necessary skills and knowledge to build relationships with stepchildren. A clear implication of these findings is that stepparents should engage in relationship-building behaviors with stepchildren.

It is not entirely clear why stepparents do not engage in trying to bond emotionally with stepchildren, although there is evidence that some stepparents opt instead to enact roles as disciplinarians (Erera-Weatherley, 1996; Ganong et al., 1999), which in their views may not include befriending stepchildren or becoming emotionally close to them. In other words, making friends with stepchildren may not feel proper or parental to some stepparents, whereas setting rules, levying discipline, and making decisions about stepchildren does. There is evidence that at least some stepparents do not think about bonding and nurturing because they have been encouraged to be tough disciplinarians by their spouses/partners. This happens when parents feel overwhelmed or incapable of managing the children, and so they seek help from stepparents. We have interviewed stepfathers who were encouraged by their wives to think their role was to shape up their "out of control" stepchildren, and we have talked to stepmothers who have been asked to "teach these kids some manners" by their beleaguered spouses. Unfortunately, stepchildren do not appreciate the "stepparent-as-sheriff" approach, and sometimes these roles are undermined by parents.

Stepparents who are uncertain about the importance of bonding with stepchildren may need help from family professionals in thinking about the logic of establishing a bond with children before trying to set rules for them. For example, most childrearing discipline methods are more effective when there is an emotional bond – parents provide care and nurture for their own children for years before trying to discipline them, and stepparents who bond before trying to discipline are imitating how relationships between parents and their children develop. Parental discipline often relies on children caring about parents, trusting them, and wanting to please them. Thus, stepparents' attempts to enforce rules and discipline are weakened without an emotional bond existing with stepchildren.

Family practitioners can help stepparents and parents think about stepparenting from a relationship-building perspective which may include assisting stepparents with how to befriend their stepchildren. Since no singular activity or strategy works for all stepchildren, helping stepparents think about what stepchildren like to do for fun and how to get to know stepchildren better is part of an effective strategy of affinity-building. This could be particularly helpful to stepparents who have not had children of their own. Information on basic child development could enlighten stepparents about developmental stages and changes in children as they age, which would help them in thinking about effective ways of building close ties with stepchildren. Although most stepparents have friendship-building skills, cross-generational friendships are somewhat unusual in industrialized societies. Therefore, family professionals can help stepparents brainstorm ways to befriend children of different ages and coach them on how to monitor themselves, their stepchildren, and the progress of the relationship and not overwhelm stepchildren who prefer a slower pace to the relationship-building process.

There is overwhelming evidence that stepchildren do not want stepparents to discipline, instead preferring stepparents support their parents' efforts (Crohn, 2010; Ganong et al., 2011; McDougal & George, 2016). Family professionals can help stepparents and parents in figuring out culturally appropriate ways for stepparents to enact household responsibilities as adults and avoid becoming primary disciplinarians of their stepchildren, particularly early in the stepfamily formation. Clinicians have written about ways that stepparents can support parents' household rules while parents make it clear to children that the stepparent is part of the coparenting team (e.g., Browning & Artelt, 2012; Papernow, 2013; Visher & Visher, 1988). Family practitioners may be needed to aid parents and stepparents in strategizing how to relieve stepparents of primary disciplinary responsibility and how to present this to stepchildren.

In addition to helping stepparents, family professionals can help parents in understanding their important roles in helping stepparents and stepchildren to bond. Parents can either help or hinder stepparents' opportunities to bond with stepchildren (Weaver & Coleman, 2005). There are many reasons why parents may gatekeep restrictively – jealousy, concerns about children's safety, concerns about stepparents' abilities to care for children, beliefs about what a good parent should do (Weaver & Coleman, 2005). Yet parents who trust their new partners should be encouraged to let them engage with children (Ganong et al., 2015). Family professionals can coach parents on ways to help stepparent–stepchild interactions in low-stress, enjoyable activities that may or may not involve parents and other stepfamily members. Parents can also be encouraged to educate stepparents about children's likes and dislikes, personalities, and behavioral quirks, while doing the same for stepchildren about the step-parent. Stepchildren in turn may also benefit from professional support as they try to figure out how to respond to their new stepparents.

Family professionals also can help parents and stepparents negoti-ate and clarify what types of roles stepparents will fill in children's lives. Our review suggests that multiple stepparent roles can work for step-parents, although stepparents who initially fulfill a friend role and avoid parent-like behaviors early in the relationship, particularly discipline, are generally more effective at establishing close relationships. Addition-ally, stepparents' roles often change over time, as stepchildren grow and mature, and relationship quality becomes clearer. Part of the challenge in clarifying stepparents' roles is that they are complex, embodying aspects of both friendships and parenthood. The lack of clear scripts for how to *do stepparenting* can be daunting, and family professionals can help step-couples navigate this ambiguity. For instance, rather than see the absence of cultural norms and standards as a deficit (Cherlin, 1978), many step-families use this freedom to imaginatively enact roles for stepparents that work for them. Not being bound by norms can be stressful, but it can also be freeing when stepfamily members are open to creating new ways of being a family. Adaptability contributes to well-being and is a functional response to challenges, and stepfamilies who are flexible in creating roles for stepparents and stepchildren have more effective relationships and functioning families (Goldberg & Allen, 2013).

Because agreement on stepparents' roles is important for stepfamily functioning, stepfamily members and family practitioners can work at reaching consensus on these roles. A stepparent's roles are not individ-ual decisions made by the stepparent alone but result from interactions among stepparents, stepchildren, and parents (Afifi, 2003). The consen-sus achieved from talking, listening, negotiating, and flexibly trying, fail-ing, and trying again to reach collaborated roles results in agreed-upon solutions that work for stepfamilies (Reid & Golub, 2018). Clinicians may help stepfamily members with negotiating and making decisions about stepparent roles and responsibilities, and family life educators may help them consider the range of role options open to them. In addi-tion, because flexibility in creating stepparent roles works for stepfamilies and stepfamily members, family practitioners should be prepared to help stepfamilies think outside of the box. Helping stepfamilies explore what they want and *what works* for them would be a central contribution that family professionals can make in helping stepfamilies choose roles that work. Instead of trying to find the "right" roles, stepfamilies should be helped to find the "best fit" of roles for their needs and wants. It may be that it is the *process* of negotiating the stepparent role rather than the final role constellation that matters. The key term may be *agreement*, rather than any specific set of roles enacted (Crosbie-Burnett, 1984; Jensen & Shafer, 2013; Quick et al., 1995; Saint-Jacques, 1995; Skopin et al., 1993; Whiting et al., 2007). Family professionals can help parents and stepparents navigate these discussions, particularly when there is spousal disagreement concerning role expectations.

Finally, family educators and clinicians can help when stepchildren reject stepparents' befriending efforts. For example, they can support parents by teaching them ways to promote the specific needs stepchildren may have. Family professionals also may help stepchildren uncover and explore deeper motivations for their resistance to stepparents' relationship-building efforts. For instance, one motive for stepchildren resisting stepparents' relationship-building is the fear that bonding with a stepparent equals disloyalty to one or both biological parents, particularly the parent in the other household. Some researchers find that stepchildren appreciate stepparents who take extra care to communicate they are not replacing a parent or trying to become a parent to the stepchild (Allan et al., 2011). These messages help stepchildren avoid *loyalty conflicts* or feeling "caught" between parents. When stepparents send these freeing messages, some stepchildren notice and welcome such messages (Allan et al., 2011). Of course, these messages do not prevent a nonresidential parent from trying to form a coalition with children against the stepparent, but family professionals can help stepchildren sort out competing messages they receive from adults in their stepfamilies (Afifi, 2003). Keeping children out of the middle of adults' disputes, a worthy goal explored more deeply in Chapter 4, may be done in multiple ways (Afifi, 2003; Allan et al., 2011). Stepparents and parents may need help from family professionals in crafting messages to children assuring them that they will not harm children's relationships with nonresidential parents.

Future Research

Although researchers have made great strides in identifying *what works* for effective stepparenting, opportunities for deeper knowledge remain. For example, studies are needed that examine how effective practices may be unique for stepparents of diverse social locations and family contexts – for example, stepparents of different genders, marital statuses (i.e., married or unmarried), and residential statuses (i.e., living full-time or part-time with stepchildren, or not living with them at all). Studies are also needed in which the effects on effective stepparenting of family experiences (e.g., domestic violence, child abuse, parental death) that preceded the formation of the stepfamily are examined. Second, study samples need to include people of color and marginalized ethnic minorities so that racial and ethnic variability in resilience processes may be examined more thoroughly. There are scholars who have asserted that African American stepfamilies have long engaged in effective childrearing behaviors obtained from cultural backgrounds and adaptations to the institutions of slavery and societal racism (Burton & Hardaway, 2012; Crosbie-Burnett & Lewis, 1993; Green & Chuang, 2021). Some of these stepfamily dynamics (e.g., flexible kinship definitions, the concepts of othermothers and otherfathers) could be adapted by stepfamilies of other racial and ethnic backgrounds, and studies could examine how effective these adaptations are. Other groups and types of stepfamilies need more study from this resilience perspective, such as gay and lesbian-headed stepfamilies and low-income stepfamilies. Context matters, and qualitative and quantitative scholars should purposefully examine under-studied groups.

Given that stepfamilies are structurally diverse, future studies that examine resilience processes within the context of different stepfamily structures would add to what is known. How might structural variations affect *what works* processes? Similarly, studies that explore how effective stepfamilies interact with other social systems (e.g., schools, hospitals, government agencies, religious systems) are needed. Effective stepparenting may be hindered or enhanced via interactions with other social systems. For instance, given the lack of legal recognition of step-relationships, stepparents often encounter challenges in legitimizing their roles when interacting with outside institutions (Acosta, 2021; Ganong & Coleman, 2017).

Future research could explore how intuitions, laws, and policies function as supportive (or unsupportive) resources for stepfamilies and stepparenting.

Additionally, although there have been a few longitudinal studies in which step-relationships have been examined, there is a need for investigations focused specifically on how effective stepparenting changes over time. For example, the importance of affinity-building in stepparent–stepchild relationships has been documented in more than 30 studies, but more research attention should be directed toward relationship maintenance and how stepparent–stepchild relationships evolve.

Another area ripe for future research involves processes underlying role negotiation and stepfamily consensus. Unfortunately, little is known about *how* individual stepfamilies come to agreements on stepparent roles that work for them. The negotiation processes alluded to above are speculative and not yet empirically supported. This is an area of study in need of investigation. What little work that has been done suggests that some stepparent roles may be related to age of the stepchildren when the relationships begin – it is easier, for instance, for stepparents to assume parent-like roles when stepchildren are infants or toddlers when the stepfamily begins than when they are adolescents (Ganong et al., 2011). Young stepchildren often grow up with multiple adults in parental roles, and they know of no other existence, unlike older children and adolescents who have clearer memories of pre-stepfamily life. Researchers should examine *how* stepparent roles are created in stepfamilies, particularly when stepchildren are of varying ages, including when there are divergent expectations among stepfamily members. Such insights would offer meaningful contributions to our understanding of *what works* for promoting effective stepparenting in stepfamilies.

References

Acosta, K.L. (2021). *Queer stepfamilies: The path to social and legal recognition*. NYU Press. http://dx.doi.org/10.18574/nyu/9781479800957.001.0001

Afifi, T.D. (2003). Feeling caught in stepfamilies: Managing boundary turbulence through appropriate communication privacy rules. *Journal of Social and Personal Relationships*, *20*, 729–756. https://doi.org/10.1177/0265407503206002

Agar, A.D., Cioe, J.D., Gorsalka, B.B. (2010). Biology matters? Intimate relationships of young adults from divorced and intact family backgrounds as a function of biological father and male model involvement. *Journal of Divorce and Remarriage*, *51*, 441–463. http://dx.doi.org/10.1080/10502556.2010.507131

Ahrons, C. (2007). Family ties after divorce: Long-term implications for children. *Family Process, 46*(1), 53–65. https://doi.org/10.1111/j.1545-5300.2006.00191.x

Allan, G., Crow, G., & Hawker, S. (2011). *Stepfamilies.* Palgrave Macmillan.

Ambert, A.M. (1986). Being a stepparent: Live-in and visiting stepchildren. *Journal of Marriage and the Family, 48*(3), 795–804. https://doi.org/10.2307/352572

Australian Bureau of Statistics. (2016). *Family blending.* Retrieved 11/6/2020 from https://profile.id.com.au/australia/family-blending

Banker, B.S., & Gaertner, S.L. (1998). Achieving stepfamily harmony: An intergroup-relations approach. *Journal of Family Psychology, 12*(3), 310–325. https://doi.org/10.1037/0893-3200.12.3.310

Baxter, L.A., Braithwaite, D.O., & Nicholson, J.H. (1999). Turning points in the development of blended families. *Journal of Social and Personal Relationships, 16*, 291–313. https://doi.org/10.1177/0265407599163002

Berger, R. (1995). Three types of stepfamilies. *Journal of Divorce & Remarriage, 24*(1/2), 35–49.

Blyaert, L., Van Parys, H., De Mol, J., & Buysse, A. (2016). Like a parent and a friend, but not the father: A qualitative study of stepfathers' experiences in the stepfamily. *Australian and New Zealand Journal of Family Therapy, 37*, 119–132. https://doi.org/10.1002/anzf.1138

Braithwaite, D.O., Waldron, V.R., Allen, J., Oliver, B., Bergquist, G., Storck, K., Marsh, J., Swords, N., & Tschampl-Diesing, C. (2018). "Feeling warmth and close to her": Communication and resilience reflected turning points in positive adult stepparent-stepchild relationships. *Journal of Family Communication, 18*, 92–109. https://doi.org/10.1080/15267431.2017.1415902

Bray, J.H. (1999). From marriage to remarriage and beyond: Findings from the Developmental Issues in Stepfamilies Research Project. In E.M. Hetherington (Ed.), *Coping with divorce, single parenting, and remarriage: A risk and resiliency perspective* (pp. 253–271). Erlbaum. https://doi.org/10.4324/9781410602893-19

Bronstein, P., Stoll, M.F., Clauson, J., Abrams, C.L., & Briones, M. (1994). Fathering after separation or divorce: Factors predicting children's adjustment. *Family Relations, 43*, 469–479. https://doi.org/10.2307/585380

Brown, A.C., Green, R.-J., & Druckman, J. (1990). A comparison of stepfamilies with and without child-focused problems. *American Journal of Orthopsychiatry, 60*(4), 556–566. https://doi.org/10.1037/h0079208

Browning, S., & Artelt, E. (2012). *Stepfamily therapy: A 10-step clinical approach.* APA. https://doi.org/10.1037/13089-000

Bryant, C.M., Futris, T.G., Hicks, M.R., Lee, T.-Y., & Oshri, A. (2016). African American stepfather-stepchild relationships, marital quality, and mental health. *Journal of Divorce & Remarriage, 57*(6), 375–388. https://doi.org/10.1080/10502556.2016.119852

Burton, L.M., & Hardaway, C.R. (2012). Low-income mothers as "othermothers" to their romantic partners' children: Women's coparenting in multiple partner fertility relationships. *Family Process, 51*(3), 343–359. http://dx.doi.org/10.1111/j.1545-5300.2012.01401.x

Bzostek, S. (2008). Social fathers and child well-being. *Journal of Marriage and Family, 70*(4), 950–961. https://doi.org/10.1111/j.1741-3737.2008.00538.x.

Campbell, C.G., & Winn, E.J. (2018). Father-daughter bonds: A comparison of adolescent daughters' relationships with resident biological fathers and stepfathers. *Family Relations, 67*, 675–686. https://doi.org/10.1111/fare.12342

Cartwright, C., Farnsworth, V., & Mobley, V. (2009). Relationships with stepparents in the life stories of young adults of divorce. *Family Matters, 82*, 30–37.

Cherlin, A. (1978). Remarriage as an incomplete institution. *American Journal of Sociology*, *84*, 634–650. https://doi.org/10.1086/226830

Clawson, J., & Ganong, L. (2002). Adult stepchildren's obligations to older stepparents. *Journal of Family Nursing*, *8*, 50–73. https://doi.org/10.1177/107484070200800104

Coleman, M., Ganong, L., Russell, L., & Frye, N. (2015). Stepchildren's views about former steprelationships following stepfamily dissolution. *Journal of Marriage and Family*, *77*, 775–790. https://doi.org/10.1111/jomf.12182

Cookston, J.T., Olide, A., Parke, R.D., Fabricius, W.V., Saenz, D. S., & Braver, S.L. (2014). He said what? Guided cognitive reframing about the co-resident father/stepfather-adolescent relationship. *Journal of Research on Adolescence*, *25*(2), 263–278. https://doi.org/10.1111/jora.12120

Crohn, H.M. (2006). Five styles of positive stepmothering from the perspective of young adult stepdaughters. *Journal of Divorce & Remarriage*, *46*(1/2), 119–134. https://doi.org/10.1300/J087v46n01_07

Crohn, H.M. (2010). Communication about sexuality with mothers and stepmothers from the perspective of young adult daughters. *Journal of Divorce & Remarriage*, *51*, 348–365. https://doi.org/10.1080/10502551003652108

Crosbie-Burnett, M. (1984). The centrality of the step relationship: A challenge to family theory and practice. *Family Relations*, *33*, 459–463. https://doi.org/10.2307/584717

Crosbie-Burnett, M., & Lewis, E.A. (1993). Use of African-American family structures and functioning to address the challenges of European-American postdivorce families. *Family Relations*, *42*, 243–248. https://doi.org/10.2307/585552

Cross, C.J. & Zhang, X. (2022). Nonresident social fathering in African American single-mother families. *Journal of Marriage and Family*, *84*(5), 1250–1269. https://doi.org/10.1111/jomf.12839

Dictionary.com (n.d.). Affinity. Retrieved from www.dictionary.com/browse/affinity.

Egginton, B., Holmes, E.K., James, S.C., & Hawkins, A, J. (2021). The power of three: A latent class analysis of the three parent-child relationships in stepfamilies and their influence on emerging adult outcomes. *Journal of Divorce & Remarriage*, *62*(5), 374–397. https://doi.org/10.1080/10502556.2021.1871841

Erera-Weatherley, P. (1996). On becoming a stepparent: Factors associated with the adoption of alternative stepparenting styles. *Journal of Divorce & Remarriage*, *25*, 155–175. https://doi.org/10.1300/j087v25n03_10

Fang, C., & Zartler, U. (2023). Adolescents' experiences with ambiguity in postdivorce stepfamilies. *Journal of Marriage and Family*, *84*, 1–21. https://doi.org/10.1111/jomf.12942

Fine, F.A., Coleman, M., & Ganong, L. (1998). Consistency in perceptions of the stepparent role among stepparents, parents, and stepchildren. *Journal of Social and Personal Relationships*, *15*(6), 810–828. https://doi.org/10.1177/0265407598156006

Fine, M., Ganong, L., & Coleman, M. (1997). The relation between role constructions and adjustment among stepparents. *Journal of Family Issues*, *18*, 503–525. https://doi.org/10.1177/019251397018005003

Forehand, R., Parent, J., Golub, A., & Reid, M. (2014). Correlates of male cohabiting partner's involvement in child-rearing tasks in low-income urban Black stepfamilies. *Journal of Family Psychology*, *28*(3), 336–345. https://doi.org/10.1037/a0036369

Forehand, R., Parent, J., Golub, A., & Reid, M. (2015). Male cohabiting partners as primary coparents in low-income Black stepfamilies. *Journal of Child and Family Studies*, *24*, 2874–2880. https://doi.org/10.1007/s10826-014-0091-5

Forehand, R., Parent, J., Golub, A., & Reid, M. (2016). Positive parenting of young adolescents by male cohabiting partners: The roles of coparenting conflict and support. *Journal of Early Adolescence*, *36*(3), 420–441. https://doi.org/10.1177/0272431614566947

Galvin, K.M., & Braithwaite, D.O. (2014). Theory and research from the communication field: Discourses that constitute and reflect families. *Journal of Family Theory & Review*, *6*(1), 97–111. http://dx.doi.org/10.1111/jftr.12030

Ganong, L., & Coleman, M. (1999). *Changing families, changing responsibilities: Family obligations following divorce and remarriage*. Erlbaum. https://doi.org/10.5860/choice.37-1854

Ganong, L., & Coleman, M. (2017). *Stepfamily relationships: Development, dynamics, and intervention* (2nd ed.). Springer. https://doi.org/10.10078/978-1-4899-7702-1

Ganong, L., & Coleman, M. (2018). Studying stepfamilies: Four eras of scholarship. *Family Process*, *57*, 7–24. https://doi.org/10.1111/famp.12307

Ganong, L., Coleman, M., Chapman, A., & Jamison, T. (2018). Stepchildren claiming stepparents. *Journal of Family Issues*, *39*(6), 1712–1736. https://doi.org/10.1177/0192513X17725878

Ganong, L., Coleman, M., Fine, M., & Martin, P. (1999). Stepparents' affinity-seeking and affinity-maintaining strategies with stepchildren. *Journal of Family Issues*, *20*(3), 299–327. https://doi.org/10.1177/019251399020003001

Ganong, L., Coleman, M., & Jamison, T. (2011). Patterns of stepchild-stepparent relationship development. *Journal of Marriage and Family*, *73*(2), 396–413. https://doi.org/10.1111/j.1741-3737.2010.00814.x

Ganong, L., Coleman, M., Jamison, T., & Feistman, R. (2015). Divorced mothers' coparental boundary maintenance after parents re-partner. *Journal of Family Psychology*, *29*, 221–231. https://doi.org/10.1037/fam0000064

Ganong, L., Jensen, T., Sanner, C., Chapman, A., & Coleman, M. (2020). Stepparents' attachment orientation, parental gatekeeping, and stepparents' affinity-seeking with stepchildren. *Family Process*, *59*(2), 756–771. https://doi.org/10.1111/famp.12448

Ganong, L., Jensen, T., Sanner, C., Russell, L., & Coleman, M. (2019a). Stepfathers' affinity-seeking with stepchildren, stepfather-stepchild relationship quality, marital quality, and stepfamily cohesion among stepfathers and mothers. *Journal of Family Psychology*, *33*, 521–531. https://doi.org/10.1037/fam0000518

Ganong, L., Jensen, T., Sanner, C., Russell, L., Coleman, M., & Chapman, A. (2019b). Linking stepfamily functioning, marital quality, and steprelationship quality. *Family Relations*, *68*(2), 469–483. https://doi.org/10.1111/fare.12380

Gath, M. (2016). Identifying stepfamilies in longitudinal data. (Statistics New Zealand Working Paper No 16–01). Retrieved from www.stats.govt.nz

Gold, S., & Edin, K.J. (2023). Rethinking stepfathers' contributions: Fathers, stepfathers, and child well-being. *Journal of Family Issues*, *44*(3), 745–765. https://doi.org/10.1177/0192513X211054471

Goldberg, A.E., & Allen, K.R. (2013). Same-sex relationship dissolution and LGB stepfamily formation: Perspectives of young adults with LGB parents. *Family Relations*, *62*(3), 529–544. https://doi.org/10.1111/fare.12024

Golish, T.D. (2003). Stepfamily communication strengths: Understanding the ties that bind. *Human Communication Research*, *29*(1), 41–80. https://doi.org/10.1093/hcr/29.1.41

Green, D.S., & Chuang, S.S. (2021). A critical exploration of biological and social fathering among Afro-Caribbean fathers. *Family Relations*, *70*(2), 282–296. https://doi.org/10.1111/fare.12479

Guisinger, S., Cowan, P., & Schuldberg, D. (1989). Changing parent and spouse relations in the first years of remarriage of divorced fathers. *Journal of Marriage and the Family*, *51*, 445–456. https://doi.org/10.2307/352506

Hannon, M.D., Ferguson, A.L., Blanchard, R.A., & Santiago-Ataande, J.E. (2023). Oth-erfathering and Black men's mental; health: A phenomenological study. *Journal of Multicultural Counseling and Development, 51*, 255–268. https://doi.org/10.1002/jmcd.12289

Henry, C.S., & Lovelace, S.G. (1995). Family resources and adolescent family life sat-isfaction in remarried family households. *Journal of Family Issues, 16*(6), 765–786. https://doi.org/10.1177/019251395016006005

Hequembourg, A. (2004). Unscripted motherhood: Lesbian mothers negotiating in-completely institutionalized family relationships. *Journal of Social and Personal Relationships, 21*(6), 739–762. Doi: 10.1177/0265407504047834

Hetherington, E.M. (1987). Family relations six years after the divorce. In K. Pasley & M. Ihinger-Tallman (Eds.), *Remarriage and stepparenting today* (pp. 185–205). Guilford. https://doi.org/10.2307/583619

Hetherington, E.M. (1993). An overview of the Virginia Longitudinal Study of Divorce and Remarriage with a focus on early adolescence. *Journal of Family Psychology, 7*(1), 39–56. https://doi.org/10.1037/0893-3200.7.1.39

Hetherington, E.M., Clingempeel, W.G., Anderson, E.R., Deal, J.E., Hagan, M.S., Hollier, E.A., & Lindner, M.S. (1992). Coping with marital transitions. *Monographs of the Society for Research in Child Development, 57*(2–3). University of Chicago Press. https://doi.org/10.2307/1166050

Hornstra, M., & Ivanova, K. (2023). Kinkeeping across families: The central role of moth-ers and stepmothers in the facilitation of adult intergenerational ties. *Sex Roles, 88*, 367–382. https://doi.org/10.1007/s11199-023-01352-2

Hutchinson, S.L., Afifi, T., & Krause, S. (2007). The family that plays together fares better: Examining the contribution of shared family time to family resilience fol-lowing divorce. *Journal of Divorce & Remarriage, 46*(3/4), 21–48. Doi:10.1300/J087v46n03_03

Ivanova, K. (2020). My children, your children, our children, and my well-being: Life satisfaction of "empty nest" biological parents and stepparents. *Journal of Happiness Studies, 21*, 613–633. https://doi.org/10.1007/s10902-019-00097-8

Ivanova, K., & Kalmijn, M. (2020a). Parental involvement in youth and closeness to parents during adulthood: Stepparents and biological parents. *Journal of Family Psychology, 34*(7), 794–803. https://doi.org/10.1037/fam0000659

Ivanova, K., & Kalmijn, M. (2020b). Heterogeneous effects of family complexity in childhood on mental health: Testing the "good divorce" and the "good stepparent" hypotheses. In M. Kreyenfeld & H. Trappe (Eds.), *Parental life courses after separa-tion and divorce in Europe*. Life Course Research and Social Policies, 12, 267–288. https://doi.org/10.1007/978-3-030-44575-1_13

Jensen, T. (2017). Constellation of dyadic relationship quality in stepfamilies: A factor mixture model. *Journal of Family Psychology, 31*(8), 1051–1062. https://doi.org/10.1037/fam0000355

Jensen, T. (2019). A typology of interactional patterns between youth and their stepfa-thers: Associations with family relationship quality and youth well-being. *Family Process, 58*(2), 384–403. https://doi.org/10.1111/famp.12348

Jensen, T. (2021). Patterns of interactions between youth and resident stepmothers: A latent class analysis. *Family Process, 60*(2), 538–555. https://doi.org/120.1111/famp.12556

Jensen, T., & Ganong, L. (2019). Stepparent-stepchild relationship quality and couple relationship quality: Stepfamily household type as a moderating influence. *Journal of Family Issues, 41*(5), 589–610. https://doi.org/10.1177/0192513X19881669

Jensen, T.M., & Ganong, L. (2023). Associations between dyadic relationship quality and stepfamily functioning: A common fate modeling approach. *Family Process, 62*(2), 641–652. https://doi.org/10.1111/famp.12803

Jensen, T.M., & Harris, K.M. (2017a). Stepfamily relationship quality and stepchildren's depression in adolescence and adulthood. *Emerging Adulthood, 5*(3), 191–203. https://doi.org/10.1177/2167696816669901

Jensen, T., & Harris, K.M. (2017b). A longitudinal analysis of stepfamily relationship quality and adolescent physical health. *Journal of Adolescent Health, 61*, 486–492. https://doi.org/10.1016/j.jadohealth.2017.04.015

Jensen, T., & Lippold, M.A. (2018). Patterns of stepfamily relationship quality and adolescents' short-term and long-term adjustment. *Journal of Family Psychology, 32*(8), 1130–1141. https://doi.org/10.1037/fam0000442

Jensen, T.M., Lippold, M.A., Mills-Koonce, R., & Fosco, G.M. (2017). Stepfamily relationship quality and children's internalizing and externalizing problems. *Family Process, 57*(2), 477–495. https://doi.org/10.1111/famp.12284

Jensen, T.M., & Pace, G.T. (2016). Stepfather involvement and stepfather–child relationship quality: Race and parental marital status as moderators. *Journal of Marital and Family Therapy, 42*(4), 659–672. https://doi.org/10.1111/jmft.12165

Jensen, T.M., & Shafer, K. (2013). Stepfamily functioning and closeness: Children's views on second marriages and stepfather relationships. *Social Work, 58*, 127–136. https://doi.org/10.1093/sw/swt007

Jensen, T., & Weller, B.E. (2019). Latent profiles of residential stepfamily relationship quality and family stability. *Journal of Divorce & Remarriage, 60*(1), 69–87. https://doi.org/10.1080/10502556.2018.1488111

Juteau, G., Westrick-Payne, K.K., Brown, S.L., & Manning, W.D. (2023). Visualizing children's family structure. *Socius: Sociological Research for a Dynamic World, 9*, 1–3. https://doi.org/10.1177/23780231231205216

Kalbarczyk, M. (2021). Non-financial support provided to parents in stepfamilies: Empirical examination of Europeans 50+. *International Journal of Environmental Research and Public Health, 18*(10), 5151. https://doi.org/10.3390/ijerph18105151

Kellas, J.K., Baxter, L., LeClair-Underberg, C., Thatcher, M., Routsong, T., Normand, E.L., & Braithwaite, D.O. (2014). Telling the story of stepfamily beginnings: The relationship between young-adult stepchildren's stepfamily origin stories and their satisfaction with the stepfamily. *Journal of Family Communication, 14*(2), 149–166. https://doi.org/10.1080/15267431.2013.864294

Kellas, J.K., LeClair-Underberg, C., & Normand, E.L. (2008). Stepfamily address terms: "Sometimes they mean something and sometimes they don't." *Journal of Family Communication, 8*, 238–263. https://doi.org/10.1080/15267430802397153

Kelley, P. (1992). Healthy stepfamily functioning. *Families in Society, 73*(10), 579–587. https://doi.org/10.1177/104438949207301001

King, V.L., Boyd, L.M., & Thorsen, M.L. (2015). Adolescents' perceptions of family belonging in stepfamilies. *Journal of Marriage and Family, 77*(3), 761–774. https://doi.org/10.1111/jomf.12181

King, V., Pragg, B., & Lindstrom, R. (2020). Family relationships during adolescence and stepchildren's educational attainment in young adulthood. *Journal of Marriage and Family, 82*(3), 622–638. https://doi.org/10.1111/jomf.12642

Kinniburgh-White, R., Cartwright, C. & Seymour, F. (2010) Young adults' narratives of relational development with stepfathers. *Journal of Social and Personal Relationships, 27*(7), 890–907. https://doi.org/10.1177/0265407510376252

Limb, G.E., Cousin, L.E., & Larkin, Z.S. (2020). Native American stepfamilies: Children's expectations concerning their residential stepparents' behavior. *Journal of Social Service Research, 46*, 149–159. https://doi.org/10.1080/01488376.2018.1532945

MacDonald, W.L., & DeMaris, A. (2002). Stepfather-stepchild relationship quality: The stepfather's demand for conformity and the biological father's involvement. *Journal of Family Issues, 23*(1), 121–137. https://doi.org/10.1177/0192513x02023001006

Maier, M., Turkiewicz, K., & Herrman, A.R. (2019). Relational maintenance strategies and satisfaction in the stepmother-stepdaughter dyad. *The Family Journal: Counseling and Therapy for Couples and Families, 27*, 377–386. https://doi.org/10.1177/1066480719852368

Marsiglio, W. (1992). Stepfathers with minor children living at home: Parenting perceptions and relationship quality. *Journal of Family Issues, 13*(2), 195–214. https://doi.org/10.1177/019251392013002005

Marsiglio, W. (2004). When stepfathers claim stepchildren. *Journal of Marriage and Family, 66*(1), 22–39. https://doi.org/10.1111/j.1741-3737.2004.00002.x

McDougal, S., Durnell, E., & Dlamini, P.Z. (2018). Social father presence: The experience of being raised by Black social fathers. *Africology: The Journal of Pan African Studies, 11*(7), 1–23.

McDougal, S., & George, C. (2016). "I wanted to return the favor": The experiences of Black social fathers. *Journal of Black Studies, 47*(6), 524–549. https://doi.org/10.1177/0021934716653346

Metts, S., Braithwaite, D.O, Schrodt, P., Wang, T.R., Holman, A.J., Nuru, A.K., & Abetz, J.S. (2013). The experience and expression of stepchildren's emotions at critical events in stepfamily life. *Journal of Divorce & Remarriage, 54*, 414–437, https://doi.org/10.1080/10502556.2013.800400

Metts, S.M., Schrodt, P., & Braithwaite, D.O. (2017). Stepchildren's communicative and emotional journey from divorce to remarriage: Predictors of stepfamily satisfaction. *Journal of Divorce & Remarriage, 58*(1), 29–43. https://doi.org/10.1080/10502556.2016.1257904

Michaels, M.L. (2006). Factors that contribute to stepfamily success: A qualitative analysis. *Journal of Divorce & Remarriage, 44*(3/4), 53–66. https://doi.org/10.1300/j087v44n03_04

Mikucki-Enyart, S.L., & Heisdorf, S.R. (2020). Obstacles and opportunities experienced by adult stepchildren in later life stepfamilies. *Journal of Divorce & Remarriage, 61*(1), 41–61. https://doi.org/10.1080/10502556.2019.1619380

Nuru, A.K., & Wang, T.T. (2014). "She was stomping on everything that we used to think of as a family": Communication and turning points in cohabitating (step)families. *Journal of Divorce & Remarriage, 55*, 145–163. https://doi.org/10.1080/10502556.2013.871957

Oliver-Blackburn, B.M., Braithwaite, D.O., Waldron, V.R., Hall, R., Hackenburg, L., & Worman, B.G. (2022). Protector and friend: Turning points and discursive constructions of the stepparent role. *Family Relations, 71*(3), 1266–1285. https://doi.org/10.1111/fare.12642

Orleans, M., Palisi, B.J., & Caddell, D. (1989). Marriage adjustment and satisfaction of stepfathers: Their feelings and perceptions of decision-making and stepchildren relations. *Family Relations, 38*, 371–377. https://doi.org/10.2307/585740

Papernow, P. (2013). *Surviving and thriving in stepfamily relationships: What works and what doesn't*. Routledge. https://doi.org/10.4324/9780203813645-32

Parent, J., Clifton, J., Forehand, R., Golub, A., Reid, M., & Pichler, E.R. (2014). Parental mindfulness and dyadic relationship quality in low-income cohabiting black stepfamilies: Associations with parenting experienced by adolescents. *Couple and Family Psychology: Research and Practice, 3*(2), 67–82. https://doi.org/10.1037/cfp0000020

Perry, C., & Fraser, R. (2020). A qualitative analysis of new norms on transition days in blended families. *Sociology Mind, 10*, 55–69. https://doi.org/10.4236/sm.2020.102005

Petren, R.E., Lardier, D.T., Jr., Bible, J., Bermea, A., & van Eeden-Moorefield, B. (2019). Parental relationship stability and parent–adult child relationships in stepfamilies: A test of alternative models. *Journal of Family Psychology, 33*(2), 143–153. https://doi-org.proxy.mul.missouri.edu/10.1037/fam0000481

Quick, D.S., Newman, B.M., & McKenry, P.C. (1995). Influences on the quality of stepmother adolescent relationship. *Journal of Divorce and Remarriage, 24*, 99–114. https://doi.org/10.1300/j087v24n01_08

Reid, M., & Golub, A. (2018). Low-income Black men's kin work: Social fatherhood in cohabiting stepfamilies. *Journal of Family Issues, 39*(4), 960–984. https://doi.org/10.1177/0192513x16684892

Saint-Jacques, M.C. (1995). Role strain prediction in stepfamilies. *Journal of Divorce & Remarriage, 24*, 51–72. https://doi.org/10.1300/j087v24n01_05

Salem, D.A., Zimmerman, M.A., & Notaro, P.C. (1998). Effects of family structure, family process, and father involvement on psychosocial outcomes among African American adolescents. *Family Relations, 47*(4), 331–341. https://doi.org/10.2307/585264

Sanner, C., Ganong, L.H., & Coleman, M. (2020). Shared children in stepfamilies: Experiences living in a hybrid family structure. *Journal of Marriage and Family, 82*(3), 605–621. https://doi.org/10.1111/jomf.12631

Schenck, C.E., Braver, S.L., Wolchik, S.A., Saenz, D., Cookston, J.T., & Fabricius, W.V. (2009). Relations between mattering to step- and non-residential fathers and adolescent mental health. *Fathering, 7*(1), 70–90. https://doi.org/10.3149/fth.0701.70

Schmeeckle, M. (2007). Gender dynamics in stepfamilies: Adult stepchildren's views. *Journal of Marriage and Family, 69*(1), 174–189. http://dx.doi.org/10.1111/j.1741-3737.2006.00352.x

Schmeeckle, M., Giarusso, R., Feng, D., & Bengtson, V.L. (2006). What makes someone family? Adult children's perceptions of current and former stepparents. *Journal of Marriage and Family, 68*, 595–610. https://doi.org/10.1111/j.1741-3737.2006.00277.x

Schrodt, P. (2006). A typological examination of communication competence and mental health in stepchildren. *Communication Monographs, 73*(3), 309–333. https://doi.org/10.1080/03637750600873728

Schrodt, P. (2016). Relational frames as mediators of everyday talk and relational satisfaction in stepparent-stepchild relationships. *Journal of Social and Personal Relationships, 33*, 217–236. https://doi.org/10.1177/0265407514568751

Schrodt, P. (2021). Disagreement in perceptions of stepfamily communication and functioning: Implications for mental health. *Journal of Social and Personal Relationships, 38*(1), 393–412. https://doi.org/10.1177/0265407520964862

Schrodt, P., Soliz, J., & Braithwaite, D.O. (2008). A social relations model of everyday talk and relational satisfaction in stepfamilies. *Communication Monographs, 75*, 190–217. https://doi.org/10.1080/03637750802023163

Schwartz, S.J., & Finley, G.E. (2006). Father involvement, nurturant fathering, and young adult psychosocial functioning. *Journal of Family Issues, 27*(5), 712–731. https://doi.org/10.1177/0192513x05284003

Shapiro, D. (2014). Stepparents and parenting stress: The roles of gender, marital quality, and views about gender roles. *Family Process, 53*(1), 97–108. https://doi.org/10.1111/famp.12062

Skopin, A.R., Newman, B.M., & McKenry, P.C. (1993). Influences on the quality of stepfather-adolescent relationships: Views of both family members. *Journal of Divorce & Remarriage, 19*(3/4), 181–196. https://doi.org/10.1300/j087v19n03_12

Speer, R.B., & Trees, A.R. (2007). The push and pull of stepfamily life: The contributions of stepchildren's autonomy and connection-seeking behaviors to role development in stepfamilies. *Communication Studies, 58*, 377–394. https://doi.org/10.1080/10510970701648590

Stern, P.N. (1982). Affiliating in stepfather families: Teachable strategies leading to step-father-stepchild friendship. *Western Journal of Nursing Research, 4*(1), 77–89. https://doi.org/10.1177/019394598200400107

Sweeney, M.M. (2007). Stepfather families and the emotional well-being of adolescents. *Journal of Health and Social Behavior, 48*(1), 33–49. https://doi.org/10.1177/002214650704800103

Vinick, B.H., & Lanspery, S. (2000). Cinderella's sequel: Stepmothers' long-term relationships with adult stepchildren. *Journal of Comparative Family Studies, 31*(3), 377–384. https://doi.org/10.3138/jcfs.31.3.377

Visher, E.B., Visher, J.S. (1979). *Stepfamilies: A guide to working with stepparents and stepchildren.* Brunner/Mazel. https://doi.org/10.4324/9781315784236-12

Visher, E.B., Visher, J.S. (1988). *Old loyalties, new ties: Therapeutic strategies with stepfamilies.* Brunner/Mazel. http://dx.doi.org/10.1037/e409992005-020

Waldron, V.R., Braithwaite, D.O., Oliver, B.M., Kloeber, D.N., & Marsh, J. (2018). Discourses of forgiveness and resilience in stepparent-stepchild relationships. *Journal of Applied Communication Research, 46*, 561–562. https://doi.org/10.1080/00909882.2018.1530447

Waldron, V., Braithwaite, D.O., Oliver-Blackburn, B.M., & Avalos, B.L. (2022). Paths to positivity: Relational trajectories and intersection in positive stepparent-stepchild dyads. *Journal of Family Communications, 22*(1), 33–54. https://doi.org/10.1080/15267431.2021.1999243

Weaver, S., & Coleman, M. (2005). A mothering but not a mother role: A grounded theory study of the nonresidential stepmother role. *Journal of Social and Personal Relationships, 22*(4), 477–497. https://doi.org/10.1177/0265407505054519

White, L.K., & Gilbreth, J.G. (2001). When children have two fathers: Effects of relationships with stepfathers and noncustodial fathers on adolescent outcomes. *Journal of Marriage and Family, 63*(1), 155–167. https://doi.org/10.1111/j.1741-3737.2001.00155.x

Whiting, J.B., Smith, D.R., Barnett, T., & Grafsky, E.L. (2007). Overcoming the Cinderella Myth: A mixed methods study of successful stepmothers. *Journal of Divorce & Remarriage, 47*(1/2), 95–109. https://doi.org/10.1300/j087v47n01_06

Willetts, M.C., & Maroules, N.G. (2004). Does remarriage matter? The well-being of adolescents living with cohabiting versus remarried mothers. *Journal of Divorce & Remarriage, 41*, 115–133. https://doi.org/10.1300/j087v41n03_06

Yuan, A.S., & Hamilton, H.A. (2006). Stepfather involvement and adolescent well-being: Do mothers and nonresidential fathers matter? *Journal of Family Issues, 27*(9), 1191–1213. https://doi.org/10.1177/0192513x06289214

4

EFFECTIVE PARENTING IN STEPFAMILIES

Effective Parenting in Stepfamilies

Parents are critically influential figures in stepfamilies. (In this chapter, we refer to biological and adoptive parents simply as parents.) Although there have been many more studies about stepparent–stepchild relationships than parent–child ties in stepfamilies, parents are important because they are the linchpins. They are the reason that stepparent–stepchild relationships exist, and they play critical roles in helping their children adjust positively to stepfamily life. How parents respond to their children's needs, and the strategies they use to foster warm, supportive, and cohesive stepfamily environments, affect children's levels of well-being.

Parents in stepfamilies face unique childrearing challenges that parents in nuclear families do not face. For instance, in stepfamilies, the parent–child relationship predates the romantic couple partnership, meaning that the parent–child dyad has more shared history than does the couple (Papernow, 1987). This shared history may facilitate closer parent–child bonds, particularly when repartnering occurs after a lengthy period residing in a single-parent household (Cartwright & Seymour, 2002). If parent–child relationships are especially close, parents may feel guilty when dividing time and attention between children and new partners. To make stepparents feel more like family members, some parents

DOI: 10.4324/9781003369073-4

focus more energy on developing a strong couple bond while reducing time with their children (Visher & Visher, 1996). Other parents may resolve loyalty dilemmas between children and new partners by primarily favoring their children. For instance, a mother in a self-help group we observed stated that she decided to always take her child's side against her new husband as a way out of this conundrum. Another mother in this group wanted to continue parenting just as she had before remarriage, essentially compartmentalizing relationships with her husband and her children. She preferred to view her husband (i.e., her children's stepfather) as her companion and not as a coparent, even though the children lived full-time with her and her husband. Parents whose former partners remarry or repartner also may experience questions about their roles in childrearing.

Parenting in stepfamilies is complex because childrearing happens simultaneously with the development of new family relationships. Parents often face multiple, sometimes competing, demands on their time and attention. Repartnered parents must build and nurture new couple bonds, as well as potentially new relationships with stepchildren and other kin (e.g., new in-laws), while maintaining and nurturing connections with their own children (Ganong & Coleman, 2017). It is not surprising that lower parenting stress in stepfamilies is related to stepcouple adjustment (Shapiro, 2014). So, *what works* for parents in stepfamilies? Parenting practices in five domains have been linked to positive outcomes for children in stepfamilies: (a) maintaining close parent–child bonds, (b) establishing appropriate parent–child communication boundaries, (c) exercising parental control (d) supporting stepparent–stepchild relationship development, and (e) facilitating stepfamily cohesion.

Maintaining Close Parent–Child Bonds

Given that stepfamily formation involves multiple transitions for parents and children (e.g., from nuclear to single-parent households to stepfamily households, often moving to new residences or communities), a major focus of researchers has been on how parents maintain closeness and continuity in parent–child relationships during and after these changes. Indeed, studies show that close parent–child relationships mitigate the stress children experience both during and after the transition to stepfamily life (Jensen et al., 2017; King, 2006). Closer parent–child ties are related to a number of positive outcomes for children in stepfamilies, including *youth flourishing* (i.e., the degree to which youth follow through with tasks, control their emotions, demonstrate curiosity, and are interested in school; Beckmeyer, Su-Russell, & Russell, 2020); *feelings of stepfamily belonging* (i.e., feelings of inclusion in stepfamilies, of being understood, of having fun together, and of being given attention; King et al., 2015); and fewer *internalizing and externalizing problems* (e.g., mental health problems, aggressive behaviors; Beckmeyer, Su-Russell, & Russell 2020; Egginton et al., 2021; Jensen, 2021; Jensen & Lippold, 2018; Jensen et al., 2017; King, 2006, 2007; Schenck et al., 2009).

Maintaining close parent–child relationships may sound straightforward, but studies suggest that some parents struggle to invest in these relationships in ways that children are satisfied with during stepfamily formation. Although parents may feel that they are successfully sharing their time between children, new partners, and new stepchildren, children may have vastly different perceptions of the changing nature of parent–child bonds. Youth perceptions of parent–child ties indicate less closeness, warmth, and parental involvement after remarriage (Day & Acock, 2004; McLanahan & Sandefur, 1994). Many children worry about and are sensitive to perceived changes in their relationships with parents when parents repartner – they experience fear, jealousy, and sadness if they perceive that the maintenance of parent–child relationships has taken a backseat to parents' efforts to bond with new partners and their partners' children (Cartwright, 2005; Landon et al., 2022). Creating a new stepfamily while keeping the old family members satisfied requires considerable effort, intentionality, and awareness by parents (Green & Chuang, 2021; Parent et al., 2014; Pylyser et al., 2019). So, what have researchers found about what parents do to effectively sustain close ties with children and bolster their well-being across the transition to stepfamily life?

Maintaining Regular Contact

First, preserving close ties with children after forming a new stepfamily requires regular contact and involvement (Petren et al., 2019). When children reside primarily with one parent after parental separation or divorce, the frequency of contact with their nonresidential parent is linked to closer relationships with that parent and greater child well-being (Bray, 1999; Bronstein et al., 1994; Bzostek, 2008; Golish, 2003; Jensen, 2021; King, 2007; Salem et al., 1998; Schwartz & Finley, 2006; Sweeney, 2007; Troilo & Coleman, 2013; Zimmerman et al., 1995). For example, among youth in father–stepmother households, more frequent contact with nonresidential mothers is linked to closer mother–adolescent and stepmother–adolescent relationships (Jensen, 2021), which in turn are linked to fewer internalizing and externalizing problems for children (Jensen, 2021; King, 2007). Similarly, among youth in mother–stepfather households, more frequent contact with nonresidential fathers is linked to children's better behavioral adjustment (Bray, 1999; Bronstein et al., 1994; Bzostek, 2008), more positive self-concepts (Bronstein et al., 1994), less substance use (Salem et al., 1998), fewer depressive symptoms (Sweeney, 2007), greater academic achievements (King et al., 2020), and fewer psychological problems, especially for boys (Bronstein et al., 1994). In addition, more frequent contact between nonresidential fathers and children was related to greater financial support for those children (Cross & Zhang, 2022). Golish (2003) found that continual contact with nonresidential parents was one of the characteristics that distinguished strong stepfamilies from stepfamilies having difficulties – 71% of strong stepfamilies reported that children had frequent contact with nonresidential parents, compared to 44% of stepfamilies having difficulties.

Clearly, the frequency of contact between parents and children matters for preserving close ties. Many types of contact can be beneficial to children. What parents do with children when they are together, also called *parental involvement*, can vary widely. Researchers have measured parental involvement in a variety of ways, including the frequency of overnight stays, in-person interactions, phone calls, and texts (e.g., King, 2007); composite scores of specific behaviors and interactions with parents, such as shopping, attending religious services, or talking about schoolwork or grades (e.g., Jensen, 2019; Sweeney, 2007); and showing affection, praising or complimenting, talking and laughing together, going on walks, and going to special events together (Montgomery et al., 1992). Fathers in one study described their efforts to engage in activities with their children that would create lasting memories, activities that included simple experiences such as a day devoted to watching science fiction movies and eating pizza and popcorn (Troilo & Coleman, 2013). Researchers suggest that children benefit from a range of interactions with parents, regardless of physical custody arrangements (Beckmeyer, Su-Russell, & Russell, 2020; Jensen, 2021; King et al., 2020; Montgomery et al., 1992; Schrodt, 2021). Effective nonresidential parents and parents who share physical custody of children figure out ways to have more frequent contact with their children – for example, attending children's soccer practices and matches to see them more frequently (Pylyser et al., 2019).

Protecting One-On-One Time

Not all time spent with children has equal benefits, however. Shared one-on-one time, or being together without other people present, appears to be particularly beneficial in maintaining parent–child closeness (Cartwright, 2005; Kelley, 1992; Pylyser et al., 2019). When parents repartner, they often are eager for their children to bond with their significant others, and so parents may use family leisure time as an opportunity to engage in collective family activities with children, partners, and stepchildren all present (Ganong et al., 2022; Pylyser et al., 2019). Although enabling shared family time is important, promoting stepfamily bonding may be successful only insofar as parents also maintain one-on-one time with their children throughout the transition to stepfamily life (Cartwright, 2005; Kelley, 1992). Losing parental time and attention after a parent repartners may be particularly difficult for children who lived in single-parent households where parent–child ties may have become especially close prior to the entrance of a stepparent. Kelley (1992) found that in well-adjusted stepfamilies, parents were intentional about setting aside one-on-one time with children, without other family members. The children in Cartwright's (2005) study who felt they had kept close relationships with parents approved of how their parents had managed the transition from single-parent household to stepfamily household, and how they had prioritized the parent–child relationships. The parent–child dyads who were most satisfied were those who carefully guarded their alone time together.

Activities such as playing games or sports, being helped with homework, shopping, going on trips, being in the car together, watching television together, or just talking one-on-one can supply important and meaningful opportunities to connect (Cartwright, 2005). What is most important is that, in addition to engaging in activities with the whole stepfamily present, parents also set aside one-on-one time with their children, without stepparents or stepsiblings present. As one Belgian father described, "we do something together as a family on the weekend, but it also happens that I do something with my children, and she does something with hers" (Pylyser et al., 2019, p. 507). These efforts appear to assuage children's concerns about losing quality time with their parents and may be especially important early in stepfamily formation, as children are adjusting to the changes of merging households.

Displaying Warmth

Children in stepfamilies also appear to benefit from regular displays of warmth and affection from their parents (Barnes & Farrell, 1992; Fine & Kurdek, 1992; Fine et al., 1993; Haberstroh et al., 1998; Hetherington et al., 1992; King et al., 2015; Rodgers & Rose, 2002; Ward et al., 2018). Examples of parental warmth toward children include praising, hugging, spending time together, playing or working on projects, reading to them, having private talks, and eating meals together (Fine et al., 1993; Green & Chuang, 2021; Jensen, 2019). When parents in stepfamilies do these behaviors more often, parent–child relationship quality is better (Jensen, 2019, 2021) and children have fewer psychological and behavioral problems (Fine et al., 1993; Jensen et al., 2017; Jensen & Lippold, 2018). Children's perceptions of parental warmth also are linked to feelings of belonging in the stepfamily (King et al., 2015), higher grades and self-esteem (Fine & Kurdek, 1992), and higher levels of child positivity (i.e., being warm, assertive, communicative, encouraging, and with a positive mood), which in turn are linked to fewer problem behaviors and higher academic achievement (Hetherington et al., 1992). Bonding with children by reading together – even picture books for younger children – also is linked to positive academic outcomes. When parents in stepfamilies read with children at least three times per week, children's standardized scores in reading improved from kindergarten to fifth grade (Shriner et al., 2009).

Establishing Appropriate Communication Boundaries

Another major focus of research on effective parenting in stepfamilies has been on setting up appropriate parent–child boundaries regarding how much and what information they communicate to children (Afifi, 2003; Braithwaite et al., 2008; Kang & Ganong, 2020). On one hand, intimate conversations between parents and children are beneficial to children's well-being (e.g., Beckmeyer, Troilo, & Markham, 2020; Beckmeyer, Su-Russell, & Russell, 2020). On the other hand, openness in some areas, such as sharing information with children about conflicts between their biological parents, can undermine child well-being and lower parent–child relationship quality (e.g., Amato & Afifi, 2006). So, how do parents effectively balance the need for both openness and closedness in parent–child communication?

Focusing on Children

When conversation is focused on children's thoughts, feelings, and needs, open communication is beneficial for children. When children freely share their ideas and talk openly with parents about what is going on in their lives (e.g., about grades, school, friends, dating), they experience more positive outcomes, including staying calm when faced with challenges, showing interest in learning new things, caring about doing well in school, and feeling that they belong in the stepfamily (Beckmeyer, Troilo, & Markham, 2020; Beckmeyer, Su-Russell, & Russell, 2020; King et al., 2015). Child-centered dialogue communicates to children that parents care about them and that they matter, and *mattering* to parents (i.e., feeling noticed and being an object of concern) is related to fewer problem behaviors and depressive symptoms for children in stepfamilies (Schenck et al., 2009). Children who maintain close relationships with parents after their parents repartner point to the importance of their parents listening to them, supporting them, and showing genuine interest in their day-to-day lives (Cartwright, 2005). In fact, parents knowing children's friends, a reflection of interest in and familiarity with children's lives, is related to children showing interest in school and in learning and participating in extracurricular activities for children in stepfamilies (Beckmeyer, Su-Russell, & Russell, 2020; Beckmeyer, Troilo, & Markham, 2020).

Openness between parents and children is not only good for the parent–child relationship, but also for the stepparent–stepchild relationship. For instance, when children perceive mothers as more responsive and available, they report closer relationships with stepfathers (Jensen & Schafer, 2013). Although open communication may be beneficial to parent–child ties, too much openness on certain topics can be problematic. Which topics should parents avoid in the best interests of their children? The following topics to avoid were gleaned from the research literature.

Avoiding Divorce Talk

Researchers generally find that effective parents in stepfamilies avoid talking with children about (a) circumstances surrounding the divorce, and (b) negative information about the child's other parent (Afifi, 2003; Braithwaite et al., 2008; Kang & Ganong, 2020; Metts et al., 2017). Researchers find that inappropriate disclosures have consequences both for child adjustment outcomes and for parent–child relationships (Afifi et al., 2007; Metts et al., 2017). Effective parents do not reveal too much information to children; they protect them from feeling as if they are taking on adult concerns that they are not emotionally or cognitively equipped to handle, and they shield them from feeling pressured to choose one parent over the other (Ahrons, 2007; Braithwaite et al., 2008; Cartwright, 2005). For example, refraining from disclosing divorce-related details is linked to positive child outcomes; children report significantly higher levels of stepfamily satisfaction when they perceive that their mothers have withheld details about the circumstances or reasons for the divorce (Metts et al., 2017). Unfortunately, many children in stepfamilies feel they are exposed by parents to more confidential information about their parents and parents' relationships than what most other children know about their parents (Braithwaite et al., 2008).

Children want their parents to understand, "at their core, the children are just children" and should not be involved in matters that are beyond the child's emotional and maturity threshold (Braithwaite et al., 2008, p. 44). Children also do not want to serve as "go-betweens," and they want to be left out of issues that make them feel caught between their parents when parents disagree (Afifi, 2003; Braithwaite et al., 2008). Children prefer that coparents communicate directly to each other.

In one study, researchers concluded that if parents find themselves prefacing or concluding their disclosures with statements such as, "I know you guys don't need to be hearing this, but …" or "I shouldn't be saying this," then parents should self-monitor and stop making such disclosures to children (Braithwaite et al., 2008, p. 41). The children whose parents exercise restraint and monitor the negative things they say about the other parent consistently report better developmental outcomes and adjustment than children whose parents badmouth the other parent (Ahrons, 2007; Arditti & Prouty, 1999). In fact, there is evidence that children are more drawn to the parent who does not over-disclose, who keeps them out of loyalty dilemmas, and who avoids retaliating against the badmouthing parent, and they respect parents for their restraint (Arditti & Prouty, 1999). Stepchildren want to feel that their parents are putting them in the center of their attention and concern, but not making them feel caught in the middle between them (Braithwaite et al., 2008). As one stepchild explained, "Think about your kids and not yourself, no matter how much pain you guys have put each other through, the effects of what is going on is going to affect your kids for a long time" (Braithwaite et al., 2008, p. 43).

Establishing Rules

Effective coparents in stepfamilies manage informational boundaries with children by making and trying to abide by explicit rules about: (a) what is appropriate and inappropriate to disclose, (b) not talking badly about the other parent, and (c) not putting children in the middle of parental conflicts (Afifi, 2003; Kang & Ganong, 2020). Effective coparents monitor the information they share with their children, so as not to overwhelm or stress them (Golish, 2003; Jamison et al., 2014). If coparents are unable to mutually agree on communication rules, individual parents who set and abide by communication rules for themselves, can also reduce harmful disclosures that benefit their children's well-being (Afifi, 2003).

Exercising Parental Control

In addition to: (a) maintaining parent–child closeness and (b) establishing appropriate parent–child communication boundaries, a third focus of effective parents in stepfamilies concerns best practices for monitoring and disciplining children. The transitions that precede or accompany stepfamily formation can disrupt family rules and routines that seem "normal" or "natural" to children and parents prior to forming a stepfamily. Once parents have repartnered, however, there are more people in the household, new family roles to determine, and many household practices and routines that must be changed to incorporate new people and new relationships. These changes may affect the extent to which parents have the capacity to monitor children's activities as they did before.

Monitoring Children

Parental control, or the extent to which parents set limits for children, monitor their activities, and enforce rules, has been linked with positive child outcomes in stepfamilies (Barnes & Farrell, 1992; Brown & Rinelli, 2010; Choquet et al., 2008; Fine & Kurdek, 1992; Fine et al., 1993; Hetherington et al., 1992; Rodgers & Rose, 2002; Sweeney, 2007; Willetts & Maroules, 2004) and closer parent–child relationships (Parent et al., 2014). For example, the extent to which parents know children's friends, their friends' parents, their teachers, and their whereabouts when not at home is related to fewer behavioral and emotional problems for children in stepfamilies (Willetts & Maroules, 2004). Parental monitoring, or *parental supervision*, also positively relates to children's grades, self-esteem, and levels of warmth and positivity (Fine & Kurdek, 1992; Hetherington et al., 1992). Higher parental control by fathers in father–stepmother families is linked to lower levels of children's psychological maladjustment (e.g., sadness, depression) and higher quality mother–child relationships (Fine et al., 1993). Higher maternal control in mother–stepfather families is linked to lower odds of adolescents smoking or drinking alcohol (Brown & Rinelli, 2010). Examples of parental control in one study included placing limits on (a) the amount of television the child watches and the type of programs he or she watches; (b) whether children are allowed to be at home alone before school, after school, at night, and overnight; (c) whether children are supposed to let parents know where they are when away from home; and (d) whether children are required to complete chores or homework before playing, watching television, or going out (Fine et al., 1993).

Disciplining Children

Consensus across studies is that child adjustment and stepfamily functioning is best when parents continue to be the primary disciplinarians, especially early in stepfamily formation, and especially with adolescents (Bray, 1999; Cartwright, 2005; Cartwright et al., 2009; Golish, 2003; Kelley, 1992; Michaels, 2006; Moore & Cartwright, 2005; Pylyser et al., 2019). Strong stepfamilies and those who struggle appear to grapple with ambiguity about parental roles, particularly surrounding the role of disciplinarian (Golish, 2003). Children and stepfamily therapists agree that parents ought to be responsible for discipline (Cartwright, 2005), and that stepparents can best contribute to effective childrearing by supporting parents' efforts (see Chapter 3 for a review of effective stepparenting, and Chapter 5 for coparenting research). Even as stepparents gradually become more actively involved in childrearing decision-making, stepfamilies appear to operate best when parents are supported by stepparents in their disciplinary decisions (Ganong et al., 2015). Finally, one study examined the specific type of disciplinary style used by parents in stepfamilies and found that, when parents use a reasoning-based disciplinary style, children in stepfamilies experience fewer depressive symptoms (Sweeney, 2007). Specifically, when adolescents did something of consequence wrong and mothers talked with them about it and helped them understand why it was wrong, adolescents in stepfamilies fared better.

Supporting Stepparent–Stepchild Relationship Development

A fourth theme in effective parenting in stepfamilies concerns parents' roles in the development of the relationship between their new partner and their children. Some researchers suggest that the stepparent–stepchild relationship may be the most critical relationship to stepfamily functioning (e.g., Crosbie-Burnett, 1984). Both researchers and clinicians have found the development of positive stepparent–stepchild ties as a critical stepfamily task (Ganong & Coleman, 2017). Given that close relationships with stepparents are linked to positive outcomes for stepchildren (King, 2006, 2007; White & Gilbreth, 2001), what parents do to support the development of these relationships is of consequence in stepfamilies.

Staying Involved with Children

First, parents support stepparent–stepchild ties by having closer relationships and greater involvement with their own children. Research supports a spillover effect between parent–child closeness and stepparent–stepchild closeness, meaning that when children feel closer to their residential parents, they also feel closer to their residential stepparents (King 2006, 2007). Moreover, when parents are more highly involved and offer more support to children (e.g., with practical matters, household chores, giving advice), their spouses also are more involved with children (van Houdt et al., 2020). Therefore, many of the behaviors examined in the section "Maintaining Close Parent–Child Bonds" (e.g., having fun together, staying in touch, communicating often, showing affection) have benefits that extend beyond the parent–child bond into stepparent–stepchild relationships.

Gate Opening

Children having close relationships with parents, however, does not guarantee they will have close relationships with stepparents. Parents support the development of stepparent–stepchild ties by *allowing* and actively encouraging stepparents to be involved. Gatekeeping is defined as "functions exercised by one or both parents that determine who will have access to their children and the nature of that access" (Pruett et al., 2003, p. 171). This may sound straightforward, but many mothers and fathers, intentionally or unintentionally, tend to limit interactions between stepparents and stepchildren, also known as *restrictive gatekeeping* (Ganong et al., 2015, 2020). Examples of restrictive gatekeeping include telling stepparents what they can and cannot do with stepchildren; supervising stepparents' interactions with stepchildren; criticizing stepparents' parenting abilities; and saying sarcastic comments while stepparents are interacting with stepchildren (Ganong et al., 2020). When parents engage in these restrictive gatekeeping behaviors more often, stepparents engage in fewer *affinity-seeking behaviors* with stepchildren, or actions intentionally performed to get stepchildren to like them and to feel positive towards them. This, in turn, negatively affects stepparent–stepchild relationship development (Ganong et al., 2020).

Parents engage in restrictive gatekeeping for a variety of reasons. For instance, they may: (a) feel uncertain about how competent stepparents are as caregivers, (b) want to protect the safety and well-being of their children, (c) want to protect their role as primary parents, and (d) want to maintain the quality of their relationships with children they had established prior to repartnering (Ganong et al., 2015; Pruett et al., 2003). If stepparents have proven themselves to be unfit caregivers or harmful influences on children, then parents have good reasons to engage in restrictive gatekeeping and to limit stepparents' access to children. Assuming, however, that stepparents are responsible and trustworthy adults, creating space for stepparents to interact with stepchildren, or *gate-opening*, is necessary for developing close ties (Schmeeckle, 2007) or maintaining step-relationships after divorce (Coleman et al., 2015). Given the potential benefits of stepparents' affinity-seeking with stepchildren (Ganong et al., 1999, 2019), parents should be aware of the extent to which they needlessly restrict stepparents' interactions with stepchildren.

Mediating Conflicts

A third way in which parents support the development of stepparent–stepchild relationships is by carefully navigating their role as mediators of stepparent–stepchild conflict. The role of mediator may begin prior to creation of the stepfamily household, when parents are dating prospective new partners (Anderson & Greene, 2011). Conflict in family relationships is inevitable, including between stepparents and stepchildren, and how parents handle conflict between their partners and children is important (Weaver & Coleman, 2010). On the one hand, when children view their mothers as open to their communications about stepfathers, and responsive to those communications, they report closer relationships with stepfathers (Jensen & Schafer, 2013). Parents' willingness to listen to children, as opposed to becoming defensive about children's issues with stepparents, may make children less likely to resent stepparents, and thus facilitate closer stepparent–stepchild relationships (Jensen & Schafer, 2013). Adolescents whose mothers helped them understand stepfathers' behaviors by explaining reasons for the behaviors felt better about themselves and their stepfathers (Cookston et al., 2014). Similarly, in father–stepmother families, fathers also can help interpret conflict between children and stepmothers (Pylyser et al., 2019).

At the same time, communication between parents and children that consistently excludes stepparents can result in what therapists call *triangulation*, whereby conflict between stepparents and stepchildren is handled solely through parents, who become the mediator of all conflicts. When parents remove themselves from the middle of stepparent–stepchild conflicts and encourage stepparents and stepchildren to discuss problems openly and directly with each other, stepchildren describe better relationships with stepparents (Afifi, 2003). A pattern of openness and direct communication in stepfamilies is one of the most effective tactics for minimizing loyalty conflicts (Afifi, 2003). Therefore, parents appear to be most effective at mediating conflict when they act as a sounding board for their children or their partner and help them engage in perspective-taking, *and also* when they encourage children and partners to address issues openly and directly with each other.

Minimizing Children's Exposure to Stepcouple Conflicts

Finally, parents support stepparent–stepchild relationships by minimizing children's exposure to conflict between parents and stepparents. Communicating a united front as a couple is effective not only for reducing triangulation in stepfamilies (Afifi, 2003), but also for promoting closer bonds between stepparents and stepchildren (Jensen & Schafer, 2013). One strategy that parents use to present a united front is to delay answers to children's questions until they have time to consult their partner and formulate a response (Afifi, 2003). When children feel that parents and stepparents agree on parenting issues and argue infrequently, they report closer relationships to their stepparents (Jensen & Schafer, 2013).

Facilitating Stepfamily Cohesion

The final theme in effective parenting in stepfamilies concerns what parents do to facilitate stepfamily cohesion. Building solidarity as a family unit is a challenge experienced by nearly all stepfamilies (Golish, 2003). Stepfamily formation involves the merging of two sets of pre-established family traditions, routines, patterns of interaction, and shared meanings, and establishing a shared identity can be challenging. Fortunately, researchers have identified specific parenting strategies that are linked to greater stepfamily cohesion.

First, efforts to organize shared family time are key; spending time together as a family is important for both individual and family well-being (Baxter et al., 1999; Beckmeyer, Su-Russell, & Russell, 2020; Fine et al., 1993; Henry & Lovelace, 1995; Hutchinson et al., 2007; Metts et al., 2013; Pylyser et al., 2019; Struss et al., 2001; Willetts & Maroules, 2004). One successful strategy is having shared family meals. The more nights per week parents in stepfamilies report having shared family meals (i.e., meals with everyone in the household present), the more positive outcomes their children experience (Beckmeyer, Su-Russell, & Russell, 2020). Specifically, having shared meals is linked to youth adjustment, stepfamily cohesion, and children's involvement in extracurricular activities (Beckmeyer, Su-Russell, & Russell, 2020; Fine et al., 1993; Hutchinson et al., 2007; Struss et al., 2001).

Other shared activities such as going for walks, playing games, and even doing household chores together has been found to contribute to feelings of continuity and stability among adolescents in stepfamilies and to generate feelings of stepfamily belonging (Hutchinson et al., 2007). When stepfamilies engage in shared activities and daily routines more often, adolescents in stepfamilies engage in fewer delinquent behaviors, use fewer illegal substances, have fewer behavioral and emotional problems, and are more satisfied with stepfamily life (Henry & Lovelace, 1995; Willetts & Maroules, 2004). Some evidence suggests that cohabiting stepfamilies particularly may benefit from shared family activities; family meals, for instance, had a stronger positive association with positive developmental outcomes for youth living in cohabiting stepfamilies compared with youth in married stepfamilies (Beckmeyer, Su-Russell, & Russell, 2020).

Although studies show that family time is indeed important, these findings should be considered alongside the evidence that protecting one-on-one time between parents and children is critical to strong parent-child bonds that promote child well-being in stepfamilies. Without a strong parent–child relationship, it is unlikely that parents' efforts to promote stepfamily cohesion will be well received by children. Parenting practices found to promote children's best outcomes appear to involve a delicate balance of facilitating shared family time and preserving one-on-one time with children (see Box 4.1).

Box 4.1 *What works* **for parents in stepfamilies**

- Set aside one-on-one time with children and spend quality time together regularly and frequently.
- Communicate frequently with nonresidential children via texts, phone calls, and in-person interactions, including overnight stays.
- Guard the time for interacting with children one-on-one. Playing games, doing homework, shopping, watching television, or just talking are important bonding activities.
- Display warmth and affection to children (e.g., praising them, hugging, reading to younger children, and talking privately with them).
- Engage in child-centered dialogue with children, focusing communications on their lives, thoughts, and feelings.
- Listen to children and show interest in their daily activities.
- Exercise restraint in talking with children about the divorce, the child's other parent, and the new stepparent.
- Establish personal and coparenting rules about:
  ○ what is appropriate to disclose to children,
  ○ not talking badly about the other parent, and
  ○ not putting children in the middle of parental conflicts.
- Monitor children's activities, set limits for them, and enforce the rules.
- Maintain the role of primary disciplinarian, making sure stepparents support disciplinary decisions.
- Use a reasoning-based disciplinary style, talk with children about what they did wrong and help them understand reasons why it was wrong.
- Support stepparent–stepchild interactions by providing opportunities for them to interact (i.e., gate opening).
- Encourage stepparents and stepchildren to discuss problems openly and directly with each other.
- Mediate stepparent–stepchild conflicts when they can't resolve a disagreement after discussions.
- Minimize children's exposure to conflict between parents and stepparents.
- Organize and plan shared family time (e.g., shared family meals, day trips, and household projects).

What Works for Older Parents and Adult Children in Stepfamilies

Compared to research on parenting minor-age children in stepfamilies, fewer studies have examined later-life relationships between parents and children in stepfamilies. There have been several studies examining intergenerational exchanges of support in stepfamilies, whereby exchanges of support between parents and children were compared to exchanges of support between stepparents and stepchildren, but these studies do not contain information about *what works* for these later-life stepfamilies.

We do know that parent–child closeness is linked to older adults' life satisfaction (Ivanova, 2020) and to greater resources exchanged between older parents and their adult children (Kalbarczyk, 2021). Emotional closeness and helping each other in later life are consequences of parents having built strong emotional attachments with their adult offspring when they were children (Ivanova & Kalmijn, 2020). When parents are more involved in children's lives when children are young, those children are more likely, as adults, to repay that support to parents as they age (Ivanova & Kalmijn, 2020; Kalbarczyk, 2021). Older parents who are more involved in helping their adult children (e.g., with chores, advice) also serve as models for stepparents, who in turn are more involved in helping their stepchildren (van Houdt et al., 2020). Additionally, similar to research on older stepparents, researchers suggest that older parents' assistance to adult offspring is often gendered. Mothers often function as kinkeepers who make sure family members stay in touch, plan family outings, and remember birthdays (Hornstra & Ivanova, 2023; Schmeeckle, 2007), while fathers have been found to provide financial and other instrumental aid, such as advice and tangible help (Schmeeckle, 2007).

We found only one study about aging parents and adult children in stepfamilies formed later in life, and most of that investigation focused on what stepparents and stepchildren could do that works (Mikucki-Enyart & Heisdorf, 2020). One action that parents did that was beneficial to children, however, was to resolve the problem faced by many older stepchildren (and younger ones, too) in how to spend time with both sets of parents on important holidays and birthdays by merging family celebrations so that adult children did not have to choose between parents or split their celebrations between them (Mikucki-Enyart & Heisdorf, 2020). For example, both parents might share a Christmas celebration with extended family, including stepparents and their kin (see Box 4.2).

Box 4.2 *What works* **for older parents and adult children in stepfamilies**

For parents who repartnered when children were younger:

- Maintain positive relationships developed when children were young.
  - Take care of children when they are young.
    - Show love and affection.
    - Help them (e.g., with school, relationships).
    - Support them emotionally, physically, and financially.
    - Teach them knowledge and skills.
    - Play with children.
  - Assist children in their adult years.
    - Babysit grandchildren.
    - Offer advice and emotional support.
    - Provide financial support (if possible and if needed).
    - Engage in kinkeeping.
      - Keep in touch with family members.
      - Arrange family gatherings.
      - Remember birthdays and other celebrations.
  - Work through conflicts by making amends and by apologizing.

For parents who repartnered in later life:

- Stay connected with stepchildren or reconnect with them.
- Merge holidays and other celebrations so children do not have to choose between parents.
- Grieve losses with children.

Finally, in two studies of widowed older adults, parents who had repartnered or started dating relatively soon after the death of their partner learned to communicate more often with their adult children, apologize to them for mistakes made, and share their collective grief as a family (Carr & Boerner, 2013; Nice et al., 2021). Retrospectively, parents realized that they needed to be more mindful and sensitive to their children's grief.

Implications for Practice

Taken together, effective parenting in stepfamilies appears to involve *managing competing family needs*. For example, there is a need for both shared family time and one-on-one parent–child time. There is a need for parents to maintain open communication boundaries in some areas while maintaining closed communication boundaries in others. There is a need for parents to be both open and responsive to children's concerns about stepparents and to encourage them to discuss problems directly. There is a need to exercise parental control (e.g., monitoring children's activities) but not so much that it restricts stepparents' involvement with children and undermines stepparent–stepchild relationship development. Parents are balancing multiple individual and family needs as they employ strategies that maximize their children's well-being across the transition to stepfamily life.

To be sure, all families and relationships involve managing competing needs. Researchers have called these opposing motivations that contradict one another *relational dialectics* (Baxter & Braithwaite, 2010; Braithwaite et al., 2008; Braithwaite et al., 1998). For instance, relationship partners manage the tension of *autonomy vs. connection*, wanting independence and freedom in relationships but also wanting intimacy and belonging. People also manage the tension of *openness vs. closedness*, wanting both self-disclosure and privacy in families. Another contradiction is *stability vs. change* – people find comfort in familiarity and routine yet yearn for novelty and excitement. Tensions and contradictions are inherent to family life, but the structural complexity of stepfamilies may make tensions surrounding competing family needs even more salient. For instance, stepfamily formation not only increases the number of family subsystems within and across households, but also brings together family members who lack shared history – a context ripe for negotiating inevitable tensions and feelings of ambivalence. Moreover, stepfamily formation happens against the backdrop of cultural narratives that paint stepfamilies as either dysfunctional (e.g., Cinderella and other wicked stepparent tropes) or always harmonious (e.g., The Brady Bunch), neither of which accurately depicts the complex, meaningful, and nuanced realities of most stepfamilies (Ganong & Coleman, 2017; Sanner & Coleman, 2017). At the same time, the bonds that hold stepfamilies together may not be as durable as first-family bonds, at least early in the lives of stepfamilies, making dialectic tensions in stepfamilies feel stressful and harder to manage.

Parents' roles in stepfamilies are in many ways like their parental roles as single parents prior to the creation of the stepfamily household, but within a socio-emotional context that is dramatically different. Parents in stepfamilies love their new romantic partners, and they love their children from prior unions, and yet those partners and children may be unsure of each other as they build new relationships, making the parent the fulcrum of an emotionally charged triangle that has enormous implications for couple and family stability. Parents are asked to do a lot to facilitate individual and stepfamily well-being. Because parents are the main reason that stepchildren and stepparents are in relationships with each other, the parental role in stepfamilies is likely stressful, and parents may need guidance in how to manage their roles and new relationships in stepfamilies.

Practitioners can help parents set priorities and plan strategies for achieving their relational goals. Effective parents know how to rear their children, but they may need regular reminders to focus attention on their children and view family changes from children's perspectives. Although parents may feel that they are successfully sharing their time between children, new partners, and new stepchildren, children appear to be hypersensitive to perceived changes in their relationships with their parents. Practitioners can remind parents of the power of acknowledging and validating children's feelings. Children may be reluctant to voice feelings of loss or sadness surrounding stepfamily formation for fear or disappointing or upsetting their parents. Encouraging parents to view these changes from children's perspectives can help parents enter children's emotional worlds, meet them where they are, and validate their feelings in ways that strengthen the parent–child bond.

Practitioners can also assist parents in how to facilitate stepfamily bonding more broadly. Parents are partly responsible for creating a new stepfamily culture, and they may need help in figuring out ways to make this happen. For instance, sharing activities as a family group builds shared memories that help build culture. In-group norms evolve as stepfamilies do projects together (e.g., painting a child's bedroom, planting flowers), have fun together playing games, and engage in everyday activities like making and eating meals. Again, parents should be reminded that, without a strong parent–child relationship, it is unlikely that parents' efforts to promote stepfamily cohesion will be well received by children. Successfully creating a new stepfamily culture may involve a balance of facilitating shared family time *and* preserving one-on-one time with children.

Practitioners also can help parents determine ways in which stepparents can be involved in childrearing and in *supporting* parental discipline and rules-setting *while also taking a back seat as disciplinarians.* Stepparents often want to be engaged with stepchildren (see Chapter 3), but they may only know how to do this by acting like a parent. Practitioners can help parents gently discuss ways that stepparents can help with childrearing without trying to replace the nonresidential (other) parent. Some stepparents are eager to come in and be the new sheriff in town by making stepchildren toe the line and "grow up." Practitioners can help these stepparents understand the inappropriateness of this approach. On the other hand, stepparents often hold more objective views about children's behaviors than their parents do and can play a role in helping the parent not to worry or overreact to children's misbehaviors.

Parents also may need guidance in how to effectively mediate between their partner and children when there are disagreements. Helping the new partner understand the child can foster interactions between the stepparent and stepchildren. "He gets cranky when his blood sugar is low. He will be ok after a snack" is a simple message that helps a partner understand a child better. Conversely, telling a child that, "Your stepdad is having a stressful time at work, so let's give him some time when he comes home to relax a bit before we ask him for a favor" can help children understand why a stepparent is grouchy. Explaining behaviors and reframing events and actions are teachable skills that parents could learn with professional guidance.

Future Research

Although our understanding of effective parenting in stepfamilies has improved over the last several decades, major gaps in knowledge remain. Consistent with research reviewed in other chapters, most problematic is that this literature overwhelmingly relies on White, middle-class samples in heteronormative stepfamilies (e.g., mother–stepfather families, father–stepmother families). The lack of attention to racial, ethnic, gender, and sexual diversity in stepfamilies is troubling – as in other areas of stepfamily research, researchers *must* do better to address the perpetual centering of White cisgender middle-class family experiences in this literature. This is particularly important given recent evidence that suggests that what we know to be true for White stepfamilies may not hold for Black, Hispanic, or Indigenous stepfamilies (Burton & Hardaway, 2012; Crosbie-Burnet & Lewis, 1993; Cross, 2020; Limb et al., 2020). For example, the very notion that family structure is consequential to child well-being appears to be true primarily for White youth (Cross, 2020). Using over 30 years of national data that tracked children's living arrangements from birth to adulthood, Cross found that living in a stepfamily does not carry the same costs for Black youth as for their White peers. For Black youth, access to resources is more important than family structure, suggesting that for families experiencing stress and unequal access to resources resulting from historic and contemporary structural racism, added stress incurred by living apart from a biological parent is only marginally impactful (Cross, 2020).

Findings such as this highlight the need to better understand *families in context*, particularly when seeking to better understand how, and under what conditions, certain parenting practices may or may not yield positive returns. Although parents may have power to promote children's well-being in stepfamilies by employing certain parenting practices, the extent to which families struggle or thrive does not rest solely in the hands of family members. The stressors families experience, and the extent to which parents have the bandwidth to employ these parenting practices, are shaped by larger social forces, including the extent to which families are supported at the local, state, and federal levels. Future research should move beyond family-level explanations of why families struggle or thrive to confront socially structured privilege and oppression; that is, to connect family-structure research to the discussion of how and why our systems, laws, and policies have been designed to benefit some family structures to the exclusion of others (Letiecq, 2019). A discussion of "*What Works* in Stepfamilies" is incomplete without recognizing that our systems, institutions, and governing officials play key roles in shaping and supporting communities that are conducive to promoting effective parenting. Families cannot be understood outside of the larger social contexts in which they are embedded, and research opportunities are ripe for better connecting family dynamics to these larger social forces.

In addition to assessing contexts, more research is needed on what parents do to help their children adjust to stepfamily changes they meet. More investigations are called for on how much, what, and when to communicate to children. Additionally, more needs to be known about how parents can facilitate stepparent–stepchild bonding. A few researchers have examined parents' roles as mediators vis à vis stepparents and stepchildren (e.g., Pylyser et al., 2019; Weaver & Coleman, 2010), but more research is needed that examines the developmental outcomes for children when parents engage in different gate-closing/gate-opening strategies. Gathering the perspectives of both adults and children may be beneficial in exploring effective behaviors that result in positive outcomes.

Finally, there is a great need for more diverse designs in studies of *what works* for effective parenting in stepfamilies. For example, much of what we know about stepfamilies comes from cross-sectional study designs. More longitudinal research is critical to examining how associations between parenting behaviors and child outcomes change over time with respect to children's ages and developmental contexts. Promising opportunities lie ahead as researchers seek to better understand the complex interactions of family contexts, parenting practices, and individual and relational well-being in stepfamilies.

References

Afifi, T.D. (2003). Feeling caught in stepfamilies: Managing boundary turbulence through appropriate communication privacy rules. *Journal of Social and Personal Relationships*, *20*, 729–756. https://doi.org/10.1177/0265407503206002

Afifi, T.D., McManus, T., Hutchinson, S., & Baker, B. (2007). Inappropriate parental divorce disclosures, the factors that prompt them, and their impact on parents' and adolescents' well-being. *Communication Monographs*, *74*(1), 78–102. https://doi.org/10.1080/03637750701196870

Ahrons, C.R. (2007). Family ties after divorce: Long-term implications for children. *Family Process*, *46*(1), 53–65. https://doi.org/10.1111/j.1545-5300.2006.00191.x

Amato, P.R., & Afifi, T.D. (2006). Feeling caught between parents: Adult children's relations with parents and subjective well-being. *Journal of Marriage and Family*, *68*, 222–235.

Anderson, E.R., Greene, S.M. (2011). "My child and I are a package deal.": Balancing adult and child concerns in repartnering after divorce. *Journal of Family Psychology*, *25*, 741–750. https://doi.org/10.1037/a0024620

Arditti, J.A., & Prouty, A.M. (1999). Change, disengagement, and renewal: Relationship dynamics between young adults and their fathers after divorce. *Journal of Marital and Family Therapy, 25*(1), 61–81. https://doi.org/10.1111/j.1752-0606.1999.tb01110.x

Barnes, G.M., & Farrell, M.P. (1992). Parental support and control as predictors of adolescent drinking, delinquency, and related problem behaviors. *Journal of Marriage and the Family, 54*(4), 763–776.

Baxter, L.A., & Braithwaite, D.O. (2010). Relational dialectics theory, applied. In S.E. Smith & S.R. Wilson (Eds.), *New directions in interpersonal communication research* (pp. 48–66). Sage.

Baxter, L.A., Braithwaite, D.O., & Nicholson, J.H. (1999). Turning points in the development of blended families. *Journal of Social and Personal Relationships, 16*(3), 291–314. https://doi.org/10.1177/0265407599163002

Beckmeyer, J.J., Su-Russell, C., & Russell, L.T. (2020). Family management practices and positive youth development in stepfamilies and single-mother families. *Family Relations, 69*, 92–108. https://doi.org/10.1111/fare.12412

Beckmeyer, J.J., Troilo, J., & Markham, M.S. (2020). Parental academic involvement and youth well-being in post-divorce families. *Journal of Divorce & Remarriage, 61*(6), 443–462. https://doi.org/10.1080/10502556.2020.768491

Braithwaite, D.O., Baxter, L.A., & Harper, A.M. (1998). The role of rituals in the management of the dialectical tension of "old" and "new" in blended families. *Communication Studies, 49*, 101–120. https://doi.org/10.1080/10510979809368523

Braithwaite, D.O., Toller, P.W., Daas, K.L., Durham, W.T., & Jones, A.C. (2008). Centered but not caught in the middle: Stepchildren's perceptions of dialectical contradictions in the communication of co-parents. *Journal of Applied Communication Research, 36*, 33–55. https://doi.org/10.1080/00909880701799337

Bray, J.H. (1999). From marriage to remarriage and beyond: Findings from the Developmental Issues in Stepfamilies Research Project. In E.M. Hetherington (Ed.), *Coping with divorce, single parenting, and remarriage: A risk and resiliency perspective* (pp. 253–271). Erlbaum. https://doi.org/10.4324/9781410602893-19

Bronstein, P., Stoll, M.F., Clauson, J., Abrams, C.L., & Briones, M. (1994). Fathering after separation or divorce: Factors predicting children's adjustment. *Family Relations, 43*, 469–479. https://doi.org/10.2307/585380

Brown, S.L., & Rinelli, L.N. (2010). Family structure, family processes, and adolescent smoking and drinking. *Journal of Research on Adolescence, 10*, 259–173. https://doi.org/10.1111/j.1532-7795.2010.00636.x

Burton, L.M., & Hardaway, C.R. (2012). Low-income mothers as "othermothers" to their romantic partners' children: Women's coparenting in multiple partner fertility relationships. *Family Process, 51*(3), 343–359. http://dx.doi.org/10.1111/j.1545-5300.2012.01401.x

Bzostek, S. (2008). Social fathers and child well-being. *Journal of Marriage and Family, 70*, 950–961. https://doi.org/10.1111/j.1741-3737.2008.00538.x

Carr, D., & Boerner, K. (2013). Dating after late-life spousal loss: Does it compromise relationships with adult children? *Journal of Aging Studies, 27*, 487–498. https://doi.org/10.1016/j.jaging.2012.12.009

Cartwright, C. (2005). Stepfamily living and parent-child relationships: An exploratory investigation. *Journal of Family Studies, 11*, 267–283. https://doi.org/10.5172/jfs.327.11.2.267

Cartwright, C., Farnsworth, V., & Mobley, V. (2009). Relationships with step-parents in the life stories of young adults of divorce. *Family Matters, 82*, 30–37.

Cartwright, C., & Seymour, F. (2002). Young adults' perceptions of parents' responses in stepfamilies: What hurts? What helps? *Journal of Divorce & Remarriage, 37*(3–4), 123–141. https://doi.org/10.1300/J087v37n03_07

Choquet, M., Hassler, C., Morin, D., Falissard, B., & Chau, N. (2008). Perceived parenting styles and tobacco, alcohol, and cannabis use among French adolescents: Gender and family structure differential. *Alcohol & Alcoholism, 43*(1), 73–80. https://doi.org/10.1093/alcalc/agm060

Coleman, M., Ganong, L., Russell, L., & Frye, N. (2015). Stepchildren's views about former steprelationships following stepfamily dissolution. *Journal of Marriage and Family, 77,* 775–790. https://doi.org/10.1111/jomf.12182

Cookston, J.T., Olide, A., Parke, R.D., Fabricius, W.V., Saenz, D.S., & Braver, S.L. (2014). He said what? Guided cognitive reframing about the co-resident father/stepfather-adolescent relationship. *Journal of Research on Adolescence, 25*(2), 263–278. https://doi.org/10.1111/jora.12120

Crosbie-Burnett, M. (1984). The centrality of the step relationship: A challenge to family theory and practice. *Family Relations, 33*(3), 459–463. https://doi.org/10.2307/584717

Crosbie-Burnett, M., & Lewis, E.A. (1993). Use of African-American family structures and functioning to address the challenges of European-American postdivorce families. *Family Relations, 42,* 243–248. https://doi.org/10.2307/585552

Cross, C.J. (2020). Racial/ethnic differences in the association between family structure and children's education. *Journal of Marriage and Family, 82*(2), 691–712. https://doi.org/10.1111/jomf.12625

Cross, C.J. & Zhang, X. (2022). Nonresident social fathering in African American single-mother families. *Journal of Marriage and Family, 84*(5), 1250–1269. https://doi.org/10.1111/jomf.12839

Day, R.D., & Acock, A. (2004). Youth ratings of family processes and father role performance of resident and nonresident fathers. In R.D. Day & M.E. Lamb (Eds.), *Conceptualizing and measuring father involvement* (pp. 273–292). Erlbaum. https://doi.org/10.4324/9781410609380

Egginton, B.R., Holmes, E.K., James, S.C., & Hawkins, A.J. (2021). The power of three: A latent class analysis of the three parent–child relationships in stepfamilies and their influence on emerging adult outcomes. *Journal of Divorce & Remarriage, 62*(5), 374–397. https://doi.org/10.1080/10502556.2021.1871841

Fine, M.A., & Kurdek, L.A. (1992). The adjustment of adolescents in stepfather and stepmother families. *Journal of Marriage and the Family, 54,* 725–736. https://doi.org/10.2307/353156

Fine, M.A., Voydanoff, P., & Donnelly, B.W. (1993). Relations between parental control and warmth and child well-being in stepfamilies. *Journal of Family Psychology, 7,* 222–232. https://doi.org/10.1037/0893-3200.7.2.222

Ganong, L., & Coleman, M. (2017). *Stepfamily relationships: Development, dynamics, and interventions* (2nd ed.). Springer.

Ganong, L., Coleman, M., Fine, M., & Martin, P. (1999). Stepparents' affinity-seeking and affinity-maintaining strategies with stepchildren. *Journal of Family Issues, 20*(3), 299–327. https://doi.org/10.1177/019251399020003001

Ganong, L., Coleman, M., Jamison, T., & Feistman, R. (2015). Divorced mothers' coparental boundary maintenance after parents repartner. *Journal of Family Psychology, 29*(2), 221. https://doi.org/10.1037/fam0000064

Ganong, L., Jensen, T., Sanner, C., Chapman, A., & Coleman, M. (2020). Stepparents' attachment orientation, parental gatekeeping, and stepparents' affinity-seeking with stepchildren. *Family Process, 59*(2), 756–771. https://doi.org/10.1111/famp.12448

Ganong, L., Jensen, T., Sanner, C., Russell, L., & Coleman, M. (2019). Stepfathers' affinity-seeking with stepchildren, stepfather-stepchild relationship quality, marital quality, and stepfamily cohesion among stepfathers and mothers. *Journal of Family Psychology, 22,* 521–531. https://doi.org/10.1037/fam0000518

Ganong, L., Sanner, C., Landon, O., & Coleman, M. (2022). Patterns of stepsibling relationship development. *Journal of Family Issues*, *43*(10), 2788–2809. https://doi.or g/10.1177/0192513X211033924

Golish, T.D. (2003). Stepfamily communication strengths: Understanding the ties that bind. *Human Communication Research*, *29*, 41–80. https://doi.org/10.1111/j. 1468-2958.2003.tb00831.x

Green, D.S., & Chuang, S.S. (2021). A critical exploration of biological and social fathering among Afro-Caribbean fathers. *Family Relations*, *70*, 282–296. https://doi. org/10.1111/fare.12479

Haberstroh, C., Hayslip Jr, B., & Essandoh, P. (1998). The relationship between stepdaughters' self-esteem and perceived parenting behavior. *Journal of Divorce & Remarriage*, *29*(3–4), 161–175. https://doi.org/10.1300/J087v29n03_10

Henry, C.S., & Lovelace, S.G. (1995). Family resources and adolescent family life satisfaction in remarried family households. *Journal of Family Issues*, *16*(6), 765–786. https://doi.org/10.1177/019251395016006005

Hetherington, E.M., Clingempeel, W.G., Anderson, E.R., Deal, J.E., Hagan, M.S., Hollier, E.A., & Lindner, M.S. (1992). Coping with marital transitions. *Monographs of the Society for Research in Child Development*, *57*(2–3). University of Chicago Press. http://dx.doi.org/10.2307/1166050

Hornstra, M., & Ivanova, K. (2023). Kinkeeping across families: The central role of mothers and stepmothers in the facilitation of adult intergenerational ties. *Sex Roles*, *88*(7–8), 367–382. https://doi.org/10.1007/s11199-023-01352-2

Hutchinson, S.L., Afifi, T., & Krause, S. (2007). The family that plays together fares better: Examining the contribution of shared family time to family resilience following divorce. *Journal of Divorce & Remarriage*, *46*, 21–48. https://doi.org/10.1300/ J087v46n03_03

Ivanova, K. (2020). My children, your children, our children, and my well-being: Life satisfaction of "empty nest" biological parents and stepparents. *Journal of Happiness Studies*, *21*, 613–633. https://doi.org/10.1007/s10902-019-00097-8

Ivanova, K., & Kalmijn, M. (2020). Parental involvement in youth and closeness to parents during adulthood: Stepparents and biological parents. *Journal of Family Psychology*, *34*(7), 794–803. https://doi.org/10.1037/fam0000659

Jamison, T.B., Coleman, M., Ganong, L.H., & Feistman, R.E. (2014). Transitioning to postdivorce family life: A grounded theory investigation of resilience in coparenting. *Family Relations*, *63*(3), 411–423. https://doi.org/10.1111/fare.12074

Jensen, T. (2019). A typology of interactional patterns between youth and their stepfathers: Associations with family relationship quality and youth well-being. *Family Process*, *58*(2), 384–403. https://doi.org/10.1111/famp.12348

Jensen, T. (2021). Patterns of interactions between youth and resident stepmothers: A latent class analysis. *Family Process*, *60*(2), 538–55. https://doi.org/120.1111/famp.12556

Jensen, T., & Lippold, M.A. (2018). Patterns of stepfamily relationship quality and adolescents' short-term and long-term adjustment. *Journal of Family Psychology*, *32*(8), 1130–1141. https://doi.org/10.1037/fam0000442

Jensen, T.M., Lippold, M.A., Mills-Koonce, R., & Fosco, G.M. (2017). Stepfamily relationship quality and children's internalizing and externalizing problems. *Family Process*, *57*(2), 477–495. https://doi.org/10.1111/famp.12284

Jensen, T.M., & Shafer, K. (2013). Stepfamily functioning and closeness: Children's views on second marriages and stepfather relationships. *Social Work*, *58*(2), 127–136. https://doi.org/10.1093/sw/swt007

Kalbarczyk, M. (2021). Non-financial support provided to parents in stepfamilies: Empirical examination of Europeans 50+. *International Journal of Environmental Research and Public Health*, *18*(10), 5151. https://doi.org/10.3390/ijerph18105151

Kang, Y., & Ganong, L. (2020). Divorced fathers' perceptions of parental disclosures to children. *Family Relations, 69*(1), 36–50. https://doi.org/10.1111/fare.12410

Kelley, P. (1992). Healthy stepfamily functioning. *Families in Society, 73*(10), 579–587. https://doi.org/10.1177/104438949207301001

King, V. (2006). The antecedents and consequences of adolescents' relationships with stepfathers and nonresident fathers. *Journal of Marriage and Family, 68,* 910–928. https://doi.org/10.1111/j.1741-3737.2006.00304.x

King, V. (2007). When children have two mothers: Relationships with nonresident mothers, stepmothers, and fathers. *Journal of Marriage and Family, 69,* 1178–1193. https://doi.org/10.1111/j.1741-3737.2007.00440.x

King, V.L., Boyd, L.M., & Thorsen, M.L. (2015). Adolescents' perceptions of family belonging in stepfamilies. *Journal of Marriage and Family, 77,* 761–774. https://doi.org/10.1111/jomf.12181

King, V., Pragg, B., & Lindstrom, R. (2020). Family relationships during adolescence and stepchildren's educational attainment in young adulthood. *Journal of Marriage and Family, 82,* 622–638. https://doi.org/10.1111/jomf.12642

Landon, O., Ganong, L., & Sanner, C. (2022). "Stop going in my room": A grounded theory study of conflict among stepsiblings. *Family Relations, 71*(1), 256–278. https://doi.org/10.1111/fare.12595

Letiecq, B.L. (2019). Surfacing family privilege and supremacy in family science: Toward justice for all. *Journal of Family Theory & Review, 11*(3), 398–411. https://doi.org/10.1111/jftr.12338

Limb, G.E., Cousin, L.E., & Larkin, Z.S. (2020). Native American stepfamilies: Children's expectations concerning their residential stepparents' behavior. *Journal of Social Service Research, 46,* 149–159. https://doi.org/10.1080/01488376.2018.1532945

McLanahan, S., & Sandefur, G. (1994). *Growing up with a single parent. What hurts, what helps.* Harvard University Press. https://doi.org/10.2307/j.ctv22tnmnn

Metts, S., Braithwaite, D.O., Schrodt, P., Wang, T.R., Holman, A.J., Nuru, A.K., & Stephenson Abetz, J. (2013). The experience and expression of stepchildren's emotions at critical events in stepfamily life. *Journal of Divorce & Remarriage, 54,* 414–437. https://doi.org/10.1080/10502556.2013.800400

Metts, S., Schrodt, P., & Braithwaite, D.O. (2017). Stepchildren's communicative and emotional journey from divorce to remarriage: Predictors of stepfamily satisfaction. *Journal of Divorce & Remarriage, 58,* 29–43. https://doi.org/10.1080/10502556.2016.1257904

Michaels, M.L. (2006). Factors that contribute to stepfamily success: A qualitative analysis. *Journal of Divorce & Remarriage, 44,* 53–66. https://doi.org/10.1300/J087v44n03_04

Mikucki-Enyart, S.L., & Heisdorf, S.R. (2020). Obstacles and opportunities experienced by adult stepchildren in later life stepfamilies. *Journal of Divorce & Remarriage, 61*(1), 41–61. https://doi.org/10.1080/10502556.2019.1619380

Montgomery, M.J., Anderson, E.A., Hetherington, E.M., & Clingempeel, G.C. (1992). Patterns of courtship for remarriage: Implications for child adjustment and parent-child relationships. *Journal of Marriage and the Family, 54*(August), 686–698. https://doi.org/10.2307/353254

Moore, S., & Cartwright, C. (2005). Adolescents' and young adults' expectations of parental responsibilities in stepfamilies. *Journal of Divorce & Remarriage, 43*(1–2), 109–128. https://doi.org/10.1300/j087v43n01_06

Nice, L.A., Jenks, D.B., Saunders, C.A., & Quintero, L.C. (2021). Regret and repair: Experiences of adult children and parents when a father remarries soon after the death of a spouse. *Omega,* July, 1–15. https://doi.org/10.1177/00302228211036315

Papernow, P.L. (1987). Thickening the "middle ground": Dilemmas and vulnerabilities of remarried couples. *Psychotherapy: Theory, Research, Practice, Training, 24*(3S), 630–639. https://doi.org/10.1037/h0085761

Parent, J., Clifton, J., Forehand, R., Golub, A., Reid, M, & Pichler, E.R. (2014). Parental mindfulness and dyadic relationship quality in low-income cohabiting black stepfamilies: Associations with parenting experienced by adolescents. *Couple and Family Psychology: Research and Practice, 3*(2), 67–82. https://doi.org/10.1037/cfp0000020

Petren, R.E., Lardier, D.T., Jr., Bible, J., Bermea, A., & van Eeden-Moorefield, B. (2019). Parental relationship stability and parent–adult child relationships in stepfamilies: A test of alternative models. *Journal of Family Psychology, 33*(2), 143–153. https://doi.org/10.1037/fam0000481

Pruett, M.K., Williams, T.Y., Insabella, G., & Little, T.D. (2003). Family and legal indicators of child adjustment to divorce among families with young children. *Journal of Family Psychology, 17*(2), 169–180. https://doi.org/10.1037/0893-3200.17.2.169

Pylyser, C., De Mol, J., Loeys, T., & Buysse, A. (2019). Father reflections on doing family in stepfamilies. *Family Relations, 68*, 500–511. https://doi.org/10.1111/fare.12377

Rodgers, K.B., & Rose, H.A. (2002). Risk and resiliency factors among adolescents who experience marital transitions. *Journal of Marriage and Family, 64*, 1024–1037. https://doi.org/10.1111/j.1741-3737.2002.01024.x

Salem, D.A., Zimmerman, M.A., & Notaro, P.C. (1998). Effects of family structure, family process, and father involvement on psychosocial outcomes among African American adolescents. *Family Relations, 47*, 331–341. https://doi.org/10.2307/585264

Sanner, C., & Coleman, M. (2017). (Re)constructing family images: Stepmotherhood before biological motherhood. *Journal of Marriage and Family, 79*(5), 1462–1477. https://doi.org/10.1111/jomf.12428

Schenck, C.E., Braver, S.L., Wolchik, S.A., Saenz, D., Cookston, J.T., & Fabricius, W.V. (2009). Relations between mattering to step-and non-residential fathers and adolescent mental health. *Fathering, 7*, 70. https://doi.org/10.3149/fth.0701.70

Schmeeckle, M. (2007). Gender dynamics in stepfamilies: Adult stepchildren's views. *Journal of Marriage and Family, 69*(1), 174–189. http://dx.doi.org/10.1111/j.1741-3737.2006.00352.x

Schrodt, P. (2021). Disagreement in perceptions of stepfamily communication and functioning: Implications for mental health. *Journal of Social and Personal Relationships, 38*(1), 393–412. https://doi.org/10.1177/0265407520964862

Schwartz, S.J., & Finley, G.E. (2006). Father involvement, nurturant fathering, and young adult psychosocial functioning. *Journal of Family Issues, 27*, 712–731. https://doi.org/10.1177/0192513X05284003

Shapiro, D. (2014). Stepparents and parenting stress: The roles of gender, marital quality, and views about gender roles. *Family Process, 53*(1), 97–108. https://doi.org/10.1111/famp.12062

Shriner, M., Mullis, R.L., & Schlee, B.M. (2009). The usefulness of social capital theory for understanding the academic improvement of young children in stepfamilies at two points in time. *Journal of Divorce & Remarriage, 50*, 445–458. https://doi.org/10.1080/10502550902970553

Struss, M., Pfeiffer, C., Preuss, U., & Felder, W. (2001). Adolescents from divorced families and their perceptions of visitation arrangements and factors influencing parent–child contact. *Journal of Divorce and Remarriage, 35*, 75–89. https://doi.org/10.1300/j087v35n01_04

Sweeney, M.M. (2007). Stepfather families and the emotional wellbeing of adolescents. *Journal of Health and Social Behavior, 48*, 33–49. https://doi.org/10.1177/002214650704800103

Troilo, J., & Coleman, M. (2013). "I don't know how much more I can take": How divorced nonresidential fathers manage barriers to involvement? *Fathering*, *11*(2), 159–178. https://doi.org/10.3149/fth.1102.159

van Houdt, K., Kalmijn, M., & Ivanova, K. (2020). Stepparental support to adult children: The diverging roles of stepmothers and stepfathers. *Journal of Marriage and Family*, *82*, 639–656. https://doi.org/10.1111/jomf.12599

Visher, E.B., & Visher, J.S. (1996). *Therapy with stepfamilies*. Psychology Press.

Ward, K.P., Dennis, C.B., & Limb, G.E. (2018). The impact of stepfamily relationship quality on emerging adult non-medical use of prescription drugs. *The American Journal of Drug and Alcohol Abuse*, *44*(4), 463–471. https://doi.org/10.1080/00952990.2017.1405010

Weaver, S.E., & Coleman, M. (2010). Caught in the middle: Mothers in stepfamilies. *Journal of Social and Personal Relationships*, *27*(3), 305–326. https://doi.org/10.1177/0265407510361729

White, L.K., & Gilbreth, J.G. (2001). When children have two fathers: Effects of relationships with stepfathers and noncustodial fathers on adolescent outcomes. *Journal of Marriage and Family*, *63*(1), 155–167.

Willetts, M.C., & Maroules, N.G. (2004). Does remarriage matter? The well-being of adolescents living with cohabiting versus remarried mothers. *Journal of Divorce & Remarriage*, *41*, 115–133. https://doi.org/10.1300/J087v41n03_06

Zimmerman, M.A., Salem, D.A., & Maton, K.I. (1995). Family structure and psychosocial correlates among urban African American adolescent males. *Child Development*, *66*, 1598–1613. https://doi.org/10.1111/j.1467-8624.1995.tb00954.x

5

Effective Coparenting in Stepfamilies

Coparenting Complexity in Stepfamilies

Diverse histories and complex family structures can make coparenting in stepfamilies a challenging endeavor. To illustrate, let's look at three relatively common stepfamilies. In Stepfamily A, a single mother who has never married weds an individual who has no children. In Stepfamily B, a woman who has children from three prior unions repartners with a man who has two children, one each from two prior relationships. Stepfamily C, somewhere between Stepfamilies A and B in complexity, is started by a mother with two children from a prior marriage that ended in divorce who then remarries a woman who also has two children from a prior marriage that ended in divorce.

Each of these stepfamilies contains different combinations of coparenting subsystems. For example, Stepfamily A has three coparenting systems that slightly overlap but which also operate separately at times (see Figure 5.1). First, there is a biological coparenting dyad on the maternal side of the stepfamily household (i.e., the mom and the dad). Then, there is a parent–stepparent coparenting system engaging in daily childrearing in the stepfamily household. Finally, there is a somewhat larger coparenting system that includes all the adults (i.e., mom, dad, and stepparent), for a total of three coparenting subsystems.

DOI: 10.4324/9781003369073-5

Stepfamily A

Coparenting subsystem
Divorced/separated
Partnered/married

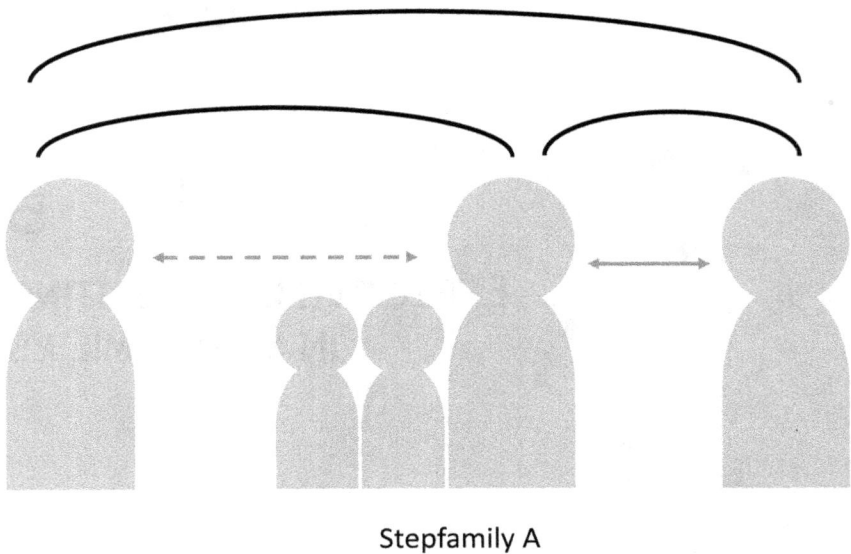

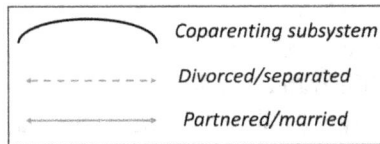

Figure 5.1 Stepfamily with three coparenting subsystems

Stepfamily B, because the mother had children with multiple previous partners, potentially contains 11 separate coparenting subsystems (see Figure 5.2). Three different biological coparenting dyads exist on the mother's side of the stepfamily household, consisting of the mother and each of her children's biological fathers. In addition, there are two biological coparenting dyads on the father's side, comprised of the father and each of his children's mothers. The stepfamily household includes a parent–stepparent coparental subsystem (the sixth coparental subsystem). Finally, there are up to five separate coparenting subsystems that include each child's biological parents plus the stepparent. Any of these three-person coparental subsystems could expand to four adults per subsystem if each child's other parent had also repartnered.

Stepfamily C likely has two biological-parent coparenting subsystems, one for each adult in the stepfamily household (with their former

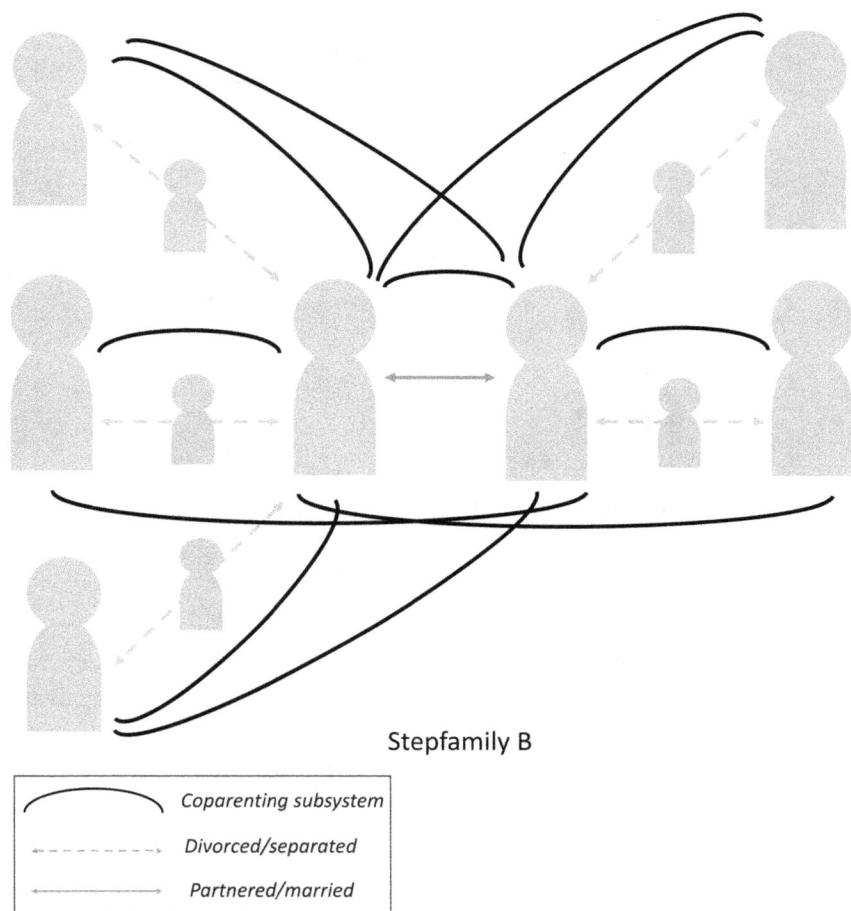

Stepfamily B

⌒	Coparenting subsystem
←------→	Divorced/separated
←——————→	Partnered/married

Figure 5.2 Stepfamily with eleven coparenting subsystems

partners), a parent–stepparent household coparenting unit, and two more multiple-adult coparenting subsystems that contain each child's two biological parents plus a stepparent (see Figure 5.3). Stepfamily C has a total of five coparenting subsystems.

If any of these repartnered couples have a child together, then an additional coparental subsystem is added for each stepfamily, because the stepcouple would be coparents of this mutual child. If the former partners of any of these adults also repartner, then the number of cross-household, multiple-person coparental subsystems in which each stepfamily adult

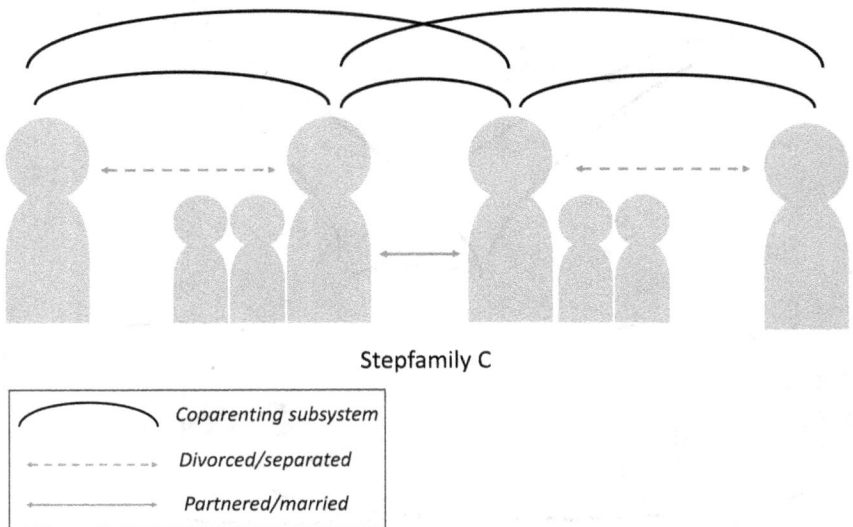

Stepfamily C

⌒	Coparenting subsystem
- - - - - - - →	Divorced/separated
←- - - - - - →	Partnered/married

Figure 5.3 Stepfamily with five coparenting subsystems

may be a member increases further. Confused yet? It is no wonder that new stepfamily members often are surprised and, sometimes, overwhelmed at their family's complexity (Visher & Visher, 1979).

Coparenting Challenges in Stepfamilies

Coparenting after separation and repartnering tends to present challenges. Parents who end their romantic relationship are faced with redefining and reconfiguring their relationships as platonic coparents living apart (Emery, 2012). This renegotiation of roles is made even more challenging because coparents may have different motivations to share childrearing after divorce/separation, they may have unresolved feelings toward each other, or they may be burdened with anger, grief, or sadness about the ending of their romantic bond (Papernow, 2013). Couples separate and divorce for reasons that are important to the partner(s) initiating the split (e.g., broken promises, unfulfilled dreams, physical or psychological abuse, infidelity), and these reasons often make it difficult for couples to continue to coparent productively or at all (Emery, 2012).

Stepcouples, in contrast, are confronted with learning how to coparent together in vastly different circumstances. First, parents and children have ongoing relationships and share a family culture in which the stepparent is an outsider. This dynamic may present challenges for couples in stepfamilies, particularly if parent–child relationships became extremely close after the divorce/dissolution. Stepparents may feel like a "third wheel" to the parent–child dyad. Second, recoupled parents may feel guilty about dividing time and attention between their children and their new partner, placing them in uncomfortable loyalty binds. Feeling caught between children and new partners may make stepcouple coparenting more complicated for both parents and stepparents. Third, stepcouples' coparenting relationships are forming at the same time as stepparents, stepchildren, and other stepfamily members are trying to build new relationships with each other, so there are many relationship changes occurring as parent–stepparent coparenting dyads are being created. In addition, parents and their exes often are in ongoing coparental subsystems when stepparents and parents are trying to work out stepfamily household roles and rules about childrearing. Stepcouple coparents are faced with figuring out how they will function as coparents in the stepfamily household alongside these existing coparental subsystems. Finally, in parents' coparenting subsystems, both adults may have legal rights and responsibilities to make childrearing decisions and to participate in children's care, while in parent–stepparent coparenting subsystems, stepparents have no rights and few legal responsibilities regarding stepchildren, even when stepchildren live with them most of the time. Over time, repartnered parents may want to create a multi-household subsystem that includes both parents and their new partners. These larger coparenting units require additional renegotiations about roles, boundaries, and decision-making (Ganong & Coleman, 2017).

Despite the complexity and challenges presented by adding new family members, new roles, and new responsibilities, coparenting in stepfamilies is essential. Effective childrearing has been shown to foster children's and adults' well-being and to benefit stepfamily relationships (Ganong & Coleman, 2017). In stepfamilies, as in other family forms, effective childrearing is not accomplished by individual parents or stepparents; instead, effective childrearing involves dyads, triads, and even larger groups working together as coparenting teams. As the old African proverb goes, *it takes a village* to raise a child well.

In this chapter, we focus on three types of coparental units: (a) the *ex-couple* (biological or adoptive parents coparenting across separate stepfamily households), (b) the *stepcouple* (parent–stepparent coparenting dyads in stepfamily households), and (c) *cross-residential coparenting teams* involving the ex-couple and one or two stepparents, depending on how many parents have repartnered. In real life, these three types of coparenting units are not independent of each other. That is, what happens in one subsystem affects the others. For example, consider a child whose parent and stepparent in one household implement a new bedtime or curfew. This likely will prompt discussions and negotiations about bedtime or curfew policies in the other household as well. Or consider a parent who loses a job or is evicted from their apartment; coparents in the other household may need to renegotiate their schedules or children's custodial arrangements to accommodate these changes. Big or small, the ebbs and flows of life often require coparents to work together, and especially in structurally complex families – where coparents may reside in multiple households and have complex histories while simultaneously working to establish new coparenting relationships with their current partners – these negotiations can be complicated.

Coparenting Among Ex-Couples in Stepfamilies

In this book we use the term *ex-couples* to refer to biological or adoptive coparents. It should be noted that there is a large body of research on coparenting after separation and divorce, with much of this research focusing on coparenting couples during the divorce process and soon after. We included these studies in our review if a substantive proportion of the sample had remarried or repartnered. Of course, we also reviewed investigations of coparents in which the entire sample were coparenting after stepfamily formation.

Outcomes of Effective Ex-Couple Coparenting in Stepfamilies

Researchers have consistently linked ex-couple coparenting practices to parent and child outcomes. Considerable prior research has indicated that interparental conflict is one of the strongest predictors of how well children adjust to the separation or divorce of their parents (Amato, 2010; Emery, 2012). Although conflict theorists assert that disagreements are inevitable in any close relationship (White et al., 2018), conflict may be especially germane for romantic partners who are no longer together. Separated and divorced couples may be prone to angry disputes, hostile interactions, and hurt feelings lingering from the break-up of the marriage or romantic partnership (Emery, 2012). Even when couples agree to remain congenial for the sake of their children, sometimes this agreement is hard to keep when one of them remarries or commits to a new romantic partner (Ganong & Coleman, 2017).

Positive coparenting relationships benefit both parents, but they especially benefit nonresidential fathers, because maintaining amicable ties with an ex is linked to fathers' having more contact and involvement in their children's lives (Carlson et al., 2008; Golish, 2003; Larouche et al., 2023; Madden-Derditch & Leonard, 2000; McClain & DeMaris, 2013; Rettig et al., 1999; Sobolewski & King, 2005; Taanila et al., 2002). More contact and greater engagement in childrearing in turn allows fathers to engage in more responsive parenting practices (Larouche et al., 2023) and establish closer relationships with their nonresidential children (Ahrons, 2007; Ahrons & Miller, 1993; Carlson et al., 2008; Forehand et al., 2016; Hornstra et al., 2020; Taanila et al., 2002). Coparents themselves benefit from cooperating with each other. Parents who are more flexible with children's schedules, while still maintaining some consistency in scheduling, are happier with their custody arrangements (Jamison et al., 2014), and nonresidential fathers who cooperatively discuss childrearing decisions with their coparents report less conflict and greater family and life satisfaction (Rettig et al., 1999).

Coparents' ability to get along with each other also has long-term benefits for children's well-being (Ahrons, 2007; Lamela et al., 2016). Constructive contact between residential and non-residential parents in stepfamilies is associated with positive emotions for children in shared physical custody as they go back and forth between parental households (Steinbach, 2023; Struss et al., 2001). It also is associated with better overall adjustment of children (Beckmeyer et al., 2020; Bronstein et al., 1994; Ferraro et al., 2016; Lamela et al., 2016; Steinbach, 2023), fewer behavioral problems in school (Bronstein et al., 1994; Taanila et al., 2002), and more prosocial behaviors (Beckmeyer et al., 2020). Additionally, parental agreement on child-rearing issues and positive interactions between coparents are linked to effective problem-solving among parents raising preadolescent sons (Vuchinich et al., 1993) and greater fathers' involvement in childrearing (Madden-Derditch & Leonard, 2000). Parents who describe their coparenting relationships as cooperative report greater cohesion and expressiveness in their relationships, and have fewer conflicts (Giles-Sims, 1987).

Clearly, positive coparental relationships have important benefits. Many *what works* strategies focus on how ex-couples avoid or reduce interparental conflicts (Jamison et al., 2014; Kelly & Ganong, 2011; Miller, 2009a, 2009b; Russell et al., 2021; Schrodt et al., 2006), while other strategies focus on what stepcouples can do to facilitate positive coparenting and promote better outcomes in children (Bermea et al., 2020; Ferraro et al., 2016; Russell et al., 2012; Schrodt & Afifi, 2007).

What Works for Ex-Couple Coparenting in Stepfamilies

Synthesizing research findings on *what works* for divorced/separated coparents in stepfamilies, we draw two major conclusions. First, high-functioning ex-couple coparents *focus mainly on what is best for the child* rather than on their own needs, the needs of the coparent, or on their past or current problems and conflicts (Braithwaite et al., 2008; Ferraro et al., 2016; Golish, 2003; Jamison et al., 2014; Kelly & Ganong, 2011; Schrodt et al., 2006). Making the children the center of their ongoing relationship and focusing their interactions on meeting the children's needs and facilitating children's development and well-being distinguishes ex-couples that work effectively as coparents from those that struggle. Second, effective ex-partner coparents communicate clearly and directly *to each other* and keep children out of the middle of their issues and conflicts (Ahrons, 2007; Braithwaite et al., 2008; Dunn et al., 2005; Ganong et al., 2012; Kang & Ganong, 2020; Russell et al., 2021; Schrodt & Afifi, 2007). This is accomplished in part by purposefully not using children as messengers or mediators between coparents and not inappropriately disclosing private information to children, or information that children are developmentally too young to hear (e.g., discussing legal or child support issues, badmouthing the other parent, or treating children as peers or confidants; Afifi, 2003; Schrodt & Afifi, 2007). Not allowing children to witness conflicts between coparents also helps keep them from feeling caught between the parents and becoming involved in parents' issues and disputes (Bermea et al., 2020; Dunn et al., 2005).

Keeping children out of the middle also means that parents try their best to convey clear messages to their coparents about the children (Carlson et al., 2008; Russell et al., 2021), while recognizing that nobody communicates clearly all the time. Below, we review specific takeaways from the findings of studies in which researchers reported what effective ex-couples think, feel, and do when childrearing that promoted positive coparenting outcomes in stepfamilies. Note that these findings include both intrapersonal (i.e., thoughts, feelings, beliefs, actions taken by only one parent) and interpersonal (i.e., interactions between parents) dynamics.

Clarifying Expectations about Roles, Rules, and Boundaries

The creation of workable ex-couple coparenting relationships in step-families is facilitated by having clear expectations for coparental roles and behaviors after a new stepparent enters the family (Carlson et al., 2008; Madden-Derditch et al., 1999; Michaels, 2006). Even ex-couples who have coparented well together prior to one or both repartnering may need to re-examine their expectations about coparenting when a remarriage or repartnering occurs. Clarifying expectations is an ongoing task – continual and steady communications between exes help them clarify roles, rules, and boundaries as children age and family circumstances change (Goldberg & Allen, 2013; Golish, 2003; Jamison et al., 2014). For example, discussions about possible changes in physical custody arrangements may occur when adolescents become more involved in school and extracurricular activities and they want to spend more time with their friends (Goldberg & Allen, 2013). Effective coparents also share with each other their goals for their children and clearly articulate their childrearing values and beliefs (Carlson et al., 2008; Jamison et al., 2014).

Once separated, and often prior to finding a new partner, coparents are faced with decisions about how much to communicate about their personal lives to each other (Miller, 2009a) and to their children (Miller, 2009b). Dating is an activity that triggers some of this decision-making, as parents may be concerned about not embarrassing their former partners by sharing too much information about their dates and dating, or by sharing information too soon (Miller, 2009a). Parents manage this by communicating little information about dating activities until they are sure a dating partner has long-term potential, only telling the coparent what he or she might need to know to keep the children safe and secure (Miller, 2009a). For example, a father in one study recalled limiting information about dating so that his coparent would not think he was trying to replace her:

> I didn't want to rub anything in her face and make her think that I had already found someone to take her place. I was very conscious of her feelings. So, she would ask me what I did last weekend, and I would say I went out.
>
> (Miller, 2009a, p. 167)

In this study, once parents decided to disclose to coparents about dating, amiable coparents had long, in-depth conversations with the coparent. Effective coparents made privacy rules about what to disclose to children about their new dating partners, including how much information would be shared and when (Miller, 2009b). Individually, parents weighed the potential costs and benefits of sharing specific content with children (e.g., about dating partners, about financial problems), with the primary goals of keeping children out of the middle of coparental issues and maintaining positive relationships with coparents (Miller, 2009b). These personal privacy rules often were shared with former partners, sometimes with the goal of agreeing on a set of rules for both coparents. When coparents respected these privacy rules, relationships were more cordial. If the rules were violated, coparents communicated ways to address these rule violations and their consequences (Miller, 2009b).

Reframing Situations

Cognitive reframing involves changing how a situation, behavior, person, or event is perceived, with the goal of altering feelings and behaviors associated with the perceived phenomenon. Replacing an old, negative perspective with a new, positive one (i.e., a positive reframe) is thought to change thoughts, feelings, and behaviors in more productive ways. Some individuals receive guidance from professionals to learn how to reframe, but reframing is also a cognitive technique that many individuals develop on their own without professional assistance, and some coparents reframe without being aware they are doing so (Jamison et al., 2014).

In coparenting, reframing situations to focus on the children and their well-being rather than on each other (e.g., "She's a good mom, and that's what matters most") is an effective way in which exes reduce conflicts and make coparenting relationships more functional (Jamison et al., 2014; Schrodt et al., 2006; Troilo & Coleman, 2013). Other reframing strategies that have been found to work include thinking about each other in new ways that make it easier to interact without rancor. For example, reframing thoughts about "my horrible ex" to thinking of the other coparent as a friend, business partner, or simply as their child's "other parent" can help reduce anger towards the coparent (Jamison et al., 2014; Troilo & Coleman, 2013). Such role reframing is related to lower levels of coparental conflict and more effective childrearing relationships (Madden-Derditch et al., 1999). One mother noted that her ex-spouse was "a good father," which she contrasted to his failures as a husband, concluding that "I don't really think he is a bad guy," a reframing which freed her to work with him for the sake of the children (Jamison et al., 2014, p. 416).

Reframing also can be a helpful strategy for nonresidential parents who miss spending more time with their children. For example, in one study, nonresidential fathers who were able to reframe concerns about *having limited time to spend with their children* to thinking about their situations as *providing opportunities to spend higher quality time with their children, where they could give their children their undivided attention* had more frequent contact with their nonresidential children than did fathers who did not do such reframing (Troilo & Coleman, 2013).

Managing Negative Emotions

Knowing how, when, and to whom to express negative emotions is another key to developing and maintaining workable coparenting relationships (Afifi, 2003; Jamison et al., 2014; Troilo & Coleman, 2013). Coparenting relationships are better, and children's well-being is better, when negative feelings between coparents are not expressed to children. For instance, reframing negative emotions into positive ones or stopping from lashing back at hurtful exchanges with an ex-spouse are productive emotion regulation strategies (Jamison et al., 2014; Troilo & Coleman, 2013). Not expressing negative feelings and judgments about the coparent to children – in other words, not *badmouthing* the other parent to the child – also is critical (Schrodt & Afifi, 2007). Children consistently say that feeling caught in the middle of their parents' conflict is the most stressful part of their family dynamic (Braithwaite et al., 2008). This is not to say that parents should bottle up their negative emotions indefinitely – chronic suppression of negative feelings can harm personal well-being and relationships (Gross, 1998) – but it is vital that coparents figure out safe and appropriate ways of expressing their negative feelings, such as venting to therapists and friends, rather than unloading negative feelings onto children. Parents' negative disclosures are associated with children's feelings of being caught between their parents, and children who feel caught report lower family satisfaction and poorer mental health (Schrodt & Afifi, 2007). The impossibility of a parent knowing how much information to disclose to children is the right amount, beyond which there are harmful intrapersonal and interpersonal costs, suggests that parents generally should refrain from communicating negative information about their child's other parent to the child.

Being Cordial and Business-Like

A longitudinal study of families after divorce found that ex-couples who maintained friendships or close ties after separating had fewer disagreements overall than other ex-couples, and their children benefited more than children whose parents were not close (Ahrons, 2007). Maintaining close emotional bonds is not feasible for many couples after separation, however, and even if relationships are not *close* per se (as most relationships between exes likely are not), cordial relationships are equally beneficial. Interacting with ex-partners in a cordial, business-like manner reduces the number of disagreements and helps both children (Afifi, 2003; Ahrons, 2007; Ferraro et al., 2016; Golish, 2003; Schrodt et al., 2006) and adults (Bermea et al., 2020; Gonzalez & Barnett, 2014) in stepfamilies. Being cordial was defined by researchers as being polite and courteous when interacting (Afifi, 2003; Ferraro et al., 2016; Golish, 2003). As one father stated, "I am not overtly rude to her, and she is not overtly rude to me, especially in front of the kids" (Bermea et al., 2020, p. 170). Being business-like meant focusing their communications on childrearing and children's issues (Ahrons, 2007; Beckmeyer et al., 2020; Schrodt et al., 2006). Ex-couple coparents are in the "business" of rearing their mutual children, so other topics, such as past relationship transgressions, are not useful for successfully conducting coparenting business. These business-like parents tended to have shorter conversations because they limited themselves to an immediate agenda, such as discussing a child's field trip at school.

Cordial exes also successfully used technological tools (e.g., texts, emails, Dropbox, Google calendar) to create more "business-like" interactions when relationships are not emotionally positive (Ganong et al., 2011; Russell et al., 2021; Schrodt et al., 2006). Technology allows coparents to flexibly communicate with each other and experiment with different communication platforms (Ganong et al., 2012; Jamison et al., 2014; Miller, 2009a; Russell et al., 2021). For example, when in-person interactions often led to angry confrontations and unproductive decision-making, effective coparents used email or texts to clearly and calmly think about what they wanted to say, edit what they communicated, choose when to send messages, and have a written record of their agreements (Ganong et al., 2012; Russell et al., 2021). Tech tools that allow parents to reflect and edit before sending may enhance the quality of coparental relationships and facilitate more effective childrearing (Russell et al., 2021). It should be noted that ineffective coparents also used technology to communicate, but they used it to punish, fight, and disrupt the other parent's plans, so it is not technology per se that helps coparents, but how it is employed (Ganong et al., 2012). The widespread use of technological devices to communicate suggests that effective coparents use multiple forms of technology to stay in touch as they communicate about their children (Russell et al., 2021).

Being Flexible

Flexibility is a hallmark of resilience in coparenting (Jamison et al., 2014), and it applies to many aspects of childrearing. For example, negotiating schedules is an ongoing challenge for coparents, and ex-couples who were "flexible with the schedule yet maintained some consistency were happier with their custody arrangements and felt better about their coparenting relationships" (Jamison et al., 2014, p. 418). Although there is evidence that effective coparents generally abide by agreed-upon schedules for children's activities, including time spent in each parent's household, which is critical to children (Bermea et al., 2020; Carlson et al., 2008; Goldberg & Allen, 2013), being willing to alter schedules to help the coparent with unexpected childcare problems is an example of how being flexible benefits coparental bonds and children's well-being (Carlson et al., 2008). This suggests that even though regular schedules may help coparents and children know what to expect (Goldberg & Allen, 2013), building flexibility into parenting plans may be helpful for some.

In one study, some parents decided to consider their custody agreements as a binding legal contract that they would follow closely as a way to limit their coparental conflicts and disagreements (Schrodt et al., 2006). These coparents saw the divorce decree as clearly articulating their rights and responsibilities, and they followed the contract to avoid arguing with ex-partners. However, other coparents agreed that the language of the legal contract was too restrictive and inflexible, and so they instead considered the legal contract as a set of broad guidelines to help them negotiate solutions that worked for their family. They employed principles of fairness and the best interests of their children in their negotiations and discussions (Schrodt et al., 2006).

Being willing to negotiate flexibly and compromise with coparents includes learning when to accommodate the coparent and when to be assertive on behalf of children (Afifi, 2003; Ahrons, 2007; Golish, 2003). Successful coparents pick their battles carefully, sometimes conceding on an issue if they are less invested in the decision than the ex-partner or if they can be more flexible than the coparent on a particular issue (e.g., scheduling a child's pick up from one household; Jamison et al., 2014). For example, a coparent who does not care which musical instrument the child learns to play advances family relationships by conceding this decision to the coparent who fervently wants the child to play the clarinet. Coparenting may be seen as the responsibility of making many decisions about childrearing, ranging from minor judgments about daily behaviors (e.g., table manners) to life-changing decisions (e.g., health care; Kelly & Ganong, 2011). Coparents who are selective in choosing when to disagree about childrearing also exhibit greater cooperation and have fewer conflicts with each other (Kelly & Ganong, 2011). There is some evidence that ex-couples who are effective coparents get better over time at knowing when and how to engage with each other when feelings are high (Jamison et al., 2014). Also, as children get older and post-separation relationships change, flexibility in how coparenting roles are defined and enacted benefits both parents and children (Goldberg & Allen, 2013). For example, as children reach adolescence, they often want to spend more time with friends than with parents, and flexible coparents work at finding ways of meeting adolescents' and parents' needs.

Box 5.1 *What works* **for ex-couple coparenting**

- Focus on what is best for children rather than on past romantic transgressions.
- Communicate directly to the other coparent instead of using children as messengers.
- Keep children out of the middle of coparenting disagreements.
- Clearly define expectations about roles, rules, and coparenting boundaries.
- Clarify coparenting expectations as children age and family circumstances change.
- Reframe situations in ways that make it easier to interact without rancor.
- Think of your coparent not as "my ex" but as "my child's other parent."
- Keep interactions cordial and business-like.
- Keep communications focused on childrearing and children's issues.
- Use technology to communicate if in-person interactions lead to conflict.
- Use technology to help improve communication clarity and frequency.
- Know how, when, and to whom to express negative emotions.
- Vent to third-party adults rather than badmouthing your coparent to your child.
- Choose your battles wisely; be willing to compromise and negotiate with coparents.
- Maintain consistency with the schedule but also be willing to be flexible.
- If the legal divorce decree works for everyone, follow it to avoid conflicts, but if the legal contract is too restrictive for both households, think of it as a guideline to use as you negotiate changes with coparents.

Stepcouple Coparenting

Some of the dynamics of effective stepcouple coparenting resemble those of effective ex-couple coparenting (e.g., cooperation between coparenting adults, reframing of behaviors), but there also are differences, most notably in assigning primary parental responsibilities to biological parents. Unlike ex-couple coparents who are both the biological and/or legal parents of the children with institutionalized rights and responsibilities, stepparents have few normative guidelines to follow and little or no legal obligations to their stepchildren. Instead, stepparents are relative newcomers to the coparenting role, so expectations for their roles are less clear and childrearing responsibilities for stepparents initially are not well-defined (Ganong & Coleman, 2017). Parents typically establish their coparenting roles with spouses/partners as their children grow from infancy, whereas stepparents and their new partners are faced with figuring out stepparents' coparenting roles when stepchildren vary in age when the relationships begin. Put another way, parental coparenting subsystems have time to evolve as children age, whereas stepcouple coparenting subsystems are created when children may be old enough to have their own ideas about how they want to be coparented. Stepparents learn to be coparents in the presence of their stepchildren, who are generally extremely interested observers in the stepparents' learning processes. Nonresidential parents also may be engaged "third parties" to stepcouple coparenting who are invested in observing how stepparents coparent their children.

What Works for Stepcouple Coparenting in Stepfamilies

Clarifying Expectations

Rarely do two people on a first date discuss their parenting philosophies. If one or both of those people have children, rarely do they assess the extent to which they are on the same page about the roles and responsibilities a stepparent should fulfill. Indeed, studies show that the majority of repartnered couples do not explicitly discuss expectations regarding parenting and stepparenting roles prior to repartnering, and to their detriment (Cartwright, 2010; Ganong & Coleman, 2017). When stepcouples do openly discuss and agree on childrearing expectations, researchers find they enjoy closer stepfamily relationships and a greater sense of well-being for children and adults (Cartwright, 2010).

Considering the ambiguity of stepparenting roles and the complexity of stepfamily coparenting, it is no surprise that failing to discuss these matters can have negative consequences. Stepfamily formation involves either the merging of two pre-established systems of roles and responsibilities that were developed in family households formed before remarriage or repartnering, or stepfamilies incorporating a new stepparent into an ongoing family system. Whether stepfamilies are merging groups or incorporating individual stepparents, clarifying expectations about household coparents' roles and responsibilities is vital to stepfamily functioning. Researchers find that stepcouples promote positive outcomes by: (a) negotiating and agreeing on rules for the children and for the household in general (Felker et al., 2002; Jensen & Shafer, 2013; Metts et al., 2013; Quick et al., 1995; Skopin et al., 1993), (b) clarifying and agreeing on stepparents' roles (Blyaert et al., 2016; Bray et al., 1994; Goldberg & Allen, 2013; Saint-Jacques, 1995), and (c) showing children that the parent and stepparent are in agreement with each other on these issues (Jensen & Shafer, 2013; Metts et al., 2013; Schrodt & Braithwaite, 2011; Skopin et al., 1993; Saint-Jacques, 1995). For example, stepchildren are closer to their stepfathers when they perceive that mothers and stepfathers agree on parenting and argue infrequently (Jensen & Shafer, 2013). Similarly, the degree of consensus among mothers and stepfathers about childrearing is positively related to the quality of the stepfather–stepchild relationship, from the perspectives of both stepfathers and adolescent stepchildren (Skopin et al., 1993). Clearly, stepcouple consensus on childrearing and coparenting yields positive outcomes for stepfamily members and relationships.

Coparental Involvement in Childrearing

Beyond agreeing on childrearing roles and responsibilities, the degree to which coparents are actively involved in their (step)children's lives also has been found to matter for child well-being (Favez et al., 2019; Yeung et al., 2002). For example, when parents and stepparents report knowing where their children are, knowing who they are with, helping them with their homework, attending their school events, and talking to their children's teachers, then their children are more likely to feel invested in school, perform better at school, and engage more positively with their friends (Beckmeyer & Russell, 2018).

Moreover, when both members of the stepcouple: (a) express solidarity and support of each other in their parenting efforts, (b) minimize criticism and undermining coparents' childrearing efforts, and (c) actively interact with children, both partners feel more satisfied in their romantic relationship (Schrodt & Braithwaite, 2011). When partners feel satisfied in their romantic relationships, they report higher quality coparenting within the parent–stepparent dyad (Golish, 2003; Hetherington, 1993; Kelley, 1992), as do their children (Parent et al., 2014).

Parents can help stepparents become more involved in childrearing. For one, when parents are more involved in childrearing, then stepparents also are more involved, so parents can facilitate stepparent involvement simply by being more involved themselves (van Houdt et al., 2020). Second, when parents engage in fewer restrictive gatekeeping behaviors (e.g., criticizing stepparents' parenting abilities, saying sarcastic comments while stepparents are interacting with stepchildren) then stepparents tend to be more involved with stepchildren and engage in more efforts to bond with them (Ganong et al., 2020).

Just like parents can help stepparents become more involved, stepparents also can help their partners be more productive as coparents. For example, childrearing support from stepmothers helped fathers be more engaged in childrearing, and support from stepmothers moderated the negative effects of daily hassles, stress, and role overload on fathers' warmth and engagement with children (DeGarmo et al., 2008). Cohabiting stepfathers whose partners think of them as coparents are more supportive of mothers and more positively involved in childrearing tasks than non-coparenting men (Forehand et al., 2014, 2015, 2016).

Parents as Primary Disciplinarians

Just as new stepcouples rarely discuss coparenting expectations, they also rarely discuss expectations about parental authority, even though this is a key issue in stepfamily adjustment. Studies consistently show that stepchildren prefer parents as the primary disciplinarians (Moore & Cartwright, 2005). Stepchildren are better adjusted (Bray, 1988;

Hetherington, 1993) and stepfamilies are more successful (Bray, 1988; Golish, 2003; Hetherington et al., 1992; Hetherington, 1993; Kelley, 1992; Schrodt & Braithwaite, 2011) when the parent plays the primary disciplinarian role and the stepparent is less active in disciplining stepchildren, a style of parent–stepparent coparenting that Repond and colleagues (2019) called *complementary coparenting*. When parents take the lead, particularly in setting rules and disciplining children, then stepparents can benefit by learning from observing what the parents' expectations for children have been; if the stepparent is inexperienced with children of that age, then they also benefit from gaining first-hand knowledge about children's development by observing the children's behaviors without engaging as a disciplinarian (Saint-Jacques, 1995). These experiences also offer opportunities for stepparents to learn more about themselves as they work to support parents' childrearing (McDougal & George, 2016).

Communicating Effectively with Coparents and Stepchildren

In addition to talking to each other about childrearing, stepcouple coparents also must communicate with their step/children. A study of stepchildren's perceptions of parent–stepparent–stepchild triads found that multiple patterns of communication work for stepfamily adjustment (Baxter et al., 2006). The most satisfying and least frequent pattern, described by many stepfamily members as their ideal, is the *clear triad* – a model of interaction in which all stepfamily members feel comfortable discussing even difficult subjects with each other, and these discussions are characterized by clear communication. Although the authors did not explore how these communication dynamics are achieved, stepparents in clear triads listen and are open to talking about any subject, and parents encourage children to deal directly with the stepparent rather than acting as a mediator of stepparent–stepchild conflict (Baxter et al., 2006; Weaver & Coleman, 2010). Some of the few stepfamilies who manage this pattern do so through considerable effort – it does not just happen.

Other communication patterns seen by stepchildren as effective and functional situationally (i.e., not used all the time) are *linked triads*, in which the stepchild speaks to the parent about a problem with the stepparent and the parent then discusses this with the stepparent to find a solution, and the *outsider triad*, where the stepparent is like an acquaintance to the stepchild and most meaningful communication occurs between the parent and child, with the stepparent as an outsider to problem-solving in the household (Baxter et al., 2006). In *linked triads*, parents are intermediaries or mediators between their spouse and their children. As intermediaries, parents interpret children's behaviors and intentions to stepparents (and sometimes the converse), because children feel more comfortable disclosing to parents and because they trust the parent to act in their best interests. Sometimes, parents serve as advocates and protectors of their children, usually when the stepparent and stepchild have distant or adversarial relationships. In this advocate role, parents are asked to address issues of fairness or other complaints against the stepparent. In the *outsider triad*, children feel close to the parent, but consider the stepparent to be unimportant. This is an extreme version of biological parent as primary and stepparent as secondary coparent – in essence, the parent continues doing what he or she had done prior to remarriage or repartnering and the stepparent does little, if any, coparenting. It is important to emphasize that these patterns of communication are from the stepchildren's perspectives. It is also important to note that linked triads and outsider triads are illustrations of parent–child coalitions in triangles with stepparents, which Bowenian family systems theory would caution against if interactions become rigid and unchanging (Hoffman & Conway, 1981).

Minimal parent–stepparent communication about child-related issues, which allows parents and children to solve problems, works situationally from some stepchildren's perspectives (Baxter et al., 2006). However, other studies find that stepchildren benefit from communication systems that resemble *complete triads*. For instance, stepchildren describe that being open and honest with stepparents strengthens the relationship and improves communication between them (Afifi, 2003), as opposed to asking biological parents to mediate. As with coparenting between biological parents, parent–stepparent dyads should also refrain from talking negatively or revealing inappropriate information about the nonresidential parent or the nonresidential parent's partner (i.e., the child's nonresidential stepparent). Parent–stepparent coparenting dyads who minimized inappropriate disclosures made explicit rules to not talk badly about the other parent and to not reveal inappropriate information to children (Afifi, 2003).

In another study of stepfamily household triads and communication dynamics, Schrodt (2021) found that conflicts, participation in family activities and celebrations, and flexibly trying new ways of solving problems were positively related to the mental health of parents, stepparents, and stepchildren. In other words, households with less conflict, greater involvement in rituals and activities, and more flexibility benefited individual family members self-reported mental health and well-being (Schrodt, 2021).

Adopting Effective Parenting Styles

Several researchers have used Baumrind's (1991) parenting style framework to investigate how parenting styles of coparents predicted stepchild outcomes. This typological model of parenting asserts that parenting consists of two behavioral components, warmth (e.g., love, care, concern) and control (e.g., authority, discipline, rule-setting), and that any given parent may be assessed as having a parenting style that is the intersection of these components (Baumrind, 1991). Before discussing findings from these studies, we caution that Baumrind's framework heavily favors a White, Western, middle-class way of thinking about parenting and parenthood. How parents express warmth (i.e., concern, caring) has found to vary across racialized and cultural groups – for instance, Black parents protecting their children from the omnipresent dangers of White supremacy may emphasize obedience over patience and negotiation. White youth may equate "strictness" with parental anger and hostility, whereas Asian youth may equate strictness with parental concern for their children's success and well-being. In sum, because Baumrind's operationalization of warmth largely reflects White Western parenting, and because the samples in the studies below are primarily White, these findings should be interpreted in the context of White stepfamilies.

Within these studies, findings suggested that, regardless of stepfamily structures and genders of stepchildren (Crosbie-Burnett & Giles-Sims, 1994), stepchildren's adjustment and well-being were better when stepparents and parents engage in high warmth parenting, coupled with either low control parenting (i.e., a permissive parenting style; Barber

& Lyons, 1994; Crosbie-Burnett & Giles-Sims, 1994) or high control parenting (i.e., an authoritative parenting style; Bray, 1999; Fine & Kurdek, 1992; Haberstroh et al., 1998; Hetherington, 1987). Expressing care and concern for step/children, low coerciveness, high monitoring and supervision, firm but responsive control, and demands and expectations for mature, responsible behaviors from children were characteristics of childrearing that promoted positive child outcomes (Hetherington, 1993). Parenting with these characteristics was related to better stepchild psychological adjustment (Nicholson et al., 2002; Shucksmith et al., 1995), fewer behavioral problems, greater social competence, and better stepfamily relationships (Bray, 1988; Crosbie-Burnett & Giles-Sims, 1994; Fine & Kurdek, 1992; Golish, 2000; Haberstroh et al., 1998; Hetherington, 1993; Shucksmith et al., 1995).

Parenting by stepparents characterized by high warmth and low control also appears to be related to better stepchild adjustment (Crosbie-Burnett & Giles-Sims, 1994) and closer step-relationships (Golish, 2000), particularly when stepchildren are younger (Hetherington et al., 1992). High-warmth and low-control stepparenting also is related to greater satisfaction with stepparenting, at least for stepfathers (Fine et al., 1997). Evidence suggests that high warmth and low control should be the initial approach by stepparents. Then, after a closer emotional bond has been made, the stepparent might move into authoritative parenting with the stepchild where levels of control (e.g., monitoring, supervision, clear expectations for responsible behavior) are higher. The best strategy for preadolescent stepchildren is for new stepparents to work at establishing relationships with them and supporting parents in their childrearing, which can be followed by more active supervision and monitoring by stepparents over time (Hetherington et al., 1992).

Developing Cohesive Stepfamily Dynamics

One major task when merging two families is beginning to *feel* like a family. Studies show that facilitating a cohesive stepfamily dynamic that includes all members is beneficial to stepchildren's well-being. Stepcouples are the architects of these dynamics, which they create via: (a) engaging in inclusive activities with step/children, (b) developing a shared family identity, and (c) modifying expectations for the stepfamily.

Engaging in Inclusive Activities with Step/children

Several researchers have focused on what stepparents and parents do to help children feel included as part of the stepfamily (Golish, 2003), a phenomenon variously labeled as belonging (King et al., 2015), mattering (Schenck et al., 2009), and claiming step-kin as family (Ganong et al., 2018; Marsiglio, 2004). Communicating to stepfamily members a sense of inclusion and belonging is a characteristic that distinguishes strong stepfamilies from stepfamilies functioning less well (Golish, 2003). Researchers framed these endeavors in various ways – creating stepfamily unity (Banker & Gaertner, 1998; Felker et al., 2002; Golish, 2003; Schmeekle et al., 2006), feeling the stepfamily was "like a family" (Baxter et al., 1999; Braithwaite et al., 1998, 2001; Hutchinson et al., 2007; Nura & Wang, 2014), and co-constructing a family identity (Golish, 2003; Pill, 1990).

Inclusive activities help stepchildren feel central to the stepfamily. Such activities may happen only once, such as involving stepchildren in the parent's wedding to the stepparent (Baxter et al., 1999; Ganong et al., 1999), or they may occur periodically, such as involving stepchildren in the stepparents' extended family gatherings, going on family vacations, or having family game nights (Ganong et al., 1999; Braithwaite et al., 2001; Mikucki-Enyart & Heisdorf, 2020). Inclusive activities either embrace the entire household or contain multiple stepfamily members (Baxter et al., 1999; Ganong et al., 1999; Golish, 2003; Hutchinson et al., 2007; Metts et al., 2013; Nura & Wang, 2014). Activities are more effective at building a sense of belonging in stepchildren when they become part of the stepfamily's regular routines (Beckmeyer et al., 2020; Braithwaite et al., 2001; Golish, 2003; Greeff & Du Toit, 2009; Hutchinson et al., 2007; Schrodt, 2016). Stepchildren who perceive that stepparents and parents try to treat all children fairly, and who listen respectfully to children, feel that their stepfamilies are more harmonious and unified (Banker & Gaertner, 1998).

Developing a Shared Family Identity

Shared identities are developed through: (a) creating family rituals, (b) establishing new routines, and (c) problem-solving as a group. Studies have found that establishing shared stepfamily rituals to celebrate holidays, birthdays, and other special occasions are common ways in which family solidarity and connections are enhanced (Baxter et al., 1999; Braithwaite et al., 1998, 2018; Felker et al., 2002; Golish, 2003; Hutchinson et al., 2007; Metts et al., 2013; Mikucki-Enyart & Heisdorf, 2020; Pill, 1990). Family rituals help families create a shared sense of family, in part by making positive memories (Baxter et al., 1999; Braithwaite et al., 1998, 2018; Felker et al., 2002; Golish, 2003; Hutchinson et al., 2007; Metts et al., 2013; Pill, 1990).

Successful rituals often celebrate both the old and the new families. Rather than asking stepfamily members to abandon older rituals, previous ways of celebrating are retained, sometimes with added elements that allow new step-kin to be included (Braithwaite et al., 1998; Golish, 2003). Rituals are more effective at bringing stepfamily members together and making stepchildren feel included when they are accepted by everyone, which is made more likely if all family members have input into creating or enacting the celebrations (Braithwaite et al., 1998). Effective stepfamily rituals, whether newly created for the stepfamily or modifications of former family rituals, usually are purposefully crafted through discussions, negotiations, and give-and-take (Braithwaite et al., 1998, 2001; Michaels, 2006). The negotiation processes by which stepfamilies construct new rituals are important parts of bonding (Braithwaite et al., 2001). For stepfamilies that share religious beliefs, attending worship services together and engaging in religious rituals help build a sense of inclusion and belonging (Ganong et al., 1999). Public rituals such as commitment ceremonies or weddings also are perceived by coparents to garner support from extended family and friends (Hequembourg, 2004; Quick et al., 1995).

Family rituals entail more than celebrations of special events and holidays (Imber-Black et al., 2003). Daily routines also are ritualized ways in which stepfamilies bond and define themselves (Baxter et al., 1999; Henry & Lovelace, 1995; Hutchinson et al., 2007). Daily routines include talking to each other every day, hanging out, going for walks, eating meals together, and doing household chores together that contribute to the overall functioning of the household and the well-being of its members (Beckmeyer et al., 2020; Greeff & DuTroit, 2009; Golish, 2003; Hutchinson et al., 2007; Willetts & Maroules, 2004). In one study, parents and adolescents in strong stepfamilies thought that the shared activities they did routinely were important for staying connected to each other, maintaining a sense of belonging, and demonstrating caring even during times of conflict (Hutchinson et al., 2007). Listening to stepchildren and giving them a voice in how the stepfamily household functions also enhances step-kin closeness and helps stepchildren feel as if their stepfamily is unified (Banker & Gartner, 1998).

Another important aspect of developing cohesive stepfamily dynamics involves problem-solving as a group. Conflict theorists assert that conflicts are normative in relationships and may benefit the development and maintenance of close relationships (White et al., 2018). Clinicians have noted that conflict is often avoided in stepfamilies because of fears that the interpersonal bonds among step-kin are too weak to withstand disagreements and disputes (Papernow, 2013; Visher & Visher, 2013). But research evidence supports that conflicts and disagreements, when engaged in with flexibility, openness to listening, and mutual respect, can lead to closer, more positive stepfamily relationships (Baxter et al., 1999; Braithwaite et al., 2018; Clawson & Ganong, 2002; Golish, 2003; Oliver-Blackburn et al., 2022). Therefore, being able to manage conflicts in the face of problems is an essential characteristic of effective functioning in stepfamilies (Braithwaite et al., 2001).

In one study, stepcouples in both strong and struggling stepfamilies experienced conflicts, but the stepcouples in strong stepfamilies accepted conflict as an inevitable part of their coparenting that was both necessary and constructive (Golish, 2003). Anticipating that there will be disagreements helped stepcouples normalize conflicts and allowed them to focus on resolving those conflicts. When parents, stepparents, and stepchildren can engage productively in talking about problems, the mental health of all family members is enhanced (Schrodt, 2021). Believing in the potential of conflict to be productive and to promote understanding among family members by bringing problems to light may help coparents approach each other more constructively.

Constructive conflict resolution in stepfamilies can occur on many levels, including intrapersonally (individually), or interpersonally, in dyads and larger groups, including the whole household or stepfamily system (Coleman et al., 2001). Unfortunately, research on stepfamily conflict does not offer many concrete suggestions for productively managing disputes and disagreements. There are some clues, however, in the terms used to describe effective stepfamily functioning regarding conflicts – words like negotiating, listening, compromising, forgiveness, and being patient provide evidence of how emotionally-close stepfamilies manage conflicts, disagreements, and change (Braithwaite et al., 2001; Carr & Wang, 2012; Cookston et al., 2014; Schrodt, 2006; Waldron et al., 2018). Members of constructive stepfamilies communicate with each other and with the linked households of nonresidential coparents, work at being aware of the needs and wants of other stepfamily members, and compromise rather than rigidly take positions when there are disagreements (Braithwaite et al., 2001).

Modifying Stepfamily Expectations

Clinicians have long noted that many people enter stepfamilies with the expectations that their stepfamily functioning should resemble that of first-marriage nuclear families (Visher & Visher, 1979). Adults forming stepfamilies often hope for the best, children may expect the worst or are unsure what to expect, and society provides them with a variety of competing, and sometimes conflicting, expectations (Ganong & Coleman, 2017). Among the competing perspectives are that stepfamilies are: (a) recreated nuclear families, (b) deviant and dysfunctional systems, (c) ambiguous and ill-understood family structures, and (d) adaptive and resilient family forms (Ganong & Coleman, 2017). Research framed from the latter perspective has revealed that members of effective stepfamilies are able to either change their unrealistic expectations or create adaptive, more flexible expectations regarding roles, relationships, and family functioning (Golish, 2003; Kelley, 1992; Pill, 1990).

Stepfamilies whose members are patient with the development of step-relationships, who expect and accept change, and who understand that it takes time to feel "like a family," tend to see closeness develop between family members over time (Braithwaite et al., 2001). Effective stepfamilies stress the importance of not forcing a sense of family on members or expecting that love will automatically flourish. Instead, they accept that there will be "differential feelings and expressions of love" within the stepfamily (Kelley, 1992, pp. 585–586). These stepfamilies believe that neither stepparents nor stepchildren should be expected to love one another effortlessly or immediately. Adults who modify their expectations of instant love between stepfamily members to a goal of creating mutual respect and caring accept that they often will feel less close to step-kin than to biological kin, while still valuing and appreciating their stepfamily relationships (Pill, 1990) (see Box 5.2).

Box 5.2 *What works* **for stepcouple coparenting**

- Explicitly discuss expectations for the roles/responsibilities step/parents should fulfill.
- Reach consensus on parenting/stepparenting roles prior to stepfamily formation.
- Show step/children that you are on the same page about coparents' roles.
- Anticipate disagreements and view them as opportunities for growth.
- Support each other in being actively involved in step/children's lives.
- Minimize criticism and undermining coparents' childrearing efforts.
- Have parents be the primary disciplinarians/decision-makers.
- Have stepparents focus on getting to know stepchildren and developing a friendship.
- Plan activities that include all members of the stepfamily household.
- Create family rituals that both honor old traditions and celebrate new ones.
- Ensure that all family members have input into the creation/enactment of new rituals.
- Establish daily routines that facilitate bonding (e.g., shared meals, playing games).
- Problem-solve as a group; listen to and validate different perspectives.
- Maintain realistic expectations; remember it takes time to feel "like a family."

Coparenting Triads and Subsystems

Few researchers have addressed coparenting subsystems that extended across households to include both parents (i.e., the ex-couple) and one or more stepparents. These researchers report that when all parents and stepparents work together cooperatively to rear children, parents and stepparents are more satisfied with coparenting (Ganong et al., 2015; Schrodt, 2011), more satisfied in their relationships (Schrodt, 2010), and parents' well-being is enhanced (Gonzalez & Barnett, 2014; Ivanova & Kalmijn, 2020; Schrodt, 2010). For example, mothers' well-being is enhanced when fathers and stepfathers are supportive coparents (Forehand et al., 2016). Children also benefit when stepparents and non-residential parents are cordial. Cooperative coparenting systems allow children to form close bonds with both stepfathers and fathers, without feeling like they have to choose or like they are being disloyal by becoming close with stepparents (Hornstra et al., 2020). Protecting children by shielding them from witnessing conflicts between mothers, fathers, and stepfathers also facilitates children's positive development (Dunn et al., 2005).

These studies, however, provide little evidence about *how* these cooperative coparenting subsystems with both parents and one or two stepparents are developed. One study found that mothers see themselves as captains of the coparenting team and expect stepparents to know when to "step back" and "step forward" as coparents (Ganong et al., 2015). These mothers welcome both stepmothers and stepfathers as members of the childrearing team, along with fathers, when the mothers: (a) perceive that stepparents are adequate caregivers (e.g., observing how stepmothers treat their own children, listening to children talk about their experiences with the stepmothers), (b) have cooperative coparenting relationships with the biological fathers, (c) perceive biological fathers as good and responsible parents, and (d) feel secure in their place as the primary parent (Ganong et al., 2015). Findings suggest that when these cross-household group-coparenting subsystems work cooperatively with low hostility, coparents report fewer mental health symptoms (Schrodt, 2010) and better functioning stepfamily relationships (Blyaert et al., 2016; Ganong et al., 2015; Reid & Golub, 2018; Schrodt, 2010, 2011; see Figure 5.4).

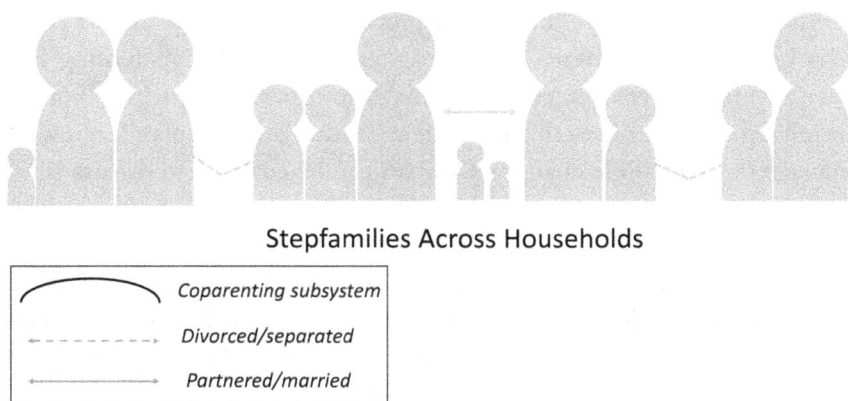

Stepfamilies Across Households

⌒	Coparenting subsystem
←- - - - - - -→	Divorced/separated
←————————→	Partnered/married

Figure 5.4 Stepfamilies across households

Implications for Practice

Effective childrearing by coparents in stepfamilies is clearly complex. Words such as compromise, negotiate, flexibility, and cooperation appear repeatedly in the investigations of effective coparenting, the underlying phenomenon being *concern for the children*. The primary aim of effective coparenting is focusing on children's well-being, a key that may help (step)parents navigating these complex dynamics. Focusing on children's well-being as a guiding principle may help coparents set reasonable goals and maintain productive childrearing dynamics after one or both have repartnered, while also being flexible when necessary. With family roles and rules in flux as stepfamilies are formed, and with new partners figuring out their roles vis-à-vis children, keeping centered on coparenting behaviors and interactions that benefit children may help all coparents make better decisions.

This principle of focusing on children's well-being applies also when separated and divorced adults cannot coparent because a former spouse has been physically or emotionally abusive or has substance abuse problems that put others at risk. There are sound reasons why some parents should not be involved in decision-making about children and should be engaged with children only in supervised or limited conditions for their safety (Ganong et al., 2015). It should again be noted that the studies we reviewed sampled individuals and families in which parents and stepparents were deemed able to coparent by family members and by the legal system.

There are many ways that family practitioners can help former partners be effective coparents after repartnering. First, if coparenting has been functioning well, practitioners may help coparents anticipate potential changes in their lives that may affect childrearing and plan for how to manage those possible changes. Couples can be coached to discuss their expectations for a new partner regarding childrearing and taking care of children while in the new partner's household. New partners, who may expect to step into the family as a parental figure or who might be unsure about their new role vis à vis stepchildren, can be educated about potential issues to anticipate. Conjoint mediation or counseling sessions might facilitate discussions about their new roles.

Second, helping professionals might assist parents in figuring out ways to use technology effectively to reduce conflicts and stress, particularly if coparenting between exes has been a persistent challenge. The goal for helping coparents might not be to "get along," but to at least be cordial and achieve some type of business-like relationship. Many parents have had the experience of getting things done at work with coworkers they do not like or find difficult, and using this as a model of coping with a coparent that is difficult may help parents strategize ways of interacting that are easier for them and for the children. A new partner is likely to be more disruptive to coparents who are challenged to work together in childrearing and decision-making about children, so helping couples focus on their coparenting relationships and how to make them more functional should be a priority before addressing issues related to adding a new adult to the coparenting "team." If coparenting challenges persist, family professionals might also help parents renegotiate their parenting plans and draft rules about privacy and the involvement of new partners.

Even if coparenting dynamics remain difficult, family professionals can help individuals cope more successfully. Reframing is a powerful tool for helping parents cognitively and emotionally manage their reactions to coparent misbehavior. Professionals also could help individuals develop privacy management rules for themselves that would lower conflicts and miscommunications with coparents. Individual coparents might also be encouraged to engage in parallel coparenting if necessary; this might entail limiting contacts to texts and emails, staying to the visiting schedule set by the court, and realizing that neither parent can control what happens in the other household. Individuals can also be helped to avoid problematic behaviors, such as confiding in children, sending messages to the coparent via children, and badmouthing the coparent in front of the children. Such individual actions are not effective coparenting per se, but they can minimize negative effects on children and adults until or if interactions become more positive.

Parents and stepparents also may need help in defining and negotiating comfortable roles for stepparents in the coparenting subsystem. Stepparents may have few ideas about how to be an adult in a household without being an active disciplinarian and rule setter. Family professionals can help stepparents envision new role possibilities, including what it might look like to be a supportive coparent who engages in caregiving tasks without being a replacement for the nonresidential parent. The ambiguity of the stepparent role may be difficult for some stepparents, and helping professionals can help them reach a level of comfort and understanding of this hybrid role set of friend and supportive, almost-a-parent that works well for many. Stepparents in some stepfamilies need support as they do the work of parenting while not being a full-fledged parent/decision-maker.

David Mills, a family therapist, used to tell stepparents and parents that it would take as many years for them to be accepted by stepchildren as the child was old when the stepparent joined the family. For instance, a 10-year-old stepchild would take ten years to accept the stepparent. We asked him why he said this to stepparents and their partners, as it was not a fact supported by any research, and he replied that he just made it up to lower their unrealistic expectations for rapid integration and acceptance. We do not support making up facts even for a good purpose, but we do think family professionals could assist parents and stepparents in managing their unrealistic expectations about how rapidly stepparents can become full-fledged coparents.

Finally, practitioners can serve as teachers, coaches, or mediators for multiple-parent/stepparent coparenting systems to help them work cooperatively. In English, there is no word for the relationship between a father and stepfather or between a mother and stepmother, which suggests that such an interpersonal connection is not thought to be likely or even possible. Researchers have reported such ties in effective coparenting subsystems, however, and so practitioners can help normalize such ties by talking about their utility and by helping families work out ways to communicate clearly across households.

Much is known about *what works* in coparenting. Family life educators have offered programs for divorced and separated parents for years, and much of the research-based content of these programs focuses on coparenting (Adler-Baeder & Higginbotham, 2020). This is an area of stepfamily living with substantive evidence about what family members can do, and with clear implications for family professionals working with them.

Future Research

Although there are some clear take-home messages from this body of research, there also are gaps in what we know. First, more attention should focus on coparenting subsystems that include both parents and one or more stepparents (i.e., coparenting "teams"). The legal systems in many countries have changed dramatically in recent years, with shared custody becoming the legal preference after divorce and separation (Blyaert et al., 2016; Emery, 2012). The reality for many stepfamilies is that coparenting often is a group effort involving stepparents and parents across households. More research is needed on how these units develop effectively. Second, more attention should be paid to fathers', children's, and stepparents' perspectives on coparenting in stepfamilies, as much of what we know comes from the perspectives of mothers in stepfamilies. Third, more research is needed in which data from multiple family members are collected, using dyadic and triadic units of analyses. More research that garners multiple perspectives would enrich knowledge about effective childrearing.

More attention also should focus on how and why coparenting and coparental behaviors change over time. Longitudinal investigations would enrich what is known, especially given that coparenting dynamics are fluid and ever-changing. Relatedly, investigations into the impacts of major life events (e.g., the birth of children to repartnered parents, changes in physical custody, stepfamily dissolution) on coparental dynamics would shed light on the fluidity of coparenting and how relationships change in response to life circumstances.

Studies are also needed on how other stepfamily members (e.g., step-grandparents, grandparents, adult siblings) affect coparenting, as well as research on what coparenting looks like in stepfamilies when the nonresidential biological parent is absent or uninvolved. If one parent is deceased or their whereabouts are unknown, then parent–stepparent coparenting is what remains. In this context, the parent–stepparent coparenting system likely functions differently than a system that also involves an active nonresidential parent. If nonresidential parents have been abusive or pose potential risks to children and ex-partners, research also is needed on the effectiveness of parallel coparenting, coparenting under legal supervision, and other situations when cordial coparenting is unlikely. Finally, studies of more diverse samples of stepfamilies are needed to explore variations in coparenting across ethnic, socioeconomic, and other social contexts.

References

Adler-Baeder, F., & Higginbotham, B. (2020). Efforts to design, implement, and evaluate community-based education for stepfamilies: Current knowledge and future directions. *Family Relations, 69*(3), 559–576. https://doi.org/10.1111/fare.12427

Afifi, T.D. (2003). Feeling caught in stepfamilies: Managing boundary turbulence through appropriate communication privacy rules. *Journal of Social and Personal Relationships, 20,* 729–756. https://doi.org/10.1177/0265407503206002

Ahrons, C. (2007). Family ties after divorce: Long-term implications for children. *Family Process, 46*(1), 53–65. https://doi.org/10.1111/j.1545-5300.2006.00191.x

Ahrons, C., & Miller, R.B. (1993). The effect of the postdivorce relationships on paternal involvement: A longitudinal analysis. *American Journal of Orthopsychiatry, 63*(3), 441–450. https://doi.org/10.1037/h0079446

Amato, P. (2010). Research on divorce: Continuing trends and new development. *Journal of Marriage and Family, 72,* 650–666. https://doi.org/10.1111/j.1741-3737.2010.00723.x

Banker, B.S., & Gaertner, S.L. (1998). Achieving stepfamily harmony: An intergroup-relations approach. *Journal of Family Psychology, 12*(3), 310–325. https://doi.org/10.1037/0893-3200.12.3.310

Barber, B.L., & Lyons, J.M. (1994). Family processes and adolescent adjustment in intact and remarried families. *Journal of Youth and Adolescence, 23*(4), 421–436. https://doi.org/10.1007/bf01538037

Baumrind, D. (1991). The influence of parenting style on adolescent competence and substance use. *The Journal of Early Adolescence, 11*(1), 56–95. https://doi.org/10.1177/0272431691111004

Baxter, L.A., Braithwaite, D.O., & Bryant, L.H. (2006). Types of communication triads perceived by young-adult stepchildren in established stepfamilies. *Communication Studies, 57,* 381–400. https://doi:10.1080/10510970600945923

Baxter, L.A., Braithwaite, D.O., & Nicholson, J.H. (1999). Turning points in the development of blended families. *Journal of Social and Personal Relationships, 16,* 291–313. https://doi.org/10.1177/0265407599163002

Beckmeyer, J.J., Krejnick, S.J., McCray, J.A., Troilo, J., & Markham, M.S. (2020). A multidimensional perspective on former spouses' ongoing relationships: Associations with children's post-divorce well-being. *Family Relations, 70*(2), 467–482. https://doi:10.1111/fare.12504

Beckmeyer, J.J., & Russell, L.T. (2018). Family structure and family management practices: Associations with positive aspects of youth well-being. *Journal of Family Issues, 39*(7), 2131–2154. https://doi:10.1177/0192513X17741921

Bermea, A.M., van Eeden-Moorefield, B., & Bible, J. (2020). Perceived boundary negotiations with former partners among queer stepfamilies. *Psychology of Sexual Orientation and Gender Diversity, 7*(2), 162–175. https://doi.org/10.1037/sgd0000370

Blyaert, L., Van Parys, H., De Mol, J., & Buysse, A. (2016). Like a parent and a friend, but not the father: A qualitative study of stepfathers' experiences in the stepfamily. *Australian and New Zealand Journal of Family Therapy, 37*, 119–132. https://doi:10.1002/anzf.1138

Braithwaite, D.O., Baxter, L.A., & Harper, A.M. (1998). The role of rituals in the management of the dialectical tension of "old" and "new" in blended families. *Communication Studies, 49*, 101–120. https://doi.org/10.1080/10510979809368523

Braithwaite, D.O., Olson, L.N., Golish, T.D., Soukup, C., & Turman, P. (2001). "Becoming a family": Developmental processes represented in blended family discourse. *Journal of Applied Communication Research, 29*(3), 221–247. http://dx.doi.org/10.1080/00909880128112

Braithwaite, D.O., Toller, P.W., Daas, K.L., Durham, W.T., & Jones, A.C. (2008). Centered but not caught in the middle: Stepchildren's perceptions of dialectical contradictions in the communication of co-parents. *Journal of Applied Communication Research, 36*(1), 33–55. https://doi.org/10.1080/00909880701799337

Braithwaite, D.O., Waldron, V.R., Allen, J., Oliver, B., Bergquist, G., Storck, K., Marsh, J., Swords, N., & Tschampl-Diesling, C. (2018). "Feeling warmth and close to her": Communication and resilience reflected turning points in positive adult stepparent-stepchild relationships. *Journal of Family Communication, 18*, 92–109. https://doi:10.1080/15267431.2017.1415902

Bray, J.H. (1988). Children's development during early remarriage. In E.M. Hetherington & J.D. Arasteh (Eds.), *Impact of divorce, single parenting, and stepparenting on children* (pp. 279–298). Erlbaum. https://doi.org/10.4324/9781315799711

Bray, J.H. (1999). From marriage to remarriage and beyond: Findings from the Developmental Issues in Stepfamilies Research Project. In E.M. Hetherington (Ed.), *Coping with divorce, single parenting, and remarriage: A risk and resiliency perspective* (pp. 253–271). Erlbaum. https://doi.org/10.4324/9781410602893-19

Bray, J.H., Berger, S.H., & Boethel, C.L. (1994). Role integration and marital adjustment in stepfather families. In K. Pasley & M. Ihinger-Tallman (Eds.), *Stepparenting: Issues in theory, research, and practice* (pp. 69–86). Greenwood. https://doi.org/10.2307/584813

Bronstein, P., Stoll, M.F., Clauson, J., Abrams, C.L., & Briones, M. (1994). Fathering after separation or divorce: Factors predicting children's adjustment. *Family Relations, 43*, 469–479. https://doi.org/10.2307/585380

Carlson, M.J., McLanahan, S.S., & Brooks-Gunn, J. (2008). Coparenting and nonresident fathers' involvement with young children after a nonmarital birth. *Demography, 45*(2), 461–488. https://doi.org/10.1353/dem.0.0007

Carr, K., & Wang, T.R. (2012). "Forgiveness isn't a simple process: It's a vast undertaking": Negotiating and communicating forgiveness in nonvoluntary family relationships. *Journal of Family Communication, 12*(1), 40–56. https://doi.org/10.1080/15267431.2011.629970

Cartwright, C. (2010). Preparing to repartner and live in a stepfamily: An exploratory investigation. *Journal of Family Studies, 16*, 237–250. https://doi.org/10.5172/jfs.16.3.237

Clawson, J., & Ganong, L. (2002). Adult stepchildren's obligations to older stepparents. *Journal of Family Nursing, 8*, 50–73. https://doi.org/10.1177/107484070200800104

Coleman, M., Fine, M., Ganong, L., Downs, K., & Pauk, N. (2001). When you're not the Brady Bunch: Identifying perceived conflicts and resolution strategies in step-families. *Personal Relationships, 8,* 55–73. https://doi.org/10.1111/j.1475-6811.2001.tb00028.x

Cookston, J.T., Olide, A., Parke, R.D., Fabricius, W.V., Saenz, D.S., & Braver, S.L. (2014). He said what? Guided cognitive reframing about the co-resident father/stepfather-adolescent relationship. *Journal of Research on Adolescence, 25*(2), 263–278.

Crosbie-Burnett, M., & Giles-Sims, J. (1994). Adolescent adjustment and stepparenting styles. *Family Relations, 43,* 394–399. https://doi.org/10.2307/585370. https://doi:10.1111/jora.12120

DeGarmo, D.S., Patras, J., & Eap, S. (2008). Social support for divorced fathers' parenting: Testing a stress-buffering model. *Family Relations, 57,* 35–48. https://doi.org/10.1111/j.1741-3729.2007.00481.x

Dunn, J., O'Connor, T., & Cheng, H. (2005). Children's responses to conflict between their different parents: Mothers, stepfathers, nonresident fathers, and nonresident stepmothers. *Journal of Clinical Child and Adolescent Psychology, 34(2),* 223–234. https://doi.org/10.1207/s15374424jccp3402_2

Emery, R.E. (2012). *Renegotiating family relationships: Divorce, child custody, and mediation* (2nd ed.). Guilford.

Favez, N., Widmer, E.D., Frascarolo, F., & Doan, M.-T. (2019). Mother-stepfather co-parenting in stepfamilies as predictor of child adjustment. *Family Process, 58*(2), 446–462. https://doi:10.1111/famp.12360

Felker, J.A., Fromme, D.K., Arnaut, G.L., & Stoll, B.M. (2002). A qualitative analysis of stepfamilies: The stepparent. *Journal of Divorce and Remarriage, 38,* 125–142. https://doi.org/10.1300/j087v38n01_07

Ferraro, A.J., Davis, T.R., Petren, R.E., & Pasley, K. (2016). Postdivorce parenting: A study of recently divorced mothers and fathers. *Journal of Divorce & Remarriage, 57*(7), 485–503. https://doi/10.1080/105025567.2016.1220302

Fine, M., Ganong, L., & Coleman, M. (1997). The relation between role constructions and adjustment among stepparents. *Journal of Family Issues, 18,* 503–525. https://doi.org/10.1177/019251397018005003

Fine, M.A., & Kurdek, L.A. (1992). The adjustment of adolescents in stepfather and stepmother families. *Journal of Marriage and the Family, 54,* 725–736. https://doi.org/10.2307/353156

Forehand, R., Parent, J., Golub, A., & Reid, M. (2014). Correlates of male cohabiting partner's involvement in child-rearing tasks in low-income urban Black stepfamilies. *Journal of Family Psychology, 28*(3), 336–345. https://doi.org/10.1037/a0036369

Forehand, R., Parent, J., Golub, A., & Reid, M. (2015). Male cohabiting partners as primary coparents in low-income Black stepfamilies. *Journal of Child and Family Studies, 24,* 2874–2880. https://doi.org/10.1007/s10826-014-0091-5

Forehand, R., Parent, J., Golub, A., & Reid, M. (2016). Positive parenting of young adolescents by male cohabiting partners: The roles of coparenting conflict and support. *Journal of Early Adolescence, 36*(3), 420–441. https://doi.org/10.1177/0272431614566947

Ganong, L., & Coleman, M. (2017). *Stepfamily relationships* (2nd ed.). Springer. https://doi.org/10.10078/978-1-4899-7702-1

Ganong, L., Coleman, M., Chapman, A., & Jamison, T. (2018). Stepchildren claiming stepparents. *Journal of Family Issues, 39*(6), 1712–1736. https://doi.org/10.1177/0192513X17725878

Ganong, L., Coleman, M., Feistman, R., Jamison, T., & Markham, M. (2012). Communication technology and post-divorce coparenting. *Family Relations, 61,* 397–409. https://doi.org/10.1111/j.1741-3729.2012.00706.x

Ganong, L., Coleman, M., Fine, M., & Martin, P. (1999). Stepparents' affinity-seeking and affinity-maintaining strategies with stepchildren. *Journal of Family Issues, 20*(3), 299–327. https://doi.org/10.1177/019251399020003001

Ganong, L., Coleman, M., Jamison, T., & Feistman, R. (2015). Divorced mothers' coparental boundary maintenance after parents re-partner. *Journal of Family Psychology, 29*, 221–231. https://doi.org//10.1037.fam0000064

Ganong, L.H., Coleman, M., Markham, M., Rothrauff, T. (2011). Predicting postdivorce coparental communication. *Journal of Divorce & Remarriage, 52*, 1–18. https://doi.org/10.1080/10502556.2011.534391

Ganong, L., Jensen, T., Sanner, C., Chapman, A., & Coleman, M. (2020). Stepparents' attachment orientation, parental gatekeeping, and stepparents' affinity-seeking with stepchildren. *Family Process, 59*(2), 756–771. https://doi.org/10.1111/famp.12448

Giles-Sims, J. (1987). Parental role-sharing between remarrieds and ex-spouses. *Youth & Society, 19*(2), 134–150. https://doi.org/10.1177/0044118x87019002003

Goldberg, A.E., & Allen, K.R. (2013). Same-sex relationship dissolution and LGB stepfamily formation: Perspectives of young adults with LGB parents. *Family Relations, 62*, 529–544. Https://doi.org/10.1111/fare.12024

Golish, T.D. (2000). Is openness always better?: Exploring the topic avoidance, satisfaction, and parenting styles of stepparents. *Communication Quarterly, 48*(2), 137–158. https://doi.org/10.1080/01463370009385587

Golish, T.D. (2003). Stepfamily communication strengths: Understanding the ties that bind. *Human Communication Research, 29*(1), 41–80. https://doi.org/10.1093/hcr/29.1.41

Gonzalez, H., & Barnett, M.A. (2014). Romantic partner and biological father support: Associations with maternal distress in low-income Mexican-origin families. *Family Relations, 63*(July), 371–383. https://doi.org/10.1111/fare.12070

Greeff, A.P., Du Toit, C. (2009). Resilience in remarried families. *American Journal of Family Therapy, 37*, 114–126. https://doi.org/10.1080/01926180802151919

Gross, J.J. (1998). The emerging field of emotion regulation: An integrative review. *Review of General Psychology, 2*, 271–299.

Haberstroh, C., Hayslip, B., & Essandoh, P. (1998). The relationships between stepdaughters' self-esteem and perceived parenting behavior. *Journal of Divorce & Remarriage, 29*(3/4), 161–175. https://doi.org/10.1300/j087v29n03_10

Henry, C.S., & Lovelace, S.G. (1995). Family resources and adolescent family life satisfaction in remarried family households. *Journal of Family Issues, 16*(6), 765–786. https://doi.org/10.1177/019251395016006005

Hequembourg, A. (2004). Unscripted motherhood: Lesbian mothers negotiating incompletely institutionalized family relationships. *Journal of Social and Personal Relationships, 21*(6), 739–762. https://doi.org/10.1177/0265407504047834

Hetherington, E.M. (1987). Family relations six years after the divorce. In K. Pasley & M. Ihinger-Tallman (Eds.), *Remarriage and stepparenting today* (pp. 185–205). Guilford. https://doi.org/10.2307/583619

Hetherington, E.M. (1993). An overview of the Virginia Longitudinal Study of Divorce and Remarriage with a focus on early adolescence. *Journal of Family Psychology, 7*(1), 39–56. https://doi.org/10.1037/0893-3200.7.1.39

Hetherington, E.M., Clingempeel, W.G., Anderson, E.R., Deal, J.E., Hagan, M.S., Hollier, E.A., & Lindner, M.S. (1992). Coping with marital transitions. *Monographs of the Society for Research in Child Development, 57*(2–3). University of Chicago Press. https://doi.org/10.2307/1166050

Hoffman, L., & Conway, M. (1981). *Foundations of family therapy: A conceptual framework for systems change.* Basic.

Hornstra, M., Kalmijn, M., & Ivanova, K. (2020). Fatherhood in complex families: Ties between adult children, biological fathers, and stepfathers. *Journal of Marriage and Family, 82*(9), 1637–1654. https://doi.org/10.111/jomf.12679

Hutchinson, S.L., Afifi, T., & Krause, S. (2007). The family that plays together fares better: Examining the contribution of shared family time to family resilience following divorce. *Journal of Divorce & Remarriage, 46*(3/4), 21–48. https://doi.org/10.1300/J087v46n03_03

Imber-Black, E., Roberts, J., & Whiting, R.A. (Eds.). (2003). *Rituals in families & family therapy.* Norton.

Ivanova, K., & Kalmijn, M. (2020). Heterogeneous effects of family complexity in childhood on mental health: Testing the "good divorce" and the "good stepparent" hypotheses. In M. Kreyenfeld & H. Trappe (Eds.), *Parental life courses after separation and divorce in Europe* (pp. 267–288). https://doi.org/10.1007/978-3-030-44575-1_13

Jamison, T.B., Coleman, M., Ganong, L.H., & Feistman, R.E. (2014). Transitioning to postdivorce family life: A grounded theory investigation of resilience in coparenting. *Family Relations, 63*, 411–423. https://doi.org/10.1111/fare.12074

Jensen, T.M., & Shafer, K. (2013). Stepfamily functioning and closeness: Children's views on second marriages and stepfather relationships. *Social Work, 58*, 127–136. https://doi.org/10.1093/sw/swt007

Kang, Y. and Ganong, L. (2020), Divorced fathers' perceptions of parental disclosures to children. *Family Relations, 69*, 36–50. https://doi.org/10.1111/fare.12410

Kelley, P. (1992). Healthy stepfamily functioning. *Families in Society, 73*(10), 579–587. https://doi.org/10.1177/104438949207301001

Kelly, K.P., & Ganong, L. (2011). Moving to place: Childhood cancer treatment decision making in single-parent and repartnered family structures. *Qualitative Health Research, 21*(3), 349–364. https://doi.org/10.1177/1049732310385823

King, V.L., Boyd, L.M., & Thorsen, M.L. (2015). Adolescents' perceptions of family belonging in stepfamilies. *Journal of Marriage and Family, 77*, 761–774. https://doi.org/10.1111/jomf.12181

Lamela, D., Figueiredo, B., Bastos, A., & Feinberg, M. (2016). Typologies of postdivorce coparenting and paternal well-being, parenting quality and children's adjustment problems. *Child Psychiatry and Human Development, 47*, 716–728. https://doi.org/10.1007/s10578-015-0604-5

Larouche, K., Pierce, T., Drapeau, S., & Saint-Jacques, M.C. (2023). Understanding fathers' involvement relative to the other parent after parental separation. *Journal of Divorce & Remarriage, 64*(7–8), 254–279. http://dx.doi.org/10.1080/10502556.2023.2290899

Madden-Derditch, D.A., & Leonard, S.A. (2000). Parental role identity and fathers' involvement in coparental interaction after divorce: Fathers' perspectives. *Family Relations, 49*, 311–318. https://doi.org/10.1111/j.1741-3729.2000.00311.x

Madden-Derditch, D., Leonard, S., & Christopher, F.S. (1999). Boundary ambiguity and coparental conflict after divorce. *Journal of Marriage and the Family, 61*(3), 588–598. https://doi.org/10.2307/353562

Marsiglio, W. (2004). When stepfathers claim stepchildren. *Journal of Marriage and Family, 66*, 22–39. https://doi.org/10.1111/j.1741-3737.2004.00002.x

McClain, L.R., & DeMaris, A. (2013). A better deal for cohabiting fathers? Union status differences in father involvement. *Fathering, 11*(2), 199–220. https://doi.org/10.3149/fth.1102.199

McDougal, S., & George, C. (2016). "I wanted to return the favor": The experiences of Black social fathers. *Journal of Black Studies, 47*(6), 524–549. https://doi:10.1177/0021934716653346

Metts, S., Braithwaite, D.O, Schrodt, P., Wang, T.R., Holman, A.J., Nuru, A.K., & Abetz, J.S. (2013). The experience and expression of stepchildren's emotions at critical events in stepfamily life. *Journal of Divorce & Remarriage, 54*, 414–437, https://doi: 10.1080/10502556.2013.800400

Michaels, M.L. (2006). Factors that contribute to stepfamily success: A qualitative analysis. *Journal of Divorce & Remarriage, 44*(3/4), 53–66. https://doi.org/10.1300/j087v44n03_04

Mikucki-Enyart, S.L., & Heisdorf, S.R. (2020). Obstacles and opportunities experienced by adult stepchildren in later life stepfamilies. *Journal of Divorce & Remarriage, 61*(1), 41–61. https://doi.org/10.1080/10502556.2019.1619380

Miller, A. (2009a). Face concerns and facework strategies in maintaining postdivorce coparenting and dating relationships. *Southern Communication Journal, 74*, 157–173. https://doi.org/10.1080/10417940802516842

Miller, A. (2009b). Revealing and concealing postmarital dating information: Divorced coparents' privacy rule development and boundary coordination processes. *Journal of Family Communication, 9*, 135–149. https://doi.org/10.1080/15267430902773287

Moore, S., & Cartwright, C. (2005). Adolescents' and young adults' expectations of parental responsibilities in stepfamilies. *Journal of Divorce & Remarriage, 43*(1/2), 109–128. https://doi.org/10.1300/j087v43n01_06

Nicholson, J.M., Phillips, M., Peterson, C.C., & Bauttistutta, D. (2002). Relationships between parenting styles of biological parents and stepparents and the adjustment of young adult stepchildren. *Journal of Divorce & Remarriage, 36*(3/4), 57–76. https://doi.org/10.1300/j087v36n03_04

Nuru, A.K., & Wang, T.T. (2014). "She was stomping on everything that we used to think of as a family": Communication and turning points in cohabitating (step)families. *Journal of Divorce & Remarriage, 55*, 145–163. https://dDoi:10.1080/10502556.2013.871957

Oliver-Blackburn, B.M., Braithwaite, D.O., Waldron, V.R., Hall, R., Hackenburg, L., & Worman, B.G. (2022). Protector and friend: Turning points and discursive constructions of the stepparent role. *Family Relations, 71*(3), 1266–1285. https://doi.org/10.1111/fare.12642

Papernow, P.L. (2013). *Surviving and thriving in stepfamily relationships.* Routledge. https://doi.org/10.4324/9780203813645

Parent, J., Clifton, J., Forehand, R., Golub, A., Reid, M., & Pichler, E.R. (2014). Parental mindfulness and dyadic relationship quality in low-income cohabiting black stepfamilies: Associations with parenting experienced by adolescents. *Couple and Family Psychology: Research and Practice, 3*(2), 67–82. https://doi.org/10.1037/cfp0000020

Pill, C.J. (1990). Stepfamilies: Redefining the family. *Family Relations, 39*, 186–193. https://doi.org/10.2307/585722

Quick, D.S., Newman, B.M., & McKenry, P.C. (1995). Influences on the quality of stepmother adolescent relationship. *Journal of Divorce and Remarriage, 24*, 99–114. https://doi.org/10.1300/j087v24n01_08

Reid, M., & Golub, A. (2018). Low-income Black men's kin work: Social fatherhood in cohabiting stepfamilies. *Journal of Family Issues, 39*(4), 960–984. https://doi/10.1177/0192513X16684892

Repond, G., Darwiche, J., El Ghaziri, N., & Antonietti, J. P. (2019). Coparenting in stepfamilies: A cluster analysis. *Journal of Divorce & Remarriage, 60*(3), 211–233. https://doi.org/10.1080/10502556.2018.1488121

Rettig, K.D., Leichtentritt, R.D., & Stanton, L.M. (1999). Understanding noncustodial fathers' family and life satisfaction from resource theory perspective. *Journal of Family Issues, 20*(4), 507–538. https://doi:10.1177/019251399020004005

Russell, L.T., Ferraro, A.J., Beckmeyer, J.J., Markham, M.S., Wilkins-Clark, R.E., & Zimmermann, M.L. (2021). Communication technology use in post-divorce co-parenting relationships: A typology and associations with post-divorce adjustment. *Journal of Social and Personal Relationships, 38*(2), 3752–3776. https://doi.org/10. 1177/0265407521043837

Saint-Jacques, M.C. (1995). Role strain prediction in stepfamilies. *Journal of Divorce & Remarriage, 24*, 51–72. https://doi.org/10.1300/j087v24n01_05

Schenck, C.E., Braver, S.L., Wolchik, S.A., Saenz, D., Cookston, J.T., & Fabricius, W.V. (2009). Relations between mattering to step- and non-residential fathers and adolescent mental health. *Fathering, 7*(1), 70–90. https://doi.org/10.3149/fth.07001.70

Schmeekle, M., Giarusso, R., Feng, D., & Bengtson, V.L. (2006). What makes someone family? Adult children's perceptions of current and former stepparents. *Journal of Marriage and Family, 68*, 595–610. https://doi.org/10.1111/j.1741-3737.2006.00277.x

Schrodt, P. (2006). A typological examination of communication competence and mental health in stepchildren. *Communication Monographs, 73*(3), 309–333. https://doi.org/10.1080/03637750600873728

Schrodt, P. (2010). Coparental communication with nonresidential parents as a predictor of couples' relational satisfaction and mental health in stepfamilies. *Western Journal of Communication, 74*, 484–503. https://doi.org/10.1080/10570314.2010.512282

Schrodt, P. (2011). Stepparents' and nonresidential parents' relational satisfaction as a function of coparental communication in stepfamilies. *Journal of Social and Personal Relationships, 28*, 983–1004. https://doi:10.1177/0265407510397990

Schrodt, P. (2016). Relational frames as mediators of everyday talk and relational satisfaction in stepparent-stepchild relationships. *Journal of Social and Personal Relationships, 33*, 217–236. https://doi.org/10.1177/0265407514568751

Schrodt, P. (2021). Disagreement in perceptions of stepfamily communication and functioning: Implications for mental health. *Journal of Social and Personal Relationships, 38*(1), 393–412. https://doi.org/10.1177/0265407520964862

Schrodt, P., & Afifi, T.D. (2007). Communication processes that predict young adults' feelings of being caught and their associations with mental health and family satisfaction. *Communication Monographs, 74*(2), 200–228. https://doi.org/10.1080/03637750701390085

Schrodt, P., Baxter, L.A., McBride, M.C., Braithwaite, D.O., & Fine, M.A. (2006). The divorce decree, communication, and the structuration of coparenting relationships in stepfamilies. *Journal of Social and Personal Relationships, 23*(5), 741–759. https://doi.org/10.1177/0265407506068261

Schrodt, S., & Braithwaite, D.O. (2011). Coparental communication, relational satisfaction, and mental health in stepfamilies. *Personal Relationships, 18*, 352–369. https://doi.org/10.1111/j.1475-6811.2010.01295.x

Shucksmith, J., Hendry, L.B., & Glendinning, A. (1995). Models of parenting: Implications for adolescent well-being within different types of family contexts. *Journal of Adolescence, 18*, 253–270. http://dx.doi.org/10.1006/jado.1995.1018

Skopin, A.R., Newman, B.M., & McKenry, P.C. (1993). Influences on the quality of stepfather-adolescent relationships: Views of both family members. *Journal of Divorce & Remarriage, 19*(3/4), 181–196. https://doi.org/10.1300/j087v19n03_12

Sobolewski, J.M., & King, V. (2005). The importance of the coparental relationship for nonresident fathers' ties to children. *Journal of Marriage and Family, 67*, 1196–1212. https://doi.org/10.1111/j.1741-3737.2005.00210.x

Steinbach, A. (2023). Coparenting as a mediator between physical custody arrangements and children's mental health. *Family Process, 62*, 1–15. https://doi.org/10.1111/famp.12844

Struss, M., Pfeiffer, C., Preuss, U., & Felder, W. (2001). Adolescents from divorced families and their perceptions of visitation arrangements and factors influencing parent–
child contact. *Journal of Divorce and Remarriage, 35,* 75–89. https://doi.org/10.1300/
j087v35n01_04

Taanila, A., Laitinen, E., Moilanen, I., & Jarvelin, M-R. (2002). Effects of family interaction on the child's behavior in single-parent and reconstructed families. *Family
Process, 41*(4), 693–708. https://doi.org/10.1111/j.1545-5300.2002.00693.x

Troilo, J., & Coleman, M. (2013). "I don't know how much more I can take": How divorced nonresidential fathers manage barriers to involvement? *Fathering: A Journal
of Theory, Research, and Practice About Men as Fathers, 11*(2), 159–178. https://doi.
org/10.3149/fth.1102.159

van Houdt, K., Kalmijn, M., Ivanova, K. (2020). Stepparental support to adult children:
The diverging roles of stepmothers and stepfathers. *Journal of Marriage and Family,
82,* 639–656. https://doi.org/10.1111/jomf.12599

Visher, E.B., & Visher, J.S. (1979). *Stepfamilies: A guide to working with stepparents and
stepchildren.* Brunner/Mazel. https://doi.org/10.4324/9781315784236-11

Visher, E.B., & Visher, J.S. (2013). *Therapy with stepfamilies.* Routledge.

Vuchinich, S., Vuchinich, R., & Wood, B. (1993). The interparental relationship and family problem-solving with preadolescent males. *Child Development, 64,* 1389–1400.
https://doi.org/10.1111/j.1467-8624.1993.tb02959.x

Waldron, V.R., Braithwaite, D.O., Oliver, B.M., Kloeber, D.N., & Marsh, J. (2018).
Discussions of forgiveness and resilience in stepchild-stepparent relationships.
Journal of Applied Communication Research, 46(5), 561–582. https://doi:10.1080/
00909882.2018.1530447

Weaver, S.E., & Coleman, M. (2010). Caught in the middle: Mothers in stepfamilies.
Journal of Social and Personal Relationships, 27(3), 305–326. https://doi.org/10.
1177/0265407510361729

White, J.M., Martin, T.F., & Adamsons, K. (2018). *Family theories: An introduction.* Sage.

Willetts, M.C., & Maroules, N.G. (2004). Does remarriage matter? The well-being of
adolescents living with cohabiting versus remarried mothers. *Journal of Divorce &
Remarriage, 41,* 115–133. https://doi.org/10.1300/j087v41n03_06

Yeung, W.J., Linver, M.R., & Brooks-Gunn, J. (2002). How money matters for young children's development: Parental investment and family processes. *Child Development,
73*(6), 1861–1879. https://doi.org/10.1111/1467-8624.t01-1-00511

6
WHAT WORKS FOR HALF- AND STEPSIBLINGS

What Works for Half- and Stepsiblings

Stepfamily formation, in addition to introducing new partners, stepparents, and stepchildren to the family system, can also introduce new sibling relationships. Three in ten American adults report having a half- or stepsibling, a number that is higher for those younger than age 30 (44%) and for Black (45%) and Hispanic (38%) adults (Pew Research Center, 2011). Unlike biological or adopted siblings, who share the same primary parents, *half-siblings* share a biogenetic connection to one parent only. *Stepsiblings* are not genetically related but are linked to each other because their parents have romantically partnered. In 35% of repartnerships, both partners bring children into the union, forming stepsibling relationships – a trend that is more common among cohabiting stepfamilies (41%) than marital stepfamilies (31%; Guzzo, 2021). If the repartnered couple goes on to have a shared child together, then that child is a half-sibling to the older stepchildren. Roughly 17% of minor-age children in the United States share a household with at least one half-sibling (Kreider & Lofquist, 2014). Half-sibling relationships are significantly more common in the U.S. than in European countries, where rates of multi-partner fertility have remained low for several decades (Thompson et al., 2020).

DOI: 10.4324/9781003369073-6

Relative to research on stepparent–stepchild relationships, less research exists on relationships between half- and stepsiblings. The lack of sibling research in stepfamilies is surprising, given evidence that siblings play important roles in family life (Gilligan et al., 2020; McHale et al., 2012). For instance, in acting as companions, role models, confidants, combatants, and "the focus of social comparisons," siblings shape development and well-being throughout the life course (Gilligan et al., 2020; McHale et al., 2012, p. 913). Because of the frequency with which siblings engage in conflict, siblings facilitate the development of skills in perspective-taking, emotional understanding, negotiation, persuasion, and problem-solving (Dunn, 2007), benefits that can extend into adulthood (Gilligan et al., 2020). Close sibling relationships in young adulthood are associated with enhanced self-esteem and decreased loneliness (Sherman et al., 2006), and siblings in middle and late adulthood have been identified as sources of support, providers of care, and trusted confidants (Reczek et al., 2021; Volkom, 2006). Siblings also can serve as valuable sources of support in times of family change; for example, supportive sibling relationships can buffer the negative effects of divorce by providing a sense of continuity and shared experience during family reorganization (Jacobs & Sillars, 2012; van Dijk et al., 2022).

Research on half- and stepsiblings has tended to focus primarily on the outcomes associated with sibling structure, often comparing children who live with half- or stepsiblings to those who live with full siblings only. Findings from these studies suggest small but consistent negative effects associated with *sibling complexity* (i.e., living with half- and/or stepsiblings), including lower levels of parental involvement, educational attainment, feelings of family belonging, and physical and economic well-being, as well as higher levels of depressive symptoms and antisocial behaviors (Apel & Kaukinen, 2008; Brown et al., 2015; Fomby et al., 2016; Halpern-Meekin & Tach, 2008; Strow & Strow, 2008; Tillman, 2008; Turunen, 2014). When comparing half- and stepsibling relationships to full sibling relationships, relationships between half- and stepsiblings appear to be less close than those between full siblings, but they also are less prone to conflict, rivalry, and aggression than are full sibling ties (Anderson, 1999; Deater-Deckard et al., 2002; Mikkelson, Myers, & Hannawa, 2011).

Given these findings, the question of *how* people develop close relationships with half- and stepsiblings is important. There is robust evidence that people benefit from close stepfamily relationships, and they suffer when stepfamily dynamics are characterized by conflict and volatility (Ganong et al., 2019; Hornstra et al., 2022; Jensen, 2022; King et al., 2015). This chapter addresses the question of *what works* in developing close and supportive half- and stepsibling ties. Because half- and stepsibling relationships are qualitatively different from each other, we distinguish research on *what works* in half-sibling relationships from research on *what works* in stepsibling relationships. We first discuss the contexts in which these relationships develop, and then we review research evidence on the things that parents and siblings can do to promote healthy half- and stepsibling bonds.

Half-Sibling Relationships

Before turning to research about *what works* for developing close half-sibling relationships, let's first consider the context in which half-sibling relationships develop. Recall that when a couple in a stepfamily has a shared child together, that child becomes the younger half-sibling to the older stepchildren in the family. Because it takes time for parents to separate/divorce, meet new partners, and have children with those partners, there often are age gaps between older half-siblings (e.g., children from a first marriage) and younger half-siblings (e.g., children from a second marriage). Older half-siblings, especially if there are large age gaps, can serve as parent-like figures in younger half-siblings' lives – as valued mentors, caregivers, and sources of love and support. As a participant in one of our studies described, "[My half-sister] was sort of a mother figure when I was an infant, you know, helping take care of me and babysitting and stuff" (Sanner et al., 2020, p. 614). Similarly, another younger half-sibling said, "I grew up with Kevin and Debbie [half-siblings] in more of an aunt and uncle role, even though they're my brother and sister … I knew they were my siblings, but they were adults, and I was a kid" (Sanner et al., 2020, p. 614).

In addition to larger age gaps, older and younger half-siblings are often raised in different family structures. In other words, older half-siblings live in a stepfamily; they have experienced their parents' separation/divorce and recoupling/remarriage – family transitions that occurred before the younger half-sibling's birth. In contrast, younger half-siblings are born *into* the stepfamily; they often grow up in a household with continuously married biological parents, meaning that their families can look to them more like nuclear families than stepfamilies. Younger half-siblings may benefit from growing up with continuously married parents in ways that their older half-siblings did not. For example, parents may be older and more mature when they are raising children from second marriages compared to first marriages (Ganong & Coleman, 2017). Depending on the quality of parents' relationships to their children from their first marriage or partnership, those children may feel resentment toward younger half-siblings who benefited from their parents' involvement in ways that they (the older half-siblings) did not (Sanner et al., 2020).

For stepfamilies in which older and younger half-siblings live together in the same household, younger half-siblings are in the unique position of sharing a biogenetic connection to everyone in the home. Shared children in stepfamilies are biologically related to both members of the stepcouple, whereas older half-siblings are related to only one member of the couple; the other person is their stepparent. Therefore, although shared children themselves may not have stepparents, they live in a household in which stepparent–stepchild relationships exist. Further, if both members of the stepcouple have children from previous relationships, then those children – all of whom are older half-siblings to the shared child – are stepsiblings to each other. If those stepchildren are part of shared custodial arrangements, then they may transition between two homes, even while their younger half-siblings are stationed in one household only. So, although younger half-siblings themselves are not transitioning between two households, their older half-siblings might be, which means that shared children indirectly experience the cyclical nature of having older half-siblings in and out of the home.

Additionally, when both members of the stepcouple had children from prior unions before the birth of their shared child, then the dynamics of stepsibling relationships can impact the lives of younger half-siblings who are biologically related to all parties. If there is stepfamily strife, for example, then friction (e.g., between stepparents and stepchildren, between stepsiblings) can put younger half-siblings, who are related to everyone, in loyalty binds (Sanner et al., 2020). Of course, half-siblings also develop close and meaningful relationships. Many people do not think of their half-siblings as "half" siblings at all, but as full siblings, especially if they lived with their half-siblings for most of their childhood (Tanskanen & Danielsbacka, 2019). These siblings may actively reject the prefix *half-* because they are resistant to a label that suggests that their relationships are anything less than fully familial (Sanner et al., 2021).

In short, there is enormous variation in the quality of half-sibling relationships. We turn now to research evidence about that variation, examining *what works* in promoting close, supportive relationships between half-siblings in stepfamilies.

What Works for Half-Siblings

Only three published studies have explicitly explored the conditions under which half-siblings develop close relationships (Michaels, 2006; Tanskanen & Danielsbacka, 2019; Sanner et al., 2020). First, relationships between half-siblings tend to be closer when they live together and spend more time with each other during childhood (Tanskanen & Danielsbacka, 2019). Individuals who co-resided for longer periods with half-siblings during childhood reported more frequent contact with them and greater emotional closeness compared to those who did not co-reside with half-siblings during childhood (Tanskanen & Danielsbacka, 2019). In fact, relationships between half-siblings were just as close as relationships between full siblings when half-siblings grew up in the same household. Therefore, to the extent that parents can advocate for custodial arrangements that allow for half-sibling co-residence, half-sibling relationships are likely to benefit. Even partial co-residence (e.g., spending time in the household with half-siblings when visiting a non-custodial parent) is likely to provide important opportunities for bonding that, if consistent, can strengthen half-sibling ties.

Research with both residential and non-residential half-siblings indicates that younger half-siblings largely perceive it to be the responsibility of the older half-sibling to steer the development of the relationship

(Sanner et al., 2020). Younger half-siblings may desire close relationships with their older half-siblings, but if their efforts to bond with older half-siblings are rebuffed, then they are unlikely to keep trying. There is evidence that the quality of half-sibling relationships may come down to the extent to which older half-siblings hold positive or negative sentiments about the stepfamily formation. Recall that older half-siblings in stepfamilies have experienced their parents' separation/divorce and partnerships/remarriage prior to the birth of the half-sibling. How they feel about those family transitions appears to "spill over" into how they feel about younger half-siblings. As a person with a half-sibling in one of our studies shared:

> Those relationships are really a product of how [older] half-siblings feel towards the [younger] half-sibling. It can go either way; they [older half-siblings] can choose to accept the situation and treat the [shared child] as a normal sibling, or they can choose to not accept it and not be a part of the family. It's really in their hands.
>
> (Sanner et al., 2020, p. 616)

If older half-siblings carry resentment about having a more difficult upbringing than the shared child(ren), then this may negatively affect half-sibling relationship quality, whereas if they are accepting (or even embracing) of family structure changes, then relationships with younger half-siblings tend to be closer (Michaels, 2006; Sanner et al., 2020). Illustrating a case where resentment can impede relationship quality, one half-sibling described this well when she shared, "I think that she [older half-sister] has always been upset that she didn't grow up with her mom and dad living together … I think that's always been the root of her problem with me" (Sanner et al., 2020, p. 615). Another person from the same study similarly said, "I know now that she [half-sister] was just really jealous … that I was raised by our father, and she wasn't … He was a great dad to me … I openly admit he … was not a good dad to his other children" (p. 615).

Therefore, the question of *what works* in promoting half-sibling ties has roots that go deeper than the immediate context of half-sibling relationship development. In other words, parents set the stage for the quality of half-sibling ties in how they handle family transitions with older children. When parents nurture their relationships with children across family transitions, their older children appear to be more receptive to the birth of a younger half-sibling than when older children feel neglected or possibly replaced by the birth of a shared child (Michaels, 2006; Sanner et al., 2020). As such, parents can take comfort in knowing that our content in Chapter 4 on *what works* in maintaining close parent–child relationships has benefits that extend to other family subsystems, including relationships between half-siblings.

There are other things that parents do to promote close half-sibling ties. For example, when parents draw boundaries of family membership that are inclusive of older half-siblings, half-sibling relationships benefit (Sanner et al., 2020). In other words, when parents and stepparents make a concerted effort to include older half-siblings in family events and communications, relationships between older and younger half-siblings appear to be closer. Half-siblings in one study described how family group texts that included all family members facilitated regular communication between half-siblings, especially when older half-siblings were away at college (Sanner et al., 2020). Others described how their parents carefully coordinated holiday or birthday parties so that all family members (including older half-siblings, whose schedules were often more complex due to having multiple parental households to visit) were able to attend. When parents clearly communicated messages of belonging, half-sibling relationships appeared to be closer. To illustrate this dynamic, consider Calli, who credited her close relationships with her older half-siblings from her father's first marriage to her parents' ability to bring everyone together. She spoke especially highly of her mother's commitment to being a devoted stepmom to her older half-siblings and how that impacted the family dynamic:

> I never felt like that they [half-siblings] were excluded or were a separate part of the family … It wasn't like "Okay, here's my mom's stepkids, and then there's us." When I was growing up, my mom would say, you know, "They aren't just my stepkids, those are my kids, and I love them the same amount as I love you and

Ian." … So, for my whole life, I would explain "Oh, I'm like one of five kids." I do not feel any differently towards them than I do towards my [biological] brother.

(Sanner et al., 2020, p. 216)

Nonresidential parents in the other household (i.e., the older half-sibling's other parent, who is unrelated to the younger half-sibling) also may have the power to subtly shape these relationships for the better. When parents across households work together to establish cooperative family systems, children may feel liberated from the possibility of loyalty binds and supported in nurturing *all* their sibling relationships. In fact, younger half-siblings sometimes enjoy close relationships with their older half-sibling's other parent, who they might think of and relate to as an aunt or uncle to them. Some even describe being close to their half-siblings' other half-siblings, who one person called their "quarter siblings" (Sanner et al., 2021). When parents establish positive coparenting networks, half-sibling relationships appear to be more likely to flourish.

Half-siblings themselves also can engage in behaviors that strengthen their relationships. For example, open conversations between half-siblings about their family history, including family experiences prior to the divorce, remarriage, and birth of a half-sibling, facilitated closer half-sibling ties (Sanner et al., 2020). Another behavior that half-siblings engage in to affirm closeness in their relationships is to omit the address term "half" when describing their relationship to others (Sanner et al., 2020). Intellectually, half-siblings may understand that they are, technically, half-siblings, but close half-siblings tend to reject this label. Half-siblings perceive that introducing each other with the address term "half" would signal a less close relationship and would make them feel less connected to their half-sibling. Not using the "half" label communicated and affirmed to siblings that they are important in each other's lives, and that their relationships were just as important as any sibling relationship. Indeed, address terms can convey powerful messages about the quality and closeness of relationships in stepfamilies (Koenig Kellas et al., 2008). With an understanding of *what works* for half-siblings, we turn now to a review of *what works* for stepsiblings (see Box 6.1).

Box 6.1 *What works* for half-siblings

Effective parents and stepparents help half-siblings bond when they:

- Provide half-siblings with opportunities to spend time together. Half-siblings are closer when they live together during childhood.
- Nurture relationships with children before and after family transitions, such as the birth of a younger half-sibling or a half-sibling changing primary residences.
- Make efforts to ensure that children do not feel replaced by new half-siblings.
- Cooperate with coparents in other households to make sure that older half-siblings are included in family events and communications (e.g., group texts).

Effective half-siblings create closer bonds when they:

- Communicate openly with half-siblings about their family history, including family experiences prior to the divorce, remarriage, and birth of a half-sibling.
- Spend one-on-one time with each other (e.g., going shopping, watching television).
- Omit the address term "half" when introducing half-siblings to others.

Stepsibling Relationships

Unlike half-siblings, who share a biogenetic connection to one parent, stepsiblings share a biogenetic connection to neither parent; they are related to each other because their parents have romantically partnered. When both partners bring children into the union – which happens in 35% of repartnerships – stepsibling relationships are formed. Complex stepfamilies may face challenges related to bringing two sets of children from prior unions together, such as (a) finding housing that can accommodate everyone; (b) moving, which may mean new schools for children, making new friends, and coping with losses; (c) adjusting to parents' efforts to bond with stepsiblings; (d) developing new household rules; (e) negotiating new family roles; and (f) establishing family rituals and routines that celebrate both the old and the new (Ganong & Coleman, 2017). Clinicians have identified several difficulties in stepsibling relationships, such as competing for resources (e.g., parental attention and physical space), adapting to changes in family size and ordinal position in the family (e.g., going from being the oldest child to the middle child), and creating bonds with individuals who may be different in personality, interests, or values (Visher & Visher, 2013).

Only a handful of studies have explored the nature of stepsibling ties, generally finding that stepsiblings have less close and less supportive relationships than full siblings, though they also exhibit less conflict and aggression in their relationships than full siblings (Campo et al., 2012; Mikkelson, Floyd, & Pauley, 2011; Mikkelson, Myers, & Hannawa, 2011). However, there is enormous variability in the quality and closeness of stepsibling relationships. In one study, six types of relationships with stepsiblings were identified: (a) strangers, (b) distant acquaintances, (c) rivals, (d) ambivalent friends or frenemies, (e) friends, and (f) siblings (Ganong et al., 2022). *Strangers* (representing 23.9% of stepsibling relationships in the sample) were stepsiblings with no relationship, who had never met or interacted rarely and who often had large gaps in age and/or geographic proximity. *Distant acquaintances* (11.3% of the sample) were stepsiblings with casual relationships, who interacted occasionally (e.g., major holidays, family events) and were cordial but did not know each other well. *Rivals* (5.7% of the sample) were stepsiblings with hostile relationships, whose interactions were competitive and conflictual and often affected the stepfamily dynamic. *Ambivalent friends* (21.1% of the sample) were stepsiblings with ambivalent (i.e., "mixed bag") relationships, who generally liked and were polite towards each other but had mild and/or occasional feelings of dislike or resentment. *Friends* (14.1% of relationships) were stepsiblings with intimate relationships, who enjoyed spending time with each other and were emotionally close. Finally, *siblings* (23.9% of relationships) were stepsiblings with familial relationships, who claimed each other as siblings and believed that relationships would continue even if parents were to divorce.

Stepsibling relationships clearly take different forms, but what accounts for why relationships develop in the ways that they do? What can parents, stepparents, and stepsiblings do to promote closer relationships? We turn now to a review of *what works* for stepsiblings.

What Works for Stepsiblings

As is true for half-siblings, the question of *what works* in promoting stepsibling ties has roots that go deeper than the immediate context of stepsibling relationship development. Parents set the stage for stepsibling relationship development in how they handle the transition to stepfamily life with their children. Perhaps the most important thing parents can do is nurture their relationships with children during stepfamily formation, when children are acquiring stepsiblings (Ganong et al., 2022; Landon et al., 2022). This can be hard for parents, who are simultaneously nurturing relationships with their children, with their new partner, and with their partner's children. There is evidence, however, that when children perceive that their relationship with their parent is taking a backseat to their parent's efforts to bond with their stepsiblings, then those feelings tend to spill over into stepsibling relationships (Ganong et al., 2022; Landon et al., 2022). For example, one stepsibling said, "The main tension [with my stepsiblings] … stemmed from each of us wanting to have alone time with our parents and not being able to have that" (Landon et al., 2022, p. 270). Another stepsibling described her concerns about the changing nature of her relationship with her father when she acquired stepsiblings:

> It was really upsetting. I felt like our [father–daughter] relationship started lacking very quickly because he was splitting his attention between not just two girls but four girls … he treated her [stepsister] very much like a daughter, like he was trying harder with her because he needed to gain her trust. And she had pet names for him, and it was just like they had this great relationship with each other, and then I would see him every other weekend and it was just not the same. It's still not the same.
> (Landon et al., 2022, p. 270)

Therefore, protecting and nurturing the parent–child relationship as children acquire stepsiblings is critical. At the root of many people's resistance to acquiring stepsiblings appears to be fear and sadness over the perceived changing nature of the parent–child bond (Ganong et al., 2022). When parents prioritize their relationships with children across family transitions, children appear to be more receptive to the acquisition of stepsiblings. For example, one son described how his father's remarriage, which resulted in three younger stepsisters, did not affect their relationship because his dad still made an effort to spend one-on-one father–son time with him, without the stepsisters (Ganong et al., 2022). Indeed, there is a positive association between post-divorce relationship quality with fathers and relationship quality with paternal stepsiblings (Ahrons, 2007; Ahrons & Tanner, 2003). Adult children who reported that their father's remarriage had a positive effect on their lives also said that they had better relationships with their stepsiblings (Ahrons, 2007).

In addition to prioritizing one-on-one time with children, parents promote closer stepsibling relationships by making deliberate attempts to build a sense of family identity (Ganong et al., 2022; Michaels, 2006). Parents and stepparents positively shape the development of relationships between stepsiblings by encouraging bonding between the children via family activities (e.g., dinners out, game nights, and family trips), and generally facilitating children's attempts to bond (Ganong et al., 2022; Michaels, 2006). They also work to establish family traditions, such as shared meals and family dates with all the children (Michaels, 2006). Stepchildren whose stepsiblings were *siblings* (as opposed to ambivalent friends, distant acquaintances, or strangers) described direct parental strategies to foster family cohesion more than other stepsiblings (Ganong et al., 2022). For example, one participant said:

> Family dinner was always central because we were always in and out of the house, but that was one thing where they [dad and stepmom] did a really good job of bringing everybody together … I played a lot of sports, and they [stepsisters] did cheer, so it was just supporting each other at activities. They came to my games. I went to cheer.

Importantly, *patience* also has been identified as critical in parents' attempts to facilitate stepsibling bonding and build family solidarity (Michaels, 2006). Parents whose stepsiblings were close understood that it would take time for families to gain a sense of family identity and merge into one new family. The first two years of stepfamily formation were perceived as the most difficult time and presented the greatest challenges. When families remained calm and patient during this time, they were more successful (Michaels, 2006).

Stepparents, who are the parents of stepsiblings, also play an important role. When stepchildren are close with their stepparents, they also tend to be closer to their stepsiblings (Ganong et al., 2022). One participant who was close to her stepfather described how this made her more inclined to bond with his children: "I would say it probably brought us closer. I wanted to make that effort to include them as part of our [family]" (Ganong et al., 2022, p. 2801). Stepparents in this study did not assume parental roles but functioned generally as older friends and mentors, and they worked to facilitate bonding between stepsiblings: "I think [my stepmother] probably presented more opportunities for bonding ... it probably helped [my stepsister relationships] because I get along with both really well" (Ganong et al., 2022, p. 2801). Therefore, content in Chapter 3 on *what works* for stepparenting is likely to have spillover effects for stepsibling ties.

Parents and stepparents also can support stepsibling relationships by being cognizant of the extent to which their interactions with children and stepchildren might inadvertently create conflict or competition for resources, whether tangible (e.g., household space) or intangible (e.g., parental time, attention, and praise). In one study, perceiving that stepsiblings were treated better created contention or jealousy between stepsiblings, especially when participants felt they were being compared to their stepsiblings (Landon et al., 2022). One stepsister said, "When my grades weren't as good as hers, my dad would downplay my grades ... I felt that wasn't fair ... she had one more A than me and would get praised" (Landon et al., 2022, p. 269). Stepsiblings who were similar in age and gender appeared to be especially sensitize to inadvertent comparisons by parents and stepparents. In contrast, stepsiblings who were close did not feel as if they were in competition with each other, nor did they feel as if they were being compared by parents. For instance, when asked why she was closer to her older than her younger stepsister, one young woman said: "We [older stepsister and I] are not being compared directly, there's not that pressure to be the same or be different. There's kind of pressure to do both with [younger stepsister]" (Ganong et al., 2022, p. 2802). Therefore, parents and stepparents can support stepsiblings' bonds by celebrating each child's unique and independent self, without making comparisons between them, even those that seem trivial or harmless.

A tougher issue for parents and stepparents to mitigate involves issues surrounding physical space as families merge households. After parents remarry or repartner, they usually join households by moving into one of the partners' homes or relocating to a new household. Either way, combining households means that children are faced with sharing a residence with stepsiblings either full-time or part-time. With rare exceptions (e.g., houses large enough to have ample space for everyone), the stepfamily household configuration often presents stepsiblings with issues of establishing and maintaining boundaries for territory, or physical space. For example, describing an issue of physical space involving stepsiblings, one stepdaughter said:

> Why do they [stepbrothers] have to play full force Battle Royale in the middle of the basement? Can't we compromise on this? That was a big issue. I would go to my dad, and then dad and [stepmom] would fight, and it was a territory thing. It was [about] who had the right to the basement.
> (Landon et al., 2022, p. 269)

Although these issues may seem trivial, issues of physical space often are manifestations of deeper feelings and anxieties about adjusting to stepfamily life. Parents can help stepsiblings manage conflict by listening to and validating their concerns, and then engaging stepsiblings on possible solutions or compromises. At the root of the matter might be the extent to which children feel *at home* in their new space. For example, one stepbrother who did not have close relationships with his stepsiblings said about going to his father's stepfamily household on the weekends: "I didn't like it. It's not my house, I didn't have stuff there, I very much felt like a guest. Wasn't really anything for me to do" (Ganong et al., 2022, p. 2803). When children do not feel that they have their own space, or they do not feel at home in the space they do have, this can breed resentment toward stepsiblings. Even parents' attempts to talk openly and honestly with children about their feelings about these changes is likely to mitigate the potential for anger to be misdirected at stepsiblings.

Taken together, there are many things that parents and stepparents can do to promote closer relationships between stepsiblings. But what do stepsiblings themselves do to build close ties? The primary process through which stepsiblings themselves develop close relationships is through *affinity building* (Ganong et al., 2022). Affinity-seeking behaviors, often studied in the context of stepparent–stepchild relationships, are intentionally performed by individuals to get to know others and establish a connection, and affinity-maintaining strategies are efforts to maintain a good connection over time (Ganong et al., 1999). Affinity-seeking and affinity-maintaining strategies involve spending time together in mutually enjoyable activities, finding common interests, helping (e.g., teaching, supporting, and assisting with tasks), giving gifts, and expressing care, affection, and concern for the other's well-being (Ganong et al., 1999).

Most individuals know how to make new friends (i.e., seek affinity), so stepchildren theoretically have the skills necessary to engage in affinity-seeking behaviors when they encounter new stepsiblings. One difference between making friends and bonding with stepsiblings, however, is the level of motivation to engage in affinity behaviors. People may be more interested in making friends when they have greater control and choice about with whom to affiliate, whereas stepsibling relationships are involuntary and seldom freely chosen. The contexts, therefore, differ, and these differences may affect stepsibling affinity-seeking and the development of relationships.

In one study, the degree and nature of affinity-building efforts among stepsiblings depended, in part, on (a) opportunities to interact, and (b) levels of reciprocity between stepsiblings (Ganong et al., 2022). The first ingredient for affinity-seeking between stepsiblings was the opportunity (real and perceived) for relationship-building to occur. When stepsiblings never shared a residence or lived far apart, they had fewer chances to bond, and were much more likely to be *strangers* or *acquaintances* than *friends* or *siblings*. Following stepsiblings on social media, although common, was not enough to foster meaningful connections. Spending time together distinguished stepsiblings who had no relationship (strangers) or distant relationships (acquaintances) from those who had relationships of some kind, whether those relationships were warm and close (friends or siblings) or ambivalent or hostile (frenemies or rivals) (Ganong et al., 2022). Opportunities to interact did not guarantee that *positive* relationships would form, but they did open the door for relationship development to occur.

Opportunities to interact were not solely contingent on geographic proximity or shared residence (though these things helped) – they also depended on stepsiblings' *perceptions* of their opportunities to engage with each other (Ganong et al., 2022). Perceived opportunities to interact included perceptions of shared interests and activities in which stepsiblings could jointly engage. If stepsiblings perceived few shared interests, they made fewer and less consistent attempts to bond. For example, a key difference between *ambivalent friends* (stepsiblings who were polite and civil towards each other) and *friends* (stepsiblings who genuinely liked and enjoyed each other) was the degree of perceived overlap in shared interests and personalities. When stepsiblings made an effort to identify shared interests and nurture those shared interests, they enjoyed closer relationships with each other (Ganong et al., 2022; Michaels, 2006). For example, one stepdaughter said of her stepsister, "She liked clothes [and so did I] so we'd go shopping, or I would give her my old clothes and she always loved it" (Ganong et al., 2020, p. 2799). Another stepdaughter who enjoyed board games said, "[My stepbrother] knows every board game under the sun … that really helped break the ice" (Ganong et al., 2020, p. 2799). Although some stepsiblings were close because of their closeness in age and shared similar interests, larger age gaps did not necessarily preclude the possibility of close relationships. In families with larger age gaps between children, stepsibling ties were closer when older children took on the role of big brothers and sisters to the younger children (Michaels, 2006).

Once stepsiblings identified shared interests and made some sort of initial attempt to get to know each other, the next thing that was critical for relationship development was that those affinity-building efforts were reciprocated in kind (Ganong et al., 2022). When initial attempts to befriend stepsiblings were ineffective, participants were not motivated to keep trying, whereas stepsiblings who responded positively were likely to become *friends* or *siblings*. The degree of reciprocity in affinity-seeking efforts was crucial. In our study, all stepchildren who identified stepsiblings as *friends* or *siblings* engaged in affinity-seeking efforts to which stepsiblings responded positively and reciprocated with their own affinity-building efforts.

Although some relationships began with almost immediate liking, others took time to develop. In fact, some stepsiblings whose initial impressions were that new stepsiblings were annoying or undisciplined went on to develop friendly or familial relationships with them if mutual efforts were made over time. Affinity-seeking ranged from playing games, pursuing shared interests, teaching each other skills and new knowledge, providing support by attending each other's events, and just hanging out. One stepsibling said, "It meant a lot. It was just nice to see people who aren't blood related wanting to come to our events like they considered us a part of their family, as we do them. It goes both ways" (Ganong et al., 2022, p. 2800). Another stepsister described how she and her younger stepbrother bonded:

> I was like, "I'm gonna get to know you [and] you're gonna know all of me," so I basically initiated that, and so he did, too – it was a mutual, "we're gonna get to know each other and say things that we wouldn't tell our parents" kind of thing.
>
> (Ganong et al., 2020, p. 2800)

When stepsiblings *did* experience conflict, as siblings inevitably do, those who had close relationships engaged in productive conflict management strategies (Landon et al., 2022). For instance, stepsiblings used cognitive reframing to change the meanings they were attributing to the annoyances, interactions, or behaviors that were sources of conflict. For example, a stepbrother with younger stepsiblings explained, "Every once in a while, they [stepsiblings] will bother me, but it's never enough to address. They just go through little phases where they'll do things just like all kids do" (Landon et al., 2022, p. 271). This stepbrother reframed annoying behaviors as natural, developmental occurrences that were due to the stepsiblings' ages. He decided that they were not trying to irritate him on purpose and that their behaviors would change as they matured. Another daughter described what she believed to be the reason for her father treating her stepsister more leniently: "We just did the same thing, why are we getting treated different? I think it was because he [father] knew I was his and she [stepsister] wasn't and that he didn't have as much [control] over her" (p. 271). This step-sister engaged in perspective-taking to reframe and alleviate a situa-tion that could otherwise instigate conflict between the stepsiblings. Finally, another stepsister was upset with her stepbrother's treatment of her father but did not approach either him or her father because she reframed this as their conflict to resolve: "It wasn't my place to say that. It was between my dad and him, and they needed to work things out" (Landon et al., 2022, p. 271).

In addition to cognitive reframing, stepsiblings privately engaged in behaviors that helped them manage their emotions stemming from conflict. One young man would "go for runs around the neighborhood" (Landon et al., 2022, p. 271). A young woman stated that when she was upset with how things were going, "I journaled. I would write about whatever upsets me.... I'd write about how it seemed like [stepbrother] was able to have more friends over.... That pissed me off, so I'd write about that." Others talked through their feelings with biological siblings or parents as an indirect way to problem-solve. For example, one young woman explained: "I do not tell my mom in hopes that she will do some-thing or [in] hopes that she'll tell [stepdad]. I just tell her because I think it helps me work through the situation" (p. 271). These strategies appear to effectively help stepsiblings work through their feelings while protect-ing the stepsibling bond.

Another thing that stepsiblings can do to facilitate closer relationships is adopting an *adaptability mindset* (Ganong et al., 2022). The stepsib-lings who had the closest relationships exhibited flexible, make-it-work attitudes that shared a message of being adaptable and doing what they could to make the stepfamily successful, including bonding with stepsib-lings. As one stepchild described, "I would say adaptability was key, not closing yourself out from the situation because that would have made it a lot worse if anybody had" (Ganong et al., 2022, p. 2803). Another stated, "I'm a believer that everything happens for a reason, and you can always learn something from what you've done and what you've gone through … I'd rather focus on the good things than the bad things" (Ganong et al., 2020, p. 2803).

Finally, like with half-siblings, stepsiblings with the closest relationships used familial address terms to refer to each other (Koenig Kellas et al., 2008; Michaels, 2006; Mikucki-Enyart & Heisdorf, 2020). A mother in one study described how her daughter introduced her stepsiblings to friends and acquaintances: "Mary doesn't say, well, Johnny and those three are my step-brothers … She goes right down the line and names all of them. There is never a thought that there is a separation there" (Michaels, 2006, p. 60). Not using the "step" label, or not distinguishing between full siblings and stepsiblings when introducing siblings to others, communicated messages of closeness and belonging.

Close relationships with stepsiblings had benefits that extended throughout the entire stepfamily system. For example, in a study of later-life stepfamilies where stepsiblings were adults (often with children of their own), close stepsibling relationships made participants feel closer to their entire extended stepfamily (Mikucki-Enyart & Heisdorf, 2020). As one adult in a later-life stepfamily explained, "I guess as my stepsiblings and I get closer, I guess the rest of the family and I get closer" (Mikucki-Enyart & Heisdorf, 2020, p. 54). Being included in stepfamily rituals appeared to foster positive regard among late in life stepfamilies. For example, one person shared:

> They do this ritual, but it's not a new one, they already had it, they like all get together, like their aunts and uncles and everyone and they make cookies all day and then eat them that night. They started inviting us to that, like years ago. And they've been so warm to us, they give our kids presents at Christmas and they're just very, very, very good people. They are nicer and treat us better than my family, like my extended family.
>
> (Mikucki-Enyart & Heisdorf, 2020, p. 54)

Box 6.2 *What works* for stepsiblings

Effective parents and stepparents help stepsiblings bond when they:

- Nurture relationships with children across family transitions, such as moving in with new stepsiblings. When children perceive their relationships with the parent are valued while parents are trying to bond with stepchildren, it is easier for children to bond with stepsiblings.
- Engage stepsiblings in family activities together (e.g., dinners out, game nights, and family trips).
- Establish family traditions, such as shared meals and family dates with all the children.
- Make efforts to build positive relationships with stepchildren. When this happens, stepsibling relationships tend to be closer.
- Celebrate each child's unique and independent self without making comparisons between children.
- Help stepsiblings manage conflict by listening to and validating their concerns and engaging stepsiblings on possible solutions or compromises.

Effective stepsiblings bond when they:

- Identify shared interests and engage in those shared interests.
- Employ productive conflict management strategies (e.g., reframing issues as normal/manageable).
- Adopt flexible, make-it-work attitudes.

As the number of later-life stepfamilies grows, making people increasingly likely to acquire stepsiblings throughout the life course (Lin et al., 2018), the question of *how* people effectively bond with stepsiblings in adulthood will continue to be important (see Box 6.2). With an understanding of extant research on half- and stepsibling relationship development, we turn now to a discussion of how helping professionals can leverage these findings when working with stepfamily clients.

Implications for Practice

When parents with children from previous relationships repartner or remarry, they generally want their children to get along. Further, if the stepcouple goes on to have a shared child together, they generally want older stepchildren to claim the younger half-sibling fully. After all, close half- and stepsibling relationships facilitate feeling "like a family," which many perceive to be an important indicator of stepfamily success (Ganong et al., 2022; Michaels, 2006). Couples who are struggling in these areas may turn to helping professionals for guidance. Fortunately, there are many insights gleaned from these studies that can inform the clinical efforts of those who work with stepfamilies.

First, if stepcouples express frustration over turbulent half- or stepsibling ties, therapists can help them consider the extent to which those difficulties may be rooted in, or a reflection of, changes in the parent–child relationship. Research with half- and stepsiblings offers a valuable window into their emotional worlds, suggesting that strained relationships with their half- or stepsiblings often have roots that implicate the parent–child bond. For example, feelings of jealousy or resentment toward stepsiblings may reflect anxieties about the stability of the parent–child relationship, which has likely undergone a series of changes as parents and children adjust to stepfamily formation. Similarly, the extent to which children embrace or reject the birth of a younger half-sibling has much to do with the quality of the parent–child relationship. For example, when children perceive that their parent was not a good parent to *them* but is a better or more involved parent to their children from a second marriage, older half-siblings may harbor feelings that indirectly affect their ability to bond with younger half-siblings (Sanner et al., 2020). Therapists can gently explore, and help parents consider, the extent to which these dynamics are at play. Strengthening the quality of half- and stepsibling relationships may first require addressing unresolved issues in the history of the parent–child relationship. Therapists may be critical resources in facilitating open and honest discussions between parents and their children, which may have healing effects that extend to half- and stepsibling ties.

Second, assuming that unresolved issues in the parent–child relationship have been addressed, therapists can offer parents concrete strategies shown to work for fostering a family identity and facilitating stepfamily cohesion. Developing a shared family identity has been identified as a major task of stepfamily life (Ganong & Coleman, 2017). As the step-family architects, parents are in charge of this task, and therapists can remind parents of the importance of engaging in these efforts. Indeed, the extent to which parents engage in deliberate attempts to build a sense of family identity is consequential to stepfamily development (Ganong et al., 2022; Michaels, 2006). Half- and stepsibling relationships benefit from parents' facilitating shared activities, such as family dinners, game nights, family trips, family date nights, and attending and supporting all children's extracurricular activities as a family. Parents also should be reminded that it takes time to build family solidarity; the first two years may be especially challenging as children adjust to family changes, which is perfectly normal and to be expected. *Patience* is critical to successfully facilitating a shared family identity (Michaels, 2006).

Importantly, given that children are sensitive to losses in their one-on-one time with parents (Ganong et al., 2022), time devoted to shared family activities should not replace one-on-one time with children. Indeed, children appear to be more receptive to developing relationships with half- and stepsiblings when they do not feel that the quality and stability of the parent–child bond is threatened. Therefore, as discussed in Chapter 4, balancing shared family time with one-on-one time is important. Therapists can encourage parents to engage in deliberate attempts to bring half- and stepsiblings together and foster a family identity *and* remind parents to set aside one-on-one time with their children.

Finally, therapists can empower half- and stepsiblings themselves to take an active role in relationship development. These relationships are not merely a byproduct of parents' influences; half- and stepsiblings themselves have agency in the types of relationships they create. Older half-siblings facilitate closer relationships with younger half-siblings by being actively involved in their lives, taking care of them when they are young, initiating shared activities, and serving as mentors to them as they age (Sanner et al., 2020). In adulthood, half-siblings maintain close connections through meaningful exchanges of communication. Meaningful self-disclosures, or open and honest conversations about life and family, also boost half-sibling relationships for the better. Stepsiblings also can be empowered to take an active role in relationship development.

Identifying shared interests and making mutual attempts to get to know each other can set the stage for strong and meaningful connections (Ganong et al., 2022).

In addition to guiding these efforts, therapists can remind stepsiblings that occasional conflicts are natural and inevitable, and they can equip them with the tools and perspectives needed to navigate conflict productively (Landon et al., 2022). It is never too late to build or rebuild close connections with half- or stepsiblings; like any relationship, these relationships are malleable, dynamic, and capable of improving over time (Ganong et al., 2022).

Future Research

Although existing research offers useful insights into *what works* for half- and stepsiblings, research on half- and stepsiblings has only begun to scratch the surface. More work is needed on nearly all fronts of this emergent body of literature. To date, this work consists primarily of deficit-comparative studies in which researchers either (a) compare the well-being of children who live with half- or stepsiblings to the well-being of those who live with full siblings only, or (b) compare the quality of half- and stepsibling relationships to the quality of full-sibling relationships. Results from these studies tend to stigmatize half- and stepsibling relationships as inferior to full sibling relationships or as harmful to children's well-being. Instead of framing half- and stepsiblings from a deficit perspective, research is needed that identifies how, and under what conditions, half- and stepsiblings develop *close and meaningful* relationships. Half- and stepsiblings can be valuable sources of love and support – perhaps especially in times of family stress – and more work is needed to uncover the ways in which these relationships can confer meaningful benefits.

In doing this work, researchers should attend carefully to whose perspective is being documented and make efforts to capture a variety of stepfamily perspectives. For example, our knowledge about half-sibling relationships comes primarily from the perspectives of younger half-siblings, who were making inferences about their older half-siblings' feelings and perspectives (Sanner et al., 2020). Future research should document the perspectives of older half-siblings and identify what *they* perceive to be the key factors that facilitate or impede the development of close relationships with younger half-siblings. Similarly, research with stepsiblings should attend to whose perspective of *what works* is being documented and how (and why) perspectives within the same stepfamily might vary. For example, paternal stepsiblings may be especially sensitive to changes in the father–child relationships after divorce compared to maternal stepsiblings, and thus may have a more difficult time developing relationships with their father's new stepchildren. Researchers have not yet attended to potential differences in stepsibling experiences based on contextual variations, and future work should explore possible variations with a more nuanced lens.

Critically, as addressed in preceding chapters, documenting a variety of perspectives means capturing racial, ethnic, gender, and class diversity as research on stepfamilies moves forward. Too often, research with White middle-class families is represented as the universal family experience, and centering diverse perspectives means *decentering* Whiteness in future research on stepfamilies. Using nationally representative samples, we encourage researchers to test propositions about *what works* in stepfamilies. Qualitative studies have been enormously valuable in uncovering critical initial evidence about *what works*, but large-scale quantitative studies that test these propositions and explore the extent to which they hold for diverse samples will be an important agenda item moving forward.

Finally, as researchers recruit half- and stepsiblings for their studies, we urge them to be mindful of the language and labels used in their research advertisements. Given that families are socially constructed, how researchers define families is not always the same as how families define themselves (Sanner et al., 2021). For example, some half- and stepsiblings do not see themselves as half- and stepsiblings, but as merely siblings. We have learned that the labels "half-siblings," or "stepsiblings" can be restricting. Some potential study participants who we would see as falling into these categories may not identify with labels that suggest (to them, not to us) that the relationship of interest is anything less than fully familial. The social construction of kinship means that recruitment efforts must be clear, yet flexible – precise, but not restrictive. For example, in our own research ads, we have used language such as: "[A] team of researchers is interested in speaking with you about your relationships with your half- or stepsiblings (*even if you think of them as brothers and sisters, or if you don't think of them as family at all*)" (Sanner et al., 2021, p. 428). Whatever language is used, it is critical that it leaves room for the many ways in which half- and stepsiblings define and organize their relationships. Many opportunities lie ahead as researchers continue to uncover evidence about *what works* in stepfamilies, including for half- and stepsiblings.

References

Ahrons, C.R. (2007). Family ties after divorce: Long-term implications for children. *Family Process, 46*(1), 53–65. https://doi.org/10.1111/j.1545-5300.2006.00191.x

Ahrons, C.R., & Tanner, J.L. (2003). Adult children and their fathers: Relationship changes 20 years after parental divorce. *Family Relations, 52*(4), 340–351. https://doi.org/10.1111/j.1741-3729.2003.00340.x

Anderson, E.R. (1999). Sibling, half sibling, and stepsibling relationships in remarried families. *Monographs of the Society for Research in Child Development, 64*, 101–126. http://doi.org/10.1111/1540-5834.00049

Apel, R., & Kaukinen, C. (2008). On the relationship between family structure and antisocial behavior: Parental cohabitation and blended households. *Criminology, 46*, 35–70. http://doi.org/10.1111/j.1745-9125.2008.00107.x

Brown, S.L., Manning, W.D., & Stykes, J.B. (2015). Family structure and child wellbeing: Integrating family complexity. *Journal of Marriage and Family, 77*, 177–190. http://doi.org/10.1111/jomf.12145

Campo, M., Fehlberg, B., Millward, C., & Carson, R. (2012). Shared parenting time in Australia: Exploring children's views. *Journal of Social Welfare and Family Law, 34*, 295–313. http://doi.org/10.1080/09649069.2012.750480

Deater-Deckard, K., Dunn, J., & Lussier, G. (2002). Sibling relationships and social-emotional adjustment in different family contexts. *Social Development, 11*, 571–590. http://doi.org/10.1111/1467-9507.00216

Dunn, J. (2007). Siblings and socialization. In J.E. Grusec & P.D. Hastings (Eds.), *Handbook of Socialization: Theory and Research* (pp. 309–327). Guilford Press.

Fomby, P., Goode, J.A., & Mollborn, S. (2016). Family complexity, siblings, and children's aggressive behavior at school entry. *Demography, 53*, 1–26. http://doi.org/10.1007/s13524-015-0443-9

Ganong, L., & Coleman, M. (2017). *Stepfamily relationships: Development, dynamics, and interventions* (2nd ed.). Springer.

Ganong, L., Coleman, M., Fine, M., & Martin, P. (1999). Stepparents' affinity-seeking and affinity-maintaining strategies with stepchildren. *Journal of Family Issues, 20*, 299–327. https://doi.org/10.1177/019251399020003001

Ganong, L., Jensen, T., Sanner, C., Russell, L., & Coleman, M. (2019). Stepfathers' affinity-seeking with stepchildren, stepfather-stepchild relationship quality, marital quality, and stepfamily cohesion among stepfathers and mothers. *Journal of Family Psychology, 33*(5), 521. https://doi.org/10.1037/fam0000518

Ganong, L., Landon, O., Sanner, C., & Coleman, M. (2022). Patterns of stepsibling relationship development. *Journal of Family Issues, 43*(10), 2788–2809. https://doi.org/10.1177/0192513X211033924

Gilligan, M., Stocker, C.M., & Jewsbury Conger, K. (2020). Sibling relationships in adulthood: Research findings and new frontiers. *Journal of Family Theory & Review, 12*(3), 305–320. https://doi.org/10.1111/jftr.12385

Guzzo, K.B. (2021). Stepfamilies among currently cohabiting and married women under 45, 1988 and 2017. *Family Profiles*, FP-21-21. Bowling Green, OH: National Center for Family & Marriage Research. https://doi.org/10.25035/ncfmr/fp-21-21

Halpern-Meekin, S., & Tach, L. (2008). Heterogeneity in two-parent families and adolescent well-being. *Journal of Marriage and Family*, *70*(2), 435–451. http://doi.org/10.1111/j.1741-3737.2008.00492.x

Hornstra, M., Kalmijn, M., & Ivanova, K. (2022). Dissonant relationships to biological parents and stepparents and the well-being of adult children. *Journal of Social and Personal Relationships*, *39*(3), 481–504. https://doi.org/10.1177/02654075211031984

Jacobs, K., & Sillars, A. (2012). Sibling support during post-divorce adjustment: An idiographic analysis of support forms, functions, and relationship types. *Journal of Family Communication*, *12*(2), 167–187. https://doi.org/10.1080/15267431.2011.584056

Jensen, T.M. (2022). Stepparent–child relationships and child outcomes: A systematic review and meta-analysis. *Journal of Family Nursing*, *28*(4), 321–340. https://doi.org/10.1177/10748407221097460

King, V., Boyd, L.M., & Thorsen, M.L. (2015). Adolescents' perceptions of family belonging in stepfamilies. *Journal of Marriage and Family*, *77*(3), 761–774. https://doi.org/10.1111/jomf.12181

Koenig Kellas, J., LeClair-Underberg, C., & Normand, E.L. (2008). Stepfamily address terms: "Sometimes they mean something and sometimes they don't." *Journal of Family Communication*, *8*(4), 238–263. https://doi.org/10.1080/15267430802397153

Kreider, R.M., & Lofquist, D.A. (2014). Adopted children and stepchildren: 2010. United States Census Bureau. www.census.gov/content/dam/Census/library/publications/2014/demo/p20-572.pdf

Landon, O., Ganong, L., & Sanner, C. (2022). "Stop going in my room": A grounded theory study of conflict among stepsiblings. *Family Relations*, *71*(1), 256–278. https://doi.org/10.1111/fare.12595

Lin, I.F., Brown, S.L., & Cupka, C.J. (2018). A national portrait of stepfamilies in later life. *The Journals of Gerontology: Series B*, *73*(6), 1043–1054. https://doi.org/10.1093/geronb/gbx150

McHale, S.M., Updegraff, K.A., & Whiteman, S.D. (2012). Sibling relationships and influences in childhood and adolescence. *Journal of Marriage and Family*, *74*(5), 913–930. https://doi.org/10.1111/j.1741-3737.2012.01011.x

Michaels, M.L. (2006). Factors that contribute to stepfamily success: A qualitative analysis. *Journal of Divorce & Remarriage*, *44*(3–4), 53–66. https://doi.org/10.1300/J087v44n03_04

Mikkelson, A.C., Floyd, K., & Pauley, P.M. (2011). Differential solicitude of social support in different types of adult sibling relationships. *Journal of Family Communication*, *11*, 220–236. http://doi.org/10.1080/15267431.2011.554749

Mikkelson, A.C., Myers, S.A., & Hannawa, A.F. (2011). The differential use of relational maintenance behaviors in adult sibling relationships. *Communication Studies*, *62*(3), 258–271. https://doi.org/10.1080/10510974.2011.555490

Mikucki-Enyart, S.L., & Heisdorf, S.R. (2020). Obstacles and opportunities experienced by adult stepchildren in later life stepfamilies. *Journal of Divorce & Remarriage*, *61*(1), 41–61. https://doi.org/10.1080/10502556.2019.1619380

Pew Research Center (2011). *Changing American family survey*. Pew Research Center. www.pewresearch.org/social-trends/2011/01/13/a-portrait-of-stepfamilies/

Reczek, R., Stacey, L., & Dunston, C. (2022). Friend, foe, or forget 'em?: The quality of LGBTQ adult sibling relationships. *Journal of Marriage and Family*, *84*(2), 415–437. https://doi.org/10.1111/jomf.12821

Sanner, C., Ganong, L., & Coleman, M. (2020). Shared children in stepfamilies: Experiences living in a hybrid family structure. *Journal of Marriage and Family*, *82*(2), 605–621. https://doi.org/10.1111/jomf.12631

Sanner, C., Ganong, L., & Coleman, M. (2021). Families are socially constructed: Pragmatic implications for researchers. *Journal of Family Issues, 42,* 422–444. https://doi.org/10.1177/0192513X20905334

Sherman, A.M., Lansford, J.E., & Volling, B.L. (2006). Sibling relationships and best friendships in young adulthood: Warmth, conflict, and well-being. *Personal Relationships, 13*(2), 151–165. https://doi.org/10.1111/j.1475-6811.2006.00110.x

Strow, C.W., & Strow, B.K. (2008). Evidence that the presence of a half-sibling negatively impacts a child's personal development. *Economic Sociology, 67,* 177–206. http://doi.org/10.1111/j.1536-7150.2008.00567.x

Tanskanen, A.O., & Danielsbacka, M. (2019). Relationship quality among half siblings: The role of childhood co-residence. *Evolutionary Psychological Science, 5,* 13–21. https://doi.org/10.1007/s40806-018-0161-9

Tillman, K.H. (2008). "Non-traditional" siblings and the academic outcomes of adolescents. *Social Science Research, 37,* 88–108. http://doi.org/10.1016/j.ssresearch.2007.06.007

Thompson, E., Gray, E., & Carlson, M.J. (2020). Multi-partner fertility in Europe and the United States. In R. Schoen (Ed.), *Analyzing Contemporary Fertility* (pp. 173–198). Springer. https://doi.org/10.1007/978-3-030-48519-1_8

Turunen, J. (2014). Adolescent educational outcomes in blended families: Evidence from Swedish Register Data. *Journal of Divorce & Remarriage, 55,* 568–589. http://doi.org/10.1080/10502556.2014 .950897

van Dijk, R., van der Valk, I.E., Buist, K.L., Branje, S., & Deković, M. (2022). Longitudinal associations between sibling relationship quality and child adjustment after divorce. *Journal of Marriage and Family, 84*(2), 393–414. https://doi.org/10.1111/jomf.12808

Visher, E.B., & Visher, J.S. (2013). *Therapy with stepfamilies.* Routledge.

Volkom, M.V. (2006). Sibling relationships in middle and older adulthood: A review of the literature. *Marriage & Family Review, 40*(2–3), 151–170. https://doi.org/10.1300/J002v40n02_08

7

WHAT WORKS FOR STEPGRANDPARENTS AND GRANDPARENTS IN STEPFAMILIES

What Works for Stepgrandparents and Grandparents in Stepfamilies

Until recently, research on stepfamilies has focused primarily on younger stepfamilies – that is, families in which parents and stepparents are actively childrearing minor-aged children. Only within the last 20 years or so has research shifted to include older stepfamilies, examining topics such as later-life remarriage and stepgrandparenthood. Consequently, knowledge about *what works* for stepgrandparents and grandparents in stepfamilies has been based on relatively recent investigations. We begin by examining the prevalence of older adults in stepfamilies, followed by discussions of (a) *what works* for stepgrandparents, and (b) *what works* for grandparents in stepfamilies.

How Many Stepgrandparents and Grandparents in Stepfamilies Are There?

In the late 20th century, an estimated 39% of all U.S. families (including 55% of Black and 40% of Latino families) had a stepgrandparent (Szinovacz, 1998). There likely are more stepgrandparents and grandparents in stepfamilies than at any other point in history, primarily because (a) people are living longer than in the past, and (b) divorce and

DOI: 10.4324/9781003369073-7

repartnering in later life are more common than in the past, resulting in more complex relational histories (Ganong & Coleman, 2017). Life spans have doubled around the world in the last century, allowing more time for people to experience family and relationship transitions (Roser et al., 2013). Consider that, in 1900, a person had reached their expected life span in every country by 40 years of age, and by 50 years of age, they were considered elderly. Now, a 50-year-old in any industrialized nation is considered middle-aged and can expect to live another three decades.

In addition, individuals are less likely to spend their lives with the same partner. For example, although general divorce rates in the United States have been stable for decades, the phenomenon of *gray divorce*, or divorce among adults aged 50+, has dramatically increased (Brown & Wright, 2017). Since 1990, the rates of divorce for adults aged 55 to 64 have risen, with divorce rates for women nearly tripling and for men almost doubling (Schweizer, 2020). Rates of cohabitation and remarriage among older adults also continue to increase in the United States (Brown & Shinohara, 2013; Lin et al., 2018; Hemez & Brown, 2016; Julian, 2022; Schweizer, 2020). Not surprisingly, older Americans have complex marital and relational histories; data from the 2008–2012 American Community Survey indicated that over 25% of men and 28% of women born between 1940 and 1959 had been married more than once, with more than 9% of men and 7% of women in these cohorts having been married three or more times (Lewis & Kreider, 2015). Because most divorced adults have children from prior unions, many people who repartner in later life will acquire adult stepchildren and possibly stepgrandchildren. In fact, in the United States in 2010, nearly 18% of women and 19% of men aged 57 to 62 were stepgrandparents (Yahirun et al., 2018). It is estimated that, by 2030, older Americans will likely have as many stepgrandchildren as they have grandchildren (Wachter, 1997).

As with trends for longevity, greater relationship instability is a global phenomenon (Tanskanen et al., 2020). There is ample evidence that many middle-aged and older adults are stepgrandparents and grandparents in multigenerational stepfamilies worldwide (Buchanan & Rotkirch, 2018; Even-Zohar, 2023; Koren & Lipman-Schiby, 2014; Leopold & Skopek, 2015; Margolis, 2016; Marhankova & Stipkova, 2015). Moreover, we are seeing demographic shifts resulting from low fertility combined with increased longevity, meaning that grandparents and stepgrandparents are making up a greater share of the population. For several decades, women in North America, Europe, and the Pacific Rim (e.g., eastern Asia, New Zealand, Australia, and the Pacific islands) have had fewer children than earlier generations (Cherlin, 2010). As a result, there are fewer children relative to older adults in multigenerational families. Families in the areas of the world with reduced fertility now have more grandparents and great-grandparents than ever before in history, but these older kin have fewer grandchildren than in the past. Structurally, multigenerational families used to resemble pyramids, with the most people (grandchildren) at the bottom, and the fewest people (grandparents) at the top. Now, families in much of the industrialized world resemble rectangles, with comparable numbers of grandchildren, parents, and grandparents. Considered alongside the demographic trends of longer life spans and serial romantic unions, we find that some multigenerational stepfamilies resemble family bushes rather than family trees, with children in the youngest generation often being outnumbered by adults in the stepgrandparent/grandparent generation.

Pathways to Stepgrandparenthood

There are multiple ways to become a stepparent. For example, stepgrandparents could be the spouse of a biological grandparent (e.g., "Grandpa's wife") or they could be the parents of a stepparent (e.g., "stepmom's parents"). Stepgrandparents could join the family before the stepgrandchildren are born, when the stepgrandchildren are quite young, or when the stepgrandchildren are adults themselves. Given the multiple pathways to stepgrandparenthood, stepgrandparenthood is an amorphous family position that can take many forms (Chapman, Sanner et al., 2016).

The pathways to stepgrandparenthood represent enormous structural variability, depending on (a) whether the stepgrandparent is the spouse of a biological grandparent or the parent of a stepparent (said differently, whether the stepgrandparent acquired stepgrandchildren through their own remarriage or through their adult child's remarriage), and (b) when in the life course of stepgrandparents and stepgrandchildren their relationships begin (Allan et al., 2011; DeGreef & Burnett, 2017; Pashos et al., 2016). Indeed, a life course perspective suggests that the *timing* of the start of the stepgrandparent–stepgrandchild relationship matters for relational development. For example, a stepgrandparent may gain stepgrandchildren who range from infants to middle-aged adults, a contextual variation that affects the development of the relationships (Ganong & Coleman, 2017). Consequently, *what works* for a 75-year-old, newlywed stepgrandfather who just met his 30-year-old stepgrandson likely will not be the same behaviors and interactions that work for a 75-year-old stepgrandfather who has known his 30-year-old stepgrandson since the stepgrandson's birth.

There are four pathways by which stepgrandparent–stepgrandchild relationships are formed (Chapman, Sanner et al., 2016; Ganong & Coleman, 2017). In three of the pathways, the stepgrandparent is the spouse of a biological grandparent. What distinguishes among these pathways is the timing of *when* stepgrandparents enter the family. In the first pathway, *long-term stepgrandparenthood*, stepgrandparents join the family long before their future stepgrandchildren are born, when those future stepgrandchildren's parents are children themselves. Said differently, a *long-term stepgrandparent* is someone who raises minor-age stepchildren who grow up and become parents themselves, making the stepparent a stepgrandparent (Chapman et al., 2018). For example, in Figure 7.1, Jay became a *long-term stepgrandparent* when his stepson,

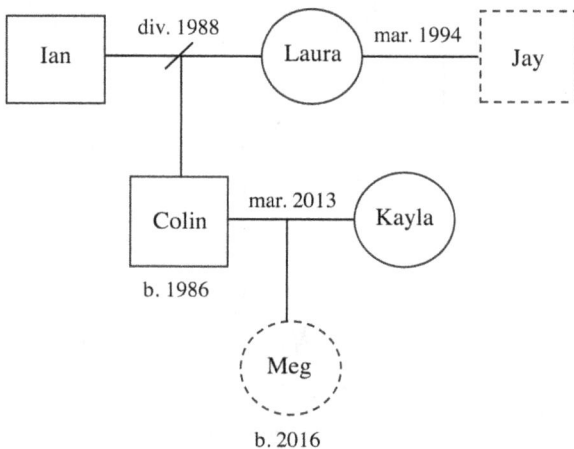

Figure 7.1 Long-term stepgrandparent pathway genogram

Colin, and Colin's wife, Kayla, had their first child, Meg. Jay has been Colin's stepfather since Colin was 8. Meg, now 6, has always known Jay as Papa (she calls Laura, Nanna, and Ian, Grandpa).

The second pathway is *later-life stepgrandparenthood*. Later-life step-grandparents enter the family much later, remarrying when their step-children are middle-aged and stepgrandchildren are adolescents or young adults (Chapman et al., 2018). For example, in Figure 7.2, Cal becomes a *later-life* stepgrandfather when, at 65, he marries 72-year-old Sue, the grandmother of Haley (30), Alex (26), and Luke (20). Sue's grandchil-dren, who are young adults, are unlikely to refer to their grandmother's new husband as *Grandpa* and are more likely to refer to him by his first name, Cal. Nonetheless, Cal is technically a stepgrandparent (a later-life stepgrandparent) to Sue's grandchildren.

A third pathway falls in between these two pathways in terms of when stepgrandparents enter the family. *Skip-generation stepgrandparents* join the family when their partner's children are young adults, but before or just after the birth of their stepgrandchildren (Chapman et al., 2017). Therefore, they have been in the family for the entire lives of their step-grandchildren, but not for the entire lives of their stepgrandchildren's parents, who were adults when the stepgrandparent joined the family. For

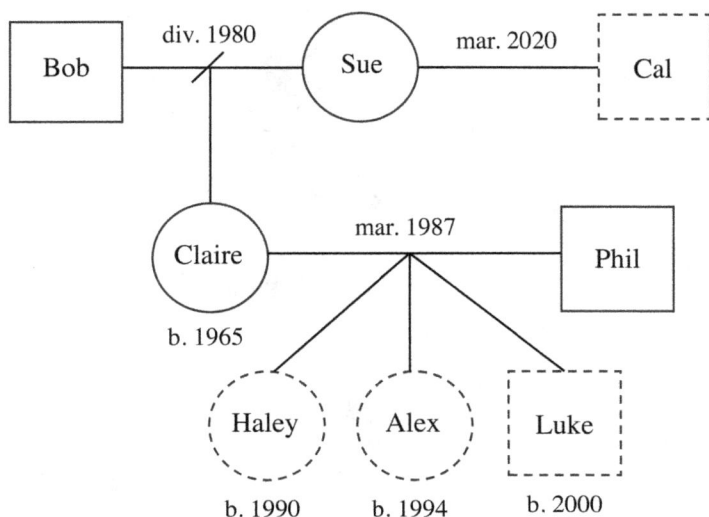

Figure 7.2 Later-life stepgrandparent pathway genogram

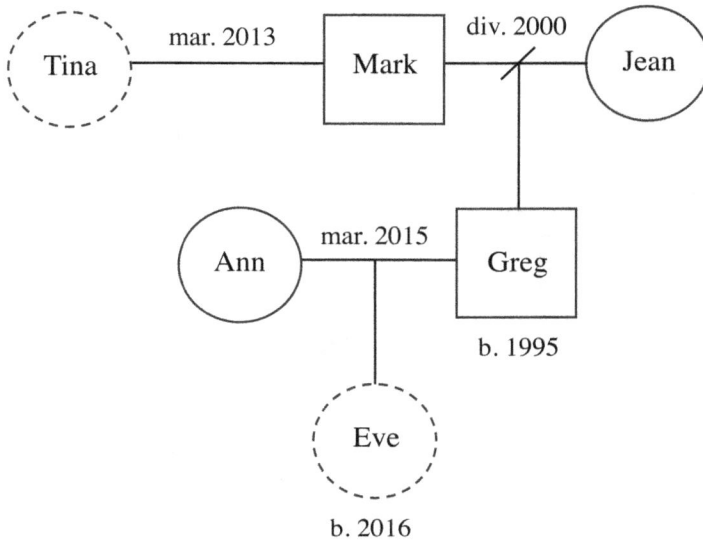

Figure 7.3 Skip-generation stepgrandparent pathway genogram

example, in Figure 7.3, Tina became a skip-generation stepgrandmother to Eve after just three years of marriage to Mark, Eve's grandfather. Tina is stepmother to Greg, who was 18 and in military service when Mark and Tina wed. Greg married two years later, never having lived with Tina and Mark as a couple. Eve, now 6 years old, has always known her family as having three grandparent figures, her biological grandparents (Amma and Gramps) and Tina (Granny T).

Unlike the previous three pathways, in which the stepgrandparent is the spouse of a grandparent, in the fourth pathway, the stepgrandparents are the parents of a stepparent. This occurs when an older adult's son or daughter marries a person who has children from previous unions. The older individuals "inherit" a new son- or daughter-in-law in addition to stepgrandchildren through their adult child's (re)marriage. Inherited stepgrandparents do not change their marital status and do not acquire a stepchild; in fact, many inherited stepgrandparents are in their first marriages and experience step-relationships for the first time (Ganong & Coleman, 2017; Sanner et al., 2019). For example, Figure 7.4 depicts Bill and Zoe, two long-married individuals who became *inherited stepgrandparents* when their son, Dan, married Lilly. Bill and Zoe did not just gain

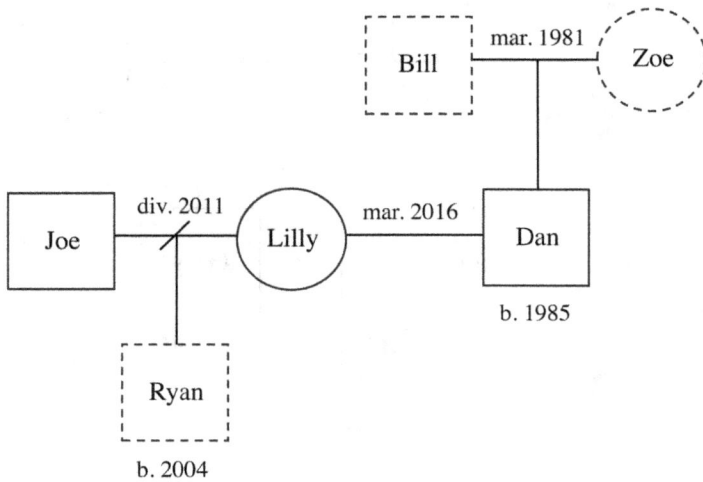

Figure 7.4 Inherited stepgrandparent pathway genogram

a daughter-in-law with Dan's marriage, they also "inherited" a stepgrandson, Lilly's son Ryan (12) from her first marriage.

Cal, Jay, Tina, and Bill and Zoe are all stepgrandparents, but the timing of their entry into the lives of their stepgrandchildren varies widely, as do their opportunities for bonding and building relationships. After all, the ages of their stepgrandchildren when they first meet range from young adulthood (Cal, the later-life grandfather), to infancy (Jay, the long-term stepgrandparent and Tina, the skip-generation stepgrandmother), to adolescence (Bill and Zoe, the inherited stepgrandparents), so that alone creates diverse contexts in which to begin relationships. We refer repeatedly to these structural differences as we explore the research evidence on *what works* for stepgrandparents.

Incompletely Institutionalized Family Position

Because stepgrandparenthood is an ambiguous family position, stepfamily members often have questions about what roles are expected of individuals in this family position, how they fit in the extended family system, and how should they interact with other family members, particularly stepgrandchildren. In many ways, stepgrandparents embody what Cherlin (1978) called an *incompletely institutionalized* family role because there are not clear norms and social guidelines for individuals and families to follow. This lack of social norms may be challenging for new stepgrand-parents and their extended family systems – not knowing what to do in a social role is stressful. On the other hand, having multiple grandparents *is* a normative expectation of contemporary families, so families are used to children having multiple grandfathers and grandmothers, which may make it easier for families to find roles for new stepgrandparents.

Research on *What Works* for Stepgrandparents

In contrast to the large body of research identifying grandparents as important sources of financial, physical, and emotional support to chil-dren and grandchildren (e.g., Cooney, 2021; Dunifon, 2013), there have been far fewer studies on stepgrandparents and their contributions to younger step-kin (Chapman, Sanner et al., 2016). Most investigators have either (a) described stepgrandparents, stepgrandchildren, and their relationships (e.g., documented the pathways to stepgrandparenthood) or (b) compared their interactions to those of biological grandparents and grandchildren (e.g., Block, 2002; Christensen & Smith, 2002; Coall et al., 2014; Gray & Brogdon, 2017; Pashos et al., 2016; Perry & Daly, 2021; Tanskanen et al., 2020). In what has been called the "step-gap" phenomenon, these latter investigations, using mainly evolutionary theories, report consistent differences between biological grandparent–grandchild relationships and stepgrandparent–stepgrandchild relation-ships in closeness, contacts, and exchanges of resources (e.g., Schoeni et al., 2022; Steinbach & Silverstein, 2020).

We found only nine studies that examined *how* stepgrandparents build close relationships with stepgrandchildren and negotiate roles for them-selves in the stepfamily system. All but two were qualitative studies. Eight of the nine studies gathered samples from the midwestern United States. Study participants mainly were White and middle class. Therefore, much of the findings on *what works* for stepgrandparents come from a lim-ited geographic area and from relatively homogeneous samples. The lone exception is an Israeli study of multiple-generation stepfamilies (Koren & Lipman-Schiby, 2014). In all but the Israeli investigation, which sampled three members of extended stepfamilies (Koren & Lipman-Schiby, 2014), data were gathered from individual stepgrandparents, step-grandchildren, and ex-stepgrandchildren. Given evidence that variations in stepgrandparent–stepgrandchild relationships are informed by a life course perspective, we distinguish *what works* for stepgrandparents based on when relationships began (*timing in lives*) and how long those relationships existed (*linked lives*).

What Works for Stepgrandparents with Younger Stepgrandchildren

Recall that long-term and skip-generation stepgrandparents have known stepgrandchildren since they were born (see Figures 7.2 and 7.3 for a quick refresher and examples of these types). Inherited stepgrandparents acquire stepgrandchildren who may be within a range of ages, from infants to adolescents (see Figure 7.4). Across these types, effective stepgrandparents of younger stepgrandchildren positively address the challenges in their incompletely institutionalized family positions by attending to and utilizing social norms about grandparenthood to find roles and places for themselves in the extended stepfamily system. In particular, these types of stepgrandparents build bonds with their young stepgrandchildren by: (1) *acting like a grandparent*, while respecting boundaries and following the lead of partners and middle-generation parents, (2) *publicly claiming their stepgrandchildren as kin*, (3) *adopting a kin-like name* that helps them with identifying as a family member, feeling included, and helping them know how to interact with other family members, and (4) *treating stepgrandchildren similarly* to how they treat their biological grandchildren.

Acting Like a Grandparent

One effective solution to the absence of clear norms about how to be a stepgrandparent is for them to enact – as much as is allowed by other family members – conventional and even stereotypical grandparent roles. In other words, in the absence of societal guidelines for stepgrandparenthood, stepgrandparents with close ties to stepgrandchildren function *as if* they are grandparents to the children, taking cues from norms about grandparents to know how to interact with their young stepgrandchildren. Researchers described this as stepgrandparents relying on *social scripts* for grandparents (Chapman et al., 2017) and enacting what they perceived to be stereotypical or common grandparental roles (Chapman, Coleman, & Ganong, 2016; DeGreef & Burnett, 2017). Even stepgrandchildren used these social conventions as they evaluated *long-term*

(Chapman et al., 2018), *skip-generation* (Chapman, Coleman, & Ganong, 2016), and *inherited* (Sanner et al., 2019) stepgrandparents' efforts to build relationships by comparing their interactions with them to how their biological grandparents treated them. Stepgrandparents who acted similarly to biological grandparents were judged more favorably by stepgrandchildren, and relationship bonds were stronger (Chapman et al., 2018; Chapman, Coleman, & Ganong, 2016; Sanner et al., 2019). One long-term stepgranddaughter, describing her relationship with her long-term stepgrandmother, said:

> She treated me like a granddaughter. Whenever I would come into town, she would take me with her ... so she could show her friends her granddaughter, and she had pictures of me on the refrigerator. I think those experiences and feelings were pretty typical of what I experienced with my other biological grandparents ... It was pretty much the same feeling, the same relationship to me.
>
> (Chapman et al., 2018, p. 107)

So, what did *acting like a grandparent* entail? When stepgrandchildren are infants and toddlers, effective stepgrandparents hold, comfort, and otherwise engage in the many necessary caretaking duties required to nurture infants and young children (Chapman, Coleman, & Ganong, 2016; Chapman et al., 2017). As children grow, stepgrandparents acting as grandparents play with them, attend their school and sports events, and host or attend extended family celebrations and gatherings (DeGreef & Burnett, 2017; Sanner et al., 2019). For stepgrandchildren of all ages, acting like a grandparent involved giving gifts on birthdays and holidays and "spoiling them rotten" (DeGreef & Burnett, 2017, p. 614) by randomly indulging them with small presents, letting them get away with things parents would not have allowed, and spending time together (DeGreef & Burnett, 2017). Engaging in these grandparent-like behaviors led stepgrandchildren to perceive stepgrandparents as kin, and relationships were closer than when stepgrandchildren did not think stepgrandparents acted like "traditional" grandparents (Chapman, Coleman, & Ganong, 2016). As one stepgrandchild noted in a study, "When you think of a grandma, she's supposed to be a good listener [and] be someone that [a] stepgrandson can relax around and have fun with" (Chapman et al., 2017).

We hasten to add that *acting like a grandparent* does not mean that effective stepgrandparents automatically expect they are going to be accepted as grandparents. Effective stepgrandparents whose stepgrandchildren are very young look not only to cultural norms and social stereotypes about grandparents (Chapman et al., 2017), but also to their partners and to other grandparents they knew, or had known, to get clues about appropriate behaviors (DeGreef & Burnett, 2017). By taking cues from biological grandparents, stepgrandparents implicitly seek permission to engage alongside them as another grandparent. One benefit of paying attention to grandparents is to sensitize stepgrandparents to boundaries – effective stepgrandparents respect the "primacy of all family-of-origin grandparents" by not overstepping and not competing with grandparents (DeGreef & Burnett, 2017, p. 619).

There is ample evidence that effective long-term and skip-generation stepgrandparents often build bonds with young (infant or toddler) stepgrandchildren in the same ways as grandparents do (Chapman et al., 2018; Chapman, Coleman, & Ganong, 2016). In these forms of multigenerational stepfamilies, by the time stepgrandchildren are aware that stepgrandparents are not genetically related to them, a strong emotional bond has often been created. Although it is far easier for long-term and skip-generation stepgrandparents to act "like a grandparent" because their stepgrandchildren have known them from infancy, some inherited stepgrandparents (i.e., the parents of a stepparent) also may benefit from engaging in grandparental behaviors by interacting with stepgrandchildren as a grandparent would, particularly if stepgrandchildren are young when their parent repartners (Sanner et al., 2019).

Publicly Claiming Stepgrandchildren

Children expect older adults to initiate interactions and relationship development, and one of the most meaningful actions is when long-term, skip-generation, and inherited stepgrandparents claim the stepgrandchildren as their kin (Chapman, Coleman, & Ganong, 2016). They do this by introducing the children to others as "my grandson" or "my granddaughter" and by making sure family outsiders knew that they were related.

They also include stepgrandchildren in family photos during holidays and extended family gatherings (Sanner et al., 2019). Publicly claiming stepgrandchildren is a way of defining external family boundaries – telling everyone who is in and who is out of the kin network. Publicly being included as family sends powerful messages about belonging, mattering, and kinship.

Adopting a Kin-Like Name

In Western societies, it is not unusual for children to have more than one grandmother and grandfather, so figuring out unique names is a normative, expected part of life in multigenerational families. Stepgrandparents pay more attention to what they are called than do younger family members, and there is evidence that kin-like names help stepgrandparents feel more included (Chapman et al., 2017) and this helps them develop identities as stepgrandparents and in feeling as if they have a place in the extended stepfamily (DeGreef & Burnett, 2017). Stepgrandchildren also use familial terms to facilitate bonding (Mikucki-Enyart & Heisdorf, 2020). Stepgrandparents who would like to adopt a kin-like name with younger stepgrandchildren can broach the subject with their partner and their stepgrandchildren's parents. As a participant in one study described:

> I'm Grandma, and we set that up ahead of time [before step-grandchildren were born] … we had the discussion … [I said], "Okay, so what, who am I gonna be" you know, cause I'm the third one in the chain here. They [several stepfamily members] wanted me to be Grandma … and the family had a warm spot for the name Grandma, so I would be Grandma.
> (Chapman, Ganong, et al., 2017, p. 1151)

Treating Stepgrandchildren Equitably

Stepgrandchildren appreciate being treated the same as biological grandchildren, seeing this as a powerful symbol of kinship that makes them feel closer to stepgrandparents (Sanner et al., 2019). For example, giving comparable gifts to grandchildren and stepgrandchildren on birthdays and holidays, interacting with them in similar ways, and spending roughly equal amounts of time with them are seen by stepgrandchildren as indicators they are considered family members (Sanner et al., 2019). As a participant in one study described, "On Christmas when they'd give us gifts, or other times that we would just be together, I was [treated] the same as Kyle and Cooper [half-brothers] and all of my cousins who are their direct blood line" (Sanner et al., 2019, p. 492). Similarly, another participant in this study said, "They [stepgrandparents] came to Grandparents Day and our sports games, you know, the same way that they would do with Amy, Nick, and Jack [stepsiblings]" (p. 492). Being included in ongoing family rituals also helps adult stepgrandchildren feel closer to stepgrandparents and other stepfamily members (Mikucki-Enyart & Heisdorf, 2020). For long-term stepgrandchildren, having stepgrandparents include them in their wills is another example of behavior seen as equitable treatment (DeGreef & Burnett, 2017).

What Works for Stepgrandparents with Older Stepgrandchildren
Respecting Boundaries

Effective later-life grandparents do *not* attempt to act like grandparents. In these cases, at the time stepgrandparents enter the family system, their stepgrandchildren are typically either adolescents about to leave their parents' households or are adults residing in their own households, often with partners and children of their own, so bonding with them differs dramatically from the productive actions of stepgrandparents with younger stepgrandchildren. Effective later-life stepgrandparents recognize that their adolescent or adult stepchildren and stepgrandchildren likely will not readily accept them as a replacement for the deceased or divorced parent or grandparent, and so they respect family system boundaries and move more slowly to create bonds. They communicate clearly to younger family members that they do not want, nor do they intend, to replace deceased or absent grandparents (Koren & Lipman-Schiby, 2014). In stark contrast to evidence that effective stepgrandparents act like grandparents when stepgrandchildren are younger, successful later-life stepgrandparents make it clear that they are *not* going to act like a grandparent. Making it clear to younger stepfamily members that they have no intention of replacing departed loved ones helps reduce defensiveness and increase acceptance (Koren & Lipman-Schiby, 2014).

In addition to stating their intentions clearly and often, limiting public displays of affection with grandparents and not infringing on rituals designed to honor deceased grandparents, enhances younger kin's
acceptance of later-life stepgrandparents (Koren & Lipman-Schiby,
2014). Instead, effective later-life (and some inherited) stepgrandparents
who have older stepgrandchildren strive to build new relationships with
stepgrandchildren as friends (Koren & Lipman-Schiby, 2014; Sanner
et al., 2019), something they have in common with other effective stepgrandparents, regardless of family members' ages.

Affinity-Seeking Behaviors with Stepgrandchildren of All Ages

All effective stepgrandparents, regardless of the pathway that led them
to stepgrandparenthood, engage in affinity-seeking behaviors designed
to build bonds with stepgrandchildren and to sustain those connections
over time. These behaviors include getting to know the stepgrandchildren and their parents, showing sincere interest in stepgrandchildren's
lives, sharing resources and assisting younger generations in the extended
stepfamily, and taking cues from younger stepfamily members and following their leads on how rapidly they want to bond. Stepgrandchildren
generally appreciate stepgrandparents' efforts to bond, and they see these
efforts as important indicators that stepgrandparents care about them
(Sanner et al., 2019). As a participant in one study shared, "This is something small, but he [stepgrandfather] sent me a card here [at my dorm]
for my birthday. He took the time to get my new address and made an
effort to stay involved with where I am" (Sanner et al., 2019, p. 490).
Similarly, a stepgrandson shared:

> My stepmother's parents tried to get to know us. Always invited
> to family events. To this day I still get cards from them, like
> "thinking of you," and so I call them on a regular basis. Like they
> would come to my sporting events in high school.
>
> (p. 490)

Some stepgrandparents' affinity-seeking behaviors aimed at getting
stepgrandchildren to like them appear to be identical to grandparenting behaviors, such as giving gifts and attending children's activities as

observers (Sanner et al., 2019), but many of the behaviors more closely resemble stepparents' affinity-seeking actions with stepchildren. For example, getting to know them, finding out what they like to do for fun and then doing those activities, showing interest in their lives by asking them questions about what they are doing, and looking for shared interests and hobbies to enjoy together are common affinity-seeking behaviors by stepparents and stepgrandparents alike (Chapman et al., 2018; Sanner et al., 2019). Affinity-building efforts are more effective when stepgrandparents take the time to get to know stepgrandchildren's interests and personalities first. For example, one participant shared a meaningful story about a hat his stepgrandparents brought back for him from their Alaskan cruise. Explaining the gift's significance, he said, "I have worn a hat every day of my life since first grade ... it's an autistic thing that I have. It's almost like a safety blanket. I feel exposed without my hat" (Sanner et al., 2019, p. 491). Compare this example of affinity-building with an attempt made by a stepgrandparent that was less effective, because the stepgrandmother had not taken her time getting to know her stepgrandchildren well:

She [stepgrandmother] sent us Christmas gifts and got me, of all things, a Hannah Montana purse and shirt, which I had never worn girls' clothing. I'm not girly at all, so she was way off with that. And then she got my brother an Iron Man T-shirt, and he's just like "I'm not an Iron Man fan." So, I think she was very much guessing on what we were like based on typical children that age instead of actually getting to know us.

(Sanner et al., 2019, p. 491)

Seeking common interests is important because when stepgrandchildren see shared similarities with stepgrandparents, they find more reasons to relate to them and become closer (Chapman, Coleman, & Ganong, 2016). For instance, one stepgrandchild described how she and her stepgrandmother both appreciated fashion, and she fondly recalled their frequent trips to outlet malls (Sanner et al., 2019). Another participant reflected on her shared interests with her stepgrandparents, which facilitated their relationship:

They would take me around the farm, which I had a big interest in because I'm going to vet school next year, and everything
[related to] animals is kind of what I'm about, so I really enjoyed
that. They would take me out when there was a new calf and let
me bottle feed it, and it was just really cool.

In the event that the remarriage which brought stepgrandparents into
the family dissolves (either through the death of a partner or separation/
divorce), what happens to stepgrandparent–stepgrandchild ties? Former
stepgrandparents can maintain relationships with former stepgrandchildren to the extent that they initiate contact and exert continued efforts
to remain involved (Sanner et al., 2018). Because bonds already exist
between the two stepfamily members, we call these *affinity-maintaining*
behaviors. Former stepgrandchildren appreciate the efforts of ex-
stepgrandparents to reach out to them after stepfamily dissolution, and
they benefit by receiving love and support from former stepgrandparents
who continue to claim them as family (Sanner et al., 2018).

What Middle-Generation Parents Do that Make Stepgrandparents More Effective

Gate-Opening

There are several actions taken by the middle-generation parents of the
stepgrandchildren that benefit the development of close stepgrandparent–
stepgrandchild bonds. Parents may be seen as "gatekeepers" of their children, especially when children still reside with them. In other words, parents either facilitate access (gate-open) or hinder access (gate-close) to
their children (Ganong et al., 2016). Gatekeeping is an expected aspect
of parenting that helps protect children from potential harm and enriches
children's lives by exposing them to constructive individuals and experiences while reducing exposure to potentially harmful individuals, ideas,
and activities (Ganong et al., 2016). In multigenerational stepfamilies,
parental gate-opening can have huge positive impacts on stepgrandparents. The primary gatekeepers in stepfamilies usually are the biological
parents of children, although when the stepgrandparents are the parents
of a stepparent, the stepparent of stepgrandchildren also acts as a gate-
opener or gate-closer.

In multigenerational stepfamilies, gate-opening involves allowing stepgrandparents to have access to stepgrandchildren (Chapman et al., 2017). Providing opportunities for older and younger generations to spend time together is one of the most basic gate-opening actions of parents. Gate-opening may begin early in the stepgrandchildren's lives. As one stepgrandmother explained: "They let me hold the baby at the hospital, and they were just very open to me watching him, keeping him" (Chapman et al., 2017, p. 1151). Parents also gate-open by allowing stepgrandparents to adopt kin-like names when stepgrandchildren are new infants (Chapman, Coleman, & Ganong, 2016; Chapman et al., 2017). Parental gate-opening makes it easier for stepgrandparents to function like grandparents as stepgrandchildren age.

For inherited stepgrandparents, who are the parents of a stepparent, parental gate-opening also is critical. As the sons- or daughters-in-law of stepgrandparents, parents are generally invested in promoting relationships between their children and their spouses' families – after all, it is the parents' remarriage that introduced the stepgrandparents to the family. Strategies for effectively promoting relationships between children and stepgrandparents vary based on children's age at the time of remarriage. When stepgrandchildren are younger when they acquire the stepgrandparents (e.g., early childhood), they tend to be more malleable and more receptive to parents' active encouragement to bond with stepgrandparents (Sanner et al., 2019). This could include arranging times to visit stepgrandparents, inviting stepgrandparents for family meals, asking stepgrandparents to babysit, reminding stepgrandchildren to talk with stepgrandparents at family gatherings, and encouraging stepgrandchildren to address stepgrandparents using a grandparent label (e.g., Grandma, Papa; Sanner et al., 2019). When stepgrandchildren are older when they acquire stepgrandparents (e.g., in adolescence), they tend to be slower to adjust to the acquisition of stepfamily members. In these circumstances, parents help facilitate intergenerational relationships by not putting pressure on children to bond with stepgrandparents. They do this by telling children that it is up to them whether or not, and how much, they bond with stepgrandparents, and they allow children to move at their own pace. The element of *choice* is key to stepgrandchildren's involvement in bonding. As one participant shared, "Having a sense of independence and control over my thoughts and feelings was extremely helpful. It allowed me to gravitate toward my stepfamily at my own pace, not the pace that my stepgrandparents may have wanted from me" (Sanner et al., 2019, p. 494).

Modeling Positive Relationships

Additionally, parents aid the development of close stepgrandparent–stepgrandchild relationships by modeling for their younger children warm and familial interactions with stepgrandparents (Chapman et al., 2017; Chapman et al., 2018). Children and adolescents look to their parents for guidance about how they are supposed to think and feel about stepgrandparents (Chapman, Coleman, & Ganong, 2016; Chapman et al., 2018; Sanner et al., 2019) and former stepgrandparents after divorce (Sanner et al., 2018). Stepgrandchildren, particularly when younger, imitate parents in their interactions with stepgrandparents. Clear messages of parental acceptance and approval of stepgrandparents positively influence stepgrandchildren perceptions of the stepgrandparents. For example, on taking cues from their parents about their skip-generation stepgrandparents, one participant shared:

> I think [my mom] made me closer to [my stepgrandfather] because she would take me to see my Papa, and I could see how happy she was when she was visiting him. I think she kind of helped … make me close to him.
> (Chapman, Coleman, & Ganong, 2016, p. 639)

Similarly, another stepgrandchild said, "I wanted to be just like my dad. So, seeing my dad get along with my stepgrandmother made me think, 'OK, well if dad can get along with her then it's OK, and you know I'll do the same'" (Chapman, Coleman, & Ganong, 2016, p. 639).

Long-term stepgrandchildren shared similar sentiments about the role their parents played in shaping the stepgrandparent–stepgrandchild relationship (Chapman et al., 2018). One participant shared, "My dad has very positive things to say about my stepgrandfather, so I'm definitely not going to think anything negative of him because he's a great guy according to my dad" (Chapman et al., 2018, p. 109). As another participant put it, "My mom really saw him as a dad figure, so to me he was a grandpa figure" Chapman et al., 2018, p. 109).

Although the quality of relationships between parents and stepgrandparents sets the stage for the relationships children develop with stepgrandparents, this does not mean that stepgrandparents cannot develop positive bonds with stepgrandchildren if relationships between the older generations are strained. They can, but the task is harder than if stepgrandparents and stepgrandchildren's parents/stepparents get along well with each other. Even long-term step-relationships are changeable; Clawson and Ganong (2002) found that adult stepchildren who had emotionally distant and even hostile ties with their older stepparents, warmed to them when they saw how stepgrandparents interacted lovingly with their new stepgrandchildren. Adult stepchildren began having second thoughts about their stepparents when they observed how much they gave to their stepgrandchildren and how much the little ones loved the stepgrandparents. The results of a single study should not be seen as a guarantee, but these results suggest that stepgrandparenthood can be a second chance for older adults to nurture and bond with younger step-kin, and that such nurturing has both direct effects (close bonds with stepgrandchildren) and indirect effects (more positive interactions with adult stepchildren).

At the very least, given the ambiguity of stepgrandparenthood, middle-generation parents can communicate clear expectations for stepgrandparents about the family roles expected from them (Chapman et al., 2017; Koren & Lipman-Schiby, 2014). Given that children follow their parents' examples, parents should be aware that (a) close relationships with stepgrandparents may benefit their children, and (b) the extent to which their children develop familial relationships with stepgrandparents is largely in parents' control.

What Biological Grandparents Do that Make Stepgrandparents More Effective

Biological grandparents also can provide helpful interpersonal contexts for stepgrandparents. Biological grandparents may be the partners/spouses of stepgrandparents, the ex-partners of those grandparents, or the parents of the stepgrandchildren's other parent (although there is little information from research about them). Researchers have reported two ways that grandparents help stepgrandparents: (a) by accepting them into the family and making it clear to the younger generations that there is a place for the new stepgrandparent, and, (b) for stepgrandparents with younger stepgrandchildren, by modeling grandparenting in the family.

Accepting Stepgrandparents

Grandparents usually cannot be gatekeepers in the same ways that parents can, primarily because they typically do not reside with the children and have less influence over them. Grandparents can facilitate gate-opening, however, by accepting and even welcoming stepgrandparents. For example, in one study, stepgrandmothers observed their husbands communicating openly with children and grandchildren about what roles they wanted their wives to play in the extended family (Chapman et al., 2017). When both husbands and husbands' ex-partners (e.g., the biological grandmother) are accepting of new partners, stepgrandmothers' comfort levels increase dramatically – "They welcomed me with no problems" (Chapman et al., 2017).

The actions of the grandparent/partner may be particularly important for later-life stepgrandparents. After all, these older adults are joining a multigenerational family whose members may have little motivation to bond with Grandpa's new wife or Grandma's new spouse. It is challenging for later-life stepgrandparents to build relationships with multiple people concurrently (i.e., adult stepchildren, adult stepgrandchildren), most of whom are busy adults with jobs, partners, and children of their own (Chapman et al., 2018). Having the partner (and ex-partner) of the new stepgrandparent assertively accept them may assist bonding with adult or older adolescent stepgrandchildren (Chapman et al., 2018; Chapman et al., 2017). As one stepgranddaughter noted:

> My stepgrandmother, my grandpa, and my grandma can get along in the same room for a reasonable period of time … and my stepgrandmother and grandpa still ask about how my grandma is doing, and she wants to know about how they're doing as well.
>
> (Chapman et al., 2018, p. 110)

Modeling Grandparenting

Although cultural norms about grandparents are widely known, each family has its own expectations for what constitutes good and appropriate grandparenting. Earlier we noted that long-term and skip-generation stepgrandparents (i.e., those who have been in stepgrandchildren's lives since they were born) look for cues on how to interact with stepgrandchildren by looking to cultural norms as well as observing and modeling their partners' grandparenting (DeGreef & Burnett, 2017; Soliz, 2007). Modeling "traditional" grandparenting may help younger family members accept stepgrandparents more easily because they are doing what grandparents are "supposed" to do in that extended family system. For grandparents with older grandchildren, making it clear via modeling and communicating that their new partners will not be replacing the deceased or absent grandparents, helps to facilitate the development of new roles for stepgrandparents (Koren & Lipman-Schiby, 2014).

What Stepgrandchildren Do that Makes Stepgrandparenting More Effective

Paying Attention to Stepgrandparents' Efforts to Bond

Although stepgrandparents' efforts to bond are critical to relationship development, these efforts do not guarantee that close relationships will form. When an individual is trying to get another person to like them (i.e., affinity-building), it is imperative that the other person note those befriending behaviors, perceive them as welcome efforts to bond, and respond accordingly with their own affinity-building behaviors (Ganong et al., 1999). Stepgrandchildren facilitate the development of close relationships by recognizing stepgrandparents' efforts to bond and responding accordingly (Sanner et al., 2018; Sanner et al., 2019; Soliz, 2007). Stepgrandchildren generally expect older adults to initiate relationship development (Sanner et al., 2019), and they notice when stepgrandparents treat them as if they were their own grandchildren, claim them publicly as their own, and make efforts to reach out to them in nurturing and supportive ways (DeGreef & Burnett, 2017; Sanner et al., 2019; Soliz, 2007). Stepgrandchildren evaluate how well stepgrandparents match cultural and personal expectations for functioning as effective grandparents, and they generally respond positively when they perceive stepgrandparents to be doing a good job (Chapman et al., 2018; Sanner et al., 2019).

Paying Attention to Parents' Relationships with Stepgrandparents

Similarly, paying attention to how parents interact with and treat step-grandparents is a requisite for stepgrandchildren imitating warm and positive bonds they witness (Chapman, Coleman, & Ganong, 2016; Chapman et al., 2018). Of course, older stepgrandchildren have greater agency to make up their own minds about how to interact with step-grandparents, but long-term and skip-generation stepgrandchildren have been socialized into their families' world views, and they internalize much of what they have witnessed from parents and step/grandparents before they become cognitively capable of making their own decisions about stepgrandparents. Even for children who are older when they acquire a stepgrandparent, the actions, attitudes, and feelings conveyed to them by parents, grandparents, and stepgrandparents help shape their perceptions of their stepgrandparents and how they will relate to them (see Box 7.1).

Box 7.1 *What Works* for stepgrandparents

When stepgrandchildren are young

Effective stepgrandparents:

- Act like a grandparent as much as possible, while also respecting boundaries.
- Publicly claim stepgrandchildren.
- Treat stepgrandchildren the same as grandchildren are treated.
- Use a kin-like name in the family, such as Meema, Nana, or Grandpa.

It helps stepgrandparents if middle-generation parents:

- Allow stepgrandparents opportunities to bond with stepgrand-children.
- Model warm relationships with stepgrandparents.
- Communicate clear expectations to new stepgrandparents.

It helps stepgrandparents if biological grandparents:

- Accept stepgrandparents as additional grandparents.
- Model appropriate grandparenting in that family system.

Stepgrandchildren help stepgrandparents be more effective in building close relationships if they:

- Pay attention to stepgrandparents efforts to bond and respond accordingly.
- Pay attention to parents' interactions and relationship quality with stepgrandparents.

When stepgrandchildren are older

Effective stepgrandparents:

- Recognize they are not seen as a replacement grandparent by younger kin.
- State intentions to younger family members that they will *not* try to replace an absent grandparent.
- Limit public displays of affection to their new partners.
- Refrain from participating in memorial services for deceased grandparents.
- Let the grandparent, adult stepchild, or stepgrandchildren lead the pace of relationship-building.

It helps stepgrandparents if middle-generation parents:

- Allow stepgrandparents opportunities to bond with step-grandchildren (shows trust).
- Model warm relationships with stepgrandparents.
- Communicate clear expectations to new stepgrandparents.

It helps stepgrandparents if biological grandparents:

- Model and communicate appropriate new roles for stepgrandparents.

Stepgrandchildren help stepgrandparents be more effective in
building close relationships if they:

- Pay attention to stepgrandparents efforts to bond and respond
  accordingly.
- Pay attention to parents' interactions and relationship quality
  with stepgrandparents.

When stepgrandchildren are any age when relationships begin

- Reach out to stepgrandchildren by getting to know them,
  showing interest in their lives, and finding common interests.
- Share resources and assist younger family members.

What Works for Grandparents in Stepfamilies

Although clinicians have written about grandparents in stepfamilies
for over 40 years (e.g., Kalish & Visher, 1981), they have been relatively
ignored by researchers. This is odd, because social scientists have studied
grandparents extensively in the past half century, as longevity increased and
the likelihood of families containing grandparents amplified (Buchanan
& Rotkirch, 2018). There are many studies about grandparents' contributions to grandchildren, to adult children, and to extended families (e.g.,
Lussier et al., 2002). If we were writing about *what works* for grandparents, regardless of family structure, this would be a lengthy section,
because grandparents often make many contributions to the well-being of
younger kin and family relationships (Buchanan & Rotkirch, 2018). For
example, grandparents (a) provide emotional support for grandchildren
(Soliz, 2008), (b) provide financial support and other tangible resources
(Cooney, 2021), (c) transmit family history and culture (Kopera-Frye &
Wiscott, 2000), and (d) provide caregiving (Tanskanen et al., 2020).

Grandparents and Divorce

Researchers of grandparents after their own or their offspring's divorces and dissolutions have focused largely on the extent to which grandparents are able to maintain contacts with grandchildren (Drew & Silverstein, 2007; Lussier et al., 2002; Schoeni et al., 2022; Westphal et al., 2015). If grandparents stay in touch with grandchildren after middle-generation adults dissolve their unions, this often is because either the adult with physical custody of the grandchildren is their offspring (Westphal et al., 2015), or their adult child and ex-partner maintain cordial relations with each other and with former in-laws (Fingerman, 2004). Cordial relationships contribute to more gate-opening by middle-generation parents, and therefore to more grandparent–grandchild contacts (Albertini & Tosi, 2018; Gladstone, 1989). In general, physical custody of children after relational dissolution predicts grandparents' involvement – the parents of nonresidential parents tend to have less contact and more emotionally distant relationships with grandchildren than grandparents whose offspring have physical custody (Doyle et al., 2010; Jappens & Van Bavel, 2016; Lussier et al., 2002).

When grandparents continue to be involved with grandchildren after the adult children's divorce, they continue to be helpful to children and grandchildren in a variety of ways (Soliz, 2008). In some studies, grandparents are reported to increase their support to children and grandchildren after middle-generation divorce, which is positive for children (Johnson, 1999; Lussier et al., 2002). For example, children's wellbeing is greater after parental divorce when grandparents are emotionally close to them (Lussier et al., 2002). When grandparents divorce, however, they tend to have less contact with grandchildren, are less involved in their lives, and feel less emotionally close to them (King, 2003). These effects are greater for grandfathers, paternal grandparents, and those with weaker ties to grandchildren before the divorce (King, 2003).

Research on *What Works* for Grandparents in Stepfamilies

So, what happens to grandparents after an offspring repartners? Early studies reported that grandparents stepped back when adult children repartnered, having less contact (Bridges et al., 2007; Lussier et al., 2002), assuming less visible involvement, and offering less assistance

(Clingempeel et al., 1992), in part to give the new couple and stepfamily household more privacy and space to bond. When grandparents repartnered, they also reduced contact and aid to grandchildren (Danielsbacka & Tanskanen, 2016). This is not to say that grandparents are not important figures in stepfamily life. Closeness between grandparents and grandchildren in stepfamilies is associated with fewer behavior problems for children (Bridges et al., 2007), suggesting that grandparents remain important characters in grandchildren's lives after parental remarriage. Additionally, clinicians Kalish and Visher (1981) asserted that grandparents could be valuable in building bridges between generations in multigenerational stepfamilies. For example, grandparents can welcome new step-kin to participate in extended family gatherings, include them in holiday celebrations, or ensure that birthdays of new extended step-kin are observed.

The research evidence for *what works* for grandparents in stepfamilies is meagre. Only six studies fit our inclusion criteria (see the Appendix for a refresher on the criteria). Once again, we bemoan the lack of diversity in the studies' samples. Although four countries are represented (UK, USA, Canada, Israel), the samples are mostly middle class and predominantly of European descent. The U.S. researchers sampled college students (Kennedy, 1991; Kennedy & Kennedy, 1993: Soliz, 2007), Gladstone (1989) interviewed Canadian grandmothers, another study contained data from 11 to 16-year-old youth in England (Attar-Schwartz et al., 2009), and the final study sampled grandparents, adult children, and grandchildren in Israeli stepfamilies (Koren & Lipman-Schiby, 2014).

Maintaining Their Grandparenting

So, *what works* for grandparents in stepfamilies? From the perspective of grandchildren, they are closest to grandparents who spend time with them, engage in fun activities, explore shared interests, and hang out in leisure time pursuits (Kennedy, 1991; Kennedy & Kennedy, 1993). Grandchildren in stepfamilies were closest to grandparents who listened carefully to them, offered advice and mentoring, and provided them with emotional and instrumental support (Attar-Schwartz et al., 2009; Kennedy, 1991; Kennedy & Kennedy, 1993; Koren & Lipman-Schiby, 2014). Grandparents to whom grandchildren were closest looked after them when they were young and attended school and social events in which children were active (Attar-Schwartz et al., 2009). The actions of effective grandparents in younger stepfamilies are similar to effective stepgrandparents in how they interact with grandchildren still residing with their parents and are similar to effective grandparents in single-parent households and nuclear families (Kennedy, 1991; Kennedy & Kennedy, 1993; Soliz, 2007). For older grandparents who repartner later in life, avoiding public displays of affection with new partners, helping new partners recognize and appreciate internal family boundaries, and allowing adult offspring and grandchildren time to accept and bond with new stepgrandparents at their own pace, are critical actions (Koren & Lipman-Schiby, 2014).

Middle-Generation Gate-Opening

As we noted earlier, parents function as gatekeepers to their children, and this gatekeeping function applies to grandparents as well as to stepgrandparents (Gladstone, 1989; Soliz, 2007). Grandmothers who maintain "friendly, good or even very good" relationships with former children-in-law have greater access to and contact with grandchildren (Gladstone, 1989, p. 359). New in-laws also play a gatekeeping role, and grandmothers who had cordial relationships with their children's new partners also have more involvement with their grandchildren (Gladstone, 1989). Grandmothers who supply resources to remarried adult children, and grandmothers who reach out to new stepgrandchildren, treating them affectionately and including them in activities with their grandchildren, found that middle-generation children and children-in-law are more willing to be gate openers and to bestow greater access to grandchildren (Gladstone, 1989) (see Box 7.2).

Box 7.2 *What Works* **for grandparents in stepfamilies**
- Continue doing what they have done prior to the formation of the stepfamily to maintain effective and satisfying relationships with grandchildren after stepfamily formation.
- Maintain at least cordial relationships with former in-laws and adult children, so that access to grandchildren is available.
- Develop cordial relationships with new in-laws, so that access to grandchildren is available.

Implications for Practice

To recap, bonding strategies for stepgrandparents depend on the ages of stepgrandchildren when those relationships begin. Internal family boundaries (e.g., the extent to which middle-generation parents welcome stepgrandparents into the family) also matter when attempting to create and maintain close bonds with stepgrandchildren. For grandparents, maintaining positive bonds with grandchildren in stepfamilies is based on how well grandparents maintain cordial or warm relationships with middle-generation parents. As with stepgrandparents, boundaries are important considerations for grandparents in multigenerational stepfamilies. Stepgrandparenting and grandparenting take place within social contexts. *What works* for stepgrandparents and grandparents involves input from multiple family members.

Although few studies have focused on *what works* for stepgrandparents and grandparents, we can draw clear clinical implications from this research. First, clinicians should be aware of the complexity of stepgrandparenthood and should know the rudiments of the different types of stepgrandparents, because *what works* for stepgrandparents is tied to when, in their own and their stepgrandchildren's life courses, they become stepgrandparents.

Stepgrandparents: Timing in Lives, Bonding Strategies, Boundaries

Although affinity-seeking behaviors with stepgrandchildren works for all types of stepgrandparents, for the most part, the widely divergent contexts of these various types of stepgrandparents mean that the process of relationship development with stepgrandchildren differs substantively.

Timing in Lives

The life course perspective concept of *timing in lives* means that *when* in life courses events occur has enormous implications for individuals and their relationships, and is key in understanding effective *what works* behaviors and interactions. Bonding behaviors with infants differ enormously from bonding approaches with adolescents. Moreover, if a grandparent repartners late in life, the likelihood of their grandchildren living far away, with busy lives of their own involving jobs, partners, and children, may make bonding with the grandparent's new partner impractical and a low priority.

Stepfamily members, and professionals working with them, may want to start with assessing the timing in lives issue by asking such questions as "What would it take to build a bond?;" "What are the stepgrandchildren's needs when these relationships begin?," and "What is realistic to expect from these relationships, given where stepgrandparents and stepgrandchildren are in their respective life courses?" These questions may seem simple and maybe even unnecessary for stepgrandparents whose adult stepchildren welcome a new baby into their lives, but they are important questions for later-life and inherited stepgrandparents. For example, adult stepchildren acquiring a stepgrandparent may not react warmly when introduced "to their new Grandmother," a poor start that could have been avoided by some advanced considerations of timing in lives issues. Similarly, adolescent and school-aged stepgrandchildren whose parents have just repartnered and who now have inherited stepgrandparents (i.e., their stepparents' parents), may not be ready to bond in the beginning, and their inherited stepgrandparents, who may be in their first marriages and unfamiliar with stepfamily dynamics, may initially be unsure how they will relate to their offspring's new stepchildren. By thinking about and discussing the questions above, and other questions regarding intergenerational ties, stepfamily members can avoid missteps and work cooperatively to build the kind of stepgrandchild–stepgrandparent bonds that make sense to them.

Bonding Strategies

Effective bonding behaviors depend on the type of stepgrandparenthood. Long-term and skip-generation stepgrandparents with close ties frame bonding behaviors as *acting like a grandparent*, starting in infancy and continuing, while later-life and inherited stepgrandparents with close ties generally view their bonding behaviors as ways of building relationships with school-age and older stepgrandchildren, which we have called *affinity-seeking behaviors* (Ganong et al., 1999). In fact, individuals who become stepgrandparents later in life should *not* expect to be accepted as grandparent replacements (Koren & Lipman-Schilby, 2014). In reading these studies, we distinguish between *acting like a grandparent* and *affinity seeking* because the stepgrandparents were clearly using cultural norms about grandparents, observations of grandparents, and their own experiences with grandchildren, to figure out their roles and ways of being in a multigenerational stepfamily. Sometimes *acting like a grandparent* and *affinity-seeking behaviors* are similar. For example, acting like a stereotypical grandparent means to engage in loving, giving, and nurturing activities and affinity-seeking and -maintaining behaviors involve paying attention to children, having fun with them, interacting in kind and caring ways, and getting to know stepgrandchildren as they grow. Effectively bonding with children entails varying amounts of practical caregiving (e.g., feeding, keeping them safe), nurturing (e.g., showing affection), sharing resources (e.g., giving money, imparting advice), and interpersonal connecting (e.g., observing, listening, disclosing). The mixture of these caregiving responsibilities varies as children age, and effective stepgrandparents enact this approach.

Family professionals can help stepfamilies navigate the nuanced differences between grandparenting and affinity-seeking. Although it is not clear how many families do this, there is evidence that communicating expectations and desires regarding stepgrandparent roles is helpful. This may be initiated by either older or younger stepfamily members, but some stepfamilies may need assistance in figuring out how to bring up topics related to stepgrandparents' roles and relationships. Stepfamilies with inherited stepgrandparents in particular may need some help in deciding how to incorporate the new stepparents' parents into the extended kin network. In these families, grandchildren may be old enough to have their own ideas about what and who they want stepgrandparents to be to them. The research suggests that these stepgrandparents can build bridges across generations by welcoming new stepgrandchildren with open arms (Sanner et al., 2018), but some older adults in these types of stepfamilies may be unsure of themselves, given that they often lack familiarity with stepfamilies.

Acting Like a Grandparent Versus Acting Like a Parent

In earlier chapters, we report evidence that for stepparents, becoming friends with stepchildren (as opposed to acting "like a parent") is a more effective path to developing emotionally close relationships. In contrast, the studies on stepgrandparents report that acting "like a grandparent" *is* an effective way to bond with young stepgrandchildren. What is the difference in these two step-kin positions?

In nearly every society, it is normative for children to have multiple (more than two) grandparents. It is also normative for families to make room for multiple grandmothers and grandfathers, and to allow children to develop ties with all of them. Therefore, it is more acceptable for extended stepfamilies to see stepgrandparents as additional grandparents rather than as replacements, especially when children are young. In addition, cultural norms about the roles of grandparents tend to be widely known (Hossain et al., 2018). Family members can rely on cultural norms about names for stepgrandparents, sharing time among extended kin households on birthdays and holidays, and other aspects of multigenerational kinship ties that reduce challenges for stepfamilies. In contrast, there are few cultures that normatively allow for more than two recognized parents, making it more of a challenge for stepparents to find space in their stepfamilies and to define relationships with stepchildren.

It is noteworthy that both stepparents and stepgrandparents often look to widespread norms about biological kin as guides for how to relate with step-kin. The goodness of fit between these step-kin positions and societal norms appears to benefit stepgrandparents more than stepparents, such that grandparenting norms align with effective stepgrandparenting more than parenting norms align with effective stepparenting. Again, it is worth pointing out the relevance of timing in lives, because modeling after biological kin relationships works primarily for stepfamilies when children are younger when the stepfamily is formed.

Boundaries Between Generations are Important

Stepgrandparents' attempts to bond with stepgrandchildren often depend on the good will of middle-generation adults. For grandparents and stepgrandparents, the middle generation serves as gatekeepers who can control access and contact to the youngest generation. If they want to maintain rigid boundaries between stepgrandparents and themselves and their children, then the degree to which intergenerational lives are linked is reduced, making it harder for bonding to happen.

Family professionals can help middle-generation adults maintain ties with older stepparents (i.e., the stepgrandparent) and repair relationships with them if needed. Gate-opening requires trusting the older adults, forgiving them for any past wrongs, and clearly communicating expectations with them. Family practitioners can assist family members in addressing unresolved issues between middle-generation parents and stepgrandparents, which is likely to have implications for the extent to which parents "let" stepgrandparents into their children's lives.

Grandparent–Stepgrandparent Boundaries

Grandparents can help their partners develop connections with grandchildren by communicating expectations to other family members, by providing opportunities for contacts between stepgrandparents and stepgrandchildren, and by modeling how to be a grandparent in that family. Professionals can help grandparents be aware of their important roles and by encouraging them to be gate openers between their partners and younger family members.

One important message that older stepgrandparents may need to hear is that others lead the pace of relationship-building with stepgrandchildren. Older adults who may have been successful in their work lives and in other relationships may feel that it is their responsibility to make things happen with stepgrandchildren. This runs the risk of creating unnecessary resistance from middle-generation adults, stepgrandchildren, and even grandparents. Family professionals can help guide these "hard-charging" stepgrandparents be better at listening and observing, encourage them to ask more questions, and help them take a slower pace as they get to know younger step-kin.

Grandparents

Grandparents in stepfamilies who have close bonds with grandchildren do the same activities with them as any good grandparent in any family structure. Of course, as noted, relationships with middle-generation adults are relevant, as access to grandchildren typically depends in part on children's parents allowing access. Family professionals can assist grandparents and their younger kin to maintain positive working connections, so that parents allow grandparents' access to grandchildren.

Future Research

The lack of research attention to intergenerational relationships in stepfamilies is puzzling. We need to know more about how stepgrandparents develop and maintain positive relationships with stepgrandchildren, and how grandparents maintain close relationships with grandchildren in stepfamilies. Moreover, information is needed on how stepgrandparents and grandparents contribute to the development and growth of stepgrandchildren, and how they achieve satisfaction in their positions in multigenerational stepfamilies. Such disinterest is not because there are few stepgrandparents or grandparents, since the numbers of stepgrandparents and grandparents are larger than ever. However, there are a few reasons why there has been little research attention on *what works* for stepgrandparents and grandparents.

First, more researchers and clinicians are interested in children and adolescents and their immediate families and households than are interested in the study of older adults and their ties to younger kin. In addition, given researchers' focus on the households of younger stepfamilies, it may be that stepgrandparents and grandparents are ignored by researchers unless they share a residence with younger kin. Even if three generations share a residence, if there is a cohabiting or remarried couple in the household, researchers in Western societies may not see older adults as integral to stepfamily functioning or to individual stepfamily members' well-being.

Second, the problems of stepgrandparents and grandparents and their relationships with younger stepfamily members may be less likely presented to family therapists and other practitioners. As a result, clinicians may write less frequently about these stepfamily issues, and therefore researchers may be less likely to notice these intergenerational relationships as needing investigations about *what works*.

Third, many stepgrandparents are hard for researchers to find because they may not *think* of themselves as stepgrandparents; they may see themselves simply as "grandparents." Stepgrandparents who see themselves as grandparents and not as stepgrandparents may not recognize themselves as step-kin on surveys, and thus they may not respond to researchers' recruitment efforts about stepgrandparenthood (Sanner et al., 2021). Still other stepfamily members may not respond to surveys and research recruitment attempts because they do not recognize that a stepgrandparent–stepgrandchild relationship even exists, such as in later-life remarriages or cohabiting unions of grandparents. In short, stepgrandparents and stepgrandchildren often may be "invisible" to researchers.

Finally, as we have noted before, a perspective that examines resilience dynamics and effective relationships is not a high priority among researchers. Instead, we often find descriptive studies that merely compare stepgrandparent–stepgrandchild relationships to biological grandparent-grandchild relationships on measures of closeness or relationship quality (i.e., "step-gap" investigations). These studies generally conclude that biological relationships are closer than step-relationships, with no guidance as to *how* close step-relationships come to be that way.

Overall, more studies are needed on *what works* for older adults and for multigenerational relationships in stepfamilies, including studies with more diverse samples that include ethnic, cultural, religious, and socioeconomic variations in multigenerational stepfamily relationships. The samples presented in this chapter are very Eurocentric and middle-class, so generalizations from them should be made cautiously. The importance of grandparents and the ease with which stepgrandparents are incorporated into family life may vary broadly across and within subcultures in societies. Large surveys should oversample for racial and ethnic diversity so that statistical analyses can be robust enough to examine racial and ethnic variation. Qualitative studies should be conducted that focus specifically on various dimensions of stepfamily diversity (e.g., racial, ethnic, SES) so that studies framed within specific contexts may be examined in-depth. The studies in this chapter focus on Western cultures for the most part, but Asian societies have different perspectives about intergenerational bonds and different roles for grandparents (Nozawa, 2020), so *what works* for grandparents and stepgrandparents is likely to vary by culture.

Whether quantitative, qualitative, or mixed-method designs are used, future research should continue to distinguish between different types of stepgrandparents. The extant literature makes it clear that how individuals enter stepgrandparent roles makes a difference in behaviors that are successful in developing close relationships, but much more in-depth analyses are needed to enrich our understanding of these resilience dynamics.

Finally, more attention should be paid to repartnered grandparents in stepfamilies and the effects of this transition on grandparent–grandchild relationships. There are a few studies of older stepparent–adult stepchild bonds (Kalbarczyk, 2021; Mikucki-Enyart & Heisdorf, 2020; Suanet et al., 2013), but there is little research about what repartnered grandparents do to maintain ties with grandchildren. *What works* for grandparents who have *living apart together* (LAT) relationships, in which they have committed relationships but do not share a residence with their partners (Benson & Coleman, 2016), also should be explored. In short, our collective knowledge of family complexity in later life has only just begun to scratch the surface. Greater understanding of these topics will enhance our ability to provide resources to individuals navigating family complexity throughout the life course.

References

Albertini, M., & Tosi, M. (2018). Grandparenting after parental divorce: The association between non-resident parent-child meetings and grandparenting in Italy. *European Journal of Ageing, 15*, 277–286. https://dx.doi.org/10.1007/s10433-018-0478-z

Allan, G., Crow, G., & Hawker, S. (2011). *Stepfamilies*. Palgrave Macmillan.

Attar-Schwartz, S., Tan, J.-P., Buchanan, A., Flouri, E., Griggs, J. (2009). Grandparenting and adolescent adjustment in two-parent biological, lone-parent, and step-families. *Journal of Family Psychology, 23*(1), 67–75. https://dx.doi.org/10.1037/a0014383

Benson, J.J., & Coleman, M. (2016). Older adults developing a preference for living apart together. *Journal of Marriage and Family, 78*, 797–812. https://dx.doi.org/10.1111/jomf.12292

Block, C.E. (2002). College students' perceptions of social support from grandmothers and stepgrandmothers. *College Student Journal, 36*(3), 419–433.

Bridges, L.J., Roe, A.E.C., Dunn, J., & O'Connor, T.G. (2007). Children's perspectives on their relationships with grandparents following parental separation: A longitudinal study. *Social Development, 16*(3), 539–554. https://dx.doi.org/10.1111/j.1467-9507.2007.00395.x

Brown, S.L., & Shinohara, S.K. (2013). Dating relationships in older adulthood: A national portrait. *Journal of Marriage and Family, 75*(5), 1194–1202. http://dx.doi.org/10.1111/jomf.12065

Brown, S.L., & Wright, M.R. (2017). Marriage, cohabitation, and divorce in later life. *Innovations in Aging, 1*(2), 90.

Buchanan, A., & Rotkirch, A. (2018). Twenty-first century grandparents: Global perspectives on changing roles and consequences. *Contemporary Social Science, 13*(2), 131–144. http://doi.org/10.1080/21582041.2018.1467034

Chapman, A., Coleman, M., & Ganong, L. (2016). "Like my grandparent but not": A qualitative investigation of skip-generation stepgrandchild-stepgrandparent relationships. *Journal of Marriage and Family, 78*, 634–643. https://doi.org/10.1111/jomf.12303

Chapman, A., Ganong, L., Coleman, M., Kang, Y.J., Russell, L., & Sanner, C. (2017). Negotiating a place in the family – A grounded theory exploration of stepgrandmothers' relationships with stepgrandchildren. *The Gerontologist, 57*(6), 1148–1157. https://doi.org/10.1093/geront/gnw112

Chapman, A., Kang, Y., Ganong, L., Sanner, C., & Coleman, M. (2018). A comparison of stepgrandchildren's perceptions of long-term and later-life stepgrandparents. *Journal of Aging Studies, 47*, 104–113. https://doi.org/10.1016/j.jaging.2018.03.005

Chapman, A., Sanner, C., Ganong, L., Coleman, M., Russell, L., Kang, Y.J., & Mitchell, S. (2016). Exploring the complexity of stepgrandparent-stepgrandchild relationships. In G. Gianseni & S.L. Blair (Eds.), *Divorce, separation, and remarriage: The transformation of family, Contemporary perspectives in family research, 10*, 101–130.

Cherlin, A. (1978). Remarriage as an incomplete institution. *American Journal of Sociology, 84*, 634–650. http://doi.org/10.1086/226830

Cherlin, A.J. (2010). Demographic trends in the United States: A review of research in the 2000s. *Journal of Marriage and Family, 72*, 403–419. http://doi.org/10.1111/j.1741-3737.2010.00710.x

Christensen, F.B., & Smith, T.A. (2002). What is happening to satisfaction and quality of relationships between step/grandparents and step/grandchildren? *Journal of Divorce & Remarriage, 37*(1-2), 117–133. http://doi.org/10.1300/j087v37n01_07

Clawson, J., & Ganong, L. (2002). Adult stepchildren's obligations to older stepparents. *Journal of Family Nursing, 8*, 50–73. http://doi.org/10.1177/107484070200800104

Clingempeel, W.G., Colyar, J.J., Brand, E., & Hetherington, E.M. (1992). Children's relationships with maternal grandparents: A longitudinal study of family structure and pubertal status effects. *Child Development, 63*, 1404–1422. http://doi.org/10.2307/1131565

Coall, D.A., Hilbrand, S., & Hertwig, R. (2014). Predictors of grandparental investment decisions in contemporary Europe: Biological relatedness and beyond. *PLOS One, 9*(1), e84082. http://doi.org/10.1371/journal.pone.0084082

Cooney, T.M. (2021). Grandparents' support to young families: Variations by adult children's union status. *Journal of Marriage and Family, 83*(3), 737–752. http://dx.doi.org/10.1111/jomf.12728

Danielsbacka, M., & Tanskanen, A.O. (2016). Grandfather involvement in Finland: Impact of divorce, remarriage, and widowhood. In *Grandfathers* (pp. 183–197). Palgrave Macmillan. http://dx.doi.org/10.1057/978-1-137-56338-5_10

DeGreef, B.L., & Burnett, A. (2017). Are you my grandmother? Constructing and maintaining stepgrandparent identity and roles. *Communication Quarterly, 65*(5), 603–623. http://doi.org/10.1080/01463373.2017.1329218

Doyle, M., O'Dywer, C., & Timonen, V. (2010). "How can you just cut off a whole side of the family and move on?" The reshaping of paternal grandparent-grandchild relationships following divorce or separation in the middle generation. *Family Relations, 59*(5), 587–598. http://doi.org/10.1111/j.1741-3729.2010.00625.x

Drew, L.M., & Silverstein, M. (2007). Grandparents' psychological well-being after loss of contact with their grandchildren. *Journal of Family Psychology, 21*(3), 372–379. http://doi.org/10.1037/0893-3200.21.3.372

Dunifon, R. (2013). The influence of grandparents on the lives of children and adolescents. *Child Development Perspectives, 7*(1), 55–60. http://doi.org/10.1111/cdep.12016

Even-Zohar, A. (2023). The relationships of divorced grandparents and their grandchildren. *Journal of Family Issues, 44*(4), 1021–1045. http://doi.org/10.1177/0192513x211055110

Fingerman, K.L. (2004). The role of offspring and in-laws in grandparents' ties to their grandchildren. *Journal of Family Issues, 25*(8), 1026–1049. http://doi.org/10.1177/0192513x04265941

Ganong, L., & Coleman, M. (2017). *Stepfamily relationships* (2nd ed.). Springer.

Ganong, L., Coleman, M., & Chapman, A. (2016). Gatekeeping after separation and divorce. In L. Drozd, M. Saini, & N. Oleson (Eds.), *Parenting plan evaluations: Applied research for the family court* (2nd ed., pp. 308–345). Oxford University Press. http://doi.org/10.1093/med:psych/9780199396580.003.0011

Ganong, L., Coleman, M., Fine, M., & Martin, P. (1999). Stepparents' affinity-seeking and affinity-maintaining strategies with stepchildren. *Journal of Family Issues, 20*(3), 299–327. http://doi.org/10.1177/019251399020003001

Gladstone, J.W. (1989). Grandmother-grandchild contact: The mediating influence of the middle generation following marriage breakdown and remarriage. *Canadian Journal on Aging, 8*(4), 355–365. http://doi.org/10.1017/s0714980800008564

Gray, P.B., & Brogdon, E. (2017). Do step-and biological grandparents show differences in investment and emotional closeness with their grandchildren? *Evolutionary Psychology, 15*, 1–9. http://doi.org/10.1177/1474704917694367

Hemez, P., & Brown, S.L. (2016). Cohabitation in middle and later life. *Family Profiles*, FP-16-20. Bowling Green, OH: National Center for Family & Marriage Research. www.bgsu.edu/resources/data/family-profiles/hemez-brown-cohabitation-middle-later-life-2014-fp-16-20.html. http://doi.org/10.1111/j.1741-3737.2012.00994.x

Hossain, Z., Eisberg, G., & Shwalb, D.W. (2018). Grandparents' social identities in cultural context. *Contemporary Social Science, 13*(2), 275–287. https://doi.org/10.1080/21582041.2018.1433315

Jappens, M., & Van Bavel, J. (2016). Parental divorce, residence arrangements, and contact between grandchildren and grandparents. *Journal of Marriage and Family, 78*, 451–467. http://doi.org/10.1111/jomf.12275

Johnson, C.L. (1999). Effects of adult children's divorce on grandparenthood. In M. Szinovacz (Ed.), *Handbook on grandparenthood* (pp. 184–199). Greenwood.

Julian, C.A. (2022). Older adult cohabiting and married couples. *Family Profiles*, FP-22-16. Bowling Green, OH: National Center for Family & Marriage Research. https://doi.org/10.25035/ncfmr/fp-22-16

Kalbarczyk, M. (2021). Non-financial support provided to parents in stepfamilies: Empirical examination of Europeans 50+. *International Journal of Environmental Research and Public Health, 18*(10), 5151. https://doi.org/10.3390/ijerph18105151.

Kalish, E. & Visher, E. (1981). Grandparents of divorce and remarriage. *Journal of Divorce, 5*, 127–140. http://doi.org/10.1300/j279v05n01_10

Kennedy, G.E. (1991). Grandchildren's reasons for closeness with grandparents. *Journal of Social Behavior and Personality, 6*(4), 697–712.

Kennedy, G.E., & Kennedy, C.E. (1993). Grandparents: A special resource for children in stepfamilies. *Journal of Divorce & Remarriage, 19*(3/4), 45–68. http://doi.org/10.1300/j087v19n03_04

King, V. (2003). The legacy of a grandparent's divorce: Consequences for ties between grandparents and grandchildren. *Journal of Marriage and Family, 65*, 170–183. http://doi.org/10.1111/j.1741-3737.2003.00170.x

Kopera-Frye, K., & Wiscott, R. (2000). Intergenerational continuity: Transmissions of beliefs and culture. In B. Hayslip, Jr., & R. Goldberg-Glen (Eds.), *Grandparents raising grandchildren: Theoretical, empirical, and clinical perspectives* (pp. 65–84). Springer.

Koren, C., & Lipman-Schiby, S. (2014). "Not a replacement": Emotional experiences and practical consequences of Israel second couplehood stepfamilies constructed in old age. *Journal of Aging Studies, 31*, 70–82. http://doi.org/10.1016/j.jaging.2014.09.002

Leopold, T., & Skopek, J. (2015). The demography of grandparenthood: An international profile. *Social Forces, 94*, 801–832. https://doi.org/10.1093/sf/sov066

Lewis, J.M., & Kreider, R.M. (2015). *Remarriage in the United States*. American Community Survey Reports, ACS-30. U.S. Census Bureau.

Lin, I.-F., Brown, S.L., & Cupka, C.J. (2018). A national portrait of stepfamilies in later life. *Journals of Gerontology: Social Sciences, 73*(6), 1043–1054. http://doi.org/10.1093/geronb/gbx150

Lussier, G., Deater-Deckard, K., Dunn, J., & Davies, L. (2002). Support across two generations: Children's closeness to grandparents following parental divorce and remarriage. *Journal of Family Psychology, 16*(3), 363–376. http://doi.org/10.1037/0893-3200.16.3.363

Margolis, R. (2016). The changing demography of grandparenthood. *Journal of Marriage and Family, 78*(3), 610–622. http://doi.org/10.1111/jomf.12286

Marhankova, J.H., & Stipkova, M. (2015). Women as care managers: The effect of gender and partnership status on grandparent care for grandchildren. *Czech Sociological Review, 51*(6), 929–958. http://doi.org/10.13060/00380288.2015.51.6.224

Mikucki-Enyart, S.L., & Heisdorf, S.R. (2020). Obstacles and opportunities experienced by adult stepchildren in later life stepfamilies. *Journal of Divorce & Remarriage, 61*(1), 41–61. https://doi.org/10.1080/10502556.2019.1619380

Nozawa, S. (2020). Similarities and variations in stepfamily dynamics among selected Asian societies. *Journal of Family Issues,* 41(7), 913–936. doi:10.1177/0192513X20917766

Pashos, A., Schwarz, S., & Bjorkland, D.F. (2016). Kin investment by step-grandparents – More than expected. *Evolutionary Psychology, 14,* 1–13. http://doi.org/10.1177/1474704916631213

Perry, G., & Daly, M. (2021). Grandparental partnership status and its effects on caring for grandchildren in Europe. *PloS One, 16*(3): e0248915. http://doi.org/10.1371/journal.pone.0248915

Roser, M., Ortiz-Ospina, E., & Ritchie, H. (2013). Life expectancy. Published online at OurWorldInData.org. Retrieved from https://ourworldindata.org/life-expectancy.

Sanner, C., Coleman, M., & Ganong, L. (2018). Relationships with former stepgrandparents after remarriage dissolution. *Journal of Family Psychology, 32,* 251–261. http://doi.org/10.1037/fam0000377

Sanner, C., Ganong, L., Chapman, A., Kang, Y., & Coleman, M. (2019). Building family relationships with inherited stepgrandparents. *Family Relations, 68,* 484–499. http://doi.org/10.1111/fare.12381

Schoeni, R.F., Freedman, V.A., Cornman, J.C., & Seltzer, J.A. (2022). The strength of parent-adult child ties in biological families and stepfamilies: Evidence from time diaries from older adults. *Demography, 59*(5), 1821–1842. http://doi.org/10.1215/00703370-10177468

Schweizer, V. (2020). Age variation in the remarriage rate, 1990 & 2018. *Family Profiles,* FP-20-13. Bowling Green, OH: National Center for Family & Marriage Research. https://doi.org/10.25035/ncfmr/fp-20-13

Soliz, J. (2007). Communicative predictors of a shared family identity: Comparison of grandchildren's perceptions of family-of-origin grandparents and stepgrandparents. *Journal of Family Communication, 7*(3), 177–194. http://doi.org/10.1080/15267430701221636

Soliz, J. (2008). Intergenerational support and the role of grandparents in post-divorce families: Retrospective accounts of young adult grandchildren. *Qualitative Research Reports in Communication, 9*(1), 72–80. http://doi.org/10.1080/17459430802400373

Steinbach, A., & Silverstein, M. (2020). Step-grandparent-step-grandchild relationships: Is there a "grand step-gap" in emotional closeness and contact? *Journal of Family Issues, 41*(8), 1137–1160. http://doi.org/10.1177/0192513x19886638

Suanet, B., Van Der Pas, S., & Van Tilberg, T.G. (2013). Who is in the stepfamily? Change in stepparents' family boundaries between 1992 and 2009. *Journal of Marriage and Family, 75,* 1070–1083. http://doi.org/10.1111/jomf.12053

Szinovacz, M.E. (1998). Grandparents today: A demographic profile. *The Gerontologist, 38,* 37–52. http://doi.org/10.1093/geront/38.1.37

Tanskanen, A.O., Danielsbacka, M., & Rotkirch, A. (2020). Grandparental childcare for biological, adopted, and step-offspring: Findings from cross-national surveys. *Evolutionary Psychology*, 18(1). https://doi.org/10.1177/1474704920907894

Wachter, K.W. (1997). Kinship resources for the elderly. *Philosophical Transactions of the Royal Society of London Biological Sciences*, *352*(13631), 1811–1817. http://doi.org/10.1098/rstb.1997.0166

Westphal, S.K., Poortman, A.-R., & Van der Lippe, T. (2015). What about the grandparents? Children's postdivorce residence arrangements and contact with grandparents. *Journal of Marriage and Family*, *77*, 424–440. https://doi/10.1111/jomf.12173

Yahirun, J.J., Park, S.S., & Seltzer, J.A. (2018). Step-grandparenthood in the United States. *Journals of Gerontology: Social Sciences*, *73*(6), 1055–1065.

8

SUMMARY OF WHAT WORKS
IN STEPFAMILIES

Summary of What Works for Stepcouples

Dating

Most divorced individuals, parents or not, are going to date and become romantically involved with other people, often soon after separating from their spouse. It also is likely that most widowed persons, particularly if they are younger adults or middle-aged, will seek companionship after the death of a spouse.

For parents who are divorced or separated and moving towards divorce, the main *what works* takeaway is awareness when dating, which is a simple-sounding task, but there are many barriers. Loneliness, fear of the unknown as a single parent, feeling the need for help with childrearing, a desire for companionship, for sex, for love – these and more are common reasons propelling separated parents into dating and the search for a new partner. From the perspective of a single parent, often the sooner, the better. Taking time and energy to be aware when dating is harder than it might seem, but the evidence suggests that awareness is key.

There are many things to be aware of when dating. Thinking about the qualities desired in a partner is a good place to start, which can occur before dating begins. Parents who are selective in their choice of dating partners do not settle or make compromises with what they want in a potential partner. They take time in choosing who to date and spend time with people who are good influences in their and their children's lives. Being aware means thinking about the well-being of themselves and their children. This means that a parent's list should include desirable characteristics for someone who someday might be a stepparent to their children, as well as qualities they would want in a companion. Being aware when dating also means thinking about the former spouse/partner, taking into consideration their feelings and concerns when faced with the possibility of a new person. This is someone they may not know and over whom they have no control, entering their lives (indirectly) and the lives of their children.

Being aware of the information that is communicated to others about dating activities and partners also is an important *what works* action. Researchers call these *privacy rules* – personal limits about how much dating information, when, and to whom to share (e.g., former partners, children, friends). These privacy rules can be changed as necessary and may be negotiated as shared privacy rules, such as agreeing with former partners and dating partners about what will be communicated to others.

Although less research has been conducted on post-bereavement dating of parents, it seems logical that much of what is found that works for post-divorce dating also may apply to widows and widowers. Instead of being aware about potential effects of dating on former spouses, bereaved parents benefit from being aware of the effects of dating on extended family members of the deceased (e.g., the deceased person's parents). In addition, allowing time for *self and children to mourn* their losses, and consulting with children prior to dating after bereavement, are *what works* behaviors found in the research on widowed parents that similarly might apply to post-divorce daters as well.

Preparing for a New Partner

The admonition to "know thyself," at least as this applies to self-in-romantic unions, is a good shorthand way of remembering the importance of awareness in repartnering preparation. Awareness is again the core of *what works* actions for individuals who have chosen a new partner and are readying themselves for stepfamily living. The list of what an adult contemplating forming a stepfamily with a new partner should be considering, according to research, is long. For example, knowing one's likes, dislikes, habits, what is wanted from a romantic relationship, what one is willing or not willing to give to a partner, pet peeves, past relationship mistakes, and past relationship strengths, have all been identified by researchers as useful self-knowledge for repartnering individuals who are creating stepfamilies.

Adults forming a stepfamily do better when they communicate their self-awareness (e.g., about their strengths and weaknesses as a romantic partner) to their new partners. In addition, it is important to know the partners – what they think they know about themselves, and their relationship needs and wants. Being aware about self and exploring the partners' awareness are critical tasks when preparing for remarriage and repartnerships. It should be noted that we know little from research about the most effective ways of sharing this knowledge. It is likely that many stepcouples who create satisfying unions identify what personal knowledge is helpful and how best to communicate it via trial and error as they interact with each other. It also is probable that some stepcouples benefit from receiving help in these awareness processes from therapists, educators, and other "third party" sources (e.g., self-help books, blogs, workshops).

Learning about Stepfamilies

Although research has yielded minimal evidence about how best to prepare for remarriage/repartnering, there is evidence that learning about stepfamilies helps stepcouples know more about what to expect. For example, it is useful for stepcouples to understand how stepfamily relationships and dynamics differ from that of first-marriage nuclear families. For instance, helping couples consider fiscal management and understanding the ranges of roles for stepparents, beyond that of being a substitute parent, may be useful to stepcouples.

Remarriage Ceremonies

Rituals are important for any organization, and not just for major life events. Most of us have daily, weekly, monthly, and annual rituals we perform, either alone or with others. Social subsystems have rituals because they hold symbolic value, indicating who, when, and sometimes why groups exist. Rituals can help group members bond, increase individuals' commitment to the group, and define boundaries (i.e., who belongs and who is excluded). Families create their own rituals, but part of family identity is generated by rituals that family members observe as members of religious, cultural, and political bodies that help family insiders and outsiders know who the family members are and what they stand for. Unfortunately, stepfamilies seldom have recognized formal rituals, and one challenge of new stepfamilies is to honor rituals of previous family groupings (households) while still developing new rituals as a stepfamily.

The relative absence of major rituals for stepfamilies may extend to remarriage ceremonies. Research findings on what works are limited, but we do know that more than the stepcouple should be involved in planning the wedding ceremony; all family members should have some input into planning, if they want it.

Constructive Individual Characteristics

We have already mentioned an important individual quality that assists stepcouples in establishing firm foundations for their stepfamilies – being aware of self and of partner's wants and needs. There are other individual attitudes that researchers have found to be useful for repartnered couples.

Confidence

A sense of optimism about the future of the relationship has been found important to effective stepcouples. Specifically, being confident that marital and familial problems can be solved together as a couple, and that the relationship will be resilient when facing stressors, form a beneficial constellation of attitudes and beliefs that serve as a valuable base for couples to build upon. Part of being confident in the couples' ability to problem-solve and address challenges is trusting the partner and feeling sure that he or she can be relied on. Individuals who start stepfamilies are more effective when they approach life's trials and tests and feel as if they, along with their new partners, will be able to overcome whatever difficulties they encounter. They are open to trying new ideas when previous problem-solving methods have been unsuccessful, and they likely stimulate a sense of confidence, trust, and loyalty in others. People who are poised, assured, and cool under fire generally are attractive to others, and inspire others to rally around them and work with them.

Cognitive Flexibility

Cognitive flexibility is being open to new ideas and experiences, being able to tolerate ambiguous situations, and being willing to change. Stepfamilies are complex and opportunities for ambiguous circumstances abound, so being able to manage in the face of unknown and unclear contexts is a positive attribute for stepcouple partners. A mindset of openness and willingness to try new things are personal attributes that make dealing with stepfamily issues less stressful and more manageable.

Repartnering Couple Dynamics

Stepcouples who enjoy each other form more effective and satisfying stepfamilies than stepcouples who do not. This sounds more like an outcome of what works practices than a strategy, but it likely is both. Couples who enjoy being together and who like and appreciate their partners, appear to share the household workload more equitably, including making decisions, childrearing, and managing money. Sharing the responsibility for household tasks and being on the same page about important issues like managing finances and taking care of children, likely means less stress for these stepcouples and lower expenditures of energy and time as they live their daily lives. After all, if partners can agree on important issues, help each other with tasks, and make decisions about subjects that both see as important, then less time is spent negotiating, and less cognitive and emotional energy is consumed trying to reach common ground.

Sharing family and household tasks fairly and jointly making decisions likely are actions that work for first partnerships as well as repartnerships. These behaviors might be the hallmarks of all satisfying marriages/romantic unions, but stepcouples face more challenges in doing so because of the complex contexts in which they live. Interested third parties, such as ex-spouses and stepchildren, can help or hinder stepcouples achieving success in doing what works for the couple bond. Context complexity means there are more relationships and more people, which means more demands for time from stepcouple partners. These demands may limit the time partners have to communicate and nurture relationships. In short, sharing workloads and decision-making tasks may be more critical for stepfamily couples than for those in first unions.

Stepcouple Communication

Stepcouple dynamics are rooted in clear communication between partners. Because stepcouples lack well-defined and distinct cultural norms and guidelines for how to create a stepfamily, they must figure out how to *do stepfamily living* on their own. Stepcouples are, therefore, what researchers have called discourse dependent relationships. Talking, engaging, clarifying, checking validity of assumptions and expectations, making few assumptions – these actions are part of creating relationships through discourse. The flip side of a lack of societal and cultural institutionalization for stepfamilies is the freedom to create and to flexibly explore what works for stepfamily members and for the whole family. Creation and exploration in stepfamily living are achieved via communication. Stepcouples who use these *what works* communication methods to connect clearly and effectively may be more willing to try new ways of thinking, being, and relating. Willingness to try new ways of being in relationships takes courage, as does willingness to fail.

It is not clear why some individuals and couples are more flexible in their thinking and doing. Are they more creative, less bound by traditional beliefs about families and family roles, better communicators, braver, more open to seeking help, more open to new ideas, more trusting, more optimistic about life in general, feel more self-confident? These are just some of the possibilities for why effective stepcouples communicate in ways that work out better for them and their children than what other stepcouples do. If the differences are better understood, perhaps clinicians and helping professionals could assist more stepcouples to be successful in meeting their goals.

On the other hand, nearly all *what works* communication skills can be learned. This is positive – a person does not have to be naturally skilled at communicating to become better at it.

Communication Topics

Talking about expectations, wants, and needs in the couple relationship is important, as are discussions about childrearing, relations with coparents, and setting boundaries around the couple subsystem and the stepfamily. It may not be an exaggeration to state that nearly all topics are relevant and crucial for stepcouples as they create their family cultures through conversation and discussion.

Clear communication is especially important because stepfamilies lack a shared history. This means that stepfamily members have different understandings about how to be a family. Merging two family cultures is challenging because people often do not think of their families as having somewhat distinctive cultural beliefs, norms for expected behaviors, and ways of behaving that are their own. Instead, family members tend to think that what they do, how they live, and how they relate are normal and the proper way to enact family life. First-time families evolve their norms for family life over time, but new stepfamilies are bringing *two established cultures* together. Communication is the key to understanding why their new family members do what they do. Inability to rely on unspoken understandings about mealtime etiquette, bedtime rituals, how laundry gets done, who makes the household rules, how children are reprimanded, and so on, makes communication more critical for stepfamilies, as they create new family realities via discourse. Clear and effective communication is a family-wide activity, but it begins with the stepcouple. Effective stepcouples communicate about a wide range of topics that help them fill the gaps in what they know about their partners and their children. Satisfied stepcouples have either recovered from being surprised at their initial naive assumptions about what stepfamily living will be like by talking about everything necessary for them to feel like a family, or they started right from the beginning by letting each other know what they felt and thought, wanted and needed, as they created their stepfamily culture.

Communication Skills that Work for Stepcouples

There appear to be two broad sets of skills that work for stepcouples. First are basic skills that improve communication abilities. These include sending clear messages, listening, responding empathically, and comforting and reassuring when partners express fears and concerns. These communication skills are the building blocks that are fundamental to successful relationships. Second are higher-order, more abstract skills that work for stepcouples. These include being open, positivity in expressing emotions and defining issues, reframing or cognitive reappraisal (i.e., attaching different meanings to the actions of others), problem-solving skills (e.g., negotiating and compromising), and setting boundaries. The distinction between basic and more abstract skills is arbitrary, and it should be emphasized that all these skills can be and are learned via trial and error or with professional assistance. These skills are essential to the content of marriage and stepfamily education, and clinical stepfamily experts have identified these skills as significant in creating and repairing relationships. Studies show that satisfied stepcouples employ these skills, which benefit couples and their stepfamilies.

Effective communication among stepcouples is especially important considering the emotional and relational histories that precede stepfamily formation. For example, because stepcouple partners often have experienced the ending of one or more close romantic relationships (i.e., marriages or cohabiting unions), and these endings may have been painful for one or both partners, that empathic responding to the expression of fears by a partner about the current relationship may be particularly pertinent and impactful. Framing interactions in more positive ways, and communicating positivity even when problem-solving with partners, are other communication skills that may have particularly beneficial effects on stepcouple relationships, given the likelihood of past relational troubles one or both may have experienced.

One phenomenon we have noticed over the years in interviewing members of long-term, stable stepfamilies, especially stepcouples, is that discourse about family interactions, how members are feeling about the stepfamily and step-kin bonds, and conversations about how things are going in the family, does not end when (step)children grow up and leave the stepcouple household. Stepfamilies that have been together for years, even decades, seem to never stop attending to and communicating about the well-being of the "state of the stepfamily." This collective awareness and attention to maintaining what is working may indicate positive habits developed over years of practice, or family procedures that serve to contribute to ensuring, as much as possible, that family members and the family unit function well.

Summary of What Works for Stepparents

Building Close Relationships with Stepchildren

Effective stepparenting involves building close relationships with stepchildren. One of the most robust *what works* findings is that stepparents have closer and more satisfying relationships with stepchildren when they focus on building a friendship with them. There are many ways to accomplish this goal, but stepparents *must* build affinity with stepchildren for step-relationships to work.

Bonding with stepchildren takes time and energy. Effective stepparents are thoughtful about their stepchildren's backgrounds, personalities, ages, wants and needs when seeking to build closer relationships with them. Affinity seeking with stepchildren involves giving – sharing knowledge, skills, resources, attention, and time. Building a bond with stepchildren is aided by positivity, which means having fun with stepchildren, giving them valued "stuff" (i.e., time, attention, goods), and reinforcing outcomes that stepchildren value (e.g., getting homework done, solving problems). The onus for initiating relationship development with stepchildren is on the stepparent. For close ties to develop, stepchildren must respond appropriately, but the process begins with the stepparents.

Building a close emotional attachment with stepchildren may take much longer than stepparents (and their partners) expect. Persistence in seeking affinity is thus another positive characteristic of successful stepparents, keeping in mind that such stepparents are aware of stepchildren's reactions to them and allow the pace of development to be led by the stepchildren. Practitioners can help stepparents with this in many ways – tempering expectations for a rapid resolution of efforts to bond, supporting them in ways to continue to bond while respecting stepchildren's needs to be in control of the pace of relational development.

The good news is that most stepparents know how to make friends and most have the necessary skills to build warm, intimate bonds with other people, which is another way of saying that most stepparents are capable of creating positive emotional ties with stepchildren. They also can learn skills that they may not have. For example, most affinity-seeking and maintaining behaviors that people in general possess are with individuals in their own age group, so some stepparents may need assistance in translating what they know about getting age peers to like them to making friends with stepchildren, who usually are from younger age cohorts than stepparents. Some stepparents also initially struggle with the idea of becoming friends or building a nurturing relationship with stepchildren. They often expect to immediately be accepted as a parent, with all that label implies – disciplinarian, rule-setter, role model, caregiver, protector, etc. Of course, some stepparents are seen as parental figures, but unless stepchildren are young when the relationships start, this usually takes time. Building affinity is a productive start to any stepparent–stepchild connection.

Clinicians can also help stepparents who become discouraged when stepchildren ignore or actively resist their efforts to become closer. Stepparent–stepchild relationships are generally involuntary connections, brought about because of the stepchild's and stepparent's attachment to the parent/partner. It may take time for stepparents to get to know the stepchildren, and even longer to become emotionally linked. Clinicians can provide support for stepparents who are distraught with their lack of progress and who may need encouragement to continue to befriend their stepchildren.

Choosing Roles for Stepparents

Research evidence indicates that multiple roles work for stepparents, stepchildren, and stepfamilies. These roles entail varying degrees of creativity. For instance, taking a parental role is assuming a role known to most stepfamily members, so taking a mother or father role involves the least amount of creativity or flexibility. Similarly, a stepparent who functions as a "casual acquaintance" of stepchildren would be taking on the generally known role behaviors of a casual acquaintance. On the opposite end of the stepparent role continuum, which involves more creativity, would be crafting a nurturing stepparent role or othermother/otherfather roles. These roles require more awareness and creativity because there are few if any cultural norms or role models to consult.

Whatever roles are chosen for stepparents, flexibility in role-taking and role-making positively contributes to well-being and satisfaction of stepfamily members. Roles may change as stepchildren get older or family situations change, so being flexible is a plus. For example, a stepparent may start out as a casual acquaintance, become a friend, and then over time may be seen as a family member (i.e., a parental figure, an othermother, a third parent, a nurturing stepparent, or a close family member without a more specific label attached to the role set).

Context is critical in stepparent role development. For example, a parental role may work better if all stepchildren are young, the nonresidential parent is uninvolved, the residential parent *and* stepchildren want the stepparent to act like a parent, and extended kin networks are supportive. Likely all these facts must be true for a parental role to work effectively, with little conflict. If the stepfamily context differs from the one just described – if stepchildren are adolescents when relationships begin, both biological parents are actively engaged in childrearing, and stepchildren reside a significant amount of time in both parents' households, then close friendships, being a loving stepparent, or other stepparent roles may be just as satisfying. Again, context matters, but flexibility in creating ways of being in relationships with stepchildren is still critically important.

Older Stepparents and Adult Stepchildren

What works for older stepparents and adult stepchildren depends on when the step-relationships began. For effective long-term stepparents whose stepchildren were not yet adults when the stepfamily began, maintaining positive relationships is critical. Research indicates that having cared for stepchildren when they were younger and continuing to help them as adults are the building blocks of having positive adult stepchild–older stepparent bonds. Biological parents are usually the primary kinkeepers with adult children, which mainly means they maintain contact and send messages of inclusion, belonging, and mattering. Older stepparents with positive ties to adult stepchildren also send these messages, and enact their meanings by helping when they can, providing a variety of emotional and tangible support, and staying in touch. Research evidence also shows that repairing relationships by apologizing and making amends for problems from the past are effective *what works* strategies for older stepparents.

For stepparents acquired in later life when stepchildren are adults, the tasks for effective stepparents are to develop positive relationships, either indirectly by taking care of the parent and loving them and encouraging them to stay in touch with their children, or directly by showing respect to adult stepchildren, and by making friends with them. As with younger stepchildren, it appears that the younger generation needs to be in control of the pace of relationship bonding for stepparents' efforts to be effective.

Summary of What Works for Parents in Stepfamilies

Parents who best support their children's adjustment to stepfamily life make an effort to prioritize one-on-one time with children amid the many changes of stepfamily formation. Children are especially sensitive to disruptions in the parent–child relationship when parents repartner, so effective parents reassure children about the stability of their bond by spending time together, checking in with them, and initiating open dialogue. Nonresidential parents in stepfamilies also influence children's well-being; they support children's development by maintaining regular contact with them and staying involved in their lives.

Effective residential parents function as the "captains" of parenting in stepfamily households. In other words, they set rules for children, are the primary disciplinarians, encourage children to spend time with the other parent and the stepparent, and protect them from coparental conflicts as much as feasible. They keep children out of coparental conflicts by not treating children as confidants or badmouthing the other parent, which can triangulate children into loyalty binds. Effective parents also engage in *gate opening* and protective *gate closing* when necessary. Parental gate opening involves helping stepparents and other step-kin spend time and build relationships with children. Parents living in stepfamily households also may be partly responsible for helping extended kin of the former spouse or partner to remain connected to children, and they are certainly responsible for maintaining children's ties with their extended kin network. Parental gate closing means making sure children feel safe and are protected from harm from others – for instance, limiting access to children or supervising interactions between children and other adults until those adults prove themselves to be responsible and trustworthy.

Effective parents also find a balance between spending one-on-one time with children and organizing shared time as a family. Spending time together as a family, with all members of the household present (e.g., having shared family meals, going for walks, playing games, going on family vacations, even doing household chores together) facilitates stepfamily cohesion, which is linked to better child outcomes.

Older Parents and Adult Children

Older parents in long-term stepfamilies who have close relationships with their children maintain close connections by staying in contact with them, providing resources to them when needed, and making sure they know they are loved. As with older stepparents who have close relationships with adult stepchildren, effective older parents cared for children when they were younger and continued to be resources for children as they became adults. Also, as with older stepparents, relational repair messages (i.e., apologizing, making amends) are often effective in nurturing or mending relationships with adult children following periods of turbulence.

Effective older parents who repartnered in later-life stay connected by kinkeeping, assisting children and grandchildren when able, and repairing past wrongs, if necessary. Repairing relationships also includes grieving losses with children if the children's other parent is deceased. All older parents, regardless of when their stepfamilies began, are more successful when they do not place undue pressure on adult children to choose between parental households on holidays, birthdays, and other special family celebrations.

Summary of What Works When Coparenting in Stepfamilies

Effective Ex-partner Coparenting

One coparenting relationship that exists in stepfamilies is that between the residential and nonresidential parent (or that between ex-partners, who are the child's parents). Evidence about what works for ex-partner coparents involves communicating clearly, lowering hostility, and interacting in ways that benefit children. The keys for ex-partners are to cooperate with each other as much as possible and keep children out of the middle of coparenting conflict. Although it may seem ideal for coparents to cooperatively raise their children with mutual affection and respect for each other, this ideal relationship is not necessary for ex-partners to effectively rear children. For many ex-partner coparents, interacting in a business-like way and being cordial with each other is sufficient for protecting children from negative outcomes. Being placed in the middle of coparenting conflict is incredibly stressful for children, who typically love both their parents and do not want to be made to choose sides. Parental behaviors that minimize putting children in the middle of parental dynamics works for children and adults. Fortunately, the research on what works for ex-partner coparents contains many examples of specific strategies used by successful coparents.

It may be oversimplified, but generally *what works* for post-divorce coparenting is likely the same as *what works* after one or both finds a new partner. In other words, if coparenting interactions work well after divorce or separation, then those interactions continue to be effective after one or both repartner if coparents are flexible and cooperative. There is a possibility this conclusion is drawn because most samples of *what works* studies included both post-divorce single parents and repartnered parents, so the findings in this book reflect adaptive behaviors and thoughts reported by both post-divorce coparents who are single and repartnered coparents. It is more likely, however, that productive ex-partner coparenting from separate households involves a common set of skills, ways of being, and ways of interacting that apply regardless of whether coparents are in new romantic relationships or not.

Stepcouple Coparenting

Another coparenting relationship that exists in stepfamilies is that between the residential parent and stepparent. Unlike parents, who are roughly equal as coparents (e.g., in how long they have known the child, the legal status of their relationship to the child, the bonds/attachments they have formed with the child), the stepparent is a newcomer to the child and to coparenting. As an outsider, the stepparent does not have the same history, bonding, and understanding of the child as the parent does. Imagine starting to binge-watch a television series by watching episode 10 – there is a lot you would not know about the main characters and their backgrounds and experiences that someone who watched from the first episode already knows. Even if your partner had started watching from the first episode and told you some things about the characters that you had not seen, starting to watch episode 10 would still not be the same for you. It would take you several more episodes to begin to sort things out, and even then, you might still have questions. For stepcouple coparents, the connection to the child and past experiences are different.

Consequently, findings about *what works* reflect this difference in status/ relationship between the two coparents (the bioparent and the stepparent). For example, in contrast to ex-partner coparents, only about one third of the findings directly deal with coparents' interactions with each other. Instead, more than half of the *what works* findings for stepcouples as coparents are about doing things to help step-kin build closer relationships. Also, rather than focusing on protecting children from coparental conflicts, *what works* for stepcouple coparenting are actions that focus on presenting a unified front to children or letting children know that the stepparent is indeed part of the coparenting team (even if as a mentor or friend or secondary parental figure). These *what works* findings for stepcouples as coparents make sense in light of the structural differences in this coparenting subsystem compared to ex-partner coparent subsystems.

Earlier, we stated that effective parents are the captains of childrearing activities in stepfamilies. One significant example of this is when successful parents in stepfamilies, create, monitor, and revise, if necessary, communication rules about adults sharing information with children about prior divorces, parental dating, and repartnering relationships. Effective parents often develop these privacy rules with their coparents to intentionally decide what information gets shared with children and what stays private.

Summary of What Works for Half- and Stepsiblings

When both partners bring children from prior relationships into the stepfamily, then stepfamily formation creates new stepsibling relationships. Additionally, if the stepcouple has a shared child together, then that child is a half-sibling to the older stepchildren. Given that the functioning of half- and stepsibling relationships can have consequences for overall stepfamily functioning, the question of how people develop close relationships with half- and stepsiblings is important.

Half-siblings

First, relationships between half-siblings tend to be closer when they live together and spend more time with each other during childhood. Therefore, to the extent that parents can negotiate custodial arrangements that allow for half-sibling co-residence, relationships among half-siblings benefit. Second, research suggests that the quality of half-sibling relationships may come down to the extent to which older half-siblings hold positive or negative sentiments about the stepfamily formation. If older half-siblings carry resentment about having a more difficult upbringing than the shared child(ren), then this may negatively affect half-sibling relationship quality, whereas if they are accepting (or even embracing) of family structure changes, then relationships with younger half-siblings tend to be closer. When parents nurture their relationships with children across family transitions, their older children appear to be more receptive to the birth of a younger half-sibling than when older children feel neglected or possibly replaced by the birth of a shared child.

Third, when parents draw boundaries of family membership that are inclusive of older half-siblings, half-sibling relationships benefit. When parents and stepparents make a concerted effort to include older half-siblings in family events and communications (e.g., group texts), relationships between older and younger half-siblings are closer. For example, coordinating holiday or birthday parties so that all family members (including older half-siblings, whose schedules were often more complex due to having multiple parental households to visit) are able to attend communicates messages about *everyone belonging*, which can indirectly strengthen half-sibling ties.

Another behavior that half-siblings engage in to affirm closeness in their relationships is to omit the term "half" when describing their relationship to others. Not using the "half" label appears to communicate and affirm to half-siblings that they are important in each other's lives, as important as any sibling relationship.

Stepsiblings

Parents set the stage for stepsibling relationship development in how they handle the transition to stepfamily life with their children. Perhaps the most important thing parents can do is nurture their relationships with children during stepfamily formation, when children are acquiring stepsiblings. When parents nurture their relationships with children across family transitions, children appear to be more receptive to stepsiblings, whereas when children perceive that their relationship with their parent is taking a backseat to their parent's efforts to bond with their stepsiblings, then they are more likely to feel jealous and resentful of stepsiblings, which undermines close relationships.

Parents also promote closer stepsibling relationships by making deliberate attempts to build a sense of family identity. Parents and stepparents positively shape the development of relationships between stepsiblings by encouraging bonding between the children via family activities (e.g., dinners out, game nights, and family trips), and establishing family traditions, such as shared meals and family dates with all the children. Parents and stepparents support stepsibling relationships by being cognizant of the extent to which their interactions with children and stepchildren might inadvertently create conflict or competition for resources, whether tangible (e.g., household space) or intangible (e.g., parental time, attention, and praise), and then doing things to reduce the conflict or competition.

Stepsiblings themselves develop close relationships with each other through affinity building (e.g., spending time together in mutually enjoyable activities, finding common interests, helping by teaching, supporting, and assisting with tasks), and expressing care, affection, and concern for the other's well-being. When conflicts arise, successful stepsiblings resolve them in multiple ways, such as directly dealing with stepsiblings or asking adults to mediate. Stepsiblings with close bonds also have figured out ways of managing stress and coping. Like half-siblings, close stepsiblings tend to not use the "step" label or distinguish between full and stepsiblings when introducing siblings to others, which communicates messages of closeness and belonging.

Summary of What Works for Stepgrandparents

Given increased longevity, it is not unusual for children to have four or more grandparents and great grandparents. This may make it easier for stepgrandparents to be accepted in multigenerational stepfamilies as just another grandparent.

When stepgrandchildren are younger when they acquire stepgrandparents, then stepgrandparents acting "like a grandparent" helps them build closer relationships. This is particularly true when partners, middle-generation adults, and stepgrandchildren do things that support cross-generational bonding. It is unlikely that everyone in every generation of the extended stepfamily will do everything in Box 7.1 for stepgrandparents to be successful. It seems likely, however, that when family members in every generation support this bonding, close relationships between stepgrandparents and stepgrandchildren are probable.

When stepgrandchildren are adolescents or older when relationships with stepgrandparents begin, then *what works* is *not* to act "like a grandparent," but instead to focus on getting to know stepgrandchildren and middle-generation parents and to work on developing friendships. This may take time, especially if younger family members feel that a stepgrandparent is "replacing" a deceased or divorced biological grandparent, so stepgrandparents should go slowly in developing close bonds with stepgrandchildren. Close relationships are more likely to develop when middle-generation adults and stepgrandchildren notice, appreciate, and reciprocate the stepgrandparent's efforts to bond.

Grandparents in Stepfamilies

In some ways, being an effective grandparent in a multigenerational stepfamily is straightforward. Grandparents with emotionally close and satisfying relationships with grandchildren can maintain these relationships by continuing what they are doing. Effective grandparents also seek affinity with the new partners of their child.

What Works in Stepfamilies? A Bird's-Eye View

In earlier chapters, we identified concrete empirical evidence about how stepfamily members individually and collectively created effective and satisfying relationships. Thus far in this chapter, we have briefly summarized the findings from those earlier chapters about *what works* in specific stepfamily relationships. In the rest of the chapter, we attempt to take a broader perspective about what works in stepfamilies.

Creating a well-functioning stepfamily takes time and effort. Some stepfamilies figure out what works on their own through trial and error, others seek professional help to get on track, and some stepfamilies do both. They all expend effort and energy determining how best to live and relate in ways that work for them. The wide array of cognitions and behaviors engaged in by members of satisfying stepfamilies suggests that there are multiple pathways by which adults and children can reach the goal of making their stepfamily work. What connects these different pathways?

To answer this question, we looked for underlying factors behind what works for each family position and each relationship to see if there were more abstract, higher-order elements that linked the specific *what works* findings. We identified five connecting elements: (a) being aware, (b) acting intentionally, (c) being positive, (d) being flexible, and (e) communicating clearly. To these we add something that may not be essential but is certainly helpful: having some knowledge about stepfamilies.

Being Aware

A word search of this chapter will show the term *awareness* appearing multiple times. Being aware, as defined here, involves both self-awareness and awareness of others. Self-awareness is defined as "understanding your own thoughts, feelings, values, beliefs, and actions. It means that you understand who you are, what you want, how you feel, and why you do the things that you do" (Cherry, 2023). Awareness of others is knowing as much as you can about the significant other people in your life – their thoughts, feelings, values, beliefs, and understanding their actions. We contend that awareness of social contexts is an important aspect of awareness, too. Awareness of contexts involves understanding self-in-relation-to others, and how those relationships may change in response to the physical and social settings, the time-in-life in which interactions occur, and other circumstances.

Self-Awareness in Stepfamilies

From the very start of contemplating whether to make a commitment to a new partner, being aware of one's wants, needs, strengths, weaknesses, capacities, values, and behaviors are essential understandings that make it easier for parents and stepparents to select a compatible partner and start relationships with new step-kin on the right footing. Self-awareness is likely helpful for children as they navigate their way in the new, complex family formation.

Being Aware of Others in Stepfamilies

Being aware of other stepfamily members should reduce the number of unexamined assumptions made about other persons. Instead of assuming what the new stepfamily members want from you or from the relationship, someone who is aware of their *not knowing* might ask them directly. For example, a new stepfamily member seeking greater awareness of the new step-kin as people might ask: What do you like to do? Who are your heroes? What do you like to eat? Oh, you are in X Organization – tell me why you joined them? What would you like me to call you? What do you want to call me? How do you want to be introduced in public when we are together? Being aware of others is only possible when an effort is made to gain that understanding, and that happens best when individuals spend time together in conversation. Increasing one's awareness of significant others is a useful goal for stepfamily members who want to have satisfying relationships in their new stepfamilies.

For example, we can think of dozens of questions a stepparent might ask themselves to help promote better understanding of their stepchildren. Here are just a few: What do my stepchildren need from me? What do they want me to do for them or for their parent? How do they respond when I do [a certain behavior]? What interests, values, or beliefs do I have in common with this stepchild? What do I share in common with this other stepchild? How do my children react when I do [a specific behavior] with their stepsiblings? How does my spouse/partner react when I do [a specific behavior] with their children from prior relationships? How can I help my parents get to know their new stepgrandchildren? What do my parents need or want to know about my new partner and new stepchildren? Questions like these, asked by a stepparent of themselves, could help them gain greater understanding and awareness of their stepchildren as people.

Being Aware of Contexts

Being aware of physical contexts helps adults in stepfamilies recognize potential problems early so that they can solve them quickly. This helps prevent problems, stops small concerns from snowballing into larger problems, and allows parents and stepparents to convey to children that they care and seek to do their best.

Awareness of Physical Contexts

Physical contexts that are relevant to consider include the households in which stepfamily members reside. For example, do stepchildren who live part of the time in another household have space to call their own in the stepfamily household? If not, can space be found and reserved for them when they are in the stepfamily household (e.g., a drawer for their clothes, a bed, a place at the kitchen table)? Thinking about physical contexts like stepchildren having space to call their own, and what having such space in the stepfamily household might mean, facilitates empathizing with the child, and leads to identifying potential solutions to a situation that an unaware stepparent or parent might not recognize as an issue.

Distance between children's coparents' households also might be a relevant physical context for better understanding stepchildren's experiences. Are stays in the other household infrequent because of distance between households? What can be done to help alleviate visiting stepchildren's homesickness, loneliness, and missing the other parent? A stepchild who can walk between parent's households lives in a different physical context than one whose parents live hundreds of miles apart. A child who spends half of their time with a mom and stepfather lives in a different physical context than a child who lives with the stepparent and parent every other winter break and six weeks in the summer. Being aware of these physical contexts, and their potential effects on stepchildren, their parents, and stepparents, is an important step in appreciating challenges encountered by the stepchild and helps in planning to maximize everyone's experiences when children go back and forth between parental residences.

Awareness of Temporal Contexts

Humans keep track of several kinds of time – clock time, calendar time, age, generations, historical eras. It is beyond the scope of this book to explore deeply all these types of temporal contexts as they relate to stepfamilies. We can, however, briefly examine examples of the relevance of being aware of these contexts.

When we think of clock time and stepfamilies, we think of challenges faced by merging two households when these households have different daily rhythms and use time differently. Even something as fundamental as bedtimes can become a meaningful contextual issue. For example, if one partner is a "lark" (early to bed and early to rise) and the other is an "owl" who loves late nights and later mornings, then compromises are in order, and accommodations may have to be made. Add children with their own circadian rhythms to the mix, and stepfamilies may have to negotiate rules about bedtimes, noise (in the morning or late at night), breakfast rituals, and so on. Ask any spouse of someone whose daily peak times are not in synch with their own peak times how much compromise this entails – being aware of stepfamily members' daily temporal contexts can be valuable in making things work more smoothly. Knowing each member's daily rhythms can enhance tolerance for others' needs and improve sensitivity to others.

The ages of stepfamily members are another type of time that merit attention. As we have noted in this book, what works with stepchildren is often related to the age of the stepchild. Younger children are often more open to stepparents' efforts to befriend them than adolescents or adult stepchildren. Stepparents who are aware of the possible effects of age as temporal context are more ready to plan how to approach stepchildren to maximize their endeavors. One way that family professionals can help stepparents prepare who have not had children before is to teach them a few things about what to expect from different age cohorts.

Acting Intentionally

Awareness is important, but being aware is not enough to ensure that stepfamily relationships work. Awareness needs to be paired with actions that are intentionally aimed at making things work well. Of course, it is feasible for stepfamily members to do the right things for themselves and their kin without being intentional about what they are doing. The likelihood, however, of engaging in *what works* behaviors are greater when aware individuals deliberately and purposefully try to make their lives and their relationships better for everyone. Consciously thinking about what will work, and then following through with action, appears to be characteristic of the members of successful stepfamilies.

Being Positive

John and Emily Visher (1988), pioneers in thinking about how stepfamilies can function well and how clinicians can help them, frequently stated that "stepfamilies are born of loss." There are many losses that precede stepfamily formation, including the loss of the marriage and nuclear family when parents divorce, loss of contact with family members who no longer share the same household, loss of family routines and traditions, legal loss of control over childrearing decisions after divorce, and loss of old identities (i.e., the oldest child, the only child) within the family (Visher & Visher, 1988). When parental unions are dissolved, families often move, generating additional losses for family members. Among the losses are friends, neighborhoods, schools, and even communities. Many events and experiences that we have described as changes in this book are experienced as losses when the stepfamily is formed. For example, children may feel as if they have lost time with their parent after remarriage/repartnering. When stepfamilies merge into living in one residence, members may feel they have lost space and privacy. We mention these losses because they provide context for understanding why being positive works so well for stepfamilies.

In addition to losses from the past, social stigma related to stepparenthood, divorce, remarriage, and being a stepchild also help explain why being positive is so important in stepfamilies. New stepfamily members know they are entering family positions and a family form that have long been the focus of social stigma and negative metaphors (e.g., "wicked stepmothers," "abusive stepfathers," and the neglected "red-headed stepchild" are common tropes). Individuals often prefer not to use stepfamily terms to describe themselves and their families, preferring more benign-sounding terms instead, such as *bonus mom* or *blended family*. It is understandable why adults and children are not eager about moving into stigmatized roles or family forms that carry negative connotations, and it is also understandable why positivity is helpful for stepfamily members.

Positivity is the practice or tendency to be positive or optimistic in life (Davis, 2023). Being positive involves engaging in constructive thinking, upbeat emotions, and encouraging and affirming behaviors. Repartnering adults are generally hopeful and optimistic about their new families, but these hopes and expectations for the future are sometimes accompanied by the sadness of past losses and stress related to current changes, and fears about redivorce. *What works* research findings support the notion that engaging in positive thoughts, feelings, and behaviors lead to good outcomes for relationships in stepfamilies.

Most of the research on stepfamily positivity emphasizes the importance of being positive for stepcouples and for coparental subsystems. As we noted earlier in this book, adults are the family architects (Satir, 1972) and parents are the captains of coparenting. Mixed metaphors aside, the primary responsibility for focusing on the bright side of things, being confident about the future and one's abilities to solve problems constructively, and interacting with family members in supporting and reassuring ways, falls to the adults in stepfamilies. The adults set the tone for children to follow, so reframing situations in positive ways, boosting the mood and affect of other family members, and generally looking for positive ways of solving problems in stepfamilies are behaviors led by parents and stepparents.

Being positive means that adults in effective stepfamilies, when communicating with partners, children or stepchildren, place an uplifting, reassuring, or constructive slant on their messages. This may take extra effort (i.e., intentionality) to accomplish, and maybe even skill, but cognitive reframing and communicating positively can be learned. Being positive does not, however, mean masking stepfamily problems or dismissing family members' concerns. For example, parents can both validate children's feelings of sadness, loss, or frustration with other stepfamily members *and* help them manage those feelings and resolve conflicts constructively.

Being positive works for children in stepfamilies as well, particularly in relationships with stepparents and stepsiblings. Bonding with stepparents happens only when stepchildren respond affirmatively to stepparents' affinity-seeking efforts. Stepsibling relationships that become friendships or siblingships become close out of bonding interactions that build on mutual interests and enjoying each other's company. Bonding with another person is primarily the result of positive interactions that benefit both parties; we find it hard to think about building relationships without them being based on positivity.

Being Flexible

Another basis for stepfamily success is being flexible. Flexibility in thoughts and behaviors is adaptive in any family structure but may be even more useful in complex family forms that lack prescribed social norms (i.e., stepfamilies). Being flexible suggests that individuals in high-functioning stepfamilies can shift gears when necessary, that they are not stuck in trying the same unproductive actions over and over, and that they are open to thinking and behaving in new and creative ways. Flexible stepfamilies are not daunted by the lack of institutional guidelines because they see that as an opportunity to adapt and be creative in how they "do family" in ways that work well for their family members.

Stepfamilies are full of ambiguity. We can think of dozens of questions that have potentially unclear or ambiguous answers – What roles should stepparents perform? How should stepsiblings relate to each other? What types of relationships between stepparents and their partners' former partners benefit children the most? How do stepparents manage when stepchildren want different types of relationships with the stepparent? What do stepgrandchildren call their stepgrandparents? What if the linked stepfamily households in which a child spends time have vastly different rules, values, and beliefs? The degree of ambiguity in stepfamilies almost demands a minimal level of cognitive flexibility by stepfamily members. Without some degree of cognitive flexibility, individuals are often frustrated by having to deal with ambiguities. This frustration may be exacerbated if individuals think rigidly about how families are "supposed" to be, and their stepfamily does not fit their inflexible expectations. We have talked to many stepfamily members who were surprised, and even shocked, to find that what they expected was not what they experienced when their stepfamilies were first formed. They often expected smooth sailing, with children eagerly accepting stepparents and family members adapting quickly to new household situations and relationships. These expectations are part of what the Vishers called the "myth of instant love." These unmet, often unrealistic expectations can be managed when stepfamily members are flexible and adjust to new realities.

Much of *what works* for individual stepfamilies is thought about intentionally, negotiated within or between households, and tried out to see if what has been negotiated works for that stepfamily. If the proposed solutions are found wanting, the process of thinking, communicating/negotiating, and evaluating is repeated. This type of real-life scientific thinking requires flexibility and a willingness to be open to new solutions if things are not working.

Communicating Clearly

We have written often about the importance of communication in this book because researchers have found that communication skills are extremely significant in making stepfamilies work. Here at a bird's-eye view, we include what we think is the umbrella concept applicable to communication, and that is clarity. All the communication skills and strategies that help stepfamilies operate more effectively serve the greater goal of helping stepfamily members clearly understand each other. Understanding the other person is one of the ultimate goals of communicating, and being clear in messaging is the pathway by which members reach understanding.

A substantive proportion of family life education programs, regardless of family structure, focuses on communication skills. Family therapists also spend considerable time with clients working with them on better communication.

The research indicates that effective stepfamily members work at maintaining and improving the clarity of their communications. We have been told by some stepfamily members, however, that having to talk about daily activities, having to negotiate rules and discuss what roles stepparents will enact, does not feel "natural." To these individuals, adults and children in a functional and happy family automatically know how to relate and what to do to make the household/family work well. Discussing things, making compromises, and working out disagreements in how daily living ought to proceed does not feel normal and may even be seen as a sign of problems. Stepfamily members who think this way often hold unrealistic expectations for how easy it will be to adapt to stepfamily living. When they find that their ideas about how to "be a family" do not coincide perfectly with those of their new partner and stepchildren, they are distraught. The cultural metaphor is apt; creating a stepfamily may involve learning new languages, customs, and new meanings for old terms. It may take an interpreter or translator to help bridge gaps in meanings (parents can serve in these roles for partners and children, or a therapist can help). Experienced travelers accept that they have much to learn about the cultures they visit, and they are respectfully observant, listen carefully, and ask questions to better understand the new culture. In short, they seek clarity via communication. Effective stepfamily members who do what works (according to research) act like experienced travelers as they explore and attempt to better understand their new family members' culture.

Knowing About Stepfamilies

The first five of the bird's-eye-view tenets of *what works* in stepfamilies are robust and pervasive. They apply to virtually all successful stepfamilies. The final one, knowing about stepfamilies, is not universal, although we argue that most families substantively benefit from having knowledge about stepfamily functioning. In fact, clinicians have long contended that problems in stepfamilies are often caused by lack of understanding about how stepfamilies function and how they differ from nuclear families. They are seldom caused by individual family members' mental health problems (Visher & Visher, 1988). If stepfamily members had more realistic expectations and greater knowledge about how to create and maintain step-relationships, then many stepfamily problems could be avoided.

Many stepfamilies successfully create their own way of being a family, forming a nurturing stepfamily model (Ganong & Sanner, 2023). Given the varied and complex family structures that stepfamilies may take, based on who had children from previous unions and where those children reside (Ganong & Coleman, 2017), it should not be surprising that the dynamics of nurturing stepfamilies vary considerably. What they have in common is that they meet the needs of individual stepfamily members and the whole family. Some stepcouples figure out how to do this on their own, maybe having learned from growing up in a stepfamily what worked and what did not. Perhaps as repartnering individuals they valued and embodied the general tenets that contribute to success (i.e., being aware, intentional, positive, flexible, and communicating clearly). Using those skills, they imagined ways of being a new kind of complex family through trial and error. Some stepcouples began recreating a nuclear family household but found this did not work well for them or their children. They then pivoted to building a functional stepfamily system (often with professional help).

Other nurturing stepfamily members, however, learned early that stepfamilies are structurally and dynamically different from first-time families, and they explored how they wanted their new families to operate. For these nurturing stepfamilies, knowing information about stepfamilies can help. Preparing stepcouples, and entire stepfamily units, helps

Table 8.1 Stepfamily Characteristics

1. Stepfamilies begin after many losses and changes.
2. Children and adults come with expectations from previous families.
3. Stepfamilies often have unrealistic expectations.
4. Stepfamilies are more structurally complex than other family forms.
5. Children often are members of two households.
6. Children have a parent who is elsewhere in actuality or in memory.
7. Co-parents of children in the stepfamily are part of the stepfamily.
8. Stepfamily members have different family histories.
9. Parent–child bonds are older than adult partner (spousal) bonds.
10. Individual, marital, and family life cycles are more likely to be incongruent
11. Stepfamilies are not well supported by society.
12. Legal relationships between stepparent and stepchild are ambiguous or nonexistent.

them think about their relationships in more complex ways. Rather than assuming that a stepfather will be welcomed by school-age and adolescent stepchildren as a new dad who can set rules and discipline children, stepcouples armed with knowledge about how step-relationships develop and what the experience of merging two households might be like for children, instead make sure children know that the mother will remain the primary parent, and that the stepfather is her support system.

From our reading of cutting-edge clinical work with stepfamilies, we identified 12 basic tenets regarding stepfamily characteristics that stepfamily members should know (see Table 8.1). The first three items focus on new stepfamilies; items 4–7 have to do with structural complexity; items 8–10 highlight variability in relational histories, individual life courses, and interpersonal relationships; and the final two items focus on cultural contexts. Knowing something about these tenets could equip family members with fresh ideas about what to do to create a workable stepfamily.

In addition to these basic tenets, knowing about some of the general issues and problems that stepfamilies face and how effective stepfamilies manage or solve them may be useful. By knowing about issues they might encounter, stepcouples and their children are made more aware of potential problems, and they can work on preventing them or more readily resolving them if they address a minor issue before it becomes a full-blown crisis. Table 8.2 contains a partial list of the issues and possible problems that stepfamily members should know about as early as feasible.

Table 8.2 Issues Often Found in Clinical Works on Stepfamilies

Family Issues:
Loyalty conflicts
Coparental conflicts
Parent–child bonds become strained
Jealousy
Custody problems
Sibling relationships
Couple relationships
Idealization of absent parent
Scapegoating
Birth of a shared child
Sexually-charged household atmosphere
Push for rapid cohesion
Names and naming
Space or territory issues
Linking two households
Boundaries
Triangulation
Rejection of stepchildren by stepparents
Discipline problems
Competition and rivalry
Grandparents' involvement
Stepchild expelled from the household
Subsystem alliances within the stepfamily
Rejection of stepparent by stepchildren
Low cohesion
Poor communication
Stepparents who lack childrearing experience
Stepsibling relationships

Transitional Adjustments:
Children's ages at parental remarriage
Lifestyle differences
Holidays and other celebrations
Birth order changes
Lack of privacy
Length of time between marriages
Adjusting to changes
Conflicts in merging households
No shared rules
Lack of shared rituals
Child surprised by remarriage
No shared history

Issues Related to Incomplete Institutionalization:
Role confusion
No legal ties
No societal rituals
Family identity confusion
Kinship terms
How much stepparents should be involved in childrearing
Ambiguous models for stepparent–child relations
How much affection to show stepchildren
Financial issues

Emotional Issues:
Guilt
Sadness and mourning
Feeling unwanted
Fantasies about parents reuniting
Ambivalence about new step-kin
Feeling responsible for parent's negative feelings
Stress
Feeling more vulnerable
Identity confusion
Fears of being misunderstood
Anger
Fears of stepfamily breaking up
Rebellion against parents and stepparents

Unrealistic Expectations:
Stepparents are mean and wicked
Love overcomes all obstacles
Stepfamilies are just the same as first-marriage nuclear families
Stepparents will rescue the family
Instant love will form between stepparents and stepchildren

In Chapter 2 of this book, we examined stepcouple preparation. As a *what works* finding, research support for preparing for stepfamily living by seeking information from multiple sources was decidedly mixed, if not weak. However, we found some evidence that stepfamily education or therapy was useful because awareness about stepfamilies (i.e., information) was increased. We think this awareness is extremely helpful when it is accompanied by other overarching tenets of *what works* in stepfamilies, namely acting intentionally, being positive, being flexible, and communicating clearly. Learning about stepfamily dynamics and how effective stepfamilies interact with each other can be key elements of enhancing individual and relational wellbeing.

What Works? What We Still Need to Know

Although a great deal is known from research about effective stepfamilies, there is still much to learn. Here we briefly identify some areas in which there are still research gaps in knowing what works.

Building on Prior Research

A major source of discovering what is not known is when researchers uncover new information, which then exposes what is not yet understood. In fact, it is a science trope that the more we learn about a topic, the more we realize how much we do not know. For example, although much is known about creating and maintaining effective stepfamily relationships, the findings from the studies reviewed in this book reveal many unknown topics. For example:

- What are effective ways in which parents introduce serious dating partners to their children?
- How do parents and stepparents plan for sharing a residence?
- What are the effects of cohabiting on subsequent remarried stepfamilies?
- What are the most effective ways to prepare for living in a stepfamily?
- Which approaches taken by stepparents to support parents' childrearing are relatively more effective?
- How do coparents reach agreement on household roles and rules?

- How do individuals and stepfamilies come to hold realistic expectations, or how are unrealistic expectations modified?
- How are effective stepfamily rituals created?
- What are the processes by which stepparent roles are determined?
- What are the processes linking couple quality and effective childrearing?
- How do interhousehold coparenting subsystems develop and maintain effective relationships?
- What are grandparents' and stepgrandparents' roles in childrearing?

Unknowns Derived from Gaps in Methods

Some *unknowns* are identified by identifying gaps in research methods and sampling that reveal under-examined content areas. We identify five major gaps in the literature.

Effective Practices Among Culturally Diverse Stepfamilies

Little is known about effective practices among racial and ethnic minority stepfamilies and other marginalized or culturally diverse stepfamilies. Study samples have been dominated by White, middle-class respondents, and most of these studies have been conducted in the United States. Although studies are increasingly being conducted in other countries, there is still a need for more ethnically, racially, structurally, and socioeconomically diverse samples in investigations about *what works* in stepfamilies. When findings are similar across cultures, researchers can point to robust phenomena with greater confidence. Dissimilar findings are also valuable, as they point to relevant contextual elements that should be considered when exploring what works for specific groups of families.

What Works for Stepfamilies Within a Variety of Social, Cultural, and Physical Contexts

Second, little is known about the structural, systemic, interpersonal, and physical environments within which stepfamilies live. Investigations are needed that examine what works for stepfamily members within a variety of social, cultural, and physical contexts. For example, more research is needed that explores the ways in which stepfamilies productively interact with other social systems (e.g., schools, hospitals, children's clubs, employers), including how institutions can better support complex families with inclusive policies. This work also should attend to stepfamilies' embeddedness within systems of privilege and oppression (e.g., racism, heterosexism), exploring how stepfamilies are differentially impacted by oppressive forces and the implications for stepfamily functioning.

Multiple Perspectives on Effective Stepfamilies

A third gap involves the dearth of research that examines the perspectives of multiple stepfamily members, particularly children. Studies examining diverse family perspectives could yield valuable insights into similarities and distinctions in how stepchildren, stepparents, and parents experience what works for them in stepfamily living. There is evidence that stepchildren perceive effective family dynamics differently from adults (see Baxter et al., 2006; Cartwright et al., 2009). Few studies have collected data from multiple stepfamily members (e.g., Baxter et al., 2006; Coleman et al., 2001), so more research is needed, particularly investigations that utilize methods to analyze data not at dyadic or higher levels.

How Sibling Complexity Affects Childrearing and Child Outcomes

A fourth gap concerns the inattention to sibling complexity within stepfamily structures. Sibling constellations in stepfamilies create considerable structural diversity that often is overlooked in stepfamily research. Children may have any combination of full siblings, half-siblings, or stepsiblings, acquired through maternal and/or paternal repartnering, with whom they may reside part-time, full-time, or not at all. Sibling complexity in stepfamilies is rich and vast, and given recent evidence that sibling structure may be more strongly associated with child outcomes than parents' marital status, greater attention to sibling complexity in stepfamilies is essential. For instance, research is needed on the processes by which sibling complexity affects child well-being, as well as how parenting practices mediate these associations. Greater attention to sibling constellations (e.g., age ranges, gender distributions) is critical for broadening our knowledge of what works in stepfamily childrearing.

What Works for Stepfamilies Over Time (Relationship Maintenance)

Finally, there is a need for more studies of how stepfamily relationships change over time. In particular, more research is needed on the strategies people use to preserve stepfamily relationships (perhaps especially in the face of challenges, such as stepfamily conflict or stepfamily dissolution), and on how effective childrearing practices change over time with respect to age, changes in stepfamily relationships, and other contexts. Longitudinal investigations would facilitate addressing this area of unknowns, but cross-sectional studies and qualitative research also could yield insights about maintaining productive practices.

Generalizing a *What Works* Mindset to Other Family Forms and Other Family Processes

We clearly are advocates for research that yields findings that are practical for family members, policy makers, and the professionals who work with families. Researchers can make their work more useful by ensuring that investigations yield clear, practical implications for how study findings might apply to "real-world" situations. This is the "*so what?*" question of family scholarship, as in, "Ok, you researchers found that X is significantly associated with Y, but what does that mean for families and family members?"

We think a *what works* research perspective sheds light on findings that can yield useful information. Family science scholars examining what individuals, relationships, and family units do that result in positive outcomes for family members and entire families are part of this *what works* approach. Identifying research findings that are transferable to real-world applications is one way that family scientists show concern about individuals and families in their scholarship.

What works perspectives also may be used in studies of the effectiveness of specific family interventions (e.g., Rauer et al., 2014) or the usefulness of specific interventions with subgroups of families, such as culturally specific programs for ethnic groups (e.g., Adler-Baeder & Higginbotham, 2020). In addition to stepfamily education, *what works* research could be done on interventions with a variety of family structures.

There are many areas of family scholarship that would benefit from a *what works* perspective, including studies of: Black families, Latinx families, Asian families, single-parent households, cohabiting households, families with chronically ill members, LGBTQIA+ families, homeless families, couples who use artificial reproduction technology, low-income families, bereaved families, immigrant families, interracial couples, foster families, work and family interface, grandparents raising children, military families, older couples, and more. Many of these and other areas of family scholarship already contain excellent examples of investigations of resilience processes, but for these and most other areas of family scholarship, more attention needs to be paid to examining effective and productive activities that benefit family members.

What Works as Translational Family Science

Most investigations we have reviewed for this book would not necessarily be considered applied research, although some would fit that label. Nonetheless, we think they are translational research, defined as "the process of turning observations in the laboratory, clinic, and community into interventions that improve the health of individuals and populations – from diagnostics and therapeutics to medical procedures and behavioral interventions" (Tufts Clinical and Translational Science Institute, 2021). Although the studies reviewed in this book were seldom laboratory- or clinic-based investigations, the research that fit our criteria for inclusion were community studies of stepfamily dynamics that contained clear, specific, and performable empirical answers about how children in stepfamilies function effectively. In short, they were like many types of investigations done by most family scholars – they were grounded on a strengths-based, normative-adaptive approach, they employed methods and theories from multiple disciplines, and they often emphasized prevention of problems for individuals, relationships, and stepfamilies (Hamon & Smith, 2017). We point this out to make clear that studies from a *what works* perspective are not necessarily limited to narrowly defined translational designs, clinical trials of interventions, or other applied field research. A *what works* focus on resilience processes is more a mindset than a specific type of research design. We encourage family researchers to pursue these investigations in their targeted areas of interest.

References

Adler-Baeder, F., & Higginbotham, B. (2020). Efforts to design, implement, and evaluate community-based education for stepfamilies: Current knowledge and future directions. *Family Relations, 69*(3), 559–576. https://doi.org/10.1111/fare.12427

Baxter, L.A., Braithwaite, D.O., & Bryant, L.H. (2006). Types of communication triads perceived by young-adult stepchildren in established stepfamilies. *Communication Studies, 57*, 381–400. https://doi.org/10.1080/10510970600945923

Cartwright, C., Farnsworth, V., & Mobley, V. (2009). Relationships with stepparents in the life stories of young adults of divorce. *Family Matters, 82*, 30–37.

Cherry, K. (2023). *What is self-awareness? Development, types, and how to improve.* www.verywellmind.com/what-is-self-awareness-2795023

Coleman, M., Fine, M., Ganong, L., Downs, K., & Pauk, N. (2001). When you're not the Brady Bunch: Identifying perceived conflicts and resolution strategies in stepfamilies. *Personal Relationships, 8*, 55–73. https://doi.org/10.1111/j.1475-6811.2001.tb00028.x

Davis, T. (2023). *Positivity: The psychology, definition, and examples.* www/berkleywellbeing.com/positivity.html

Ganong, L., & Coleman, M. (2017). *Stepfamily relationships* (2nd ed.). Springer. https://doi.org/10.1007/978-1-4899-7702-1

Ganong, L., & Sanner, C. (2023). Stepfamily roles, relationships, and dynamics: A review of stepfamily typologies. *Journal of Child and Family Studies*, 1–20. http://dx.doi.org/10.1007/s10826-023-02558-4

Hamon, R.R., & Smith, S.R. (2017). Family science as translational science: A history of the discipline. *Family Relations, 66*, 550–567. https://doi.org/10.111/fare.12273

Rauer, A.J., Adler-Baeder, F., Lucier-Greer, M., Skuban, E., Ketring, S.A., & Smith, T. (2014). Exploring processes of change in couple relationship education: Predictors of change in relationship quality. *Journal of Family Psychology, 28*(1), 65. https://doi.org/10.1037/a0035502

Satir, V. (1972). *Peoplemaking.* Science and Behavior Books.

Tufts Clinical and Translational Science Institute. (2021, March 8). www.tuftsctsi.org/about-us/what-is-translational-science/

Visher, E.B., & Visher, J.S. (1988). *Old loyalties, new ties: Therapeutic strategies with stepfamilies.* Brunner/Mazel. https://doi.org/10.4324/9781315803814

APPENDIX

THE RESEARCH BASES FOR
WHAT WORKS IN STEPFAMILIES

Methods Used in Identifying *What Works* Studies for this Book

Searching for What Works Studies

This book was based on a review of over 2,500 English-language publications on stepfamilies and stepfamily relationships. The large task of reviewing this literature was made possible because we have maintained a database of stepfamily research for over 40 years. We began by conducting hand searches of all articles in our database. We then conducted computer searches of studies published since 2010, using several academic databases, including *Academic Search Complete*, *Ebscohost*, and *PsycInfo*. We used the key words *stepparent, stepchild, stepmother, stepfather, stepfamily, coparents, coparenting, remarriage, repartnering, stepsiblings, half-siblings,* and *stepgrandparents*. Key terms of *parent* and *grandparent*, used in combination with the term *stepfamily*, also were searched in these databases. Our computer searches were limited to studies published since 2010 (a) to ensure that our database did not overrepresent studies from earlier decades, when the database began, and (b) to sensitize us to new directions in stepfamily research. Ancestry searches, or examinations of the reference lists of published reports, also were conducted to find additional studies that might meet our criteria for inclusion as a *what works* investigation. In addition, we received weekly announcements from Google

Search and APA Search engines about new studies, using the key words identified previously, so that we could continuously update our database. We focused on studies that potentially met the inclusion criteria for our review of research on *what works* in stepfamilies.

We reviewed studies published in peer-reviewed journal articles as well as chapters in edited books. We also included book-length studies (e.g., Allan et al., 2011) but excluded books or chapters that were compilations of findings from prior multiple studies (e.g., Hetherington & Kelly, 2002) or were descriptive studies that did not meet the inclusion criteria (e.g., Burgoyne & Clark, 1984; Papernow, 1993; Stacey, 1990).

Inclusion Criteria

Research studies had to meet four criteria to be included in this book. First, a report had to be either primary research (i.e., researchers collected data exclusively for that study) or investigations based on secondary data sets (i.e., large data sets collected for general purposes in which researchers extracted relevant data for the investigation being reported). Studies could employ quantitative, qualitative, or mixed methods. Although scoping reviews, systematic reviews, and meta-analytic reviews are empirical research, we excluded all literature reviews, theory-based commentaries, reports written by clinicians based on their clinical expertise or practice, and first-person accounts.

A second criterion for inclusion was that the study had to include at least one research question or hypothesis related to individual or relational well-being in stepfamilies. We defined individual well-being broadly, to include cognitive, behavioral, physical, and mental health outcomes. We defined relational or relationship well-being as measures of satisfaction, adjustment, or relationship quality. Given that the goal of this book was to present evidence-based statements about *what works* in stepfamilies, we sought to locate studies containing evidence regarding actions that were effective in promoting positive individual or relational outcomes. This meant that studies were excluded in which individual or interpersonal behaviors were *described*, but no evaluative, explanatory components about what actions were effective and what were not were presented. For example, studies in which stepparents' and parents' behaviors were described or assessed but contained no outcome measures related to their own or their children's well-being, did not meet this inclusion criterion, as we could not tell from study designs if the assessed childrearing behaviors were effective or ineffective (e.g., Coley, 1998; Kelly & Ganong, 2011; Marsiglio & Hinojosa, 2007).

The third criterion for inclusion was that at least one of the independent or predictor variables in quantitative studies or one of the phenomena explored in qualitative studies had to be under the control of at least one stepfamily member. We were seeking evidence of what stepfamily members could do to promote and maintain individual well-being and effective relationships, so characteristics beyond any individual's control did not fit this criterion. For example, finding that cohabitation was positively associated with higher quality stepparent–stepchild relationships would not be considered a finding about *what works*, but a finding that spending more time with a stepchild engaging in specific activities was positively associated with better relationships, was included as a *what works* finding. Similarly, age of stepchildren when they acquired a stepparent, gender, ethnicity, and socioeconomic status are variables that may be related to stepchildren's outcomes but are either immutable or not easily changeable characteristics. Knowing how these variables are associated with well-being might be interesting and informative, but they cannot be directly applied by stepfamily members and family practitioners wanting to know how to effectively create and maintain close relationships and enhance individual well-being in stepfamilies. Consequently, we included only studies that examined at least one variable or phenomena that were, or feasibly could be, under a person's control.

The fourth and final inclusion criterion was that studies had to include at least one finding related to what works in stepfamilies that was concrete, tangible, and operationalized clearly and in a way that stepfamily members potentially could enact the finding. This meant excluding some studies because their findings were so abstract that they could not easily be translated into *what works* statements that could be performed by stepfamily members. For instance, the positive association between marital relationship quality and children's well-being, (e.g., Willetts & Maroules, 2005; Yu & Adler-Baeder, 2007) was insufficient to be a "*what works*" finding. The explanatory mechanisms underlying this finding lacked specifics and the finding would be hard to put into practice.

Therefore, abstracted findings that could not be translated into performable statements about *what works* in stepfamilies were excluded. Many excellent, well-written studies with appropriate methods, sound theoretical underpinnings, and well-defined results nonetheless did not yield clear, concrete findings about what worked in stepfamilies, and so they were excluded from this book. We do cite some of these studies, however, because they provided relevant context for understanding *what works* findings.

This final inclusion criterion was the most challenging to apply because abstract concepts are widely employed in both quantitative and qualitative family science research. Consequently, many findings contained abstract concepts. Often, when we read a study in which an abstracted concept was related to positive outcomes, we searched tables and text for evidence about how that concept was operationalized, to determine if we could use more concrete, specific language to describe the concept, and thereby make it more demonstrable and clearer. For instance, "open communication" could have many meanings, but "everyday talk," when defined in the study's text as daily small talk, asking a stepchild about their day, and joking around, conveys concrete ways in which stepparents can communicate with their stepchildren (Schrodt et al., 2008). Similarly, "prosocial action" is a broad and abstract label, but giving unexpected gifts, loaning money for a major purchase (e.g., a car), and unexpected acts of kindness (e.g., helping a stepchild administer a deceased parent's estate) are clearer and more specific examples of prosocial actions (Braithwaite et al., 2018). Note that in some studies researchers examined a combination of unalterable demographic variables, abstracted variables, and tangible variables that could be performed by stepfamily members, but only the performable findings were included as evidence of *what works*.

Reviewing and Coding Studies

After reading abstracts and skimming results sections, studies were categorized initially as: (a) meeting the criteria for inclusion and containing relevant findings, (b) not meeting the criteria for inclusion, or (c) unclear as to whether the study met inclusion criteria. All studies were reviewed several times by more than one member of our research team. Studies that were deemed to meet the criteria for this review of *what works* in stepfamilies were made by consensus, after discussion by the research team. After screening articles, a total of 268 studies were found that contained at least one finding related to what works in stepfamilies.

Coding Processes

Each study that met inclusion criteria was reviewed using a code sheet that elicited information including: (a) type of research design (e.g., quantitative, qualitative, mixed methods); (b) sample information, including the name of secondary data sets, the country in which the study was conducted, sample size and description (e.g., age, race, socioeconomic status); (c) who supplied data for the study (e.g., stepchildren, stepparents, parents, others, or a combination of individuals); and (d) theories employed. Finally, we included *what works* statements on the code sheets, using the researchers' own words if possible, and noting the page numbers where *what works* statements were located.

Identifying what works

We derived findings about what worked directly from each study, identifying specific ways in which stepfamily members contributed to individual or relationship well-being. We extracted verbatim statements from study results or extracted findings from tables if those were more detailed than information in the text. We also occasionally found *what works* statements in the discussion sections of research reports if the conclusions were clearly and closely tied to the research findings. For example, in a study about shared children in stepfamilies (i.e., children born into the stepfamily), Sanner and colleagues (2020) reported that parents of shared children often actively engaged in efforts to disguise their family structure from them (e.g., telling shared children that their half-siblings were their full siblings), and some study participants had painful memories of learning later that their siblings were, in fact, half-siblings. In the discussion section, Sanner and colleagues wrote, "communication with shared children surrounding family histories and connections is likely to reduce the confusion they [shared children] experience in figuring these things out for themselves" (p. 619). This was a clear statement about *what works*.

If researchers' inferences in discussion sections were vague, or if their generalizations were not supported clearly by the data, then those inferences were not included. Although researchers often appropriately draw speculative implications from their data, we took a conservative approach of limiting *what works* inferences to specific concrete findings of the studies. In short, we wanted to err on the conservative side to include only *what works* statements that we could clearly identify in the findings.

Analyzing the Study Findings

From the coding sheets, we created documents that contained all *what works* statements and the citations for those statements. Separate documents were created for findings that addressed what works for (a) stepcouples, either remarried or cohabiting, (b) stepparents, (c) biological/adoptive parents, (d) coparents, (e) half- and stepsiblings, and (f) grandparents and stepgrandparents. Every coded *what works* statement was assigned to one of the documents, based on the primary content and focus of the statement. This meant that for some studies, all bulleted statements were categorized as being about one subject, such as stepparents' childrearing (e.g., Braithwaite et al., 2008), while for other studies, *what works* statements were assigned to different documents because they had to do with multiple relationships, such as parent–child, stepparent–stepchild, or coparenting (e.g., Kelley, 1992).

Coding the Content of Studies

What works findings were coded and analyzed using a content analysis approach (Schreier, 2012). The unit of analysis for content analysis coding was a single idea about *what works* in stepfamilies. A sentence in a journal article could contain one or more *what works* ideas. Concepts were identified and coded directly from *what works* statements derived from the text and tables of studies. These concepts were then clustered together with other concepts that had similar meanings or shared attributes. For example, the coded concepts of *accepting* stepchildren, *approving* of stepchildren, and *praising* stepchildren were clustered together as similar concepts, as was another cluster consisting of *being supportive, encouraging*, and *nurturing*. These two clusters both fell under a larger category of concepts labeled *conveying positive messages*. This category was in turn a sub-category of *communicating with stepchildren*. Another example was that concepts such as *focusing on children's needs*; *using communication technology to plan, schedule, and make childrearing decisions*; and *sharing childcare* were codes that were subsumed under the category of *cooperative coparenting between parents*. Coding and analyzing the content of studies continued throughout the project. As experienced qualitative researchers, we are comfortable with inductive approaches to collecting and making sense of data. If results from newer studies could not be placed in an existing category of findings, we added new codes and categories, a process that continued until we stopped adding studies on January 1, 2024.

References

Allan, G., Crow, G., & Hawker, S. (2011). *Stepfamilies*. Palgrave Macmillan.

Braithwaite, D.O., Toller, P.W., Daas, K.L., Durham, W.T., & Jones, A.C. (2008). Centered but not caught in the middle: Stepchildren's perceptions of dialectical contradictions in the communication of co-parents. *Journal of Applied Communication Research*, 36(1), 33–55. http://dx.doi.org/10.1080/00909880701799337

Braithwaite, D.O., Waldron, V.R., Allen, J., Oliver, B., Bergquist, G., Storck, K., Marsh, J., Swords, N., & Tschampi-Diesing, C. (2018). "Feeling warmth and close to her": Communication and resilience reflected in positive adult stepchild-stepparent relationships. *Journal of Family Communication*, 18(2), 92–109. https://doi.org/10.1080/15267431.2017.1415902

Burgoyne, J., & Clark, D. (1984). *Making a go of it: A study of stepfamilies in Sheffield*. Routledge & Kegan.

Coley, R.L. (1998). Children's socialization experiences and functioning in single-mother households: The importance of fathers and other men. *Child Development*, 69, 219–230. http://dx.doi.org/10.1111/j.1467-8624.1998.tb06144.x

Hetherington, E.M., & Kelly, J. (2002). *For better or for worse*. Norton.

Kelley, P. (1992). Healthy stepfamily functioning. *Families in Society*, 73(10), 579–587. http://dx.doi.org/10.1177/104438949207301001

Kelly, K., & Ganong, L. (2011). "Shifting family boundaries" after the diagnosis of childhood cancer in stepfamilies. *Journal of Family Nursing*, 17, 105–132. http://dx.doi.org/10.1177/1074840710397365

Marsiglio, W., Hinojosa, R. (2007). Managing the multifather family: Stepfathers as father allies. *Journal of Marriage and Family*, 69(3), 845–862. http://dx.doi.org/10.1111/j.1741-3737.2007.00409.x

Papernow, P. (1993). *Becoming a Stepfamily: Patterns of development in remarried families*. Jossey-Bass.

Sanner, C., Ganong, L.H., & Coleman, M. (2020). Shared children in stepfamilies: Experiences living in a hybrid family structure. *Journal of Marriage and Family*, 82, 605–621. http://doi.org:10.1111/jomf.12631

Schreier, M. (2012). *Qualitative content analysis in practice*. Sage.

Schrodt, P., Soliz, J., & Braithwaite, D.O. (2008). A social relations model of everyday talk and relational satisfaction in stepfamilies. *Communication Monographs*, 75(2), 190–217. https://doi.org/10.1080/03637750802023163

Stacey, J. (1990). *Brave new families*. NY: Basic Books.

Willetts, M.C., & Maroules, N.G. (2005). Parental reports of adolescent well-being: Does marital status matter? *Journal of Divorce & Remarriage*, 43(1/2), 129–148. http://dx.doi.org/10.1300/j087v43n01_07

Yu, T. & Adler-Baeder, F. (2007). The intergenerational transmission of relationship quality: The effects of parental remarriage quality on young adults' relationships. *Journal of Divorce & Remarriage*, 47(3/4), 87–102. http://dx.doi.org/10.1300/j087v47n03_05

INDEX